POLITICS AND POLICIES
OF THE
TRUMAN ADMINISTRATION

Politics and Policies of the Truman Administration

Edited with an Introduction
by

BARTON J. BERNSTEIN

CHICAGO
QUADRANGLE BOOKS
1972

SECOND PRINTING

Library of Congress Catalog Card Number: 70-78302

CONTENTS

POLITICS AND POLICIES
OF THE
TRUMAN ADMINISTRATION

Introduction

As THE MEMORIES of deep freezes, Russian spies, and foreign wars have faded, Americans have come to express grudging respect for Harry S. Truman and the accomplishments of his administration. Many scholars have ranked him as a "near great" President, and a few have placed him among the "great." Judging him in part by his expansion of presidential power and his extension of the nation's influence abroad, they have found much to applaud in his administration. As admirers of the liberal tradition, they praise him for continuing the New Deal program and seeking to expand its benefits through his own Fair Deal. Sharing the consensus on Soviet responsibility for the Cold War, they endorse his foreign policy, seeing his resistance to the Soviet "threat" as visionary and courageous. For these historians, Truman's postwar administration cast off the shackles of American innocence and moved to a wise and necessary foreign policy. His intervention in Korea, his determined efforts to halt communism elsewhere, and his containment policy in Europe—the Truman Doctrine, the Marshall Plan, and NATO—all command their respect.

In the late forties and early fifties, politicians and scholars sometimes challenged this emerging interpretation. Most dissenters questioned the administration's will or its ability to resist communism, and criticized the government for belated and timid responses to the Soviet "menace." Others, like Walter Lippmann and George Kennan, lamented the excessive moralism and legalism of American policy-makers, their loss of faith in traditional diplomacy, their unwillingness to seek a relaxation of Cold War antagonisms, and their inability to define and act upon the national interest. A few scholars, most notably William Appleman Williams, questioned the emerging consensus from a different and surprising perspective. Moving beyond the naive criticisms of American Cold War policies by Henry Wallace and Wilsonian internationalists, Williams explained the Cold War not by Soviet malevolence but by American ideology, which he traced back to the nineteenth century. Not the innocence of American policy-makers but their conception of the national interest produced the Cold War. The national interest, for these policy-makers, depended upon an expanding domestic economy which required equal access to international markets and the relaxation of trade barriers (the Open Door). By their analysis, economies which moved to bilateral trading, or revolutions which overturned capitalism, were a menace to the international order, upon which American prosperity, as well as domestic liberties, seemed to depend.

Initially, in *American-Russian Relations, 1781–1947* (1952), and then more fully in *The Tragedy of American Diplomacy* (1959, rev. ed., 1962), Williams emphasized that American policy-makers had sought to impose upon the postwar world their own design for peace and prosperity. America's Open Door policy, he argued, had directly threatened Russian security, provoking her fears of a renewed *cordon sanitaire*. The American struggle to roll back Soviet influence, he stressed, was not a response to feared aggression but part of the larger strategy of trying to create a world in which the American political economy could survive. Williams denied that Russia was a military threat to the United States or Western Europe, pointing out that the United States, not Russia, was the dominant military power in the postwar years.

Often ignored or rejected at first, the *Tragedy* has won great respect in the past few years, particularly as the breakdown of liberalism and the disastrous war in Vietnam have compelled many Americans to reexamine the Cold War. Under the impact of these events, scholars and others are questioning anti-communism, the uses of national power, and the belief in national innocence. They are emphasizing the importance of ideology, and some stress the relationship between ideology, the political economy, and foreign policy. Williams, more than any other man, has defined these issues and broken the path for many who have followed: the critical studies of the Cold War by three of his students, Lloyd Gardner, Gar Alperovitz, and Walter LaFeber,* as well as the recent book by Gabriel Kolko and the four essays on foreign policy in this volume. Based upon archival sources unavailable to earlier scholars, these recent studies challenge many of our fondest assumptions about the Cold War.

My own essay on American foreign policy emphasizes that American leaders sought to reshape much of the world according to American needs and standards, and thereby contributed significantly to the origins of the Cold War. By refusing to respect Soviet spheres of influence in Eastern Europe, the Truman administration in 1945 reversed Franklin Roosevelt's tactics of acceding (reluctantly) to a division of Europe. Soon the possibility of accommodation between the Great Powers collapsed under the pressure of continuing disputes. Truman's government sought briefly to follow a policy of liberation, and retreated to containment only when atomic diplomacy failed to roll back Soviet influence from Eastern Europe. Failures to reach agreement on international control of atomic energy, efforts to use economic aid to coerce the Soviet Union, and disagreements on Germany contributed to the antagonisms even before Truman, in seeking aid for Greece and Turkey, declared a war of ideology in his "Truman Doctrine" speech of March 1947. Blinded by their own ideology to evidence of indigenous revolution in Greece, American policy-makers wrongly interpreted it as a Soviet plot, part

---

*Alperovitz was an undergraduate in Williams' course at the University of Wisconsin; LaFeber, who wrote his thesis there under Fred Harvey Harrington, did not take a formal course with Williams but assisted in his course and acknowledges his influence.

of the program for the expansion of monolithic communism. Their opposition to communism sprang from a "cluster of related attitudes—humanitarianism, expectations of military attack in the short or long run, and the fear of economic encirclement." In particular, many emphasized the dangers to the American political economy from expanding communism: it might injure American foreign trade, disorder the American economic system, and thereby threaten the political freedoms which many thought rested upon capitalism at home.

In examining this ideology, Thomas G. Paterson in his essay has concentrated upon the relationship between international trade, American fears of communism, and the Marshall Plan. Peace, freedom, and world trade, he explains, were the key links in the widely held conception which shaped foreign policy and led to an extensive foreign aid program and a vigorous foreign trade. Impoverished people, according to the American outlook, were more likely to turn to totalitarianism, and particularly to communism, thereby threatening international stability. In turn, world prosperity, and hence peace, could be promoted only by strong world trade, which required the destruction of economic bilateralism and the creation of multilateralism. Because policymakers emphasized the interdependence of the world economy, they concluded that an American depression could only injure it—and reflexively plunge the United States deeper into economic distress. Accordingly, world peace and prosperity rested on a healthy and expanding foreign trade. It is partly within this framework of the ideology of political economy, concludes Paterson, that the Marshall Plan should be understood. It was generated not simply by humanitarianism but by fears that a prostrate Europe would be a breeding ground for communism, that a faltering European economy would be unable to provide the goods and markets so essential to the world and American economies, and that the American conception of peace would be endangered. In addition, as Paterson explains, the terms of the Marshall Plan, especially after the abortive Russian loan and the Truman Doctrine, threatened Russian influence in her own sphere and were, predictably, unacceptable to the Soviet Union.

Moving beyond Williams, Paterson stresses the importance of tactics in American foreign policy and implies that ideology did not dictate the way in which the United States used its economic power. In fact, he suggests that a central question for historians is how, and not whether, the United States used its economic power abroad.

Near the center of the problems separating the United States and Russia was the persistent issue of Germany. Even before Roosevelt's death, as Lloyd Gardner points out in his essay, Russian fears of a separate Anglo-American surrender and of diversion of German forces to the Soviet front had strained the fragile wartime alliance. More troubling over the long run was the difficulty of reaching and implementing a program of German reparations. For the war-ravaged Soviet economy there were only two likely sources of economic assistance—an American loan and German reparations. As the likelihood of the loan faded, the issue of reparations became even more important. At Potsdam the Great Powers reached a settlement which (in the words of Samuel Lubell) "produced . . . an economic iron curtain splitting Europe in two." Though General Lucius Clay, the American Deputy Military Governor in Germany, was initially optimistic about creating a unified economy in Germany (under the Potsdam agreement), French obstructionism, shifting American policy, and economic difficulties led him in May 1946 to cut off reparations to Russia. The United States and the Soviet Union soon began competing openly for the favor of the German people. Though both nations endorsed the principle of a united Germany, the events of 1947 established that each feared the other's proposal. Under the Marshall Plan the West German economy was reintegrated into the international capitalist economy. The Berlin blockade, rather than halting this process, Gardner concludes, solidified the establishment of the two Germanies.

For American policy-makers during the early Cold War, Latin America never merited the attention that Europe received, and even the plans for economic assistance to these southern neighbors faded with the need for European reconstruction. In his essay David Green explains that the Roosevelt administration hoped to maintain the prosperity and welfare of the United States through the establishment of an "Open World," in which all areas would be open to American trade and capital. The administration therefore generally opposed economic nationalism and state control of economic life in Latin America. According to Green, Roosevelt was reluctant to establish a closed or self-contained security system in the Western Hemisphere for fear of sanctioning parallel Russian actions in Eastern Europe; Truman's government abandoned this policy of restraint, however, and prepared to erect a hemispheric "defense against communism," even while trying to roll back Russian influence in Eastern Europe. Construction of this military alliance was temporarily delayed until 1948 because of opposition in the United States to the inclusion of fascist Argentina. But Latin America did not need military assistance against a nonexistent threat, concludes Green. What she did need was industrial and agricultural development within a nationalist-statist framework to help resolve the social crises produced by her economic underdevelopment. U.S. policy precluded aid on that basis. Such aid was not forthcoming. Also, between 1946 and 1953, U.S. private investment resulted in a 20 per cent loss of working capital in Latin America. While American policies failed to help overcome the widespread poverty and misery, Latin American governments frequently used American military aid to maintain social control and to suppress demands for social reform. Thus in Latin America the United States encouraged and assisted stability enforced by guns. For Truman and his advisers this was the only alternative to communism, which they wrongly held responsible for the periodic eruptions in the hemisphere.

II

These struggles against foreign instability and communism were intimately linked with the administration's concern about domestic loyalty and security. Yet, ironically, by 1950 the administration could no longer persuade Americans that it was resisting communist expansion abroad and rooting out subversives at home. Instead, the Republican party, particularly the so-called isolationists who often had opposed collective security and containment, successfully charged the administration with being "soft on communism."

Historians have usually explained that the administration was the victim of the widespread belief in national omnipotence: when victories were not won, when the communists were not turned back, and when China was lost, baffled and frustrated Americans blamed their government. Some charged the administration with bungling, others charged disloyalty. For many historians, however, the error of the administration was that it had failed to recognize American innocence, or what Sir Denis Brogan called the "illusion of omnipotence," and therefore had failed to educate Americans to the realities and limitations of power. Americans had not been prepared for revolutions and limited wars, for setbacks and stalemates, and it was this innocence that the GOP, and particularly Joseph McCarthy, exploited.

In 1955, in *The New American Right,* a group of prominent social scientists, including Daniel Bell, Seymour M. Lipset, and Richard Hofstadter, moved beyond this interpretation to analyze McCarthyism in terms of "status politics." Denying the importance of (economic) interest-group politics in the presumably prosperous nation, they emphasized that politics was no longer ideological but had come to express the needs and anxieties of status groups. Some groups, uneasy in a mobile and ethnically mixed society, sought to resolve anxieties by affirming their Americanism through anti-communism and attacks upon established leaders. According to this analysis, the major source of the "new American right" (what Hofstadter called the "pseudo-conservative revolt") were déclassé, old-family, Anglo-Saxon Protestants and upwardly mobile, new immigrant groups, particularly the Germans and Irish. Some contributors to *The New American Right* located status anxiety and support for McCarthy in such groups as the new rich, the lower middle class, the less educated, Midwestern isolationists, small-town residents, hick Protestants, "cankered intellectuals," small businessmen, and manual workers.

Clearly, as Nelson Polsby later demonstrated, the hypothesis of status anxiety was "much too inclusive to have much explanatory power." Though the hypothesis may explain the behavior of specific members of groups, it fails to differentiate among groups or to provide adequate criteria for exclusion of groups. Worse yet, when the theory was checked against survey data, additional flaws appeared: two groups excluded by the theory— farmers and New Englanders—proved to be pro-McCarthy, while some groups named by the theory as supporters were not. In place of this dubious theory, Polsby offered a political interpretation: McCarthy succeeded at the grass roots primarily among Republicans.*

Building upon the interpretations of Polsby and Brogan, Athan Theoharis, in his essay on "The Rhetoric of Politics," concludes that the administration's public pronouncements reinforced American innocence and the myth of omnipotence. In opposing communism, Truman equated compromise and concession with appeasement. He promised success, not stalemate or setback. Containment would block communism: military expansion could be halted and revolutions prevented. Since revolutions, by Truman's definition, were forced upon people by a tiny alien minority, a vigilant and resolute American government could stop them. When communism was not restrained, when China fell, what could the American people think? Applying the administration's own test, many concluded that the government's *will* was inadequate and attributed America's failure to bungling or subversion.

Through its domestic loyalty-and-security program, the administration also contributed to its own difficulties. By promising a perfect program and by emphasizing the danger of reds in government—whether as ambassadors or gardeners—the administration exaggerated the perils of domestic communism and the efficiency of its own program. Truman emphasized the need for *absolute* protection and promised *absolute* security. As a result, the discovery that even a single communist might have slipped through the program could raise doubts about the administra-

---

*More recently, Michael Rogin, in an important volume, *McCarthy and the Intellectuals* (1967), has analyzed the theories of many contributors to *The New American Right* and explained the defects in their application of the theory of mass politics to American industrial society.

tion's will or ability. And after 1948 there seemed to be ample evidence of slips—Alger Hiss, William Remington, Judith Coplon, Julius and Ethel Rosenberg. Later, when yielding to criticisms from the right and making the standard of loyalty even more rigid, the administration seemed to acknowledge flaws in its earlier program and raised additional doubts about its commitment to protecting the nation from the grave peril it had defined. By their rhetoric and actions, Truman and his associates thus contributed to the loss of public confidence which the Republicans, and particularly McCarthy, were able in turn to exploit.

In his related essay on "The Escalation of the Loyalty Program," the first published study of the subject based upon the Truman papers, Theoharis charts the administration's erosion of civil liberties. Agreeing with some contemporary liberal critics of the program, he laments the unfortunate break with Roosevelt's practices, attributes the program in large measure to limited vision and partisan politics, and criticizes its standards and procedures. He has also moved beyond earlier analyses to examine the impact of Attorneys General Tom Clark and J. Howard McGrath on the impairment of civil liberties, and to assess the administration's tactics in declaring as unpatriotic criticisms of its foreign policy and loyalty program. By failing to distinguish between disloyalty and political radicalism, and by justifying investigations of political activity, the administration encouraged right-wing attacks upon the liberal past. In conclusion, Theoharis notes, the "loyalty program legitimized the tactics of McCarthy and similar procedures by state and local governments and by private industry."

III

In domestic policy, as historians generally acknowledge, the Truman administration's record is rather dismal. Rebuffed by Congress on such major issues as the Brannan Plan, civil rights, price controls, and health insurance, the administration secured from Congress only a few liberal reforms—improved social security, higher minimum wages, some reclamation and public power projects, a weak employment act, and public housing. Truman's greatest achievement, then, aside from protecting the New Deal, may not have been the legislation he gained but his periodic endorsement of liberal measures—in effect, the education he (perhaps unintentionally) offered.

In analyzing Truman's difficulties, many scholars have explained that a conservative reaction set in after the war, and some have concluded that the President was simply the victim of inevitable deadlock. Confronting a hostile Congress which had become surly under Roosevelt, Truman could not impose his will. After a brief honeymoon, the conservative alliance of Northern Republicans and Southern Democrats thwarted his efforts. He could not lead a crusade against this coalition. He had to follow cautious policies at home because his party was torn by dissension. Unwilling to destroy the Democratic coalition, he needed the support of both wings in foreign policy, and was compelled sometimes to sacrifice domestic policies to this cause.

In contrast, other scholars like Samuel Lubell, in *The Future of American Politics* (1952), have cast upon Truman much of the responsibility for stalemate: "All his skills and energies . . . were directed to standing still. . . . When he took vigorous action in one direction it was axiomatic that he would contrive soon afterward to move in the conflicting direction. In the end he managed to work himself back close to the center spot of indecision from which he started."

This view has found sympathy among some younger historians and has contributed to the reassessment of the Truman administration. Exploiting archival materials unavailable in the fifties, and focusing on such issues as inflation, agriculture, and labor, they have emphasized the frequent discrepancy between liberal rhetoric and conservative action. They have charted Truman's strategy of asking for legislation he could not get, while frequently avoiding executive action which would achieve portions of the program he claimed to endorse. In various areas of economic and welfare policies, they have shown that conservative administrators undercut liberal programs. Generalizing from these events, some have questioned Truman's capacity as an administrator and criticized his procedure of "cabinet government," of permitting assistants virtual autonomy in their fields.

They have also questioned the popular image of Truman as a decisive President, as a man who subscribed to the principle (as stated by the sign on his desk) that "the buck stops here." They have found a different pattern—of drift and vacillation. As a politician and a leader, Truman, they find, was a man of limited ability. The administration's poor domestic record, they conclude, was often the fault of Harry S. Truman.

Some of these themes are found in my own appraisal of Truman's civil rights program. Often he asked for legislation he knew Congress would not authorize, while he frequently refused to use his executive powers to advance civil rights. In this disjunction between legislative requests and executive actions, Truman's effort to desegregate the armed forces stands as the major exception, but even there his caution, as well as considerations of international prestige and domestic politics, must be emphasized. Despite his periodic requests for legislation to bar racial discrimination in employment, his own government seldom enforced these policies on government contractors. Nor, despite his words in behalf of civil rights, did his own government even cease to inquire about support of racial integration as possible evidence of disloyalty. Certainly civil rights never received from Truman and his associates the support and enthusiasm that anticommunism commanded. The felt political necessities of those years, as well as his own convictions, moved him beyond Roosevelt and many white Americans, but he remained cautious and sometimes reluctant in the effort to extend legal equality to America's black citizens. And though he challenged the separate-but-equal doctrine, his understanding of the conditions essential to equality was severely limited. In summary, he left to the nation a mixed legacy: he recognized some of the problems and responded part way to the challenges, and thereby encouraged blacks to work through the political process; but he also increased expectations which his government and American society were not prepared to fulfill.

IV

In the past few years, as interest in the Truman years has grown, a number of young scholars have begun to reassess the

Truman administration. Unlike most of the earlier and more flat-
tering scholarship, these newer studies have had access to many
of the unpublished documents of the period, and the critical
judgments have been based on these new sources. For example,
these scholars have found that few policy-makers in the immediate postwar years expected an imminent Soviet attack upon
Western Europe. (In 1947, according to George Kennan, "it was
perfectly clear to anyone with even a rudimentary knowledge of
the Russia of that day that the Soviet leaders had no intention
of attempting to advance their cause by launching military attacks with their own armed forces across frontiers.") And they
have uncovered in private papers frequent evidence of the gap
between public rhetoric and administrative commitment in domestic policy. Despite differences among them, their work breaks
with the consensus on the Truman administration, and judged
by that general standard their analyses do signify the emergence
of a "school." Indeed, at the very time liberalism is breaking
down, when America no longer seems exempt from charges of
racism and imperialism, many of these young scholars are critical
of the liberal tradition—in foreign policy, civil liberties, civil
rights, economic policy, and social welfare.

So far their work has appeared separately, often in scattered
essays or monographs, and there has been no effort to bring together some of this new "revisionism" in order to make it more
available to the public and to scholars outside the Truman years.
Consequently, a number of these young scholars were invited
to participate in this collection, and fortunately most were able
to join the venture.

Obviously, because this new scholarship is still comparatively
young, some important topics remain unexamined. Nevertheless,
the following essays on the origins of the Cold War, on the
nation's policy toward Germany, on the Marshall Plan and the
ideology of political economy, on Latin American policy, on the
loyalty and security programs, and on civil rights express the
emerging reinterpretation of the Truman administration.

BARTON J. BERNSTEIN

Stanford, California
July 1969

BARTON J. BERNSTEIN

American Foreign Policy
and the Origins
of the Cold War

---

*"There is no nation which has
attitudes so pure that they cannot
be bettered by self-examination."*
—John Foster Dulles (1946)

*"We are forced to act in the world
as it is, and not in the world as
we wish it were, or as we would
like it to become."*
—Henry L. Stimson (1947)

DESPITE SOME dissents, most American scholars have reached a
general consensus on the origins of the Cold War. As confirmed

The author wishes to express his gratitude for generous counsel to Gar
Alperovitz, H. Stuart Hughes, Gabriel Kolko, Walter LaFeber, Lloyd Gardner, Allen J. Matusow, Thomas G. Paterson, Athan Theoharis, and Samuel
Williamson. Research was conducted with the assistance of grants from the
Rabinowitz Foundation, the American Philosophical Society, the Harry S.
Truman Library Institute, the Charles Warren Center of Harvard University, and the Institute of American History at Stanford University. Portions
of this paper were presented at the Warren Center in November 1967, at
the John F. Kennedy Institute at Harvard in 1967–1968, and at the annual
meeting of the Southern Historical Association in November 1968.

internationalists who believe that Russia constituted a threat to America and its European allies after World War II, they have endorsed their nation's acceptance of its obligations as a world power in the forties and its desire to establish a world order of peace and prosperity. Convinced that only American efforts prevented the Soviet Union from expanding past Eastern Europe, they have generally praised the containment policies of the Truman Doctrine, the Marshall Plan, and NATO as evidence of America's acceptance of world responsibility. While chiding or condemning those on the right who opposed international involvement (or had even urged preventive war), they have also been deeply critical of those on the left who have believed that the Cold War could have been avoided, or that the United States shared substantial responsibility for the Cold War.[1]

Whether they are devotees of the new realism or open admirers of moralism and legalism in foreign policy, most scholars have agreed that the United States moved slowly and reluctantly, in response to Soviet provocation, away from President Franklin D. Roosevelt's conciliatory policy. The Truman administration, perhaps even belatedly, they suggest, abandoned its efforts to maintain the Grand Alliance and acknowledged that Russia menaced world peace. American leaders, according to this familiar interpretation, slowly cast off the shackles of innocence and moved to courageous and necessary policies.

Despite the widespread acceptance of this interpretation, there has long been substantial evidence (and more recently a body of scholarship) which suggests that American policy was neither so innocent nor so nonideological; that American leaders sought to promote their conceptions of national interest and their values even at the conscious risk of provoking Russia's fears about her security. In 1945 these leaders apparently believed that American power would be adequate for the task of reshaping much of the world according to America's needs and standards.[2]

By overextending policy and power and refusing to accept Soviet interests, American policy-makers contributed to the Cold War. There was little understanding of any need to restrain American political efforts and desires. Though it cannot be proved that the United States could have achieved a *modus vivendi* with the Soviet Union in these years, there is evidence that Russian policies were reasonably cautious and conservative, and that there was at least a basis for accommodation. But this possibility slowly slipped away as President Harry S. Truman reversed Roosevelt's tactics of accommodation. As American demands for democratic governments in Eastern Europe became more vigorous, as the new administration delayed in providing economic assistance to Russia and in seeking international control of atomic energy, policy-makers met with increasing Soviet suspicion and antagonism. Concluding that Soviet-American cooperation was impossible, they came to believe that the Soviet state could be halted only by force or the threat of force.[3]

The emerging revisionist interpretation, then, does not view American actions simply as the necessary response to Soviet challenges, but instead tries to understand American ideology and interests, mutual suspicions and misunderstandings, and to investigate the failures to seek and achieve accommodation.

I

During the war Allied relations were often marred by suspicions and doubts rooted in the hostility of earlier years. It was only a profound "accident"—the German attack upon the Soviet Union in 1941—that thrust that leading anti-Bolshevik, Winston Churchill, and Marshal Josef Stalin into a common camp. This wartime alliance, its members realized, was not based upon trust but upon necessity; there was no deep sense of shared values or obvious similarity of interests, only opposition to a common enemy. "A coalition," as Herbert Feis has remarked, "is heir to the suppressed desires and maimed feelings of each of its members." Wartime needs and postwar aims often strained the uneasy alliance. In the early years when Russia was bearing the major burden of the Nazi onslaught, her allies postponed for two years a promised second front which would have diverted German armies. In December 1941, when Stalin requested recognition of 1941 Russian borders as they had been before the German attack (including the recently annexed Baltic states), the British were willing to agree, but Roosevelt rebuffed the proposals and aroused Soviet fears that her security needs would not be recognized and that her allies might later resume their anti-Bolshevik policies. So distrustful were the Allies that both camps feared the making of a separate peace with Germany, and Stalin's suspicions erupted into bitter accusations in March 1945, when he discovered (and Roosevelt denied) that British and American agents were participating in secret negotiations with the Germans. In anger Stalin decided not to send Vyacheslav Molotov, the Foreign Minister, to San Francisco for the April meeting on the founding of the United Nations Organization.[4]

So suspicious were the Americans and British that they would not inform the Soviet Union that they were working on an atomic bomb. Some American leaders even hoped to use it in postwar negotiations with the Russians. In wartime, American opposition to communism had not disappeared, and many of Roosevelt's advisers were fearful of Soviet intentions in Eastern Europe. In turn, Soviet leaders, recalling the prewar hostility of the Western democracies, feared a renewed attempt to establish a *cordon sanitaire* and resolved to establish a security zone in Eastern Europe.

Though Roosevelt's own strategy often seems ambiguous, his general tactics are clear: they were devised to avoid conflict. He operated often as a mediator between the British and Russians, and delayed many decisions that might have disrupted the wartime alliance. He may have been resting his hopes with the United Nations or on the exercise of America's postwar strength, or he may simply have been placing his faith in the future. Whatever future tactics he might have been planning, he concluded that America's welfare rested upon international peace, expanded trade, and open markets:

> . . . it is our hope, not only in the interest of our own prosperity, but in the interest of the prosperity of the world, that trade and commerce and access to materials and markets may be freer after this war than ever before in the history of the world. . . . Only through a dynamic and soundly expanding world economy can the living standards of individual nations be advanced to levels which will permit a full realization of our hopes for the future.

His efforts on behalf of the postwar world generally reflected this understanding.[5]

During the war Roosevelt wavered uneasily between emphasizing the postwar role of the great powers and minimizing their role and seeking to extend the principles of the Atlantic Charter. Though he often spoke of the need for an open postwar world, and he was reluctant to accept spheres of influence (beyond the Western hemisphere, where American influence was pre-eminent), his policies gradually acknowledged the pre-eminence of the great powers and yielded slowly to their demands. By late 1943 Roosevelt confided to Archbishop Francis Spellman (according to Spellman's notes) that "the world will be divided into spheres of influence: China gets the Far East; the U.S. the Pacific; Britain and Russia, Europe and Africa." The United States, he thought, would have little postwar influence on the continent, and Russia would probably "predominate in Europe," making Austria, Hungary, and Croatia "a sort of Russian protectorate." He acknowledged "that the European countries will have to undergo tremendous changes in order to adapt to Russia; but he hopes that in ten or twenty years the European influence would bring the Russians to become less barbarous."[6]

In 1944 Roosevelt recognized the establishment of zones of influence in Europe. The Italian armistice of the year before had set the pattern for other wartime agreements on the control of affairs of liberated and defeated European nations. When Stalin requested the creation of a three-power Allied commission to deal with the problems of "countries falling away from Germany," Roosevelt and Churchill first rebuffed the Russian leader and then agreed to a joint commission for Italy which would be limited to information gathering. By excluding Russia from sharing in decision-making in Italy, the United States and Great Britain, later concluded William McNeill, "prepared the way for their own exclusion from any but a marginal share in the affairs of Eastern Europe."[7]

When Roosevelt refused to participate in an Anglo-American invasion of southeastern Europe (which seemed to be the only way of restricting Russian influence in that area), Churchill sought other ways of dealing with Russian power and of protecting British interests in Greece. In May 1944 he proposed to Stalin that they recognize Greece as a British "zone of influence" and Rumania as a Russian zone; but Stalin insisted upon seeking

Roosevelt's approval and refused the offer upon learning that the United States would not warmly endorse the terms. When the Soviets liberated Rumania in September they secured temporarily the advantages that Churchill had offered. They simply followed the British-American example in Italy, retained all effective power, and announced they were "acting in the interests of all the United Nations." From the Soviet Union, W. Averell Harriman, the American ambassador, cabled, "The Russians believe, I think, that we lived up to a tacit understanding that Rumania was an area of predominant Soviet interest in which we should not interfere. . . . The terms of the armistice give the Soviet command unlimited control of Rumania's economic life" and effective control over political organization.[8]

With Russian armies sweeping through the Balkans and soon in a position to impose similar terms on Hungary and Bulgaria, Churchill renewed his efforts. "Winston," wrote an associate, "never talks of Hitler these days; he is always harping on the dangers of Communism. He dreams of the Red Army spreading like a cancer from one country to another. It has become an obsession, and he seems to think of little else." In October Churchill journeyed to Moscow to reach an agreement with Stalin. "Let us settle our affairs in the Balkans," Churchill told him. "Your armies are in Rumania and Bulgaria. We have interests, missions and agents there. Don't let us get at cross-purposes in small ways." Great Britain received "90 per cent influence" in Greece, and Russia "90 per cent influence" in Rumania, "80 per cent" in Bulgaria and Hungary, and "50 per cent" in Yugoslavia.[9]

In the cases of Hungary and Bulgaria the terms were soon sanctioned by armistice agreements (approved by the United States) which left effective power with the Soviets. "The Russians took it for granted," Cordell Hull, then Secretary of State, wrote later, "that . . . Britain and the United States had assigned them a certain portion of the Balkans, including Rumania and Bulgaria, as their spheres of influence." In December Stalin even confirmed the agreement at a considerable price: he permitted British troops to put down a rebellion in Greece. "Stalin," wrote Churchill later, "adhered strictly and faithfully to our agree-

ment . . . and during all the long weeks of fighting the communists in the streets of Athens, not one word of reproach came
from *Pravda* or *Izvestia*."[10]

At Yalta in February 1945 Roosevelt did not seem to challenge
Soviet dominance in east-central Europe, which had been established by the Churchill-Stalin agreement and confirmed by the
armistices and by British action in Greece. What Roosevelt did
seek and gain at Yalta was a weak "Declaration on Liberated
Europe"—that the powers would consult "where in their judgment conditions require" assistance to maintain peace or to establish democratic governments. By requiring unanimity the
declaration allowed any one power to veto any proposal that
seemed to threaten that power's interests. In effect, then, the
declaration, despite its statements about democratic governments, did not alter the situation in Eastern Europe. The operative phrases simply affirmed the principle that the three powers
had already established: they could consult together when all
agreed, and they could act together when all agreed. At Yalta
the broadly phrased statement provoked little discussion—only a
few pages in the official proceedings. Presumably the Russians
did not consider it a repudiation of spheres of influence, only
as rhetoric that Roosevelt wanted for home consumption. Despite later official American suggestions, the Yalta agreement
was not a product of Roosevelt's misunderstanding of the Soviet
meaning of "democracy" and "free elections." Rather, it ratified
earlier agreements, and the State Department probably understood this.[11]

While accepting the inevitable and acknowledging Russian
influence in these areas, Roosevelt had not been tractable on
the major issue confronting the three powers: the treatment of
postwar Germany. All three leaders realized that the decisions
on Germany would shape the future relations of Europe. A dismembered or permanently weakened Germany would leave Russia without challenge on the continent and would ease her fears
of future invasion. As Anthony Eden, the British Foreign Minister explained, "Russia was determined on one thing above all
others, that Germany would not again disturb the peace of Europe. . . . Stalin was determined to smash Germany so that it

would never again be able to make war." A strong Germany, on the other hand, could be a partial counterweight to Russia and help restore the European balance of power on which Britain had traditionally depended for protection. Otherwise, as Henry Morgenthau once explained in summarizing Churchill's fears, there would be nothing between "the white snows of Russia and the white cliffs of Dover."[12]

The Allied policy on Germany had been in flux for almost two years. At Teheran in 1943 the Allies had agreed in principle (despite Churchill's reluctance) that Germany should be dismembered, and in 1944 Roosevelt and a reluctant Churchill, much to the distress of Foreign Minister Anthony Eden, had agreed on a loosely phrased version of the Morgenthau Plan for the dismemberment and pastoralization of Germany. Not only would the plan have eliminated German military-industrial potential and thereby allayed Russian fears, but by stripping Germany it would also have provided the resources for Russian economic reconstruction. Churchill, despite his fear of Russia and his desire for Germany as a counterweight on the continent, had temporarily agreed to the plan because it seemed to be a prerequisite for increased American economic aid and promised to eliminate German industry as a postwar rival for the trade that the debt-ridden British economy would need. Many in the State and War Departments charged that the plan was economic madness, that it would leave not only Germany but also much of war-torn Western Europe (which would need postwar German production) without the means for economic reconstruction. (Secretary of the Treasury Morgenthau concluded after discussion with many officials that they wanted a strong Germany as a "bulwark against Bolshevism.") Yielding to the pleas of the War and State Departments, Roosevelt decided upon a plan for a stronger postwar Germany, and Churchill, under pressure from advisers, also backed away from his earlier endorsement of the Morgenthau Plan and again acted upon his fears of an unopposed Russia on the continent. At Yalta, he resisted any agreement on the dismemberment of Germany. Stalin, faced with Anglo-American solidarity on this issue, acceded. The final communiqué patched over this fundamental dispute by announcing that the three powers had pledged to "take such steps including the complete disarmament, demilitarization, and dismemberment of Germany as they deem requisite for future peace and security." The strategy of postponement had triumphed. Unable to reach a substantive agreement, the Big Three agreed to submit these problems (and the related, vital issues of reparations and boundaries) to three-power commissions.[13]

Though Yalta has come to represent the triumph of the strategy of postponement, at the time it symbolized Allied accord. Stalin accepted a limitation of the veto power on certain quasi-judicial issues in the U.N. Security Council; Roosevelt conceded to Russia the return of the Kurile Islands, which stretched between Japan and Siberia, and special rights in Dairen and Port Arthur in Manchuria; Stalin promised to enter the Pacific war within three months of the end of the European conflict. "Stalin," as William McNeill explained, "had conceded something to the British in Yugoslavia; and Churchill had yielded a good deal in Poland."[14]

II

Roosevelt's successor was less sympathetic to Russian aspirations and more responsive to those of Roosevelt's advisers, like Admiral William Leahy, Chief of Staff to the Commander in Chief; Harriman; James Forrestal, Secretary of the Navy; and James F. Byrnes, Truman's choice for Secretary of State, who had urged that he resist Soviet efforts in Eastern Europe. As an earlier self-proclaimed foe of Russian communism, Truman mistrusted Russia. ("If we see that Germany is winning the war," advised Senator Truman after the German attack upon Russia in 1941, "we ought to help Russia, and if Russia is winning we ought to help Germany and in that way kill as many as possible.") Upon entering the White House, he did not seek to follow Roosevelt's tactics of adjustment and accommodation. Only eleven days in the presidency and virtually on the eve of the United Nations conference, Truman moved to a showdown with Russia on the issue of Poland.[15]

Poland became the testing ground for American foreign policy, as Truman later said, "a symbol of the future development of our international relations." At Yalta the three powers had agreed that the Soviet-sponsored Lublin Committee (the temporary Polish government) should be "reorganized on a broader democratic basis with the inclusion of democratic leaders from Poland itself and from Poland abroad." The general terms were broad: there was no specific formula for the distribution of power in the reorganized government, and the procedures required consultation and presumably unanimity from the representatives of the three powers. The agreement, remarked Admiral Leahy, was "so elastic that the Russians can stretch it all the way from Yalta to Washington without ever technically breaking it." ("I know, Bill—I know it. But it's the best I can do for Poland at this time," Roosevelt replied.)[16]

For almost two months after Yalta the great powers haggled over Poland. The Lublin Committee objected to the Polish candidates proposed by the United States and Great Britain for consultation because these Poles had criticized the Yalta accord and refused to accept the Soviet annexation of Polish territory (moving the eastern boundary to the Curzon Line). In early April Stalin had offered a compromise—that about 80 per cent of the cabinet posts in the new government should be held by members of the Lublin Committee, and that he would urge the committee to accept the leading Western candidates if they would endorse the Yalta agreement (including the Curzon Line). By proposing a specific distribution of power, Stalin cut to the core of the issue that had disrupted negotiations for nearly three months, and sought to guarantee the victory he probably expected in Poland. Roosevelt died before replying, and it is not clear whether he would have accepted this 4 to 1 representation; but he had acknowledged that he was prepared to place "somewhat more emphasis on the Lublin Poles."[17]

Now Truman was asked to acknowledge Soviet concern about countries on her borders and to assure her influence in many of these countries by granting her friendly (and probably non-democratic) governments, and even by letting her squelch anti-communist democrats in countries like Poland. To the President and his advisers the issue was (as Truman later expressed Har-

riman's argument) "the extension of Soviet control over neighboring states by independent action; we were faced with a bar-
barian invasion of Europe." The fear was not that the Soviets
were about to threaten all of Europe but that they had designs
on Eastern Europe, and that these designs conflicted with traditional American values of self-determination, democracy, and
open markets.[18]

Rushing back to Washington after Roosevelt's death, Harriman found most of FDR's advisers (now Truman's) sympathetic
to a tougher approach. At a special White House meeting Harriman outlined what he thought were the Soviet Union's two
policies—cooperation with the United States and Great Britain,
and the creation of a unilateral security ring through domination
of its border states. These policies, he contended, did not seem
contradictory to Russian leaders, for "certain elements around
Stalin" misinterpreted America's generosity and desire to cooperate as an indication of softness and concluded "that the
Soviet Government could do anything that it wished without
having any trouble with the United States." Before Roosevelt's
death, Harriman had cabled: "It may be difficult . . . to believe,
but it still may be true that Stalin and Molotov considered at
Yalta that by our willingness to accept a general wording of the
declaration on Poland and liberated Europe, by our recognition
of the need of the Red Army for security behind its lines, and
of the predominant interest of Russia in Poland as a friendly
neighbor and as a corridor to Germany, we understood and were
ready to accept Soviet policies already known to us."[19]

Harriman wanted the American government to select a few
test cases and make the Russians realize they could not continue
their present policies. Such tactics, he advised, would place Russian-American relations on a more realistic basis and compel the
Soviet Union to adhere to the American interpretation of the
issues in dispute. Because the Soviet government "needed our
[economic assistance] . . . in their reconstruction," and because
Stalin did not wish to break with the United States, Harriman
thought Truman "could stand firm on important issues without
running serious risks." As early as January 1944 Harriman had
emphasized that "the Soviet Government places the utmost im-

portance on our cooperation" in providing economic assistance, and he had concluded: "it is a factor which should be integrated into the fabric of our overall relations." In early April Harriman had proposed that unless the United States were prepared "to live in a world dominated largely by Soviet influence, we must use our economic power to assist those countries that are naturally friendly to our concepts." In turn, he had recommended "tying our economic assistance directly into our political problems with the Soviet Union."[20]

General George Marshall, the Army Chief of Staff, and Secretary of War Henry Stimson, however, recommended caution. Stimson observed "that the Russians perhaps were being more realistic than we were in regard to their own security," and he feared "that we would find ourselves breaking our relations with Russia on the most important and difficult question which we and Russia have gotten between us." Leahy, though supporting a firm policy, admitted that the Yalta agreement "was susceptible to two interpretations." Secretary of State Edward Stettinius read aloud the Yalta decision and concluded "that this was susceptible of only one interpretation."[21]

Having heard his advisers' arguments, Truman resolved to force the Polish question: to impose his interpretation of the Yalta agreement even if it destroyed the United Nations. He later explained that this was the test of Russian cooperation. If Stalin would not abide by his agreements, the U.N. was doomed, and, anyway, there would not be enough enthusiasm among the American electorate to let the United States join the world body. "Our agreements with the Soviet Union so far . . . [have] been a one-way street." That could not continue, Truman told his advisers. "If the Russians did not wish to join us, they could go to hell." ("FDR's appeasement of Russia is over," joyously wrote Senator Arthur Vandenberg, the Republican leader on foreign policy.) Continuing in this spirit at a private conference with Molotov, the new President warned that economic aid would depend upon Russian behavior in fulfilling the Yalta agreement. Brushing aside the diplomat's contention that the Anglo-American interpretation of the Yalta agreement was wrong, the President accused the Russians of breaking agreements and scolded the Russian Foreign Minister. When Molotov replied, "I have never been talked to like that in my life," Truman warned him, "Carry out your agreement and you won't get talked to like that."[22]

At the United Nations conference in San Francisco, when Anthony Eden, the British Foreign Minister, saw a copy of Truman's "blunt message" about Poland to Stalin, "he could scarcely believe his eyes . . . and cheered loudly," reported Vandenberg. But the policy of firmness was not immediately successful. American-Russian relations were further strained by the disputes at the meeting to create the U.N.—over the veto, the admission of fascist Argentina, and the persistent question of Poland. Despite Soviet objections and Roosevelt's promise at Yalta to exclude Argentina from the U.N., the United States supported the Latin American state's candidacy for membership. In committee Molotov, whom Stalin had sent to establish good will with the new President, tried to block the admission of Argentina until the Lublin Poles were also admitted, but his proposed bargain was overwhelmingly defeated. Later in the plenary session, when only three nations voted with Russia, the Soviets found additional evidence for their fears of an American bloc directed against their interests. The Truman administration's action also gave the Soviets more reason to doubt America's explanations that her interests in Poland were inspired simply by a desire to guarantee representative, democratic governments. Moreover, because of the American bloc and Soviet fears that the U.N. (like the League of Nations) might be used against her, Molotov was at first unwilling to accede to the demands of the United States and the smaller nations who wished to exclude procedural questions before the Security Council from the great power veto.[23]

The Soviets were further embittered when the United States abruptly curtailed lend-lease six days after V-E Day. Though Truman later explained this termination as simply a "mistake," as policy-making by subordinates, his recollection was incomplete and wrong. Leo Crowley, the director of lend-lease, and Joseph Grew, the Under Secretary of State, the two subordinates most closely involved, had repeatedly warned the President of the likely impact of such action on relations with Russia, and the evidence suggests that the government, as Harriman had counseled, was seeking to use economic power to achieve diplomatic means. Termination of lend-lease, Truman later wrote, "should have been done on a gradual basis which would not have made it appear as if somebody had been deliberately snubbed." Yet, despite this later judgment, Truman had four days after signing the order in which to modify it before it was to be implemented and announced, and the lend-lease administrator (in the words of Grew) had made "sure that the President understands the situation." The administrator knew "that we would be having difficulty with the Russians and did not want them to be running all over town for help." After discussing the decision with Truman, Grew, presumably acting with the President's approval, had even contrived to guarantee that curtailment would be a dramatic shock. When the Soviet chargé d'affaires had telephoned Grew the day before the secret order was to become effective, the Under Secretary had falsely denied that lend-lease to Russia was being halted. Harriman, according to Grew's report to the Secretary of State, "said that we would be getting 'a good tough slashback' from the Russians but that we would have to face it."[24]

Presumably to patch the alliance, Truman dispatched to Moscow Harry Hopkins, Roosevelt's former adviser and a staunch advocate of Soviet-American friendship. Hopkins denied that Truman's action was an American effort to demonstrate economic power and coerce Russia ("pressure on the Russians to soften them up," as Stalin charged). Instead he emphasized that "Poland had become a symbol of our ability to work out our problems with the Soviet Union." Stalin acknowledged "the right of the United States as a world power to participate in the Polish question," but he stressed the importance of Poland to Soviet security. Within twenty-five years the "Germans had twice invaded Russia via Poland," he emphasized. "All the Soviet Union wanted was that Poland should not be in a position to open the gates to Germany," and that required a government friendly to Russia. There was "no intention," he promised, "to interfere in Poland's internal affairs" or to Sovietize Poland.[25]

Through the Hopkins mission, Truman and Stalin reached a compromise: 70 per cent of the new Polish government (fourteen of twenty ministers) should be drawn from the Lublin Committee. At the time there was reason to believe that such heavy communist influence would not lead to Soviet control. Stalin had reaffirmed the pledge of free elections in Poland, and Stanislaw Mikolajczyk, former Prime Minister of the exile government in London and Deputy Prime Minister in the new coalition government, was optimistic. He hoped (in Harriman's words) that "a reasonable degree of freedom and independence can be preserved now and that in time after conditions in Europe can become more stable and [as] Russia turns her attention to her internal development, controls will be relaxed and Poland will be able to gain for herself her independence of life as a nation even though he freely accepts that Poland's security and foreign policy must follow the lead of Moscow."[26]

Truman compromised and soon recognized the new Polish government, but he did not lose his hopes of rolling back the Soviets from their spheres of influence in Eastern Europe. Basing most of his case on the Yalta "Declaration on Liberated Europe" (for which he relied on State Department interpretations), Truman hoped to force Russia to permit representative governments in its zones, and expected that free elections would diminish, perhaps even remove, Soviet authority. Refusing to extend diplomatic recognition to Rumania and Bulgaria, he emphasized that these governments were "neither representative of nor responsive to the will of the people."[27]

"The opportunities for the democratic elements in Rumania and Bulgaria are not less than, say, in Italy, with which the Governments of the United States and the Soviet Union have already resumed diplomatic relations," replied Stalin, who was willing to exaggerate to emphasize his case. The Russians were demanding a *quid pro quo,* and they would not yield. At Potsdam, in late July, when Truman demanded "immediate reorganization" of the governments of Hungary and Bulgaria to "include representatives of all significant democratic elements" and three-power assistance in "holding . . . free and unfettered elections," Stalin pointed to Greece, again to remind Truman of the earlier agreements. The Russians were "not meddling in Greek affairs," he noted, adding that the Bulgarian and Rumanian governments were fulfilling the armistice agreements while in Greece "terrorism rages . . . against democratic elements." (One member of the American delegation later claimed that Stalin at one point made his position clear, stating that "any freely elected government [in Eastern Europe] would be anti-Soviet and that we cannot permit.") In effect, Stalin demanded that the United States abide by his construction of earlier agreements, and that Truman acknowledge what Roosevelt had accepted as the terms of the sphere-of-influence agreements—that democratic forms and anti-communist democrats of Eastern Europe be abandoned to the larger cause of Russian-American concord.[28]

Though the Allies at Potsdam were not able to settle the dispute over influence in Eastern Europe, they did reach a limited agreement on other European issues. In a "package" deal the Soviets accepted Italy in the U.N. after a peace treaty could be arranged; the United States and Great Britain agreed to set the temporary western border of Poland at the Oder-Neisse line; and the Soviets settled for far less in reparations than they had expected. The decisions on Germany were the important settlements, and the provision on reparations, when linked with American avoidance of offering Russia economic aid, left Russia without the assistance she needed for the pressing task of economic reconstruction.[29]

Russia had long been seeking substantial economic aid, and the American failure to offer it seemed to be part of a general strategy. Earlier Harriman had advised "that the development of friendly relations [with Russia] would depend upon a generous credit," and recommended "that the question of the credit should be tied into our overall diplomatic relations with the Soviet Union and at the appropriate time the Russians should be given to understand that our willingness to cooperate wholeheartedly with them in their vast reconstruction problem will depend upon their behavior in international matters." In January 1945 Roosevelt had decided not to discuss at Yalta the $6 billion credit to the Soviet Union, explaining privately, "I think it's very important that we hold this back and don't give them any promises until we get what we want." (Secretary Morgenthau, in vigorous disagreement, believed that both the President and Secretary of State Stettinius were wrong, and "that if they wanted to get the Russians to do something they should . . . do it nice. . . . Don't drive such a hard bargain that when you come through it does not taste good.") In future months American officials continued to delay, presumably using the prospect of a loan for political leverage. Shortly before Potsdam, the administration had secured congressional approval for a $1 billion loan fund which could have been used to assist Russia, but the issue of "credits to the Soviet Union" apparently was never even discussed.[30]

Shunting aside the loan, the United States also retreated from Roosevelt's implied agreement at Yalta that reparations would be about $20 billion (half of which the Soviets would receive); Truman's new Secretary of State, James F. Byrnes, pointed out that the figures were simply the "basis" for discussion. (He was technically correct, but obviously Roosevelt had intended it as a general promise and Stalin had so understood it. Had it not been so intended, why had Churchill refused to endorse this section of the Yalta agreement?) Because Byrnes was unwilling to yield, the final agreement on reparations was similar to the terms that would have prevailed if there had been no agreement: the Soviet Union would fill her claims largely by removals from her own zone. That was the substance of the Potsdam agreement. The Russians also surrendered any hopes of participating in control of the heavily industrialized Ruhr, and confirmed the earlier retreat from the policy of dismemberment of Germany. They settled for an agreement that they could trade food and raw materials from their zone for 15 per cent of such industrial capital equipment from the Western Zones "as is unnecessary for the German peace economy," and that the allies would transfer from the Western Zones "10 per cent of such industrial capital equipment as is unnecessary for the German peace economy"—but the agreement left undefined what was necessary for the economy.[31]

Potsdam, like Yalta, left many of the great questions unresolved. "One fact that stands out more clearly than others is that nothing is ever settled," wrote Lord Alanbrooke, Chief of the British Staff, in his diary. As he observed, neither the United States nor Russia had yielded significantly. Russia had refused to move from the areas that her armies occupied, and the United States had been vigorous in her efforts, but without offering economic assistance to gain concessions. Though the atomic bomb may not have greatly influenced Truman's actions in the months before Potsdam, the bomb certainly influenced his behavior at Potsdam. When he arrived he still wanted (and expected) Russian intervention in the Japanese war. During the conference he learned about the successful test at Alamogordo. With Russian intervention no longer necessary, Truman's position hardened noticeably. As sole possessor of the bomb, he had good reason to expect easier future dealings with Stalin. For months Stimson had been counseling that the bomb would be the "master card," and Truman, acting on Stimson's advice, even delayed the Potsdam Conference until a time when he would know about the bomb. On the eve of the conference the President had confided to an adviser, "If it explodes, as I think it will, I'll certainly have a hammer on those boys [the Russians]."[32]

III

At Potsdam President Truman was "delighted" when Stimson brought him the news about the bomb on July 16. Upon learning more about the results of the test, Truman (according to Stimson) said "it gave him an entirely new feeling of confidence and he thanked me for having come to the conference and being present to help him in this way." The President's enthusiasm and new sense of power were soon apparent in his meetings with the other heads of state, for as Churchill notes (in Stimson's words), "Truman was evidently much fortified by something that had happened and . . . he stood up to the Russians in a most emphatic and decisive manner." After reading the full report on the Alamogordo explosion, Churchill said, "Now I know what happened to Truman yesterday. I couldn't understand it. When he got to the meeting after having read this report he was a changed man. He told the Russians just where they got off and generally bossed the whole meeting."[33]

"From that moment [when we learned of the successful test] our outlook on the future was transformed," Churchill explained later. Forced earlier to concede parts of Eastern Europe to the Russians because Britain did not have the power to resist Soviet wishes and the United States had seemed to lack the desire, Churchill immediately savored the new possibilities. The Prime Minister (Lord Alanbrooke wrote in his diary about Churchill's enthusiasm) "was completely carried away . . . we now had something in our hands which would redress the balance with the Russians. The secret of this explosive and the power to use it would completely alter the diplomatic equilibrium. . . . Now we had a new value which redressed our position (pushing out his chin and scowling); now we could say, 'If you insist on doing this or that well . . . And then where were the Russians!' "[34]

Stimson and Byrnes had long understood that the bomb could influence future relations with Russia, and, after the successful test, they knew that Russian entry was no longer necessary to end the Japanese war. Upon Truman's direction, Stimson conferred at Potsdam with General Marshall and reported to the President that Marshall no longer saw a need for Russian intervention. "It is quite clear," cabled Churchill from Potsdam, "that the United States do not at the present time desire Russian participation in the war against Japan."[35]

"The new explosive alone was sufficient to settle matters," Churchill reported. The bomb had displaced the Russians in the calculations of American policy-makers. The combat use of the bomb, then, was not viewed as the only way to end the Far Eastern war promptly. In July there was ample evidence that there were other possible strategies—a noncombat demonstration, a warning, a blockade. Yet, before authorizing the use of the bomb at Hiroshima, Truman did not try *any* of the possible strategies, including the three most likely: guaranteeing the position of the Japanese Emperor (and hence making surrender conditional), seeking a Russian declaration of war (or announcement of intent), or waiting for Russian entry into the war.[36]

As an invasion of the Japanese mainland was not scheduled until about November 1, and as Truman knew that the Japanese were sending out "peace feelers" and that the main obstacle to peace seemed to be the requirement of unconditional surrender (which threatened the position of the Emperor), he could wisely have revised the terms of surrender. At first Under Secretary of State Grew and then Stimson had urged Truman earlier to revise the terms in this way, and he had been sympathetic. But at Potsdam Stimson found that Truman and Byrnes had rejected his advice. As a result the proclamation issued from Potsdam by the United States, Great Britain, and China retained the demand for unconditional surrender when a guarantee of the Emperor's government might have removed the chief impediment to peace.[37]

Nor was Truman willing to seek a Russian declaration of war (or even an announcement of intent). Even though American advisers had long believed that the *threat* of Russian entry might be sufficient to compel Japanese capitulation, Truman did not invite Stalin to sign the proclamation, which would have constituted a statement of Russian intent. There is even substantial evidence that Truman sought to delay Russian entry into the war.[38]

Pledging to maintain the position of the Emperor, seeking a Russian declaration of war (or announcement of intent), awaiting Russian entry—each of these options, as well as others, had been proposed in the months before Hiroshima and Nagasaki. Each was available to Truman. Why did he not try one or more? No *definite* answer is possible. But it is clear that Truman was either incapable or unwilling to reexamine his earlier assumption (or decision) of using the bomb. Under the tutelage of Byrnes and Stimson, Truman had come to assume by July that the bomb should be used, and perhaps he was incapable of reconsidering this strategy because he found no compelling reason not to use the bomb. Or he may have consciously rejected the options because he wanted to use the bomb. Perhaps he was vindictive and wished to retaliate for Pearl Harbor and other atrocities. (In justifying the use of the bomb against the Japanese, he wrote a few days after Nagasaki, "The only language they seem to understand is the one we have been using to bombard them. When you have to deal with a beast you have to treat him as a beast.") Or, most likely, Truman agreed with

Byrnes that using the bomb would advance other American policies: it would end the war before the Russians could gain a
hold in Manchuria, it would permit the United States to exclude
Russia from the occupation government of Japan, and it would
make the Soviets more manageable in Eastern Europe. It would
enable the United States to shape the peace according to its own
standards.[39]

At minimum, then, the use of the bomb reveals the moral
insensitivity of the President—whether he used it because the
moral implications did not compel a reexamination of assumptions, or because he sought retribution, or because he sought to
keep Russia out of Manchuria and the occupation government of
Japan, and to make her more manageable in Eastern Europe. In
1945 American foreign policy was not innocent, nor was it unconcerned about Russian power, nor did it assume that the
United States lacked the power to impose its will on the Russian state, nor was it characterized by high moral purpose or
consistent dedication to humanitarian principles.

IV

Both Secretary of War Stimson and Secretary of State Byrnes
had foreseen the importance of the bomb to American foreign
policy. To Stimson it had long promised to be the "master card"
for diplomacy. After Hiroshima and Nagasaki Byrnes was eager
to use the bomb as at least an "implied threat" in negotiations
with Russia, and Truman seems to have agreed to a vigorous course in trying to roll back Russian influence in Eastern
Europe.[40]

Truman seemed to be rejecting Stimson's recommendations
that international control of atomic energy be traded for important Russian concessions—"namely the settlement of the Polish, Rumanian, Yugoslavian, and Manchurian problems." In his
report on the Potsdam Conference the day after the second
bomb, the President asserted that Rumania, Bulgaria, and Hungary "are not to be spheres of influence of any one power" and
at the same time proclaimed that the United States would be
the "trustees" of the atomic bomb.[41]

Following Truman's veiled threat, Byrnes continued his efforts to roll back the Soviet Union's influence. Assisted by a similar protest by the British, who clearly recognized the power of the bomb, he gained postponement of the Bulgarian elections, charging that the government was not "adequately representative of important elements . . . of democratic opinion" and that its arrangements for elections "did not insure freedom from the fear of force or intimidation." In Hungary, Russia also acceded to similar Anglo-American demands and postponed the scheduled elections. It is not unreasonable to conclude that the bomb had made the Russians more tractable. "The significance of Hiroshima was not lost on the Russians," Alexander Werth, British correspondent in the Soviet Union, later reported. "It was clearly realized that this was a New Fact in the world's power politics, that the bomb constituted a threat to Russia. . . . Everybody . . . believed that although the two [atomic] bombs had killed or maimed [the] . . . Japanese, their real purpose was, first and foremost, to intimidate Russia."[42]

Perhaps encouraged by his successes in Bulgaria and Hungary, Byrnes "wished to have the implied threat of the bomb in his pocket during the [September] conference" of foreign ministers in London. Stimson confided to his diary that Byrnes "was very much against any attempt to cooperate with Russia. His mind is full of his problems with the coming meeting . . . and he looks to having the presence of the bomb in his pocket . . . as a great weapon to get through the thing he has. He also told me of a number of acts of perfidy . . . of Stalin which they had encountered at Potsdam and felt in the light of those that we would not rely upon anything in the way of promises from them."[43]

The London conference ended in deadlock, disbanding without even a joint communiqué. Despite American possession of the bomb, Molotov would not yield to American demands to reorganize the governments of Bulgaria and Rumania. In turn, he demanded for Russia a role in the occupation government of Japan, but Byrnes rebuffed the proposal. Unprepared for this issue, Byrnes was also unwilling or unable to understand Soviet anxieties about the security of their frontiers, and he pressed

most vigorously for the reorganization of the Rumanian government. He would not acknowledge and perhaps could not understand the dilemma of his policy: that he was supporting free
elections in areas (particularly in Rumania) where the resulting
governments would probably be hostile to the Soviet Union, and
yet he was arguing that democracy in Eastern Europe was
compatible with Soviet demands for security. Unable to accept
that Byrnes might be naive, Molotov questioned the Secretary's
sincerity and charged that he wanted governments unfriendly
to the Soviet Union. From this, Byrnes could only conclude later,
"It seemed that the Soviet Union was determined to dominate
Europe."[44]

While the United States in the cases of these Eastern European nations chose to support traditional democratic principles
and neither to acknowledge its earlier agreements on spheres of
influence nor to respect Russian fears, Byrnes would not admit
the similarity between Russian behavior in Rumania and British
action in Greece. As part of the terms of his agreement with
Churchill, Stalin had allowed the British to suppress a revolutionary force in Greece, and as a result the Greek government
could not be accurately interpreted as broadly representative nor
as a product of democratic procedures. Yet, as Molotov emphasized, the United States had not opposed British action in Greece
or questioned the legitimacy of that government, nor was the
United States making a reversal of British imperialism in Greece
a condition for the large loan that Britain needed.[45]

Some American observers, however, were aware of this
double standard. In the northern Pacific and in Japan, America
was to have the deciding voice, but in Eastern Europe, emphasized Walter Lippmann, "we invoke the principle that this is
one world in which decisions must not be taken unilaterally."
Most Americans did not see this paradox, and Byrnes probably
expressed crystallizing national sentiment that autumn when he
concluded that the dispute with Russia was a test of whether
"we really believed in what we said about one world and our
desire to build collective security, or whether we were willing
to accept the Soviet preference for the simpler task of dividing
the world into two spheres of influence."[46]

Despite Byrnes's views, and although he could not secure a reorganization of the Rumanian government, communist influence was weakened in other parts of Eastern Europe. In Budapest free elections were held and the Communist party was routed; and early in November, just two days after the United States recognized Hungary, the Communists lost in the national elections there. In Bulgaria elections took place in "complete order and without disturbance," and, despite American protests, a Communist-dominated single ticket (representing most of the political parties) triumphed.[47]

While the Soviet Union would not generally permit in Eastern Europe conditions that conformed to Western ideals, Stalin was pursuing a cautious policy and seeking accommodation with the West. He was willing to allow capitalism but was suspicious of American efforts at economic penetration which could lead to political dominance. Though by the autumn of 1945 the governments in Russia's general area of influence were subservient in foreign policy, they varied in form and in degree of independence—democracy in Czechoslovakia (the only country in this area with a democratic tradition), free elections and the overthrow of the Communist party in Hungary, a Communist-formed coalition government in Bulgaria, a broadly based but Communist-dominated government in Poland, and a Soviet-imposed government in Rumania (the most anti-Russian of these nations). In all of these countries Communists controlled the ministries of interior (the police) and were able to suppress anti-Soviet groups, including anti-communist democrats.[48]

Those who have attributed to Russia a policy of inexorable expansion have often neglected this immediate postwar period, or they have interpreted it simply as a necessary preliminary (a cunning strategy to allay American suspicions until the American Army demobilized and left the continent) to the consolidation and extension of power in east-central Europe. From this perspective, however, much of Stalin's behavior becomes strangely contradictory and potentially self-defeating. If he had planned to create puppets rather than an area of "friendly governments," why (as Isaac Deutscher asks) did Stalin "so stubbornly refuse to make any concessions to the Poles over their eastern frontiers?" Certainly, also, his demand for reparations from Hungary, Rumania, and Bulgaria would have been unnecessary if he had planned to take over these countries. (America's insistence upon using a loan to Russia to achieve political goals, and the nearly twenty-month delay after Russia first submitted a specific proposal for assistance, led Harriman to suggest in November that the loan policy "may have contributed to their [Russian] avaricious policies in the countries occupied or liberated by the Red Army.")[49]

Russian sources are closed, so it is not possible to prove that Soviet intentions were conservative; nor for the same reason is it possible for those who adhere to the thesis of inexorable Soviet expansion to prove their theory. But the available evidence better supports the thesis that these years should be viewed not as a cunning preliminary to the harshness of 1947 and afterward, but as an attempt to establish a *modus vivendi* with the West and to protect "socialism in one country." This interpretation explains more adequately why the Russians delayed nearly three years before ending dissent and hardening policies in the countries behind their own military lines. It would also explain why the Communist parties in France and Italy were cooperating with the coalition governments until these parties were forced out of the coalitions in 1947. The American government had long hoped for the exclusion of these Communist parties, and in Italy, at least, American intimations of greater economic aid to a government without Communists was an effective lever. At the same time Stalin was seeking to prevent the revolution in Greece.[50]

If the Russian policy was conservative and sought accommodation (as now seems likely), then its failure must be explained by looking beyond Russian actions. Historians must reexamine this period and reconsider American policies. Were they directed toward compromise? Can they be judged as having sought adjustment? Or did they demand acquiescence to the American world view, thus thwarting real negotiations?

There is considerable evidence that American actions clearly changed after Roosevelt's death. Slowly abandoning the tactics of accommodation, they became even more vigorous after Hiroshima. The insistence upon rolling back Soviet influence in Eastern Europe, the reluctance to grant a loan for Russian reconstruction, the inability to reach an agreement on Germany, the maintenance of the nuclear monopoly—all of these could have contributed to the sense of Russian insecurity. The point, then, is that in 1945 and 1946 there may still have been possibilities for negotiations and settlements, for accommodations and adjustments, if the United States had been willing to recognize Soviet fears, to accept Soviet power in her areas of influence, and to ease anxieties.

V

In October 1945 President Truman delivered what Washington officials called his "getting tough with the Russians" speech. Proclaiming that American policy was "based firmly on fundamental principles of righteousness and justice," he promised that the United States "shall not give our approval to any compromise with evil." In a veiled assault on Soviet actions in Eastern Europe, he declared, "We shall refuse to recognize any government imposed on any nation by the force of any foreign power." Tacitly opposing the bilateral trading practices of Russia, he asserted as a principle of American foreign policy the doctrine of the "open door"—all nations "should have access on equal terms to the trade and the raw materials of the world." At the same time, however, Truman disregarded the fact of American power in Latin America and emphasized that the Monroe Doctrine (in expanded form) remained a cherished part of American policy there: ". . . the sovereign states of the Western Hemisphere, without interference from outside the Western Hemisphere, must work together as good neighbors in the solution of their common economic problems."[51]

"Soviet current policy," concluded a secret report by the Deputy Director of Naval Intelligence a few months later, "is to establish a Soviet Monroe Doctrine for the area under her shadow, primarily and urgently for security, secondarily to facilitate the eventual emergence of the USSR as a power which could not be menaced by any other world combination of powers." The report did not expect the Soviets ". . . to take any action during the next five years which might develop into hostilities with Anglo-Americans," but anticipated attempts to build up intelligence and potential sabotage networks, "encouragement of Communist parties in all countries potentially to weaken antagonists, and in colonial areas to pave the way for 'anti-imperialist' disorders and revolutions as a means of sapping the strength of . . . chief remaining European rivals, Britain and France." "Present Soviet maneuvers to control North Iran," the report explained, were conceived to "push . . . from their own oil . . . and closer to the enemy's oil." There was no need to fear military expansion beyond this security zone, suggested the report, for the Soviet Union was economically exhausted, its population undernourished and dislocated, its industry and transportation "in an advanced state of deterioration." Despite suggestions that Soviet policy was rather cautious, Truman was reaching a more militant conclusion. "Unless Russia is faced with an iron fist and strong language," asserted Truman to his Secretary of State in January, "another war is in the making. Only one language do they understand—'how many divisions have you' . . . I'm tired of babying the Soviets."[52]

During the winter months Byrnes, Senator Vandenberg, and John Foster Dulles, a Republican adviser on foreign policy, publicly attacked Russian policies. Vandenberg warned "our Russian ally" that the United States could not ignore "a unilateral gnawing away at the status quo." After these attacks, Churchill, accompanied by the President, delivered at Fulton, Missouri, a speech that announced the opening of the Cold War. "From Stettin in the Baltic to Trieste in the Adriatic, an iron curtain has descended across the Continent," declared the former British war leader. Condemning the establishment of "police governments" in Eastern Europe and warning of "Communist fifth columns or . . . parties elsewhere," Churchill, with Truman's approval, called for an Anglo-American alliance to create "conditions of freedom and democracy as rapidly as possible in all [these] countries." The Soviet Union, he contended, did not want war, only "the fruits of war and the indefinite expansion of their power and doctrines." Such dangers could not be removed "by closing our eyes to them . . . nor will they be removed by a policy of appeasement." While he said that it was "not our duty *at this time* . . . to interfere forcibly in the internal affairs" of Eastern European countries, Churchill implied that intervention was advisable when Anglo-American forces were strengthened. His message was clear: ". . . the old doctrine of the balance of power is unsound. We cannot afford . . . to work on narrow margins, offering temptations to a trial of strength."[53]

This was, as James Warburg later wrote, the early "idea of the containment doctrine . . . [and] the first public expression of the idea of a 'policy of liberation,'" which Dulles would later promulgate. Truman's presence on the platform at Fulton implied that Churchill's statement had official American endorsement, and though the President lamely denied afterward that he had known about the contents of the speech, he had actually discussed it with Churchill for two hours. Despite official denials and brief, widespread popular opposition to Churchill's message (according to public opinion polls), American policy was becoming clearly militant. It was not responding to a threat of immediate military danger; it was operating from the position of overwhelming power, and in the self-proclaimed conviction of righteousness.[54]

Undoubtedly Truman had also agreed with the former Prime Minister when Churchill said at Fulton:

> It would . . . be wrong and imprudent to intrust the secret knowledge of experience of the atomic bomb, which the United States, Great Britain and Canada now share, to the world organization. . . . No one in any country has slept less well in their beds because this knowledge and the method and raw material to apply it are at present . . . in American hands. I do not believe that we should all have slept so soundly had the positions been reversed and some Communist or neo-Fascist state monopolized, for the time being, these dread agencies. . . . Ultimately, when the essential brotherhood of man is truly embodied and expressed in a world organization, these powers may be confided to it.

Here, in classic form, was a theme that would dominate the American dialogue on the Cold War—the assertion of the purity of Anglo-American intentions and the assumption that the opposing power was malevolent and had no justifiable interests, no justifiable fears, and should place its trust in a Pax Americana (or a Pax Anglo-Americana). Under Anglo-American power the world could be transformed, order maintained, and Anglo-American principles extended. Stalin characterized Churchill's message as, "Something in the nature of an ultimatum: 'Accept our rule voluntarily, and then all will be well; otherwise war is inevitable.' "[55]

VI

Churchill's assurances notwithstanding, Russia had reason to fear the atomic bomb, particularly after Byrnes's efforts to use it as an "implied threat." For Byrnes the nuclear monopoly seemed to promise the possibility of creating on American terms a lasting structure of peace. Since this monopoly would last at least seven years, according to his estimates, America could achieve its objectives and presumably avoid an arms race. (A few days after Hiroshima, Byrnes instructed J. Robert Oppenheimer, the nuclear physicist, that "for the time being . . . international agreement was not practical and that he and the rest of the gang should pursue their work [on the hydrogen weapon] full force.")[56]

Byrnes's strategy was briefly and unsuccessfully challenged by another member of the administration, Henry Stimson. Earlier Stimson had hoped that America's possession of the bomb could lead to the offer of a partnership with the Russians in return for a *quid pro quo*—"the settlement of the Polish, Rumanian, Yugoslavian, and Manchurian problems," and liberalization of the Soviet regime. Russia would have to roll back her curtain of secrecy and move toward an open society, reasoned Stimson, for "no permanently safe international relations can be established between two such fundamentally different national systems." The bomb, he believed, could not be shared until Russia liberalized her regime, and he hoped that the need for international controls would pry back the lid of secrecy. But his conversations with Harriman at Potsdam had made Stimson pessimistic about Russia's easing her restrictions, and after the bombing of Japan, as he watched Byrnes's strategy unfolding, he moved more strongly toward international cooperation. On September 5 the Secretary of War met with the President, explaining "that both my plan and Byrnes's plan contained chances which I outlined and I said that I thought that in my method there was less danger than in his and also we would be on the right path towards establishment of an international world, while on his plan we would be on the wrong path in that respect and would be tending to revert to power politics."[57]

Rejecting his earlier idea of using possession of the bomb "as a direct lever" to produce "a change in Russian attitudes toward individual liberty," Stimson urged the President to invite the Soviet Union to share the secret "upon a basis of cooperation and trust."

> It is true [he wrote to the President] if we approach them now, as I would propose, we may be gambling on their good faith and risk their getting into production of bombs sooner than they would otherwise. To put the matter concisely, I consider the problem of our satisfactory relations with Russia as not merely connected with but virtually dominated by the problem of the atomic bomb. Except for the problem of the control of that bomb, those relations, while vitally important, might not be immediately pressing. The establishment of relations of mutual confidence between her and us could afford to await the slow process of time. But with the discovery of the bomb, they become immediately emergent. *Those relations may be irretrievably embittered by the way in which we approach the solution of the bomb with Russia. For if we fail to approach them now and merely continue to negotiate with them, having this weapon rather ostentatiously on our hip, their suspicions and their distrust of our purposes and motives will increase.*

"The chief lesson I have learned in a long life," concluded Stimson, "is the only way you can make a man trustworthy is to trust him; and the surest way you can make a man untrustworthy is to distrust him and show your distrust." A week after learning that Byrnes planned to use the bomb as an "implied threat," Stimson warned Truman that a direct and forthright approach should be made before using *"express or implied threats* in our peace negotiations."[58]

While Byrnes was at the unsuccessful London conference in mid-September, Stimson was lining up support for his new approach. The President seemed to approve of Stimson's memorandum. Truman "thought that we must take Russia into our confidence," wrote Stimson in his diary. Dean Acheson, the Under Secretary of State, also seemed "strongly on our side in the treatment of Russia," Stimson recorded. Robert P. Patterson, Stimson's Under Secretary who was scheduled to replace the Secretary upon his retirement later in the month, was convinced (in Stimson's words): "The safest way is not to try to keep the secret. It evidently cannot be kept . . . and that being so it is better to recognize it promptly and try to get on [better] terms with the Russians."[59]

At a special cabinet meeting on September 21, Stimson outlined his proposal: "(1) that we should approach Russia at once with an opportunity to share on proper *quid pro quo* the bomb and (2) that this approach to Russia should be to her directly and not through the . . . [United Nations] or a similar conference of a number of states." He received support from Patterson, Robert Hannegan, the Postmaster General, Henry Wallace, the Secretary of Commerce, and Acheson, who was representing the State Department in Byrnes's absence. Explaining that he could not "conceive of a world in which we were hoarders of military secrets from our Allies, particularly this great Ally," Acheson (reported Forrestal) "saw no alternative except to give the full information to the Russians . . . for a *quid pro quo*."[60]

Forrestal, Fred Vinson, the Secretary of the Treasury, Tom Clark, the Attorney General, and Clinton Anderson, the Secretary of Agriculture, opposed sharing the secret. Vinson compared it to the decision at the end of World War I to sink ships, and Anderson emphasized that the President must retain the confidence of the nation in his ability to "handle Russia." He warned that giving up information on atomic energy and the bomb would dangerously weaken that confidence. Forrestal, apparently the most vigorous opponent, objected to any attempt to "buy [Russian] understanding and sympathy. We tried that once with Hitler." Concluding that "trust had to be more than a one-way street," he recommended that the United States exercise "a trusteeship over the . . . bomb on behalf of the United Nations."[61]

Twelve days later, on October 3, Truman publicly announced his decision: the United States would seek international control of atomic energy but would not share the secret of the bomb. Byrnes, who had just returned from the London conference, resisted even this plan: he opposed the sharing of any information with the Russians. Since he believed that his diplomacy had been frustrated by Russian secrecy and suspicions, he did not see how inspection could operate. Convinced that the United States should delay until it had achieved a "decent" peace, he urged the President to stall. He realized that the United States was relying more heavily on the bomb and sharply cutting back conventional forces, and he was unwilling to risk yielding nuclear mastery.[62]

For more than two months the American government delayed even approaching the Russians. "The insistence by the inventors of mankind's most horrible weapon on withholding the secret from their ally has produced a most evident reaction in Moscow," reported the *New York Times*. It also led to Molotov's uneasy public boasting in November that Russia too would develop the bomb. ("We will have atomic energy and many other things too.") Finally, four months after Hiroshima, at the Moscow Conference of Foreign Ministers in late December, Byrnes invited Russia to join in recommending that the United Nations establish a commission on atomic energy.[63]

During the next five months, while the Cold War intensified, the Truman administration organized to formulate a policy. In March it released a preliminary study (the Acheson-Lilienthal report) which sought to minimize the problems of inspection by recommending the establishment of an international Atomic Development Authority (ADA), which would control all significant nuclear activities. The ADA would be established in stages, and at each stage the United States would provide the necessary information, with the specific information on the bomb withheld until the final stage.[64]

Probably this plan would have been unacceptable to the Russians. It would have left the secret of the bomb as an American trust for at least a few years, and it would have meant Russia's relinquishing possible control of a source of great economic potential to an international authority dominated by Western powers. In its emphasis, however, the report also conflicted with the desires of many American officials. It stressed generosity and negotiations when most were emphasizing fear and suspicion. It saw no need for punishment. A violation by any nation, under the proposed arrangements, would have been obvious and would have been a warning to other nations, and all would have returned at that point to big-power politics. The plan emphasized the necessity of international control and was willing to countenance small risks for world security when most emphasized the primacy of American security. ("We should not under any circumstances throw away our gun until we are sure that the rest of the world can't arm against us," asserted Truman.[65])

The final American plan was formulated and presented by Bernard Baruch, whom Truman had appointed as American representative to the U.N. Atomic Energy Commission. It emphasized "sanctions" and "condign punishments," and called for the elimination of the Security Council veto on matters of atomic energy. The issue of the veto was unnecessary; if any nation violated the treaty after the sharing of atomic energy, what action could be vetoed? In turn, until the nations reached the last stages of the plan, a violation, whatever the situation in the U.N., would lead to the withdrawal of other nations from the plan. Also, rather than following Stimson's advice and first approaching the Soviets privately on control of atomic energy, Baruch insisted upon negotiations in the public forum where positions could easily harden. Lacking the flexibility of the earlier plan but relying upon similar stages, the Baruch plan guaranteed the United States a nuclear monopoly for some years. Thus it left the United States with the option of using the bomb for leverage or even blackmail. While Byrnes and Truman may no longer have wanted to use the bomb as an "implied threat," its value was clear to the Joint Chiefs of Staff who had so counseled Baruch. The atomic bomb, "because of its decisive power is now an essential part of our military strength," explained General Carl Spaatz, the Air Force Chief of Staff. "Our monopoly of the bomb, even though it is transitory, may well prove to be a critical factor in our efforts to achieve [peace]." Separately the military chiefs had outlined the strategy which the Baruch plan followed: "We should exploit [the nuclear monopoly] to assist

in the early establishment of a satisfying peace. . . . It will be
desirable for international agreements concerning the atomic
bomb to follow the European peace treaties and definitely to
precede the time when other countries could have atomic
bombs."[66]

Though the Western world generally viewed the plan as mag-
nanimous and interpreted Russia's objections as further evidence
of her refusal to negotiate sincerely, the Soviet criticisms were
actually quite reasonable. The Baruch plan in its early stages
did endanger Soviet security. Russia would have had to allow
investigations of natural resources and mapping of the interior—
thus surrendering a principal military advantage. The Baruch
plan, charged Molotov, "proceeds from the desire to secure for
the United States the monopolistic possession of the bomb."
(Vandenberg had reportedly told Molotov privately, "We have
the atomic bomb and we are not going to give it up. We are
not going to compromise or trade with you. We are not going
to give up our immortal souls.") American leaders, as the Soviets understood, were demanding absolute security for their
own nation and refusing to trust Russia at the same time that
they were demanding that the Soviets trust the United States
and risk the possibility of having the American nuclear monopoly
frozen.[67]

The Russian plan, on the other hand, was clearly unacceptable
to American leaders. It called for nuclear disarmament and the
sharing of secrets first while delaying the establishment of controls. In effect it asked the United States to surrender its nuclear advantage and promised that the nations could thereafter
wrestle with the problems of controls. For the Truman administration the Russian plan was further evidence of Soviet insincer-
ity. American leaders could not understand objections to the suspension of the veto, nor, perhaps, why the Soviets feared a plan
that could guarantee the American monopoly. Yet Baruch had
been explicitly counseled earlier on the advantages of the monopoly, Byrnes had tried to exploit the monopoly, and presumably Truman had understood it. Perhaps because these men so
thoroughly believed that their intentions were honorable, that
their aim was to establish a just and lasting peace, and that the

United States would never use the bomb first, they could not grant the validity of Soviet objections.[68]

VII

As the great powers moved toward a stalemate on atomic energy, the dispute over Germany contributed to the growing mistrust. At the root of many of the difficulties were the French. Though not a signatory to the Potsdam declaration, they had a zone in Germany and were frustrating efforts at cooperation. They feared a revived Germany, preferred to weaken their enemy of the last three wars, and hoped also to profit at her expense. Seeking to annex territory west of the Rhine, they also wanted to participate in control of the Ruhr and to dismember Germany. When the French were blocked in the four-power council, they vetoed proposals for interzonal trade and economic unification. The other Western powers tolerated these obstructions, but the Russians believed the actions were American-inspired. "After six months of French obstruction," a high Russian official told James Warburg in the summer of 1946, "we began to suspect that this was a put-up-job—that you did not like the bargain you had made at Potsdam and that you are letting the French get you out of it."[69]

"Our first break with Soviet policy in Germany came over reparations," later wrote Lieutenant General Lucius Clay, Deputy Military Governor of the American zone. With the German economy in disorder and the United States and Britain contributing food to their zones while the Soviet Union made its zone live on its own resources and pay reparations, Clay in May terminated reparations deliveries to the Russians from the American zone. "This situation could not be permitted to continue as it represented indirect payment for deliveries to the Soviet Union." This, Clay wrongly contended, violated the Potsdam agreement by withdrawing reparations from a deficient economy. (Despite the provision in the Potsdam protocol that Germany would be treated as "one economic unit," the poorly worded, rather muddled agreement also provided that the Russians should take reparations from their own zone and that these reparations were not contingent upon the import-export balance of the Western zones. In arguing for the plan adopted at Potsdam, Byrnes had explained that the Russians "would have no interest in exports and imports from our zone.")[70]

Lashing out at the United States after Clay's decision, the Russians charged that the Potsdam agreement had been violated. And Russian policy toward Germany soon changed. On July 10, the day after Molotov attacked the Western zonal authorities for failing to destroy fascism and its economic base, the cartels and landed estates, he reversed his tactics and made a bid for German support. Implying that the Morgenthau plan still shaped Western policy, he urged the development of peaceful basic industries in a politically unified Germany. The sudden emphasis on greater industrialization followed abruptly upon Soviet demands for less industrialization. Perhaps the reversal was simply a cynical response to fears of continuing Western violations. Whatever its inspiration, the speech seemed to be an attempt to kindle antagonism against the West.[71]

Byrnes promptly countered with a proposal for economic (but not political) unification, which the Russians could not accept without halting reparations. When France and Russia refused to participate, the British and Americans moved to create a bizonal economy. Because of the failure to establish a unified economy, explained Byrnes in his famous Stuttgart speech of September, the United States no longer felt bound by the earlier agreement to maintain a low level of industry. He emphasized that a prosperous Germany was essential to European recovery. In addition, he called into question the temporary Neisse River boundary with Poland and implied that the United States would support a return of the eastern territory to Germany. By affirming that the United States would stay in Germany "as long as there is an occupation army," he declared in effect that the country would not be abandoned to Russia. The government of Germany, he promised, would be returned to the people so that there could be a "peaceful, democratic" nation which would remain free and independent. "It is not in the interest of the German people or in the interest of world peace that Germany should become a pawn or a partner in a military struggle for power between the East and West," concluded the Secretary.

Yet, as the Potsdam agreement crumbled and the United States and Russia quarreled, Germany would remain a key issue in the Cold War struggle.[72]

VIII

How do American actions since V-J Day appear to other nations? [asked Secretary of Commerce Henry Wallace in a private letter to the President in mid-July 1946]. I mean by actions the concrete things like $13 billion for the War and Navy departments, the Bikini tests of the atomic bomb [begun just before Baruch presented his proposal at the U.N.] and continued production of bombs, the plan to arm Latin America with our weapons, production of B-29s and planned production of B-36s, and the effort to secure air bases spread over half the globe from which the other half of the globe can be bombed.

. . . it follows that to the Russians all of the defense and security measures of the Western powers seem to have an aggressive intent. Our actions to expand our military security system . . . appear to them as going far beyond the requirements of defense. I think we might feel the same if the United States were the only capitalistic country in the world, and the principal socialistic countries were creating a level of armed strength far exceeding anything in their previous history. From the Russian point of view, also, the granting of a loan to Britain and the lack of tangible results on their request to borrow for rehabilitation purposes may be regarded as another evidence of the strengthening of an anti-Soviet bloc.

Finally, our resistance to her attempts to obtain . . . her own security system in the form of "friendly" neighboring states seems, from the Russian point of view, to clinch the case. . . . Our interest in establishing democracy in Eastern Europe, where democracy by and large has never existed, seems to her an attempt to re-establish the encirclement of unfriendly neighbors which was created after the last war and which might serve as a springboard for still another effort to destroy her.[73]

Wallace could not reverse the course of American policy, and Truman was not sympathetic to the letter, later claiming that Wallace had proposed "surrendering" to the Soviet Union. In September the Secretary of Commerce openly criticized the administration's policies while Byrnes was in Paris negotiating peace treaties for the Balkan states. Calling for cooperation between the two great powers, Wallace warned against a " 'get tough with Russia' policy. . . . The tougher we get the tougher the Russians will get." While recommending "an open door for trade throughout the world" as the way to promote peace and prosperity, he contended that the United States should recognize that "we have no more business in the *political* affairs of Eastern Europe than Russia has in the *political* affairs of Latin America, Western Europe, and the United States."[74]

Perhaps Wallace was naive to think that economics and politics could be so easily separated, and clearly he did not understand that Russia, particularly after American efforts to use a loan to pry open trade, feared Western economic penetration of Eastern Europe. "In the situation which is likely to prevail in Poland and the Balkan states . . . the United States can hope to make its influence felt only if some degree of equal opportunity in trade [and] investment . . . is preserved," the State Department had advised earlier. Though trade need not lead to political dominance, the Soviets not unreasonably expressed fears of American economic power. (At Potsdam Stalin had thwarted Truman's attempts to open the Danube to free navigation and to create a multination commission for the river with American representation.) If the " 'principles of equality' are applied in international life," Molotov had argued, "the smaller states will be governed by the orders, injunctions, and instructions of strong foreign trusts and monopolies." Molotov had already seen the United States withhold aid from Poland when it would not accede to American demands for the "open door," and the State Department had insisted that the Czech government in order to be eligible for a loan must accept "the United States proposals for the expansion of world trade and employment." And Molotov knew that the United States had tried to use its economic power to coerce the Soviet Union into creating an "open door" in Eastern Europe and changing her own state-regulated trade. While negotiating a loan of $3.75 billion for Great Britain, at a low interest rate and without demanding liquidation of the Empire, the United States had falsely claimed to have lost for five months the Soviet request for a loan of $1 billion. The Truman administration belatedly offered in February to consider the Soviet Union's request, then insisted upon more stringent terms than for the British loan—Russia would have to reject state-trading and bilateralism, accept multilateralism, join the American-dominated World Bank and International Monetary Fund, reveal secret information about her economy, and disclose the terms of the favorable trade treaties that she had imposed on the nations of Eastern Europe.[75]

Though Wallace never seemed to understand specificially why these demands were unacceptable to the Soviet Union, he did not want to use American economic power to coerce the Russians. Freer trade, he believed, would advance world peace and prosperity only if nations negotiated agreements without economic blackmail. As early as March he had sufficiently distrusted the American negotiators on the loan to urge the President to appoint a group more sympathetic to the Soviet Union. Truman, by his later admission, "ignored" Wallace's request, and in July, just before Wallace's lengthy lecture, the President had foreclosed the possibility of a loan.[76]

Still believing that Truman was an unknowing captive of Secretary Byrnes and his cohorts, Wallace sought to carry the battle on foreign policy into the public forum. But, often naive and perhaps foolishly optimistic, he could not provoke a dialogue within the administration on a policy that had long been endorsed by the President. Eight days after his speech Wallace was fired for publicly criticizing foreign policy, and the last dissenter against Truman's foreign policy left the cabinet. By then, negotiations on atomic energy were proving useless, and the American staff was casting about for new ways to compel Russian approval. A much-respected foreign service officer, George Kennan, offered his analysis. The Russians, he suggested, had probably concluded "that we will do nothing" if they did not agree to the American proposal. Under such circumstances he proposed that the United States "begin a series of moves designed to convince the Russians of our serious intent and of the consequences if they choose to continue their present course."[77]

IX

As early as February 1946 Kennan had formulated the strategy—later called "containment"—which became acknowledged official policy in 1947 and was dramatically expressed in the Truman Doctrine. In explaining Soviet behavior Kennan expressed the emerging beliefs of American leaders about Soviet irrationality and the impossibility of achieving agreements. Kennan disregarded the history of Western hostility to the Soviet Union and concluded that Soviet policy was *unreasonably* based upon a fear of Western antagonism. Russian leaders, he warned, had a "neurotic view of world affairs. And they have learned to seek security only in patient but deadly struggle for total destruction of rival power, *never in compacts and compromises with it.*"[78]

Soviet power, however, "is neither schematic nor adventuristic," he said. "It does not take unnecessary risks. For this reason it can easily withdraw—and usually does—when strong resistance is encountered at any point. Thus, if the adversary has sufficient force and makes clear his readiness to use it, he rarely has to do so." (In an extended development of the same theme in 1947, Kennan warned that the Soviets move "inexorably along the prescribed path, like a persistent toy automobile wound up and headed in a given direction, stopping only when it meets unanswerable force." It was necessary to "confront the Russians with unalterable counterforce at any point where they show signs of encroaching," to stop the Russians with "superior force.")[79]

Read eagerly by policy-makers, Kennan's message seemed to represent only a slight shift in emphasis from Byrnes's policies. In 1945 and early 1946 the Secretary sought through diplomacy (and apparently "implied threats") to roll back Soviet influence in Eastern Europe. Kennan apparently accepted the situation in Eastern Europe, seemed to recommend military resistance to future expansion, and, by implication, supported a stronger military force and foreign bases. In late 1946, as Byrnes moved reluctantly toward accepting the governments of Eastern Europe, he seemed temporarily to accede to Soviet power there. But he never surrendered his hope of pushing the Soviets back, and he was prepared to resist Soviet expansion. The containment doctrine, by urging continued pressure and predicting that Soviet power would either mellow or disintegrate, promised the success that Byrnes sought; but the doctrine, according to Kennan's conception, did not emphasize the heavy reliance upon armaments and alliances that developed. (Though Kennan never explicitly discussed in his famous cable the issue of economic aid to the Soviet Union, it was clear from his analysis and from his other recommendations that disintegration could be speeded by denying economic assistance.) To the goals that Byrnes and most American officials shared, Kennan added a tactic—patience.[80]

The policies of Byrnes and Kennan were based upon what Walter Lippmann diagnosed as "a disbelief in the possibility of a settlement of the issues raised by . . . [the Cold War. The government] has reached the conclusion that all we can do is 'to contain' Russia until Russia changes." This conclusion, wrote Lippmann, was unwarranted and dangerous. "The history of diplomacy is the history of relations among rival powers which did not enjoy political intimacy and did not respond to appeals to common purposes. Nevertheless, there have been settlements . . . to think that rival and unfriendly powers cannot be brought to a settlement is to forget what diplomacy is about."[81]

Giving up diplomacy, the government prepared to declare publicly a war of ideologies—the struggle between the forces of light and darkness. On March ·12, just a year after Churchill's Iron Curtain speech, the President officially proclaimed the containment policy as the Truman Doctrine: ". . . it must be the policy of the United States to support free peoples who are resisting subjugation by armed minorities or by outside pressures." In urging financial aid for Greece and Turkey, the administration relied upon arguments that would become a familiar part of the American Cold War rhetoric. Truman justified opposition to the Greek revolution by defining it not as a revolution but as a struggle between totalitarianism and freedom. The insurgents, he believed, were communist-directed and represented part of the Soviet scheme for expansion. Their victory in Greece would probably lead to the victory of communism in other European countries, and the spread of communism automatically undermined the foundations of world peace and hence the security of the United States.[82]

Though there is still considerable controversy about the situation in Greece, it was a dangerous oversimplification to view the conflict as a struggle between freedom and totalitarianism. Greece, as many American liberals then emphasized, was not a free, democratic nation, and indeed many of the guerrillas were not communists. Rather than being part of the Soviet design for expansion (as American policy-makers wrongly believed), the revolution was opposed by Stalin and it apparently continued despite his opposition. In effect the United States was blocking a revolutionary group, often led by communists and aided by neighboring communist states, which was seeking to overthrow a corrupt, harsh, British-imposed government.[83]

Partly because American policy-makers wrongly viewed communism as monolithic and Soviet-directed, they preferred a repressive but anti-communist regime to a pro-communist or communist regime. Because many were coming to view communism as a radical evil, as simply a totalitarianism of the left (and identifying it with Hitler's Nazism), they felt justified in taking vigorous action to halt its advance. Their vaguely formulated assumption seemed to be that communism, once it gained control, would never relax its grip or even ease restraints on liberty; but other forms of repression were milder and would probably yield, ultimately conforming more closely to American democratic aspirations. Significantly, though there were occasional admissions that Greece was not really democratic, American policy-makers did not broaden the public dialogue and adequately explain that they were supporting counter-insurgency to keep open the options for democracy. Rather, in terms reminiscent of the earlier discussion about the Balkans, they publicly discussed the conflict in unreal terms distorted by ideology, as a struggle between freedom and tyranny.[84]

There were of course other reasons why the administration was concerned about Greece and Turkey, for these nations controlled the sea trade to the Middle East and were close to important oil resources on which Anglo-American interests depended. The United States wanted to retain access to these vital resources and to keep them out of the Soviet sphere of influence. "These raw materials have to come over the sea," Forrestal explained privately, and "that is *one* reason why the Mediterranean must remain a free highway." In an earlier draft of Truman's speech, advisers had stressed that Greece and Turkey were areas of great natural resources which "must be accessible to all nations and must not be under the exclusive control or domination of any single nation." But, significantly, this theme was removed from the speech, and neither the private nor public arguments that followed generally emphasized such a narrow conception of national economic interest. Instead, American policy-makers painted a larger and more frightening picture: a defeat in Greece, by sapping the will of anti-communists elsewhere and encouraging their communist enemies, would lead to the collapse of governments in Western Europe and, through a mixture of infiltration, subversion, and indirect aid, even to the fall of Africa and Asia. "If Greece and then Turkey succumb, the whole Middle East will be lost," explained William Clayton, the Under Secretary of State for Economic Affairs. "France may then capitulate to the Communists. As France goes, all Western Europe and North Africa will go."[85]

The specter of expanding communism did not simply outrage American humanitarianism; more seriously, it seemed to threaten the national interest in the largest sense. For some it simply meant that world resources—populations and materials for war—would fall to the enemy and might give it the strength to conquer the United States. (During the years when America relied upon a nuclear monopoly for protection, this view was certainly unrealistic in the short run and dubious even in the long run.) For others there was another and more subtle fear, not of attacks on the United States but of the menace of expanding communism to the American economy: it could cut off supplies of raw materials for America and curtail trade, eliminating markets for investment capital and for surpluses.[86]

Such restrictions would compel a drastic readjustment of the American economy and greatly reduce the standard of living. Unless communism was halted, according to this view, it might economically encircle the United States and disorder the American economic system. "If these countries [Greece and Turkey] and the other countries should adopt closed economies," warned Clayton, "you can imagine the effect that it would have on our foreign trade . . . it is important that we do everything we can to retain those export markets." Looking at the economic crises in the world in early 1947, Joseph Jones, a major draftsman of the Truman Doctrine speech, explained the fears of the administration. If the British Empire, Greece, France, and China "are allowed to spiral downwards into economic anarchy, then at best they will drop out of the United States orbit and try an independent nationalistic policy; at worst they will swing into the Russian orbit." The result, he predicted, would be a disastrous depression, far worse than the Great Depression.[87]

"A large volume of soundly based international trade is essential if we are to achieve prosperity, build a durable structure of world economy and attain our goal of world peace and security," explained Harry S. Truman. Linking national prosperity to international peace and prosperity, American leaders acknowledged their nation's overwhelming economic power and assumed that it was essential to the advancement of world peace and prosperity. According to this analysis, the conditions necessary for American economic expansion also promoted international economic and political good health, *directly* (through the flow of benefits from America) and *indirectly* (because other economies would emulate the American). In turn, however, nations like Russia, which engaged in state-trading and bilateralism, endangered the world economy and the American economy. "Nations which act as enemies in the marketplace," explained Clayton, "cannot long be friends at the council table."[88]

"If, by default, we permit free enterprise to disappear in the other nations of the world, the very existence of our own economy and our own democracy will be threatened . . ."—these were the words penned by some of Truman's assistants in an earlier draft of the Truman Doctrine speech. Not only did most American leaders believe that communism threatened the American economy, but they often expressed the belief that traditional freedoms rested upon the prevailing forms of the economy. "Under a different system in this country," explained Dean Acheson, "you could use the entire production of the country in the United States. If you wished to control the entire trade and income of the United States, which means the life of the people, you could probably fix it so that everything produced here would be consumed here, but that would completely change our Constitution, our relations to property, human liberty, our very conceptions of law."[89]

"Foreign trade is vitally necessary to an expanding American economy," Truman explained. "Our system cannot survive in a contracting economy." Less than a week before announcing the Truman Doctrine, the President offered a more complete analysis of the American political economy, of the relation of cherished freedoms to corporate capitalism:

> There is one thing that Americans value even more than peace. It is freedom. Freedom of worship—freedom of speech—freedom of enterprise. It must be true that the first two of these freedoms are related to the third. . . . So our devotion to free enterprise has deeper roots than a desire to protect the profits of ownership. It is part and parcel of what we call American.
> . . . The pattern of trade that is *least* conducive to freedom of enterprise is one in which decisions are made by governments.
> . . . If this [international] trend is not reversed, the Government of the United States will be under pressure . . . to fight for markets and raw materials. And if the Government were to yield to this pressure, it would shortly find itself in the business of allocating foreign goods among importers and foreign markets among exporters, and telling every trader what he could buy or sell. . . . It is not the American way.[90]

Opposition among policy-makers to communist expansion in the immediate postwar years sprang from a cluster of related attitudes—humanitarianism, expectation of military attack in the short or long run, and the fear of economic encirclement. It is this fear of economic danger, so closely linked to the political economy of American liberalism, which has often constituted much of the basis for American intervention in other lands. American efforts, as William Appleman Williams has emphasized, have frequently been directed toward maintaining an economic open door. To do so, at times the United States has been compelled to subdue or limit challenges, and in the postwar years the most serious challenges were communist. The justification usually offered—that these challenges are totalitarian —is not false but, rather, often incomplete.[91]

X

The fear of communism, often mixed with a misunderstanding of Munich and the sense that compromise may be appeasement, has led policy-makers generally to be intransigent in their re-

60 BARTON J. BERNSTEIN

sponse to communism. They have allowed their fears to distort their perceptions and their ideology to blur reality. This is part of the legacy of the Truman administration in the development of the Cold War.

In these years American liberal democracy became visibly defensive. Though espousing humanitarian ideals and proclaiming the value of self-determination, Americans have often failed to exhibit a tolerance or understanding of the methods of other people in pursuing social change and establishing governments in their own (non-American) way. Revolutions have been misunderstood, seldom accepted, never befriended. Fearing violence, respecting private property, and believing in peaceful reform, Americans have become captives of an ideology which interprets revolution as dysfunctional and dangerous to American interests. Opposing these radical movements in the name of freedom, America has turned often to oligarchies and dictators instead. By falsely dividing the world into the free and the unfree, and by making alliances in the name of freedom (not security) with the enemies of freedom, America has often judged world events by the standards of the crusade against communism, and thus it has been unable to understand the behavior and problems of the underdeveloped nations. It is this defective world view, so visible in the early Cold War, that has led some to lament that the American self-conception has lost its utopian vision.

NOTES

1. For the most notable dissents, see D. F. Fleming, *The Cold War and Its Origins* (Garden City, 1961, 2 vols.); William Appleman Williams, *American-Russian Relations, 1781–1947* (New York, 1952), and *The Tragedy of American Diplomacy* (New York, 1962, rev. ed.); Gar Alperovitz, *Atomic Diplomacy* (New York, 1965); Walter La Feber, *America, Russia and the Cold War, 1945–1966* (New York, 1967); Gabriel Kolko, *The Politics of War* (New York, 1968); and Walter Lippmann, *The Cold War* (New York,

1947). My own interpretations have been influenced particularly by the work of Williams and Lippmann. It appears that some scholars who generally accepted the consensus may be moving to a new position. See Arthur M. Schlesinger, Jr., "Origins of the Cold War," *Foreign Affairs,* XLVII (October 1967), 22–51, which accepts portions of recent reinterpretations before abruptly moving back to the more traditional position.

2. Among the major collections are the Henry Stimson and Arthur Bliss Lane Papers at Yale University; the Joseph Grew Papers at Harvard University; the William Leahy, Joseph Davies, Laurence Steinhardt, J. Robert Oppenheimer, and Robert P. Patterson Papers at the Library of Congress; and the Bernard Baruch, Harry Dexter White, and James Forrestal Papers at Princeton University; the William Clayton Papers at Rice University; and the Papers of Harry S. Truman and many of his advisers and subordinates at the Truman Library.

3. Williams, *Tragedy,* pp. 204–226, concludes that Roosevelt's ideology would have led to similar results.

4. Herbert Feis, *Churchill-Roosevelt-Stalin* (Princeton, 1957), p. 22. On the postponed second front, see Robert Sherwood, *Roosevelt and Hopkins* (New York, 1948), pp. 562–565, 618–620, 638–642; *Stalin's Correspondence with Roosevelt and Truman* (New York, 1965), pp. 33, 51–52, 74–76 (hereafter *Stalin's Corr.* I); *Stalin's Correspondence with Churchill and Attlee* (New York, 1965), pp. 60–62, 105–106, 131–135 (hereafter *Stalin's Corr.* II); Cordell Hull, *Memoirs,* II, 1173–1184, 1231–1280; Winston Churchill, *The Hinge of Fate* (Boston, 1952), pp. 479–487. On Russian borders and early fears, see Cordell Hull, *Memoirs* (New York, 1948), II, 1165–1175, 1247–1254; Churchill, *The Grand Alliance* (Boston, 1950), pp. 621–630, 695; Sherwood, *Roosevelt and Hopkins,* pp. 708–716; Anthony Eden, *The Memoirs of Anthony Eden: The Reckoning* (Boston, 1965), pp. 330–347. On the separate peace and negotiations, see *Stalin's Corr.* I, pp. 195–214; II, pp. 313–314, 316–318; Churchill, *Triumph and Tragedy* (Boston, 1953), pp. 441–442; John Ehrman, *Grand Strategy* (London, 1956), pp. 122–128; Allen W. Dulles, *The Secret Surrender* (New York, 1966); Henry Stimson Diary, March 13, 1945, Yale University; Alperovitz, *Atomic Diplomacy,* pp. 256–260. There were already bad feelings about the Russian encouragement of the uprising of the Polish resistance movement, which the Russians then abandoned without aid, and of Russian treatment of liberated American and British prisoners. Also see Davies Diary, September 16, 1946.

5. On Roosevelt's use of American economic power to gain Soviet concessions, see John Morton Blum, *From the Morgenthau Diaries* (Boston, 1967), III, 304–306; James Byrnes, *All in One Lifetime* (New York, 1958), pp. 309–310; Williams, *American-Russian Relations,* p. 274, and *Tragedy,* pp. 218–225; Hull to Roosevelt, June 2, 1944, OF5528, Franklin D. Roosevelt Library. Quotes from Roosevelt's speech of January 6, 1945, in Samuel Rosenman, ed., *Public Papers and Addresses of Franklin D. Roosevelt* (New York, 1952, 13 vols.), XIII, 502–503, and his speech of June 29, 1944, *ibid.,* XIII, 186. Also see his speeches of January 11, 1944, and March 26, 1945, *ibid.,* XIII, 32–43, 595–600; Hull, *Memoirs,* II, 970–977; Edward Stettinius, *Department of State Bulletin* (hereafter *SDB*), XII (April 1, 1945), 531–533; Will Clayton, *ibid.* (April 8, 1945), p. 620. State Department officials, in *SDB,* XII (March 11, 1945), 401–407.

6. "Atlantic Charter" is in *A Decade of American Foreign Policy*, 81st Cong., 1st sess., S. Doc. 123, pp. 1–2. Churchill declared that it did not apply to the British Empire. (Speech to House of Commons, September 9, 1941, *House of Commons Debates*, 5th series, CCLXXIV, 68–69.) The Soviet Union, though not a signatory, endorsed the principles with the reservation that their "practical application . . . will necessarily adapt itself to the circumstances, needs, and historical peculiarities of particular countries." (I. M. Maisky, Soviet ambassador to Britain. Report of Proceedings, *Inter-Allied Meeting Held in London at St. James Palace on September 24, 1941* [London, 1941], p. 6315.) On Soviet fears that the Atlantic Charter was directed against the Soviet Union, see Eden, *Reckoning*, pp. 335–344. Quotes are from a memorandum prepared by Spellman after his meeting of September 3, 1943, with Roosevelt, in Robert Gannon, *The Cardinal Spellman Story* (Garden City, 1962), pp. 222–224.

7. On Stalin's request, see *Stalin's Corr.* I, p. 84; II, pp. 148–149. On Italy, *ibid.*, I, pp. 85–102; II, pp. 149–170; "Military Armistice" and "Allied Control Commission" documents, *Decade of Foreign Policy*, pp. 456–459; William McNeill, *America, Britain, and Russia* (London, 1953), p. 310; cf. Herbert Feis, *Churchill-Roosevelt-Stalin*, pp. 182–188. For warnings about the Italian precedent, see *Foreign Relations of the United States* (hereafter *FR*), *1943*, III, 26, 556.

8. On the rejected invasion, see Hull, *Memoirs*, II, 1231. For early negotiations, see *Stalin's Corr.* II, pp. 235–236, 238; Churchill, *Triumph and Tragedy*, pp. 74–81; Hull, *Memoirs*, II, 1456–1459. Hull wrongly concludes that the agreement then went into effect. On the agreement, see also Davies Diary, October 9, 13, 1945. Armistice agreements for three nations are in *Decade of Foreign Policy*, pp. 486–500; Feis, *Churchill-Roosevelt-Stalin*, pp. 415–419. Quoted from Harriman's cable of September 15, 1944, in *FR, Diplomatic Papers, 1944* (Washington, D.C., 1966), IV, 234–236. On earlier U.S. reluctance to become involved, see Eden, *Reckoning*, p. 542.

9. Quoted from Charles Wilson, *Churchill: Taken from the Diaries of Lord Moran* (Boston, 1966), p. 185. Churchill, from his *Triumph and Tragedy*, pp. 226–227. Percentages from Llewelyn Woodward, *British Foreign Policy in the Second World War*, p. 308; cf. Churchill, *Triumph and Tragedy*, p. 227. For Harriman's correspondence with Washington, see *FR, 1944*, IV, 1003–1014.

10. Agreements are in *Decade of Foreign Policy*, pp. 482–486, 494–499. On the agreements, see Department of State, *Conference of Berlin (Potsdam)* (Washington, D.C., 1960), I, 215; Feis, *Churchill-Roosevelt-Stalin*, pp. 450–453. On the understanding of the agreements, see Hull, *Memoirs*, II, 1459; *Stalin's Corr.* I, 164–167; Sherwood, *Roosevelt and Hopkins*, pp. 833–837; Davies Diary, January 2, 1945. For other evidence that American officials understood the implications of the armistice agreements, see *FR, 1944*, III, 438–439, 443–446, 455–456, 463, 469–470, 472–473, 475–478, 482–483, 941–943, 951, 963, 969–972; IV, 243, 275–277; *ibid., 1945*, IV, 151–152. The Churchill quote is from *Triumph and Tragedy*, p. 293. See also Churchill to Roosevelt, March 8, 1945, in *FR, 1945*, V, 505–506; Department of State, *The Conferences at Malta and Yalta* (Washington, D.C., 1955), pp. 105–106.

11. For the text, see *Yalta Conference*, pp. 977–978. On discussions and revisions, *ibid.*, pp. 854, 860–863, 873, 899, 908, 913, 918-924, 948. On later suggestions, see James F. Byrnes, *Speaking Frankly* (New York, 1947), pp. 32–33. A State Department draft which Roosevelt had rejected did not require unanimity for consultation, only for action. The results would have been largely the same. (*Yalta Conference*, pp. 97–109, and for warnings by W. A. Harriman, see pp. 64–66; also see Edward Stettinius, Jr., *Roosevelt and the Russians* [Garden City, 1949], pp. 88–89; Byrnes, *Speaking Frankly*, pp. 32–33.) Churchill also acted on the basis that the earlier "spheres of influence" agreement continued to operate. (*Triumph and Tragedy*, pp. 560–561, 636. Cf. McNeill, *America, Britain, and Russia*, p. 559; and Alperovitz, *Atomic Diplomacy*, pp. 132–135.) For State Department views of the Balkans, see *Yalta Conference*, pp. 234–249, and 234–236 on economic power. For State Department understanding of the declaration, see *FR, 1945*, V, 515–516, 520–524, 835–836.

12. Eden is quoted in Department of State, *The Conferences at Cairo and Teheran* (Washington, D.C., 1961), p. 882; Churchill is quoted in *Morgenthau Diaries*, III, 277.

13. On Germany and Roosevelt's shift, see John Snell, "What to Do with Germany?" in Snell, ed., *The Meaning of Yalta* (Baton Rouge, 1956), pp. 43-49; Kolko, *Politics of War*, pp. 324–333, 352–356. For Churchill, see Wilson, *Churchill*, pp. 190–192; Eden, *Reckoning*, pp. 552–553; Blum, *Morgenthau Diaries*, III, 369–372; cf. Churchill, *Triumph and Tragedy*, p. 157. For Morgenthau, see Blum, *Morgenthau Diaries*, III, 394–395; for State and Hull, see Hull, *Memoirs*, II, 1602–1629. For Stimson and War, see Henry Stimson and McGeorge Bundy, *On Active Service in Peace and War* (New York, 1948), pp. 568–582. For Robert Murphy, later General Lucius Clay's political adviser in Germany, see Davies Diary, July 13, 1945. On Yalta, see *Yalta Conference*, pp. 299–309, 874–882; Stettinius, *Roosevelt and the Russians*, pp. 41, 230–231; Byrnes, *Speaking Frankly*, p. 26; Churchill, *Triumph and Tragedy*, pp. 349–353; *Yalta Conference*, pp. 978–979.

14. *Yalta Conference*, pp. 975–984; McNeill, *America, Britain, and Russia*, pp. 539–566, and quote from p. 564. This analysis, unlike later right-wing charges of a "sell-out," does not assume a conspiracy nor an enthusiasm for acceding to Russian power.

15. On resistance to the Soviets, see Truman, *Memoirs*, I, 69–82; William Leahy, *I Was There* (New York, 1950), pp. 347–355; Walter Millis, ed., *The Forrestal Diaries* (New York, 1951), pp. 35–51; and Harriman's cables, April 4, 6, 1945, in *FR, 1945*, V, 817–820, 821–824. Truman is quoted in *New York Times*, June 24, 1941.

16. Quotes from Truman are in *Memoirs* (Garden City, 1955, 2 vols.), I, 76; "Protocol," *Yalta Conference*, p. 980; Leahy, *I Was There*, pp. 315–316. On Yalta and Poland, see Adam B. Ulam, *Expansion and Coexistence* (New York, 1968), pp. 373–377.

17. On the dispute, see *Stalin's Corr.* I, pp. 201–204, 211–222; II, 309–316, 322–325; *FR, 1945*, V, 123, 157, 180–182, 194, and 189, the source of the quote from FDR (message to Churchill, March 29, 1945). On April 1 Roosevelt warned Stalin against "a thinly, disguised continuance of the present Warsaw regime."

64 BARTON J. BERNSTEIN

18. Truman's paraphrase and quotation from Harriman are from
Truman, *Memoirs*, I, 70–72. On the meeting of April 20, also see *FR, 1945*,
V, 231–234. See *Forrestal Diaries*, p. 47, for fears of ideological expansion,
and Stimson Diary, July 15, 1945, for Harriman's fears that Russia would
even monopolize trade in Manchuria. Also see *FR, 1944*, IV, 283–289,
1025; *Conference of Yalta*, pp. 234–237, 243–246, and for Harriman's
fears of continued Soviet penetration, see *FR, 1945*, V, 821, 841–843.

19. *FR, 1945*, V, 231–234, and 232 is the source of the first two quotes.
Similar message is in Harriman's cable of April 6, 1945, *ibid.*, *1945*, V,
821–826, the source of the last quote.

20. Truman's paraphrase of Harriman is from Truman, *Memoirs*, I, 70.
See also *FR, 1945*, V, 232. On the issue of economic assistance to Russia,
see *FR, 1944*, IV, 1032–1078. Other quotes are from Harriman's message
to Secretary of State, January 9, 1944, in *FR, 1944*, IV, 1035; and Harriman's message of April 4, 1945, *ibid.*, *1945*, V, 819–820.

21. Paraphrase of Stimson is quoted from Bohlen's notes on meeting
of April 23, 1945, *FR, 1945*, V, 254; and also in Truman, *Memoirs*, I, 78.
The second Stimson quote is from Stimson Diary, April 23, 1945. Leahy's
statement is from paraphrase in Bohlen's notes. All the sources—Truman,
Memoirs, I, 70–78; Leahy Diary, April 23, in Library of Congress; Leahy,
I Was There, pp. 351–353; *Forrestal Diaries*, pp. 48–51; and Stimson Diary,
April 23—agree on the substance, and Forrestal and Truman both mention
that Leahy used the phrase "two interpretations." Stettinius is also from
paraphrase in Bohlen's notes.

22. Truman, quoted from Bohlen's notes of April 23, 1945, meeting,
FR, 1945, V, 253. Vandenberg in his diary entry of April 24, Arthur H.
Vandenberg, Jr., ed., *The Private Papers of Senator Vandenberg* (Boston,
1952), p. 176. Truman's second statement is quoted from his *Memoirs*, I,
82, and see 80–82. For corroboration, Davies Diary, April 30, 1945.
Cf. Bohlen's notes of April 23 meeting, in *FR, 1945*, V, 256–258. For a
similar economic threat by Stettinius, see entry of April 24 in *Vandenberg
Papers*, p. 176.

23. Quoted from entry of April 24, *Vandenberg Papers*, p. 176; for a
summary of these disputes, see McNeill, *America, Britain, and Russia*, pp.
591–603. On Argentina, see *FR, 1945*, I, 36, 199–201, 396–398, 483–488,
500–501. In part, the United States believed that it had to yield to Latin
America's wishes in return for its support of admission for the Ukraine
and White Russia.

24. For Truman's later explanation, see Truman, *Memoirs*, I, 225.
On Truman's knowledge, see Grew, "Memorandum of [Telephone] Conversation" with Leo Crowley, May 11; for other evidence on this subject,
see Grew, "Conference with the President," May 11; "Memorandum of
[Telephone] Conversation" with Stettinius, McCloy, Harriman, May 12;
and "Memorandum of Telephone Conversation" with Crowley, May 12.
For the phone conversation, see Grew, "Memorandum of [Telephone]
Conversation" with the Soviet chargé d'affaires, May 12, 1945; and for
Harriman, see Grew, "Memorandum of [Telephone] Conversation" with
Harriman, Stettinius, McCloy, May 12. All of the preceding in Grew
Papers. On Harriman, see his cable to State Department, April 11, and
parts of *Forrestal Diaries*, pp. 39–40, and *FR, 1945*, V, 998–1000, 1018–
1021. On lend-lease and Russia, see also Stimson Diary, May 14, 1945.

On the fear of using lend-lease for reconstruction, in violation of promises
to Congress, see Harold Smith Diary, April 26, 1945, Smith Papers,
Bureau of the Budget Library; Leo Crowley to Bernard Baruch, February
13, Baruch Papers. On the strategy behind termination, cf. Herbert
Feis, *Between War and Peace: The Potsdam Conference* (Princeton, 1960),
pp. 28–30, 101. The mistake, it appears, was not cutting off lend-lease
abruptly but turning around the ships at sea that were carrying lend-
lease; that was the decision of subordinates. See "Minutes of Meeting
of Soviet Protocol Subcommittee on Shipping," May 12, 1945, Edgerton
folder, Director of Matériel, Records of Army Service Forces, National
Archives. George Herring, "Lend-Lease to Russia and the Origins of the
Cold War, 1944–1945" (unpublished manuscript, 1968), emphasizes the
legal and domestic political reasons for termination, and argues that
subordinates misinterpreted the administration's intentions.

25. Quoted from paraphrases of conversations, *Conference of Berlin,*
I, 33–39.

26. Based on Harriman to Secretary of State, June 21, 1945, *FR, 1945,*
V, 352–354, and his message of June 28, in *Conference of Berlin,* I, 727–
728. Alperovitz, *Atomic Diplomacy,* 75n, concludes two-thirds. Harriman
is quoted from *Conference of Berlin,* I, 728. Also see *FR, 1945,* V, 372–
374.

27. *Conference of Berlin,* I, 357–434, and quote is from Truman's
message, 358n. For earlier advice on recognition, see Harriman to State,
May 30, 1945, *FR, 1945,* V, 548.

28. Quotes, in order, are from *Stalin's Corr.* I, 244; State Department
proposals, *Conference of Berlin,* II, 53, 643–644; Churchill's paraphrase,
Triumph and Tragedy, 636; Soviet proposals, *Conference of Berlin,* II,
1044; Philip Mosely, "Hopes and Failures: American Policy Towards East
Central Europe, 1941–1947," in Stephen Kertesz, ed., *The Fate of East
Central Europe* (South Bend, Ind., 1956), p. 40.

29. Byrnes insisted upon the "package." *Conference of Berlin,* II, 491–
492. On aid, see *Conference of Berlin,* II, 1477–1497. However, the OSS
Report, *Russian Reconstruction and Postwar Foreign Trade Developments,*
September 9, 1944, enclosure with Samuel Lubell to Baruch [about March
1945], Baruch Papers, concluded that Russia could rebuild its economy
by 1948 if the war ended in 1944, and that reconstruction "will depend
very little on foreign loans." For a similar position, see *Yalta Conference,*
pp. 321–322; cf. *FR, 1945,* V, 935–936, which notes that a loan of $6
billion "would speed up the Soviet economic development by at least
two years, and probably more." Based on these reports, America's offer
of credits seemed to be a useful but limited bargaining point. Cf. Martin
Herz, *Beginnings of the Cold War* (Bloomington, Ind., 1966), pp. 153–174;
and Albert Z. Carr, *Truman, Stalin, and Peace* (Garden City, 1950), p. 41.

30. Harriman is quoted from his dispatch, *Yalta Conference,* p. 313, and
for his earlier thoughts, see *FR, 1944,* IV, 1032–1035. FDR is quoted
from Morgenthau's notes on the President's comments and the Secretary's
reaction, in Blum, *Morgenthau Diaries,* III, 305. On German reparations
and political leverage, see *FR, 1945,* III, 1186, 1211–1213; *New York Times,*
January 24, 1945; Grew, "Memorandum of Conversation with Morgenthau," January 24, 1945, Grew Papers; *Yalta Conference,* p. 319; Harriman
cable of April 11, 1945; on the loan, see Fred Vinson to Truman, July

66   BARTON J. BERNSTEIN

14, 1945, Central Files, Box 29, Office of War Mobilization and Reconversion (OWMR) Records, National Archives (NA); *Conference of Potsdam*, I, 181; *New York Times*, February 14, 1950.

31. Byrnes is quoted from paraphase, *Conference of Berlin*, II, 474. On Churchill, see *Yalta Conference*, p. 983. *Conference of Berlin*, II, 1481–1487, for the final agreement; *ibid.,* II, 490–491, 520–521, 291, 450, 473, 476, 485–492, 822, 827, 932, for their understanding on reparations; and cf. *ibid.*, 944, and *FR, 1945*, III, 1253–1254, for a later American interpretation. On earlier negotiations, see *Yalta Conference*, pp. 808–809, 822, 874.

32. Diary entry of July 23, Arthur Bryant, *Triumph in the West* (based on the diaries of Lord Alanbrooke), (Garden City, 1959), p. 364; Churchill, *Triumph and Tragedy*, p. 668. "This is some conference. We are getting some good things from it," wrote Truman to Henry Wallace, July 27, 1945, OF27-B, Truman Papers. On economic assistance, see *Conference of Berlin*, I, 181; Alperovitz, *Atomic Diplomacy*, pp. 129–131; Williams, *Tragedy*, pp. 244–252. On the influence of the bomb before Potsdam, Alperovitz, *Atomic Diplomacy*, argues a different thesis. My position is very close to that of Athan Theoharis, "Review of Atomic Diplomacy," *New University Thought*, V (May–June 1967), 12 ff. Cf. Kolko, *Politics of War*, pp. 532–543, 556–567, 595–598. For evidence that Truman delayed the Potsdam Conference until he expected to have knowledge about the bomb, see Stimson Diary, June 6, 1945; Davies Diary, May 21, 1945. On Truman's arrival, see Truman, *Memoirs*, I, 417. On the bomb, see Stimson Diary, July 23 and 24, 1945. On Truman's reaction, see Stimson Diary, July 22, 23, 24, 1945. On Stimson's concern about the bomb and its value in diplomacy, see Stimson Diary, April 24 and 25, May 10, 14, 15, 16, March 15, 1945. Truman is quoted by Jonathan Daniels, *The Man of Independence* (Philadelphia, 1950), p. 266. My analysis does not rest upon this quotation, and I have purposely avoided relying upon later statements that may be rather dubious: for example, such statements as Truman's paraphrase in 1955 (in his partly "ghosted" memoirs) of Byrnes's statements of April 1945 that "the bomb might well put us in a position to dictate our own terms at the end of the war" (*Memoirs*, I, 87). When relying upon post-Hiroshima sources for evidence of pre-Hiroshima attitudes, I have particularly avoided using their phrasing as precise expressions of earlier attitudes or conversations. In seeking to interpret attitudes toward the atomic bomb, it is important to rely *primarily* upon those sources—contemporaneous manuscripts and published diaries (which seem faithfully to use contemporaneous materials)—which cannot, or are unlikely to, represent post-Hiroshima attitudes or, still worse, Cold War attitudes of 1947 and after.

33. First quote from Stimson Diary, July 16, 1945; second from *ibid.*, July 21, and others from *ibid.*, July 22; also see *ibid.*, July 18.

34. Churchill from his speech of August 16, 1945, House of Commons Debates, 5th Series, CDXIII, 78–79; Alanbrooke in his diary entry of July 23; *Triumph in the West*, pp. 363–364. Lord Cherwell had recognized earlier (in Margaret Gowing's words) "that whoever possessed . . . [atomic capability] would be able to dictate terms to the rest of the world" (*Britain and Atomic Energy* [London, 1964], pp. 100–105). Sir John Ander-

son expressed similar thoughts (Samuel Pickersgill, *The Mackenzie King Record* [Chicago, 1960], p. 532).

35. On Byrnes, see Leahy Diary, May 20, 1945; Richard Hewlett and Oscar Anderson, Jr., *The New World* (University Park, 1962), pp. 354–357; J. W. Wheeler-Bennett, *King George VI* (New York, 1958), p. 644; Byrnes, *Speaking Frankly*, pp. 261–262; *All in One Lifetime*, p. 300; Stimson Diary, July 17, 24, 1945; Davies Diary, July 28, 1945. All this evidence indicates strongly that Byrnes understood the significance for Russia, but the clearest evidence (though unfortunately from post-1945) is Leo Szilard, "A Personal History of the Atomic Bomb," University of Chicago *Roundtable,* 601 (September 25, 1949), 14–15; and "Was A-Bomb on Japan a Mistake?" *U.S. News and World Report* (August 15, 1960), pp. 65–71. On Russian entry as unnecessary, see Stimson Diary, July 20–24, 1945. On Marshall's report, *ibid.,* June 24. Churchill's cable of July 25, 1945, in Ehrman, *Grand Strategy,* p. 292. Churchill had reached this conclusion after a discussion with Byrnes (Hewlett and Anderson, *The New World,* p. 391).

36. Churchill is quoted from entry of July 23 (paraphrase by Alanbrooke of conversation with Churchill), in *Triumph in the West.* On the warning, see Alice K. Smith, "Behind the Decision to Use the Atomic Bomb," *Bulletin of the Atomic Scientists,* XIV (October 1958), 288–312; John J. McCloy, *The Challenge to American Foreign Policy* (Cambridge, Mass., 1953), pp. 40–44. Shortly after the Interim Committee's approval of combat use of the bomb, Ralph Bard, Under Secretary of the Navy, had dissented and suggested other alternatives—a warning about the bomb, a warning about Russia's likely entry into the war, and relaxation of the requirement of unconditional surrender (Bard memorandum of June 27, 1945, reprinted in "Was A-Bomb on Japan a Mistake?," p. 64). Admiral Ernest King claims that he had pointed out many times that a naval blockade could have been successful (King and Walter Muir Whitehall, *Fleet Admiral King* [New York, 1952], p. 621). Of course, King's views reflect the pride of the Navy and could easily and not unreasonably have been discounted on those grounds. Generals Henry Arnold and Curtis LeMay of the Air Force believed that continued bombing of Japan would have been successful (Wesley Craven and James Cate, eds., *The Army Air Forces in World War II* [Chicago, 1953, 6 vols.], V, 711, 726, 747). These judgments were not after the fact, but there was no good evidence that saturation bombing would have had the very prompt results expected of the atomic bomb. The employment of heavy bombing and a blockade had been accepted earlier as complementary tactics and as preliminaries to invasion (Department of Defense, *The Entry of the Soviet Union into the War Against Japan* [mimeographed, 1955], pp. 78–83).

37. The invasion of Kyushu was scheduled for the fall, but the full-scale invasion was not scheduled until the spring, so there was no reason to fear losses of 500,000 or 1,000,000 in the autumn, as later statements by officials charged. Indeed, the estimates were about 31,000 for the first thirty days on Kyushu (*Entry of the Soviet Union,* pp. 64–66, 79–83; Truman, *Truman Speaks* [New York, 1960], p. 67; Stimson, "The Decision to Use the Atomic Bomb," *Harper's,* CXCIV [February 1947], 97–107; Churchill's speech of August 16, 1945). On Truman's knowledge, see

Conference of Berlin, I, 873–876, II, 87, 1262–1263, 1264–1267; on the knowledge of policy-makers, see *Forrestal Diaries*, pp. 74–76, and *Conference of Berlin*, II, 1265–1267; Byrnes, *All in One Lifetime*, p. 297, and see in general, *Conference of Berlin*, I, 873–948, II, 1248, 1376. On May 28 Grew suggested to the President that he should guarantee the position of the Emperor, and Truman directed the Under Secretary to discuss the issue with military leaders. Stimson, Forrestal, and Marshall "were all in accord with the principle but for certain military reasons, not divulged, it was considered inadvisable for the President to make such a statement now," recorded Grew. "The question of timing was the nub of the whole matter according to the views present" ("Memorandum of Conversation," May 29, 1945, Grew Papers). Years later Stimson claimed that "the difficulty at the time was that we were having considerable trouble with the Japanese . . . on Okinawa and some of us were afraid that any possible concession at that time might be taken as an indication of weakness" (Stimson to Grew, June 19, 1947, Grew Papers). But Grew regarded Stimson's letter as "no less disingenuous than his article in *Harper's*," and pointed out that, by the end of May, "the fighting on Okinawa was practically over, or at least the issue was no longer in doubt" (Grew to Eugene H. Dooman, June 30, 1947. Cf. Grew, *Turbulent Era* [Boston, 1952, 2 vols.], II, 1421–1431.) On attempts at revision of the formula, see Stimson Diary, June 19, July 24; *Conference of Berlin*, I, 889–894, II, 1265–1267; *Soviet Entry into the War*, pp. 87–88. On Stimson, see also Stimson Diary, July 17, 24, 1945. Despite the use of the term "unconditional surrender," the proclamation did make certain promises about the future treatment of Japan *(Conference of Berlin*, II, 1280). On the Japanese response, see *Conference of Berlin*, I, 1292–1293; Katzu Kawai, "'Mokusatsu', Japan's Response to the Potsdam Declaration," *Pacific Historical Review*, XIX (November 1950), 409–414; Robert Butow, *Japan's Decision to Surrender* (Stanford, 1954), pp. 140–149.

38. There had been considerable discussion of the "shock" of Soviet entry into the war, and sometimes policy-makers felt that a declaration or announcement might have the same effect. *Conference of Berlin*, I, 173, 891–897, 905; II, 36; *Entry of the Soviet Union*, pp. 78–80. On expectations of Soviet entry, see *New York Times*, April 6, 1945; *Soviet Entry into the War*, pp. 70–72; Leahy Diary, May 11, July 17, 24, 1945; Alperovitz, *Atomic Diplomacy*, pp. 91–128. On Russia and the proclamation, see Byrnes, *Speaking Frankly*, pp. 207–213. Also see Davies Diary, July 27, 1945. On delaying Russian entry, see Churchill cable of July 23, in Ehrman, *Grand Strategy*, p. 292; Byrnes, *All in One Lifetime*, pp. 290–298; *Speaking Frankly*, pp. 68, 205–209; *Conference of Berlin*, II, 1585–1588. On Truman's order to use the bomb, see Feis, letter to the editor, *American Historical Review*, LXVIII (October 1962), 309–310; Patterson to Stimson, December 11, 1946, Patterson Papers, No. 22.

39. For Truman's statement, see Truman to Samuel McCrea Cavert, August 11, 1945, OF692-A, Truman Papers. Perhaps there were also racist impulses behind this statement. Also see Alperovitz, *Atomic Diplomacy*, p. 190n. "Byrnes said he was most anxious to get the Japanese affair over with before the Russians got in, with particular reference to Dairen" *(Forrestal Diaries* [July 28], p. 78). For agreement, see "Was

A-Bomb on Japan a Mistake?," p. 66. On the other hand, General Marshall had concluded (in Stimson's words) "that even if we went ahead in the war without the Russians, and compelled the Japanese to surrender to our terms, that would not prevent the Russians from marching into Manchuria anyhow and striking, thus permitting them to get virtually what they wanted in surrender terms" (Stimson Diary, July 23, 1945). Norman Cousins and Thomas Finletter, "A Beginning for Sanity," *Saturday Review,* XXIX (June 15, 1946), 5–9ff; and P. M. S. Blackett, *Fear, War and the Bomb* (New York, 1949), pp. 127–143, conclude that *political* considerations led to the use of the bomb—the desire to keep Russia out of Manchuria and to exclude Russia from decision-making in the occupation of Japan. For earlier consideration of breaking the Yalta agreement on the Far East, see Edward Stettinius, "Memorandum for the Secretary of War," May 12, 1945, Stettinius Papers, University of Virginia. In 1949 Szilard reported his conversation of May 1945 with Byrnes: "Mr. Byrnes did not argue that it was necessary to use the bomb against the cities of Japan in order to win the war. . . . [He believed] that our possessing and demonstrating the bomb would make Russia more manageable in Europe" ("Personal History," pp. 14–15). Williams, *Tragedy,* p. 254, and Alexander Werth, *Russia at War* (London, 1964), pp. 936–942, conclude that this was the purpose, and Alperovitz, *Atomic Diplomacy,* believes that "the evidence strongly suggests" that Byrnes's view (as recalled by Szilard) "was an accurate statement of policy." Cf. Herbert Feis, *The Atomic Bomb and the End of World War II* (Princeton, 1966), *passim,* and pp. 194–195. My own study of the decision to use the bomb has benefited from the work of Blackett, Williams, and Alperovitz.

40. Stimson Diary, August 12, September 3, 4, 5, 1945.

41. Quoted from Stimson Diary, June 6, 1945; Truman's address of August 9, 1945, in *Public Papers of the Presidents: Harry S. Truman* (hereafter *Truman Papers*), (Washington, D.C., 1961), 1945, pp. 210–213.

42. Byrnes's note of August 13 is in *SDB, XIII* (August 19, 1945), 274. On American maneuvering and the British reversal, see *FR, 1945,* IV, 282–385. *Conference of Berlin,* II, 689–690, 1494–1495, includes the revision of administrative procedures for the Allied Control Council in Hungary. For revisions on Bulgaria and Rumania, see *Conference of Berlin,* I, 406–408; II, 690–692, 1494–1495. Fleming, *Cold War,* I, 308–357, suggests, and Williams, *Tragedy,* pp. 252–261, and Alperovitz, *Atomic Diplomacy,* pp. 188–225, conclude that the administration used atomic diplomacy. But Alperovitz, p. 205, also suggests that Russia might have yielded on Hungary anyway. Lend-lease was quickly terminated after the Japanese surrendered, and Alperovitz, p. 223, sees the decision as part of a larger strategy; cf. Leahy Diary, August 17, 1945. On Soviet responses see Werth, *Russia at War,* pp. 934, 940, the source of quotes; *FR, 1945,* II, 82–84. Cf. Ulam, *Expansion and Coexistence,* p. 414. The termination of lend-lease shocked and dismayed British leaders, and made Britain more dependent upon, and more anxious for, a large American loan; see Richard Gardner, *Sterling-Dollar Diplomacy* (Oxford, 1956), p. 185.

43. John McCloy is quoted from Stimson Diary, August 12, September 3, 1945. Stimson from Stimson Diary, September 4, 1945.

44. On Rumania, see Henry Roberts, *Rumania* (New Haven, 1951),

p. 269; McNeill, *America, Britain, and Russia*, pp. 698–702. On Byrnes and Molotov, see *FR, 1945*, II, 243–245. The quote is from Byrnes, *Speaking Frankly*, p. 99.

45. On Greece, see William McNeill, *The Greek Dilemma* (Philadelphia, 1947), pp. 162–173; Todd Gitlin, "Counter-Insurgency: The Myth and Reality in Greece," in David Horowitz, ed,. *Containment and Revolution* (Boston, 1967). On Molotov, see *FR, 1945*, II, 197, 246–247. Also see *FR, 1946*, VI, 681–682.

46. Lippmann, *New York Herald Tribune*, October 21, 1945. Byrnes, *Speaking Frankly*, p. 105. See also *FR, 1946*, VI, 681–682.

47. On the election in Budapest, see *FR, 1945*, IV, 883. Quoted from *New York Times*, November 21, 1945. Some opponents of the Communists had withdrawn from the election when the Communists and the major parties agreed upon a single ticket. *FR, 1945*, IV, 374–375.

48. V. M. Molotov, *Problems of Foreign Policy: Speeches and Statements* (Moscow, 1949), pp. 44–45, 116–117, 213–214. On American policy, see *Conference of Berlin*, I, 179, 186, 366, 369, 370–373, 420–426, 715, 786–787; II, 477; *Conference of Yalta*, 234–235, 237, 243, 246; *FR, 1945*, IV, 889–890, 908, 915–916, 922–925; II, 236–238.

49. On Soviet policy, see Mark Ethridge and C. E. Black, "Negotiating on the Balkans," in Raymond Dennett and Joseph Johnson, eds., *Negotiating with the Russians* (Boston, 1951), pp. 203–204. Cf. George Kennan, *Memoirs* (Boston, 1967), pp. 255–258, and his memorandum in *FR, 1945*, V, 853–860. Isaac Deutscher, *Stalin* (New York, 1960), pp. 536–541. Harriman in "Certain Factors Underlying Our Relations with the Soviet Union," November 14, 1945, Harriman Papers, cited by Paterson. "The Abortive Russian Loan" (unpublished manuscript, 1967). On Stalin and Greece, see Milovan Djilas, *Conversations with Stalin* (New York, 1962), pp. 181–184, 246–247.

50. Deutscher, *Stalin*, pp. 518, 536–547, offers a similar theisis and has influenced my thought. Also see Blackett, *Fear, War*, pp. 80–81; Alperovitz, "How Did the Cold War Begin?," *New York Review*, VIII (March 23, 1967), 6–12; and Williams, *Tragedy*, pp. 259–276. On Czechoslovakia, see Hubert Ripka, *Czechoslovakia Enslaved*, pp. 304–310. On Italy, see H. Stuart Hughes, *The United States and Italy* (Cambridge, Mass., 1965, rev. ed.), p. 135; on France, see Philip Williams, *Politics in Post-War France* (New York, 1954), pp. 16–20. On the Communist party in France, see *FR, 1946*, V, 471–477.

51. First quote from interview with Chester Bowles, September 13, 1962. Truman address of October 27, 1945, is in *Truman Papers 1945*, pp. 433–434; cf. transcript of conversation between McCloy and Stimson, May 8, 1945, Stimson Papers.

52. Thomas Inglis (Deputy Director, Office of Naval Intelligence), "Memorandum of Information," January 21, 1946. On Harriman, see *FR, 1945*, V, 901–908; Leahy Diary, February 21, 1946. On Iran, see George Kirk, *The Middle East, 1945–1950* (London, 1954), pp. 56–105; LaFeber, *America, Russia*, pp. 28–29, and McNeill, *America, Britain, and Russia*, pp. 560, 561, 608, 626, 711–714; *FR, 1945*, II, 629–631, 685–687. N. S. Fatemi, *Oil Diplomacy* (New York, 1954), pp. 6, 59–60, 99–125, 233–288. Truman memo of January 5, 1946, which he allegedly read to Byrnes (*Memoirs*, I, 605–606; cf. Byrnes, *All in One Lifetime*, p. 403).

Though the interpretations of Soviet actions *supra* are dated after Truman's memo, there is no reason to assume that they are uncharacteristic of secret reports during this period. Some scholars have cited Stalin's speech of February 9, 1946, as evidence that the Soviets believed that war between the U.S. and the USSR was inevitable, but actually his speech was far more conservative. He did emphasize the likelihood of war between capitalist nations and also called for an economic build-up to insure the country "against any eventuality." For the text, see Morray, *Yalta to Disarmament*, pp. 339–349, and for Molotov's speech of February 6, see Molotov, *Problems of Foreign Policy*, pp. 21–36. For interpretations of Stalin's speech as bellicose, see *Forrestal Diaries*, pp. 134–135, and Walter Bedell Smith, *My Three Years in Moscow* (Philadelphia, 1950), p. 62. For Soviet estimates of an Anglo-American clash, see *FR, 1946*, VI, 683–685.

53. On Byrnes, see *SDB*, XIII (March 10, 1946), 355–358; on Vandenberg, see *Vital Speeches*, XII (March 15, 1946), 322–326; on Dulles, see *New York Times*, March 2, 1946. All quotes from Churchill's speech are from *Congressional Record*, 79th Cong., 2nd sess., pp. 45–47, but emphasis is added.

54. James P. Warburg, *Germany: Key to Peace* (Cambridge, Mass., 1953), pp. 36–37. On Truman, see President's Press Conference, March 8, 1946, Truman Library. On responses, see Fleming, *Cold War*, I, 348–357. For his knowledge, see Leahy Diary, February 10, 1946; Official Appointment Book, February 10, 1946, Truman Library; Davies Diary, February 11, 1946. For estimates of Soviet capability, see Inglis, "Memorandum," and Leahy Diary, February 21, 1946. In May General Joseph McNarney, anticipating a communist uprising in France, secured permission from Truman (despite Acheson's opposition) to move troops into France if necessary (Leahy Diary, May 3, 1946). By late spring the Truman administration judged that its military strength in Germany and Italy was inadequate to stop a Soviet attack or even to permit evacuation of troops in case of an attack. But top leaders believed (in Leahy's words) "that the Soviet government did not wish to start a war in the early future" (Leahy Diary, May 28, June 11, 1946). Also see *FR, 1946*, V, 435–438.

55. Quoted from *Pravda* interview of March 13, 1946, in Morray, *Yalta to Disarmament*, p. 50. For earlier Soviet responses, see *FR, 1946*, V, 712–713.

56. The only evidence on Byrnes's efforts is substantial but indirect—Stimson's reports that Byrnes planned to use the bomb as a threat, and Hewlett and Anderson, *The New World*, pp. 417, 456–461. The official *published* materials on the London conference contain no evidence of this. On his aims, see Byrnes, *Speaking Frankly*, pp. 179, 203. For a disclaimer of atomic diplomacy, *ibid.*, p. 265. Byrnes, quoted in Oppenheimer to Stimson, August 17, 1945, quoted in Hewlett and Anderson, *The New World*, p. 417. (This letter is not available in Oppenheimer Papers, Library of Congress.) Also see Oppenheimer to Ernest Lawrence, August 30, 1945, Oppenheimer Papers.

57. Quotes, in order, are from Stimson Diary, June 6, 1945; Stimson, "Reflections on the Basic Problems Which Confront Us," July 19, 1945, in *Conference of Berlin*, II, 1155–1158; Stimson Diary, July 20 and 22, September 17, 1945.

58. Stimson to President, September 11, 1945, in Henry Stimson and McGeorge Bundy, *On Active Service in Peace and War* (New York, 1948), p. 642. Emphasis provided by Stimson after giving the letter to Truman. Stimson, "Memorandum for the President," September 11, 1945, *ibid.*, pp. 642–646, emphasis added.

59. First quote is from Stimson Diary, September 12, 1945. Also see Davies Journal, September 18, 1945, for other evidence of Truman's agreement. Other quotes, in order, are from Stimson Diary, September 13 and 17, 1945.

60. Quoted from Stimson Diary, September 21, 1945, dictated December 11, 1945. Forrestal, "Cabinet" (notes on the meeting, including a paraphrase of Acheson), September 21, 1945; cf. *Forrestal Diaries*, pp. 93–96, for evidence that Millis erred. On Acheson, see *FR, 1945*, II, 49–50, and on Patterson, *ibid.*, pp. 54–55. Also see Dean Acheson, *Present at the Creation* (New York, 1969), pp. 123–125; Vannevar Bush to James Conant, September 24, 1945, and reply, September 27, Bush Papers, Library of Congress.

61. Quotes are from "Cabinet" and from *Forrestal Diaries*, p. 96.

62. Truman's address of October 3 is in *Truman Papers 1945*, pp. 362–366; President's Press Conference, October 8, 1945, Truman Library; Robert Gard, "Arms Control Policy Formulation and Negotiation, 1945–1946" (unpublished Ph.D. dissertation, Harvard University, 1961). On Byrnes, see Hewlett and Anderson, *The New World*, pp. 456–457. See also *FR, 1945*, II, 55–57.

63. C. L. Sulzberger, *New York Times*, December 16, 1945. Also see *FR, 1945*, V, 922–923. Molotov's speech of November 6 is in Embassy of the Soviet Socialist Republics, *Information Bulletin*, V (November 27, 1945). On Byrnes, see *Decade of Foreign Policy*, pp. 65–66; Byrnes, *Speaking Frankly*, 111–122. For congressional fears, see Hewlett and Anderson, *The New World*, pp. 475–477.

64. "A Report on the International Control of Atomic Energy" (Acheson-Lilienthal Plan), March 28, 1946, which was first leaked and then issued as Department of State pub. 2498. My analysis follows closely the study by Rosalind Navin Rosenberg, "Origins of American Policy on Atomic Energy" (unpublished manuscript, 1967).

65. Truman to Baruch, July 10, 1946, Baruch Papers. Also see Gard, "Arms Control," pp. 334–335.

66. *United States and the United Nations: United States Atomic Energy Proposals* (Washington, D.C., 1946), pp. 1–12. On the veto, see Wallace to Truman, July 23, 1946, reprinted in *New York Times*, September 18, 1946; David Lilienthal to Walter Lippmann, June 20, 1946, Lilienthal Papers, Princeton; Acheson in (unsigned) "Memorandum of Meeting on May 40, 1946, in the State Department," Baruch Papers; Chester Barnard, "Atomic Energy Control," *Dartmouth Alumni Magazine* (February 1948), p. 35. Quoted from Spaatz to Baruch (undated but about June 5–11), 1946; for similar views, see General Dwight Eisenhower to Baruch, June 14, 1946; Admiral Ernest King to Baruch, June 5, 1946; Admiral William Leahy to Baruch, June 11, 1946; General Joseph McNarney to Baruch (undated but about June 5–11), 1946; all in response to Baruch's letters of May 24 and in Baruch Papers. Final quote is from Admiral Chester Nimitz to Baruch, June 11, 1946, Baruch Papers. On Byrnes and fear that nuclear tests might

be viewed as threats by the Russians, see Howard Peterson to Patterson, March 22, 1946, Patterson Papers, No. 19.

67. On American interpretations, see Walter Bedell Smith to Byrnes, June 26, 1946; Harold Ickes to Baruch, August 22 and September 16, 1946. For a puzzling reversal of position by Stimson, see his letters to Baruch, May 28 and June 18, 1946, March 8, 1947; all in Baruch Papers. Molotov is quoted in Morray, *Yalta to Disarmament*, p. 88. Vandenberg was quoted by Senator Brien McMahon, as reported in Davies Diary, May 25, 1946. Also see *FR, 1946,* VI, 766, 806–808.

68. On American interpretations, see Baruch to Truman, July 2, 1946, August 1, 1946; R. G. Arneson, "Notes of Meeting," Baruch to editor of *Albany Times Union,* November 27, 1946; "Notes on Staff Conference," with Mr. Wallace and his aide, Mr. Hauser (September 27, 1946); all in Baruch Papers; Truman, *Memoirs,* II, 10–12; Byrnes, *Speaking Frankly,* p. 308. "Mr. President," remarked Harold Smith, "you have an atomic bomb up your sleeve." Truman replied, "Yes, but I'm not sure that it can ever be used" (Smith Diary, October 5, 1945). In 1948, records Leahy, "The President . . . directed me to direct the Joint Chiefs of Staff to prepare an alternate plan to resist Russian attack without using atomic bombs . . . either because they might at the time be outlawed or because the people of the United States might not . . . permit their use for aggressive purposes" (Leahy Diary, May 6, 1948). On the strategic weaknesses of atomic diplomacy, see Blackett, *Fear, War,* pp. 81–82. On Soviet understanding, see H. S. Dinnerstein, *War and the Soviet Union* (New York, 1963, rev. ed.), pp. 174–175.

69. Quoted from Warburg, *Germany,* p. 22, and this paragraph relies on pp. 17–25. For explanations of why U.S. economic aid was not used to coerce France to reverse her German policy, *FR, 1946,* V, 413, 505–511, 516–520.

70. Quoted from Clay, *Decision in Germany* (Garden City, 1950), p. 122. Paraphrase of Byrnes's statement, *Conference of Berlin,* II, 491. See Manuel Gottlieb, *The German Peace Settlement and the Berlin Crisis* (New York, 1960), pp. 35–42; John Gimbel, *The American Occupation of Germany* (Stanford, 1968), pp. 58–62; E. F. Penrose, *Economic Planning for the Peace* (Princeton, 1953), pp. 282–291; Edward Mason. in House Special Committee on Postwar Economic Policy and Planning, *Statistical Analyses of the Economic Conditions of Selected Countries of Europe and the Middle East* (February 7, 1946), H. Report 1527, 79th Cong., 2nd sess., p. 68. On reparations, also see Patterson, "Notes on a Cabinet Meeting," June 27, 194(6?), Patterson Papers, No. 19. For the dispute on reparations, *FR, 1946,* V, 520–521, 538, 545–556.

71. Molotov, speeches of July 9 and 10, in Molotov, *Problems of Foreign Policy,* pp. 55–71. On Soviet policy, see Vladimir Rudolph, in Robert Slusser, ed., *Soviet Economic Policy in Postwar Germany* (New York, 1953), pp. 18–86. *FR, 1946,* V, 576–577.

72. Clay, *Decision in Germany,* pp. 130–132. Byrnes's speech of September 6, 1946, *Decade of Foreign Policy,* pp. 522–536. On French and Soviet responses, see *FR, 1946,* V, 584–585, 600–605.

73. Wallace to Truman, July 23, 1946, also Wallace to Truman, March 15, 1946, Office of the Secretary, Department of Commerce Record, National Archives. For Truman's reply of March 20, see Ronald Radosh, "The

Economic and Political Thought of Henry A. Wallace" (unpublished M.A. thesis, University of Iowa, 1960), p. 99.

74. Truman, *Memoirs*, I, 557. Wallace speech of September 12, 1946, is in Alfred Schindler Papers, Truman Library, emphasis in original. For evidence that Wallace believed Truman had read and endorsed the speech, see Davies Diary, September 11, 1946.

75. Briefing paper, *Yalta Conference*, p. 235. Molotov speech of October 10, 1946, in *Problems of Foreign Policy*, pp. 213–214; and see pp. 125–127, for similar sentiments on August 15, and pp. 117–119 for August 13. On the Polish loan, see Arthur Bliss Lane, *I Saw Poland Betrayed*, pp. 225–239, 318–320; *New York Times*, June 23 and 27, 1946; *FR, 1945*, V, 388, 402–403, 411, 419. On the Czech loan, see James Riddleberger to Laurence Steinhardt, December 2, 1946, Francis Williamson to Laurence Steinhardt, July 1 and August 1, 1946, Box 51, Steinhardt Papers. Department of State, *Proposals for the Expansion of World Trade and Employment* (Washington, D.C., 1945). The United States had also ended the United Nations Relief and Rehabilitation Administration (to which the U.S. had contributed about 70 per cent of the funds) in favor of using relief as a lever to achieve political and diplomatic goals. *SDB*, XV (August 1, 1946), 249; Senate, Committee on Foreign Relations, *Hearings, Assistance to Greece and Turkey*, 80th Cong., 1st sess., p. 37. For earlier U.S. efforts to use aid for political purposes, see Bela Gold, *Wartime Planning in Agriculture* (New York, 1953), pp. 434–454; Stimson memorandum of conversation with Herbert Hoover, May 13, 1945; and Stimson to Truman, July 22, 1945, Stimson Papers. On the loan request, see *FR, 1945*, V, 878, 881, 1034, and *ibid.*, pp. 1048, 1049, for evidence that it was not lost. On later "negotiations," see *New York Times*, March 2 and 3, April 11, 18, 21, May 18, 1946. On the loan, also see House Special Committee on Postwar Economic Policy and Planning, *Postwar Economic Policy and Planning*, 8th Report, H. Rept. 1205 (November 12, 1945), 79th Cong., 2nd sess., pp. 9–10, 29–32, 44–45. For a smaller credit on lend-lease orders, see *FR, 1945*, V, 1048. The United States was also trying to pry open the British system for American trade and sought to move the British toward multilateralism. See William Clayton to Bernard Baruch, April 26, 1946, Baruch Papers; Richard Gardner, *Sterling-Dollar Diplomacy*. Additional information on the Russian loan is in *FR, 1946*, VI, 820–853.

76. Wallace to Truman, March 15, 1946; Truman, *Memoirs*, I, 556. President's News Conference, July 18, 1946. For Stalin's later interest in the loan, see *New York Times*, October 29, 1946; and also see House Special Committee on Postwar Economic Policy and Planning, Supplement to 11th Report, H. Rept. 2737 (December 30, 1946), pp. 24–28.

77. Quoted from paraphrase of Kennan's comments, Franklin Lindsay to staff, November 12, 1946; Baruch Papers. See also *FR, 1945*, V, 884.

78. Kennan to State Department, February 22, 1946, Forrestal Papers; also source of first quotation in next paragraph, emphasis added.

79. George Kennan, "The Sources of Soviet Conduct," *Foreign Affairs*, XXV (July 1947), 566–582.

80. On the message, see *Forrestal Diaries*, pp. 135–140. On Byrnes, see George Curry, "James F. Byrnes," in Robert Ferrell, ed., *The American Secretaries of State and their Diplomacy* (New York, 1965), XIV, 191–297; *Forrestal Diaries*, pp. 233–235, 262; Byrnes, *Speaking Frankly*, p. 203; cf.

Alperovitz, *Atomic Diplomacy*, p. 234. Truman had confided to Leahy that he had not known that his government was recognizing Yugoslavia until he read about it in the newspaper (Leahy Diary, January 4, 1946). On Kennan's later interpretation, see *Memoirs*, pp. 268–270.

81. Quoted from Lippmann, *The Cold War*, p. 60, in which he is specifically discussing "Mr. X's" (Kennan's) thought. For similar thoughts, see Clifford to Truman, "American Relations with the Soviet Union," September 1946, Clifford Papers.

82. Truman's address of March 12, in *Truman Papers, 1947*, pp. 76–80, and quote at pp. 79–80. As a spokesman for the administration, Dean Acheson, Under Secretary of State, later backed away from this open-ended commitment. He tried to limit the objectives to Greece and Turkey, leaving open the issue of policy in future cases (Senate, Committee on Foreign Relations, *Hearings, Assistance to Greece and Turkey*, 80th Cong., 1st sess., p. 42). Opposing an earlier and more temperate draft of the presidential message, Kennan did not endorse aid to Turkey, wanted small military aid to Greece, but objected most to the tone and ideological content of the message. "The Russians might even reply by declaring war!" (Paraphrase of Kennan by Joseph Jones, *Fifteen Weeks* [New York, 1955], pp. 154–155). For earlier evidence of British financial difficulties and the cutback of aid to Greece, see *New York Times*, January 26, February 4, 1947. On earlier American involvement in and commitments to Greece, see Stephen Xydis, *Greece and the Great Powers* (Thessaloniki, 1963), pp. 91–100, 143–160, 187–189, 257–265, 317–318, 379–396, 400–401, 433, 513–514, 652; Byrnes, *Speaking Frankly*, pp. 300–302. On Turkey and the rebuff to Russian efforts to share control of the Dardanelles, see LaFeber, *America, Russia*, pp. 28–29. Truman's address of March 12; Acheson in Senate, *Assistance to Greece and Turkey*, p. 24; and State Department answers, in House, Committee on Foreign Affairs, *Assistance to Greece and Turkey*, 80th Cong., 2nd sess., pp. 341–386.

83. On Greece, see L. S. Stavrianos, *Greece: American Dilemma and Opportunity* (Chicago, 1952); Frank Smothers, *et al.*, *Report on the Greeks* (New York, 1948); D. G. Kousoulas, *Revolution and Defeat* (London, 1965); Xydis, *Greece*.

84. This is an attempt to reconstruct the thought of the administration as reflected particularly, but not exclusively, in: Truman's address of March 12; Acheson in Senate, *Assistance to Greece and Turkey*, p. 10; and State Department answers, House, *Assistance to Greece and Turkey*, pp. 850–865.

85. Forrestal quoted from transcript of his phone conversation with Paul Smith, March 19, 1947, in Forrestal Papers No. 91. Second quote from "Draft" (of Truman Doctrine speech), March 10, 1947, Clark Clifford Papers (used while in his possession but now at Truman Library). Also see Acheson's private explanations in Joseph Jones, *The Fifteen Weeks*, pp. 139–142; Address of May 5, 1947, by Henry Villard, Deputy Director of Office of Near Eastern and African Affairs, Joseph Jones Papers, Truman Library; House, *Assistance to Greece and Turkey*, pp. 375–376; Forrestal, telephone conversation with Paul Shields, March 20, 1947, Forrestal Papers No. 91. Third quote is from Clayton, Memorandum, March 5, 1947, Clayton Papers, Rice University, and it is almost identical to Acheson's words, as reported in Patterson, "Memorandum on Cabinet Meeting," March 7, 1947, Patterson Papers, No. 19.

86. For the largest sense, see Jones, *Fifteen Weeks*, pp. 139–142. Ambassador W. B. Smith, according to Leahy, did not anticipate a war in the near future, but "he was convinced that the Soviet government confidently expects to conduct a successful war against the capitalistic governments . . . at some time in the future" (Leahy Diary, October 17, 1947). Harriman agreed that the Soviets "will not take any steps which they feel would bring them into a major conflict in the foreseeable future" ("Statement Before President's Air Policy Commission," September 8, 1947, Commission Papers, Truman Library). Kennan, *Memoirs, passim,* expressed fears of the Russians' gaining more resources for war and overturning the balance. The most overt public statement of the threat to the U.S. economy (in connection with communism) is by Clayton in Senate, *Assistance to Greece and Turkey,* p. 81. Also see Dean Acheson, House Committee on Postwar Policy and Planning, 79th Cong., 1st sess., p. 1082; Truman's statement of March 4, 1946, in *Truman Papers, 1946,* p. 140; and Truman's address of March 6, 1947, in *Truman Papers, 1947,* pp. 167–172; Clayton, House, Committee on Banking and Currency, *Anglo-American Financial Agreement,* pp. 191–192, and in *SDB,* XII (April 22, 1945), 760–762; Fred Vinson, *ibid.,* pp. 2–4; Byrnes, in *SDB,* XIII (November 18, 1945), 783–786; Clair Wilcox, in *ibid.,* XV (October 6, 1946), 640. Also, for similar views, see Research Committee of Committee on Economic Development (including Donald David, Gardner Cowles, Chester Davis, Beardsley Ruml, Ernest Kanzler, Eric Johnston, and Paul Hoffman), "International Trade, Foreign Investment and Domestic Employment, Including Bretton Woods Proposals," May 29, 1945; U.S. Chamber of Commerce, "Wartime National Foreign Trade Week" (1945); "Report to the President on Activities of the National Advisory Council on International Monetary and Financial Problems" (about March 1946), OF85E, Truman Library; Herbert Hoover to Baruch (between May 10 and August 5, 1945), Baruch Papers; Charles Taft, in *SDB,* XII, April 25, 1945), 826–831, and in *ibid.* (May 20, 1945), pp. 942–946. For a similar analysis, see Williams, *Tragedy, passim,* and Kolko, *Politics of War,* pp. 242–279. On economic needs, see Kolko, *The Roots of American Foreign Policy* (Boston, 1969), pp. 48–87.

87. Quoted from Senate, *Assistance to Greece and Turkey,* p. 81. This view also entails concern about communism's developing in *any one country* because of the effect on American trade with that country; but the larger fear cannot be proved unreasonable or unlikely simply by establishing that relations with *that country* are not in themselves economically significant to the American economy. Normally, those who expressed concern about communism in a *particular country* shared the larger fear, but they often emphasized the *specific* problem at hand. Consider, for example, Stimson and Harriman on maintaining the "open door" in Manchuria (Stimson Diary, July 15, 1945). Of course, businessmen with interests in a particular country may limit their concern to threats to those interests without considering larger issues. (This analysis has been influenced by Williams, *Tragedy.*) In turn, businessmen, once convinced of the danger of international communism, have been willing to halt or trim trade with communist states. Between 1944 and 1947 businessmen slowly moved from enthusiasm for trade with Russia to willingness, and sometimes enthusiasm, for cutting trade with the Soviet bloc. See *Nation's Business,* XXXII (October 1944), 21–22; *Fortune,* XXXII (September 1945), 238; Baruch, draft of speech,

July 21, 1947, Baruch Papers; *Steel,* CXX (June 9, 1947), 64; *Report of the Thirty-Fourth National Foreign Trade Convention* (New York, 1947), p. 457. For the quote, see Joseph Jones to William Benton, February 26, 1947, Jones Papers. Significantly, when Jones discussed in *Fifteen Weeks* the thought behind the Truman Doctrine, he neglected this theme.

88. Truman statement of July 23, 1946, in *Truman Papers, 1946,* pp. 353–354. Clayton in *SDB,* XII (May 27, 1945), 979. Not all, however, who accepted the theory of peace and prosperity emphasized Russian restrictions on trade as necessarily hostile to the world or to America.

89. Quoted from "Draft" (of Truman Doctrine speech), March 10, 1947. Dean Acheson directed that this statement be deleted because it gave undue public attention to economic factors (Jones, *Fifteen Weeks,* pp. 156–157). For Acheson, see *Postwar Policy and Planning,* p. 1082.

90. First quote is from statement of March 4, 1946. Long quote is from speech of March 6, 1947. Cf. Allen J. Matusow, *Farm Policies and Politics in the Truman Years* (Cambridge, Mass., 1967), pp. 79–110, for the defeat of free trade by others in the government. Also see James Warburg, *Put Yourself in Marshall's Place* (New York, 1948), pp. 12–46. On economic relations with the nations within the Soviet sphere, see McNeill, *America, Britain, and Russia,* pp. 690–699; Byrnes, *Speaking Frankly,* pp. 116, 142–144.

91. By design, this essay has sought to analyze American policy and the ideology of policy-makers and only to suggest (in these closing paragraphs) the influence upon public understanding. It is clear that the *public* fear of Soviet communism and the commitment to internationalism (in the forms of intervention, economic assistance, or even concern about international economic relations) lagged behind the concern of policy-makers in 1945–1947. It may be a false question to ask whether the public's increasing fear of communism was a result of the efforts of American policy-makers *or* of the publicity about communist action. The two are so intimately linked as to make definitive analysis difficult, if not impossible. On general public attitudes, see *Public Opinion Quarterly* (1945–1948) for polls. The essay does not attempt to analyze congressional-executive relations on foreign policy, but my research indicates that Vandenberg and the internationalist wing of the Republican party provided sufficient votes and support for the administration's general foreign policy in this period to substantiate the conventional characterization of a bipartisan policy. Of course, bipartisanship did not eliminate the need for minor concessions to Vandenberg, nor did it prevent squabbles about details, and Vandenberg and his followers did constitute a strong anti-Soviet force which would have politically restricted the administration if it had sought a compromise with the Soviet Union after the autumn of 1945.

THOMAS G. PATERSON

The Quest for Peace and Prosperity: International Trade, Communism, and the Marshall Plan

In October 1947 President Harry S. Truman summed up the elementary objectives of his administration: "We have sought peace and prosperity—prosperity for all our people, peace for all the world." He had earlier explained how in large part he hoped to fulfill such objectives, and in so doing he revealed the postwar American conception of the world and America's place in it: "A large volume of soundly based international trade is essential if we are to achieve prosperity in the United States, build a durable structure of world economy and attain our goal of world peace and security." On another occasion he told a Baylor University audience: "In fact the three—peace, freedom, and world

I would like to thank the Harry S. Truman Institute, the University of California, Berkeley, and the University of Connecticut for financial grants which enabled me to reach widespread manuscript sources. I am also grateful to Professors Barton Bernstein, Robert Smith, Richard Abrams, and Armin Rappaport for their critical comments on various drafts of this essay.

trade—are inseparable." Just before his death President Franklin D. Roosevelt had informed Congress that "we cannot succeed in building a peaceful world unless we build an economically healthy world." Roosevelt and Truman expressed the ubiquitous theme of "peace and prosperity," which motivated and explained much of postwar American foreign policy.[1]

Most segments of the American political spectrum accepted, expressed, and acted upon the goals and ideology of this concept, with variations, but there were some differences over the question of tactics. The *New Republic* demonstrated its adherence to the widespread theme in an editorial: "One of the foundations of peace and prosperity in the future must be an expansion of world trade." A leading official of the National Association of Manufacturers spoke in the same vein: "We are convinced that sound economics in the rest of the world, and mutually beneficial international trade are important not only to the prosperity, but also the peace of the United States."[2]

As American leaders defined it, the peace and prosperity theme had several neatly interlocking components, which, taken together, gave American foreign policy a direction requiring an extensive foreign aid program and a vigorous foreign trade, both of which were realized in the Marshall Plan. The first premise of the concept was that world peace required global economic well-being. "It is by restoring normal production and trade throughout the world, and thereby supplying peoples with necessities," reasoned the Cleveland Trust Company, "that peace can be maintained." A State Department official dramatically stated the consequences of world economic chaos:

> Hungry people are not reasonable people. Their thoughts are concerned with their own misery and particularly with the tortured cries of their hungry children. They are easy victims of mass hysteria. When people become frightened elements of a mob, democratic precepts mean nothing.

Indeed, destitute people were prone to accept totalitarian and undemocratic political movements. The Counselor of the State Department, Benjamin V. Cohen, concluded shortly after the June 5, 1947, call for the Marshall Plan that "People long tired, cold, hungry, and impoverished are not wont to examine critically the credentials of those promising them food, shelter and clothes." In arguing for the European Recovery Program, businessman H. J. Heinz, II, saw a remedy: "Adequately fed people are generally productive workers; with jobs they can buy food, and with opportunity they will cherish their freedom and will deny totalitarian extremes." The Economic Cooperation Administration found the postwar economic recovery of Western Germany necessary "to avoid the political dangers which might result from economic distress."[3]

Peace in the American definition meant political and social stability, and as W. Averell Harriman, former Ambassador to the Soviet Union and Secretary of Commerce, put it, "Political stability can only be attained through improving economic conditions." The staff of the Council of Economic Advisers wrote similarly about conditions in Europe: "The lingering economic illness . . . retards the attainment of the political stability which is the prerequisite to the maintenance of free institutions." The council itself urged foreign aid in late 1947 for Italy and France, because industrial paralysis there might mean "serious social disturbance and political reorientation." Earlier, presidential assistant Samuel Rosenman had predicted "political upheavals" and "bloodshed and revolution" unless Europe recovered economically. Indeed, Eugene Thomas, president of the National Foreign Trade Council (comprised of large corporations), saw in "adequate employment" and "orderly international trade" the means to protect the world from "revolutionary tendencies." In brief, impoverished people tended to be revolutionary in politics, a status which Americans considered a threat to peace.[4]

Many American leaders translated "revolution" as "communism," and this challenge to peace was an omnipotent political force which "uses poverty to advance itself," as a prominent publisher suggested. George Meany of the American Federation of Labor agreed that "Nothing helps the Communist cause more effectively than hunger and misery and economic chaos." One presidential committee studying the Marshall Plan minced no words: "Without economic assistance Europe is lost to us and World War III becomes inevitable." A Policy Planning Staff memorandum of May 23, 1947, urging that Secretary of State

George C. Marshall undertake a more extensive foreign aid program, stressed that the Western confrontation with Russian communism could be met effectively by correcting "the economic maladjustment which makes European society vulnerable to exploitation by any and all movements." The Under Secretary of State for Economic Affairs, Will Clayton, after a visit to Europe, wrote what was to be an influential report on the continent's needs: "Europe is steadily deteriorating. The political position reflects the economic. One political crisis after another merely denotes the existence of grave economic distress." The leaders of America's postwar anti-communist effort thus saw prosperity as one of their most effective tools. "It is logical," said Secretary Marshall in his famous speech at Harvard on June 5, 1947, "that the United States should do whatever it is able to do to assist in the return of normal economic health in the world, without which there can be no political stability and no assured peace."[5]

Another important component of the postwar outlook held that world prosperity, and hence peace, could be fostered only by healthy world trade. Truman's statements above make this point clear. A congressional committee expressed a widely held view in 1945: "If a high level of exports and imports is essential for a prosperous and balanced economy in the United States, it is even more essential for peace and prosperity in the rest of the world." The National Foreign Trade Council extolled world trade for contributing to higher living standards, and the Committee on International Economic Policy told the Senate that "World peace and world trade are natural partners."[6]

Some commentators pointed out that economic blocs, such as the British Sterling Area and the Soviet network in Eastern Europe, as well as bilateral treaties, impeded world trade. "Nations which act as enemies in the marketplace," Will Clayton told the Detroit Economic Club, "cannot long be friends at the council table." Some prominent industrialists emphasized publicly that wide-open trade would be conducive to friendlier international political relations. Thus Studebaker's Paul Hoffman, later to head the Marshall Plan, applauded the $3.75 billion loan to Britain in 1946 and its provisions for relaxation of Sterling

Bloc trade restrictions as "a first step toward international economic coordination. And international coordination is in turn a first step toward world peace."[7]

The United States in the postwar period attempted to combat trade restrictions through a multilateral, non-discriminatory, most-favored-nation trade policy. The concept of the "open door"—equal trade and investment opportunity—was considered by some government and business spokesmen to be a traditional one from which the United States itself had strayed with a protectionist tariff policy. Truman intended to effect the "open door" through multilateral trade agreements and the Reciprocal Trade Agreements program. Winthrop Aldrich, chairman of the Chase National Bank and a frequent government adviser, summarized the American position: "Bilateralism is the road to war; multilateralism is the highway of peace." The President spelled out some of the principles of American economic foreign policy in his Navy Day speech of 1945:

> 7. We believe that all nations should have the freedom of the seas and equal rights to the navigation of boundary rivers and waterways and to rivers and waterways which pass through more than one country.
> 8. We believe that all states which are accepted in the society of nations should have access on equal terms to the trade and raw materials of the world. . . .
> 10. We believe that full economic collaboration between all nations, great and small, is essential to improvement of living conditions all over the world, and the establishment of freedom from fear and freedom from want.

The National Foreign Trade Council agreed wholeheartedly with these goals and expressed them in the peace-and-prosperity idiom:

> Since the American people are united in their desire for a prosperous and peaceful world, and since foreign trade is such an important factor in the prosperity and economic stability of our country, the Convention urges continued bipartisan support of a foreign economic policy dedicated to the restoration of multilateral, non-discriminatory foreign trade.

These principles were included in almost every international economic agreement the United States entered shortly after

World War II. And when they were strenuously promoted by American negotiators, the principles fostered intense international debate. The questions of the British Loan, trade with and investment in eastern Europe, and the abortive International Trade Organization (ITO), for example, heatedly confronted the open door policy. The Point Four program, the International Bank, and the International Monetary Fund were essentially efforts to enhance the open door. The latter, then, was an integral part of American foreign policy, and the very expression itself was frequently used by American leaders.[8]

But observers pointed out that Truman's trade goals sometimes conflicted with American practice. The disparities arose from the President's inability to control protectionist congressmen or his own Department of Agriculture (USDA), and from the chaos of the world economy. The USDA, especially in 1945–1946, advocated international commodity agreements to set minimum and maximum prices, and regarded "free trade with fear." The State Department, then, had to fight skirmishes at home as well. As *Fortune* noted: " . . . when the U.S. is cast as the standard bearer of enterprise and liberal trade principles, agriculture is conveniently forgotten." Domestic price supports, the subsidizing of agricultural exports by the Commodity Credit Corporation and by the Economic Cooperation Administration, and tariffs and quotas on agricultural imports all violated the announced Truman trade program. Subsidies to shipping interests and sugar producers, governmental purchasing of rubber, barter deals with India for manganese, and "buy America" provisions in the Stockpiling Program were other examples. The State Department's Winthrop G. Brown had to admit that "we have had in this country a certain amount of State trading. . . ." The United States also entered into a postwar international commodity agreement in wheat. In the Middle East, American oil companies, with Washington's backing, entered into cartel arrangements with British firms, virtually closing the door on the Soviet Union's desire for oil concessions there. American companies were involved in cartels in matches, screws, and electrical equipment, among others, and some companies simply continued their prewar activity in cartels.[9]

Although the government reduced American tariff schedules after World War II, the United States still was left with a protectionist program. The State Department often felt handicapped in trade negotiations, such as those of 1947 for the General Agreement on Tariffs and Trade (GATT). The United States also established preferential trade relations with Cuba and the Philippines, prompting both the British and Russians to comment on the inconsistencies in American principles and practice. *Pravda* wrote that "economic relations between the Philippines and the USA have been reestablished on the old notorious basis of 'free trade' of economic preference for the USA, and discrimination in regard to other countries." And the (London) *Economist* chided Americans for a double standard in 1946:

> In spite of their loudly proclaimed devotion to free enterprise and competition, they regard competitive imports as an evil to be guarded against by prohibitive import duties, embargoes, and quotas. Many of them object to the continued presence of European possessions in the Western Hemisphere, but see no incompatibility in American requisition of bases on the far sides of the Pacific and Atlantic Oceans—nor in telling the Russians what they should do in Poland and the Balkans, and the British what they should do in Palestine, India, and Siam.[10]

Some American leaders saw the conflict clearly. Lamar Fleming, of Clayton, Anderson, large cotton exporters, opposed an international cotton agreement, arguing that "what we are proposing is the application on a world scale of the cartel system, which we brand as unlawful and immoral when practiced by our private enterprises and as economic piracy when practiced by Germany and the other nations." Eugene Black, president of the International Bank, attacked American import barriers in 1949: "Despite a rather remarkable shift in the attitude of the United States in recent years, some of its policies are still basically inconsistent with its position as the great creditor nation of the world." And Will Clayton, who bore the task of having to bring goals and practice into some kind of alignment, admitted that, "if we want to be honest with ourselves, we will find that many of the sins that we freely criticize other countries for practicing have their counterpart in the United States."[11]

Some leading businessmen and government officials came to

realize that the economically disrupted postwar world was hardly conducive to multilateralism, and the American government itself moved further and further away from this policy. By 1950 the State Department noted that the United States conducted the "great mass of our business through bilateral relations with more than 70 governments. These involve questions of trade and travel, private investment and governmental assistance, and countless matters of daily business which affect us all." Arrangements with recipients under the Marshall Plan were bilateral, and the Chamber of Commerce found the experience so "favorable" that it insisted on bilateral agreements under Point Four.[12]

But American leaders did not think their advocacy of the open door and their contradictory actions placed them in a hypocritical position. They argued that tariff reductions and a more liberal trade practice would simply take time, and that critics should not expect the United States to change its habits drastically in a few years. Commodity agreements and subsidies for American domestic interests, argued Clayton, were temporary measures for the adjustment to peace. A House committee approved commodity agreements in 1945 as "a means of making the transition from surplus production to normal conditions. In no case, however, are they to be regarded as permanent marketing arrangements." In both the British Loan agreement and the abortive ITO charter, the United States provided for the gradual abolition of discriminatory trade practices. Bilateralism, state trading, import and export controls, and cartels, then, whether practiced by the United States or other nations, were presumably accepted only as tolerable and temporary evils. Once the world regained its economic health, argued the Truman administration, such trade impediments could be eliminated.[13]

The Interdependent World Economy

Another major element of the peace and prosperity concept was the interdependence of the world economy—the potential impact of an American depression on the world and a global depression on the United States. Henry Wallace, ousted later by Truman from the Cabinet, put it bluntly when he contended that "full employment in the United States means prosperity all over the world." Harriman, who replaced Wallace as Secretary of Commerce in 1946, pictured the United States as the "financial and economic pivot of the world," and he agreed with the prevalent view "that economic stagnation in the United States would drag the rest of the world down with us." The Advertising Council and the National Planning Association both pointed to American prosperity as the key to the economic well-being of other countries. George Kennan cabled from Moscow:

> Much depends on health and vigor of our own society. World communism is like malignant parasite which feeds only on diseased tissue. This is point at which domestic and foreign policies meet.

Secretary of State James Byrnes was alarmed, too, that "Depressions move easily across our boundaries." And a writer in the *New Republic* demonstrated the widespread popularity of this notion in 1945: "The greatest single requirement for the future peace of the world is a successful design for avoiding a serious depression in the United States during the next decade."[14]

American leaders were also alert to the potential effect of a world depression on the American economy. President Truman noted in 1947 that "Our prosperity is endangered by hunger and cold in other lands," and his Secretary of the Interior, Julius Krug, quipped that "depressions are as catching as the common cold." The Council of Economic Advisers publicly supported increased foreign aid by arguing:

> There is abundant evidence that in the longer run the foreign aid program will add to the strength and security of our own economy for the simple reason that we live in a world economy from which we cannot disassociate ourselves.

In short, said Secretary of the Treasury Fred Vinson, "You cannot maintain American production and employment in the midst of worldwide depression." American business was quite alive to this question, too. The head of General Electric, among other industrialists, lectured the small businessman that he too was involved in the interlocking world economy and that he should concern himself with international events.[15]

A healthy and growing American trade was seen as the key to

both world and American prosperity. Should that trade fail, it would cause the spindly-legged world economy to tumble to the ground, leaving totalitarianism, war, and revolution in firm control. Postwar American foreign trade was a significant and perhaps crucial element in the welfare of other countries, because the United States was the largest supplier of goods to world markets. In 1947 American exports accounted for one-third of total world exports, one-fourth in 1948, and one-fifth in 1949, compared to one-seventh in 1936–1938. And American direct investments abroad, amounting to $12 billion in 1950, provided precious capital and revenue-producing export goods for hungry and war-devastated European nations.[16]

The United States' economic power in the world was measured in other impressive figures related to foreign trade and investment. American interests owned or controlled 59 per cent of total known world oil reserves in 1947. In the same year American automobile production was eight times that of France, England, and Germany combined, and four years later the United States turned out seven million cars, compared to Russia's 65,000. In the immediate postwar period, the United States was the largest producer and consumer of both coal and steel in the world, and at mid-century the United States had one-third of the world's merchant fleet (gross tonnage). General Motors' Charles Wilson bragged in 1948 that with only 6 per cent of the world's area and 7 per cent of its population, the United States had 46 per cent of the world's electric power, 48 per cent of its radios, 54 per cent of its telephones, and 92 per cent of its modern bathtubs. The economic power of American bathtubs may have been lost on foreigners, but not the strength of America's capital and durable goods manufacturing. Countries in dire need of economic rehabilitation could not ignore the conspicuous fact that in 1948 the United States produced about 41 per cent of the world's goods and services, and accounted for almost half the world's industrial output.[17]

American economic power was recognized by William K. Jackson, president of the Chamber of Commerce: "Only our America has the capital, the productive capital, the technical personnel to save the world from economic disaster—and from

the political consequences of such disaster." The Secretary of
State who gave his name to the Marshall Plan agreed: "The
United States is the only country in the world today which has
the economic power and productivity to furnish the needed assistance." The President put it simply: "We are the giant of the
economic world."[18]

American Foreign Trade and Domestic Prosperity

The peace and prosperity concept held, next, that foreign
trade was vital to the economic power and prosperity of the
United States. In 1947 Willard L. Thorp, Assistant Secretary of
State for Economic Affairs, declared that "Any serious failure to
maintain this flow [exports and imports] would put millions of
American businessmen, farmers, and workers out of business."
The president of the American Merchant Marine Institute expressed a widely held business attitude: "To put it briefly, our
foreign trade represents the difference between depression and
prosperity."[19]

Government and business executives amassed impressive statistics to support their contention that foreign trade was a prime
segment of the American economy. When the Secretary of Agriculture presented his department's case for the Marshall Plan,
he listed surpluses in citrus fruits, potatoes, eggs, some dairy
products, wheat, rice, cotton, and tobacco, all of which, he said,
needed foreign markets. World food shortages and the American
foreign aid and relief expenditures in the 1946–1947 period insured large exports of American agricultural goods, although
there was some friction between domestic demands and foreign
needs. In 1947 almost half of the American production of wheat
went abroad, and 15 per cent of fats and oils. One-third of
unmanufactured leaf tobacco was sent to foreign outlets in
1946–1947. Thirteen per cent of total farm income was derived
from farm exports in 1947.[20]

American leaders also emphasized that, although exports
represented only about 7 per cent of the gross national product
and approximately 10 per cent of the production of movable
goods, certain key industries, such as automobiles and trucks,
coal, machine tools, railroad locomotives, steel products, and

farm machinery, relied upon foreign trade for an important part of their income. During 1947, for example, exports of the Monsanto Chemical Company accounted for one-eighth of total sales, and General Motors exported about 10 per cent of its sales in the postwar period. The promotion manager of Time-Life International concluded that "our 10 per cent production for overseas sales is the spearhead of our whole economic system."[21]

Foreign trade was also important to employment. Both Henry Wallace and businessman Eric Johnston were counting on foreign trade to contribute from four million to five million jobs at the close of the war, and H. J. Heinz claimed that in fact the export trade supported five million workers. Actually, according to the Bureau of Labor Statistics, in the first half of 1947, 2,364,000 of 41,963,000 employees were directly or indirectly employed because of the export trade. These people accounted for 5.6 per cent of all *nonagricultural* employees. In some industries, the percentage far exceeded this figure. In steel companies, for example, the figure was almost 20 per cent, in rubber 15 per cent, in coal mining 18 per cent, and in chemicals 11 per cent.[22]

Secretary of the Treasury John Snyder summarized the interplay between foreign trade and the domestic economy in the postwar period:

> The export of goods and services has recently been running at a rate of about $15 billion a year, compared with only $4 billion prior to the war. The importance of U.S. exports to the American economy is evidenced by the fact that they exceed in volume such important single elements of the national product as expenditures on producers' durable equipment, consumers' expenditures on durable goods, the net change in business inventories, the total expenditures by State and local governments or even private construction.

In short, concluded the State Department, "Participation in a flourishing world trade means domestic prosperity and higher employment in the United States."[23]

"Theoretically," wrote one observer in the *Harvard Business Review*, "the United States can achieve full employment without any exports whatsoever." But such a condition would require grave changes in the American economy, as well as increased government controls. The Committee for Economic Development predicted a "great readjustment, much inefficient production, and a lower standard of living" for the United States were it to cut back its foreign trade. Eric Johnston, who served as president of the United States Chamber of Commerce from 1942 to 1946, thought a curtailment of American foreign trade "would mean vast population shifts, and . . . new ways of subsistence would have to be found for entire geographic regions." A study for the President's Committee on Foreign Aid stated that the United States could probably survive the collapse of Europe and hence our trade with that area. "But it would take at least a generation to effect the necessary readjustments—readjustments which would inevitably be accomplished by acute distress in important sectors of the economy and a long period of economic and financial instability."[24]

This kind of observation, coupled with the conspicuous fact that Europe in 1946 took 42 per cent of American exports, in part encouraged the United States to undertake a more extensive foreign aid program in 1947. Postwar Europe was an economically depressed area, and "A progressive decline in the producing and buying power of 270,000,000 people in Western and Central Europe would have a powerful impact upon American prosperity," noted the President's Committee on Foreign Aid. Then, too, argued this committee, "prosperous conditions in Europe are essential to the maintenance of American trade in other parts of the world." Will Clayton explained that priority was given to Western Europe in the foreign aid program in the belief that the prosperity of the "underdeveloped nations of the world would follow to some extent." Such an emphasis would reduce the susceptibility of all nations to communism and increase their ability to purchase American goods—two conditions of peace and prosperity as defined in postwar America.[25]

The "Have-not" Nation

It was convincingly argued, too, that exports paid for the imports required by American industry and consumers. It was fashionable to speak of the United States as a "have-not" nation after the war, because of the wartime drain on its resources. The director of the Bureau of Mines, for example, reported that the United States was "self-sufficient in only eleven of the most critical industrial minerals." American leaders itemized domestic deficiencies in zinc, tin, mercury, manganese, lead, cobalt, vanadium, tungsten, chromite, industrial diamonds, nickel, asbestos fiber, bauxite, petroleum, and copper, or a total of over fifty materials. President Truman was emphatic about the need for raw materials for security reasons: "Without foreign trade . . . it would be difficult, if not impossible, for us to develop atomic energy." Some forty materials from fifty-seven different countries were necessary for the production of steel, and Secretary of the Interior Harold Ickes warned in early 1946 that American supplies of manganese ore (essential for steel) would be exhausted in two years. *Steel* magazine, two years later, was alarmed to find the prediction off by only six months. "The handwriting on the wall is clear. We should get busy pronto." Various government acts and appropriations, including the Marshall Plan, attempted to purchase and stockpile vital raw materials.[26]

Among other policy-makers, Secretary James Forrestal saw a direct link between foreign aid and the shortage in critical materials. For Forrestal, aid to Greece and Turkey under the Truman Doctrine was more than a simple effort to contain communism, and he labeled the doctrine "hard and selfish." What did he mean? Seventy-three per cent of America's imports consisted of raw materials for the production of necessities for the United States, and 55 per cent of these needed imports came from areas within the British Empire, mostly in the Far East. Forrestal went on: "These raw materials have to come over the sea and a good many have to go through the Mediterranean. That is *one* reason why the Mediterranean must remain a free highway." Again, Forrestal told one skeptical friend that the materials problem "is the only thing that makes any impression on me at all," and his listener observed that the "average fellow in this country" was not aware of the raw materials consideration. Few Americans were aware either that the March 10 draft of the Truman Doctrine speech stated (later removed) that

Greece and Turkey were areas of "great natural resources which must be accessible to all nations and must not be under the exclusive control or domination of any single nation. The weakening of Turkey, or the further weakening of Greece, would invite such control." The materials question was a significant component of the peace and prosperity theme of an interdependent economic world and an America in need of strategic imports for its security and prosperity.[27]

Recession Fears

Both during and after World War II, many Americans and foreigners waited expectantly for the United States to suffer a postwar economic collapse. When the French Institute of Public Opinion asked its countrymen in 1947 why the United States had proposed the Marshall Plan, over half of those who replied said that the program was designed to insure foreign markets for American goods, and thereby to avert an American economic crisis. American leaders always protested this assessment of their intentions and were quick to label it communist propaganda. Indeed, the Soviet Union and Communist parties throughout Europe did harp on this issue. Yet the idea that the United States gave foreign aid to head off a depression was not the creation of Russian propagandists, although they no doubt inflated it, for the belief was already widespread in the world (Great Britain and Czechoslovakia, for example) and in the United States itself.[28]

American decision-makers were aware too that their references to depression fortified Russian charges. Secretary Forrestal recorded that several passages in a draft of the President's message to Congress in early 1948 about "the low standard of living in this country on the part of millions of families and the foreboding of a coming depression" would serve as "excellent propaganda for the Kremlin." During the 1948 presidential campaign John Foster Dulles informed the Republican candidate that:

I have learned reliably, though not in form for attribution, that Soviet foreign policy is encouraged and stiffened by predictions in high quarters in the United States that Republican victory will bring serious internal depression to our country.[29]

That prominent Americans feared economic decline—and the resultant dangers to American well-being, to survival of a world free from the entanglements of communism, or, in brief, to a world at peace—was in large part a throwback to the depression of the 1930's. Would the United States, without wartime expenditures, resume the shaky economy it had suffered before the war intervened? Would the experience of boom-bust-quasi-boom in the 1919–1921 period be repeated? The Committee for Economic Development noted public sentiment shortly after the war: "Memories of depression and mass unemployment in the last decade are still vivid—thrown into strong relief by the recent experience of wartime full employment." During the war, public anxiety over the postwar period was reflected in several public and private studies which tried to deal with the question of an economic slump, but which failed to provide careful charts for the future. Throughout 1945 and 1946 American observers offered a divided assessment of the business outlook, with those predicting a downturn having a slight edge. Amidst the pessimism, Secretary of the Treasury Snyder tried to lift spirits by declaring it "bad psychology to be continually talking about 'depression' and 'recession' when we have all the elements for a continued prosperous period."[30]

In early June 1947 the *Journal of Commerce* reported that "An international economic crisis is being freely predicted today. . . . In this country, an approaching collapse is ascribed to the exhaustion of purchasing power abroad." President Truman, demonstrating that his immediate problem was inflation, tried at the same time to dispel the pessimistic climate when he vetoed the tax-reduction bill: "Despite many gloomy predictions, there is no convincing evidence that a recession is imminent." It was around the middle of 1947 that forecasts predicting recession were the most vociferous. This may be partly explained by the economic distress in Europe and the administration's dire warnings at that time that continued European depression would have unfortunate domestic and international economic and political consequences unless programs such as the Truman Doc-

trine and the Marshall Plan were approved. There was mounting
concern, too, over inflation and the trend of rising prices. Also
playing a part was an attempt to use history. Some commentators compared the post–World War II period with the pattern
of the early 1920's. Thus the middle of 1947 would coincide with
the start of the recession in 1920, when a sharp decline in exports
and a slowdown in construction had brought an economic
slump.[31]

The Truman administration in mid-1947 did not, however,
argue that European aid was essential to head off an *imminent*
recession. Rather, it stressed the *long-range* economic and political importance of such assistance in the familiar peace and
prosperity idiom. In November 1947 the Council of Economic
Advisers predicted an $8 billion decline in exports unless there
was a new foreign aid program. Although this rapid reduction
would not "inflict serious short-run damage on our economy,
substantial problems of readjustment would be generated. Moreover, the industrial paralysis which could be expected to result
in some other countries would have repercussions of major proportion upon our own economy and upon world stability." The
Interim Aid program ($400 million to Austria, China, France,
and Italy during the winter of 1947–1948) and the Marshall
Plan provided the dollars in the hope of preventing such an
occurrence, and continued a trend set in 1945–1947, when foreign aid extended by the United States government financed one-
third of American exports. In the second quarter of 1947, aid
to Europe financed our entire export surplus to that area.[32]

The decision to continue the foreign aid program had a stimu-
lating effect on Americans who had been pessimistic about the
business outlook. Machine-tool manufacturers looked upon the
Marshall Plan as a much-needed vehicle for profit, and *Fortune*
found business executives much more optimistic by November
1947. A White House memorandum of March 1948, looking back
on the spring of 1947 when people expected an economic decline, considered the Marshall Plan "very important" in providing
"a powerful psychological stimulus to a resumption of the up-
ward spiral," because "people generally interpreted [it] as providing for a tremendous increase in the level of exports." And

there was no question that wheat prices were kept up by relief shipments.[33]

Yet the recession that came in the third quarter of 1948 and lasted until the second quarter of 1950 was not blocked by the foreign aid program. Exports continued to decline, and one writer estimates that 26 per cent of the total drop in output during the recession was due to the slackening of the export trade. But foreign aid unquestionably blunted some of the sharper edges of the export decline and the recession by placing $6.45 billion in the hands of Europeans and other foreign people buying in American markets in 1948–1949. And it was mild in part because, due to American aid, European business activity did not slacken at the same time.[34]

Although many American leaders thought a decline in exports would bring the expected recession, this was not the only consideration in predicting an economic slump. Some people never mentioned the effect of European crisis or reduced foreign trade. They often thought excessively high domestic prices would cause the collapse. Inflation rather than deflation was stressed by some businessmen. And the president of Republic Steel, for example, blamed American "generosity abroad" for high prices at home. Other Americans feared that the Marshall Plan and other foreign aid plans would inflate the economy. Inflationary tendencies *were* at work in the economy, and Europe's demand for goods scarce in the United States did contribute somewhat to inflation.[35]

Americans had a cruel decision to make. As the *Journal of Commerce* put it in the case of foreign aid, the country had been given "the choice . . . between higher prices or lower exports." Neither of the alternatives was welcome, but government officials and some labor and business leaders thought that at least prices could be controlled through anti-inflationary policies. When the President went before a special session of Congress in November 1947, he asked for two programs: economic controls to manage inflation, and Interim Aid. The request for price controls was definitely a political move to embarrass the Republican Congress, for Truman had no plan in mind when he spoke. What took "precedence over all other questions," argued assistant

Clark Clifford, was aid to Western Europe. If the administration could have achieved some controls with the foreign aid bill, it would have been satisfied. But Truman did not intend to make foreign aid contingent upon controls. Foreign aid and foreign trade were simply too important to both American and world prosperity, to the American effort to defeat communist movements, and hence to world peace, to allow them to fade. Secretary of State Marshall, in defending the program that bore his name against the charges that it would be inflationary, and in emphasizing the long-range concern, argued that inflation "would not create a situation for us that was serious compared to the troubles that we are trying to meet abroad." Most Americans accepted the 1946 report of the National Advisory Council on International Monetary and Financial Problems, which held that "any temporary sacrifice" caused in the American economy because of a foreign assistance program "will be small compared to the long-range advantages to the United States of a peaceful, active, and growing world economy."[36]

The words "long-range" are important to the peace and prosperity concept. When discussing inflation and exports, American leaders emphasized the temporary and controllable nature of inflation and the long-run and world-wide importance of exports to "peace and prosperity." Although many, as shown above, feared an immediate economic decline in 1947, in part because of an expected drop in foreign trade, the predominant concern was more long-range. Could the United States remain at peace in a world courting communism because of international poverty and economic dislocation? Could the American people be secure and prosperous in an economically weak world increasingly embracing state-regulated economic systems, which challenged both American ideals and foreign trade? Could the United States afford to lose its lucrative European markets and its sources of strategic raw materials? Could the nation withstand both the economic and political consequences of global economic chaos? The significant question, then, was not whether a decline in foreign trade would bring an immediate American recession or depression, but whether the interdependent world economy, linked by American exports and economic power, would be viable and prosperous enough to stave off unstable and revolutionary politics—in short, communism. This was the burden of the peace and prosperity theme of American foreign policy, which serves as a useful explanation of the development of the Marshall Plan.

The Marshall Plan

After European officials responded to the call in Secretary Marshall's commencement address at Harvard University on June 5, 1947, for European initiative in a large-scale foreign aid plan, the Truman administration began to cultivate public endorsement of a European Recovery Program (ERP). Its task was not an easy one, for as late as November 1947, 40 per cent of the American people had never heard of the Marshall Plan. With the help of the State Department, the Committee for the Marshall Plan to Aid European Recovery was organized to combat that ignorance. Comprised largely of prominent business executives, such as Robert Patterson, former Secretary of War and Wall Street corporation lawyer, Philip Reed of General Electric, Allen Dulles of Sullivan and Cromwell, Thomas Lamont of J. P. Morgan, and H. D. Collier of Standard Oil of California, this committee joined with leading farm and labor groups to publicize the ERP in full-page newspaper advertisements, circulate petitions, organize speaker forums, and initiate letter campaigns directed at Congress. The very stature of the members, the close cooperation with the State Department, and the access to audiences assured the committee a considerable influence.[37]

Standing with the almost solid front of business leadership in endorsing the Marshall Plan were the American Federation of Labor, the Congress of Industrial Organizations, Americans for Democratic Action, Veterans of Foreign Wars, and the American Farm Bureau Federation. A significant ally of the administration was Republican Senator Arthur Vandenberg of Michigan. Vandenberg helped head off opposition to the plan by suggesting the appointment of the bipartisan Harriman Committee (President's Committee on Foreign Aid), which shared much material and many ideas with the Department of Interior (Krug Committee), and the Council of Economic Advisers. These three committees issued similar reports in the fall of 1947 indicating that the United States could undertake a large foreign aid program without seriously straining the economy, but with some controls, and arguing that indeed such a program was vital to the goals of American foreign and domestic policy. Vandenberg also assured his colleagues that the ERP would be a "business venture," and, as James Forrestal put it, with "business management." It was assumed by many congressmen before the passage of the ERP that the administrator of the program would be a prominent industrialist (Paul Hoffman, president of Studebaker, was named by Truman).[38]

Events in Europe also spurred passage of the Marshall Plan. The dollar shortage in Europe was becoming more acute. The fear that the Communist party would win the Italian elections in April 1948 persuaded some to vote acceptance before then, to influence the outcome. Soviet pressures on Finland, and the communist *coup d'état* in Czechoslovakia in February also aroused congressional concern. And by early 1948 it was clear that West Germany would be included in the ERP, as the United States drastically trimmed back its decartelization and dismantling operations there. The Truman administration used these events to help create a crisis atmosphere. The President appeared before Congress in mid-March to plead alarmingly for temporary selective service, universal military training, and the Marshall Plan, and leaks from American military officials suggested administration fears of a serious and sudden conflict with the Soviet Union.[39]

The administration's propaganda job was helped by the Soviet Union's rejection of the Marshall Plan, thus assuring Americans that the plan would be an anti-communist effort. In fact, the plan was presented in such a way that the Soviet Union and the Eastern European countries could not participate. Russian Foreign Minister V. M. Molotov had gone to the Paris meeting of European nations interested in Marshall's proposal in June 1947 with a staff of eighty-nine, but the conferees encountered disputes immediately. The Russians were suspicious of a private French-British meeting before the conference began, and the British were frankly cool to Molotov's delegation in Paris. Fearful that the United States would manipulate the Marshall Plan for diplomatic purposes, Molotov rejected the British-French call for a Big Three steering committee to draw up country surveys. He responded that the sovereignty of each potential recipient had to be maintained, and that a Big Three committee, with American overlordship, might meddle in internal affairs. The Soviet Union could not accept the "decisive hold" of the United States over the recovery program, especially since the Marshall Plan followed so closely behind the Truman Doctrine and many anti-Soviet speeches by government officials like Dean Acheson, and after the United States had refused to grant a loan to the Russians in 1945–1946 unless they accepted American trade principles and opened up Eastern Europe to American trade. Soviet control over Eastern Europe was not firm or decided in early 1947 (the Czechoslovak *coup*, for example, was in part a response to the Marshall Plan), and the massive influx of American-directed dollars would challenge Russian influence.[40]

The Soviet Union was also wary of the French-British proposal, prepared before the Paris gathering, that the European economies be integrated. Russia interpreted this to mean that the *status quo ante bellum* would be perpetuated; that is, that Western Europe would be the industrial center, with Eastern Europe the supplier of raw materials, especially grains and coal. The Russians feared the subordination of the agricultural East to the industrial West. The Eastern European countries had developed plans, probably with Russia's prodding, for industrialization. They were undeveloped countries, and their economic difficulties had been augmented by the war's destruction. Vera Micheles Dean wrote in 1948 that "experts on Eastern Europe believe that only through industrialization accompanied by modernization of agriculture can the countries of this region solve their rural overpopulation problems, and ultimately raise their living standards." And a student of Eastern European history adds: "It is also understandable that the new regimes would wish, from a general feeling of patriotism, to diminish their countries' economic dependence on foreign countries." George Kennan later stated that in fact the United States expected from Russian participation the flow of raw materials to help the revival of the Western European economy.[41]

The Soviet Union, then, considered the Marshall Plan another example of American pressure to isolate and challenge communist nations, and *Pravda* asked: "Why . . . deliberately obscure the phraseology of Mr. Marshall's presentation of the Truman doctrine to the world?" The Soviet Union's response was to tighten its grip on Eastern Europe. Between July 12 and July 29, 1947, Russia secured a number of trade agreements with her neighbors and eventually attempted to mold them into a cumbersome "Molotov Plan." The International Communist Information Bureau (Cominform) was organized in September 1947 as the Russian propaganda agency. In February 1948 Czechoslovakia was dragged into the communist camp, after Jan Masaryk had tried desperately to steer a middle course between East and West and had failed to attract American foreign aid. The Marshall Plan, as it was presented, served to solidify developing international blocs and to realize Secretary of State James Byrnes's simplistic division of the world in 1946 into "friends" and "enemies."[42]

The Soviet Union might have asked, if the Marshall Plan was not a weapon of American foreign policy, why the United States did not work through the United Nations or the existing and viable Economic Commission for Europe (ECE), rather than through a nationalistic, American-directed organization. Perhaps there *was* an alternative for the United States. The United Nations' Economic Commission for Europe was a working body which counted the Soviet Union as a member. Kennan had suggested a program utilizing the ECE, and Walt W. Rostow, assistant to the ECE Executive Secretary, wrote in 1949 that many world leaders saw the ECE as a means of reducing Soviet-American tensions. He pointed out that Russia did not disrupt the ECE, even after the Marshall speech. But the United States chose to form an organization it could control directly, and rejected the offer of the United Nations' Trygve Lie for a program through the ECE.[43]

Perhaps the question of the invitation to Russia in the first place is not terribly relevant. It would have been the utmost of illogic and contradiction for Congress to approve funds for the Soviet Union so shortly after the passage of the anti-Soviet Truman Doctrine, the curtailment of United Nations Relief and Rehabilitation Administration supplies to Russia, and at a time when vociferous complaints were being made against trade with the Soviets. From fragmentary evidence it appears that American leaders did not expect the Soviet Union to accept. Clayton and Kennan told Marshall to "Play it straight," and Clayton made it emphatic that although Russia would be invited, the United States would "run this show." It may have been Henry Wallace who prompted the State Department not to exclude Russia from the offer of aid. Both State Department staffman Joseph Jones and Ambassador to Great Britain Lewis Douglas have mentioned as relevant Wallace's early 1947 speech in which he advocated a massive European reconstruction plan with a large part of the assistance going to Russia. Yet there was really no gamble in offering Russia access to a recovery program. As indicated, the Soviet Union could not have accepted membership in an administration dominated and directed by Americans and motivated by a desire to curb Soviet influence in the world. Thus many Europeans and Americans interviewed in the "Marshall Plan Project" considered the American invitation a gesture and diplomatic finesse, placing the burden of rejection on the Soviet Union.[44]

American leaders judged the Marshall Plan a success. By the end of 1952 Marshall Plan aid alone to the ERP countries amounted to $13 billion, and an additional $5 billion had been given to European members of the North Atlantic Treaty Organization. The proportion of American exports going to the ERP countries was maintained at about 33 per cent, with over half of United States exports to Western Europe financed with Economic Cooperation Administration (ECA) funds. Vital raw materials were added to American stockpiles by the ECA. With the help of an extensive ECA propaganda program, seemingly stable political regimes friendly to the United States were elected. Americans believed that the Marshall Plan thwarted communist victories in Italy and France. Kennan began to see results in early 1948:

> The economic plight of the continent [in 1947] was rapidly revealing itself as far worse than anyone had dreamed, and was steadily deteriorating. . . . A pall of fear, of bewilderment, of discourage-

ment, hung over the continent and paralyzed all constructive activity. . . . Compare that with today?. . . . Recovery is progressing rapidly in the West. New hope exists. People see the possibility of a better future. The Communist position in France has been deeply shaken.[45]

The Uses of Economic Power

American foreign policy after World War II was more than simply "stop communism" and more than simply "avert depression" or "expand markets." The three objectives were intimately linked in the peace and prosperity concept, which explained the containment policy well and was its rationale. To the Truman Doctrine and the Marshall Plan was added the North Atlantic Treaty Organization (NATO). Although Kennan considered NATO a perversion of his view of containment, other government officials argued that military bases and alliances—in short, security—were needed to achieve peace and prosperity. Thus James G. Blaine, a New York banker and chief of the Marshall Plan mission to Belgium, labeled the ERP and NATO "the concrete means to implement a Peace by Strength."[46]

Coupled with the shift to an emphasis on the military were certain weaknesses of the peace and prosperity notion itself. At a time when the United States was an economic behemoth, wealthy and expanding, and Europe lay prostrate, many foreigners interpreted the American desire to extend United States foreign trade and investment as an attempt to dominate foreign markets and perhaps politics. Thus Henry Wallace's challenge to Stalin to enter into a production race with the United States must have seemed blatantly ridiculous to the Russian dictator, who was quite aware of the economic superiority of his wartime ally and the comparative weakness of his own war-wracked nation. In an October 10, 1946, speech, Molotov dipped into the 1946 *World Almanac* to remind Americans how World War II had strengthened their economy. He asked what "equal opportunity" would really mean in Europe. How long, for example, he inquired, would Rumanian and Yugoslavian industry remain independent after the penetration of American-controlled capital? It is not easy to dismiss this as communist propaganda. Leopold S. Amery, British Conservative and former Secretary of State for India, observed: "American industry in all its phases is obsessed with the idea of conquering every market in the world. . . . They are out to capture aviation, sea transport and finance, the fields of invisible as well as visible exports." And Senator Robert Taft, a major dissenter from the peace and prosperity ideology, warned that economic expansion might "build up hostility to us rather than any genuine friendship. It is easy to slip into an attitude of imperialism and to entertain the idea that we know what is good for other people better than they know themselves." The president of the National Association of Wool Manufacturers did not share the foreign trade enthusiasm of much of the rest of the business community in 1947: "The emphasis which this country is currently putting on foreign trade is much more aptly characterized as 'economic aggression' than a means of promoting peace." Nondiscriminatory multilateral trade was inappropriate to a postwar world lacking economic stability and a supply of goods to conduct multilateral trade. Few countries were eager to lay bare their economies to American goods with which they could not compete. In other words, international trade in the immediate postwar period led perhaps as much to tension as to peace.[47]

A writer for *Nation's Business* later spotted an inherent contradiction in the peace and prosperity concept. "The twin goals of American policy are peace and prosperity. Could it be that a realization of the first might endanger the second, that an understanding with Russia and an end of the cold war might upset the economy at home?" American postwar prosperity was in part supported by military expenditures and foreign aid. One businessman in 1949 expressed a widely held attitude: "How would you feel if the political situation between Russia and ourselves was eliminated? For the United States this would entail the cutting of our Federal budget by one-half and a drastic reduction of taxes, both leading to many economic adjustments." This should not be taken to mean that businessmen or government officials supported a military build-up and a continuous Cold War in order to reap profits. That was simply not the case. Businessmen complained about the uncertainties of keeping store under conditions of semi-mobilization. They had to make what seemed to them agonizing decisions of whether to take on new

commercial orders or hold space for possible industrial mobilization. Then, too, many businessmen found government controls
and allocation systems anathema. And in foreign areas, businessmen worried about the status of their properties and investments.
Would they be nationalized or become targets of international
political enemies? The Cold War may have been good to American businessmen, and it may have fostered a contradiction in
the American hope for peace and prosperity, but they would
rather have made their profits an easier way—preferably through
secure, unencumbered, and ardent economic expansion at home
and abroad. Yet the question raised by this contradiction went
unanswered: Could the United States achieve economic stability
in genuine peacetime, or were unemployment and violent business cycles inherent in American capitalism? Or could a New
Deal response to depression ever succeed?[48]

There was also a shortcoming in the fulfillment of the peace
and prosperity concept: it was not applied universally or consistently. In Latin America, for example, American policy-makers
ignored deep-seated poverty, believing that American military,
economic, and political power would prevent revolutionary and
communist movements. Americans naively and stubbornly assumed, too, that their dollars could shape an American-oriented
world, desirous of American institutions and values. Yet American aid often went to regimes, such as in Latin America, Spain,
and monarchical Greece, which were resisting the very social
changes that could have brought about American-like institutions. Peace and prosperity usually meant stability, often without
regard for democracy, in a world of change and revolution. Professor Arnold Toynbee recently spelled out the consequences:

> Today America is no longer the inspirer and leader of the World
> Revolution. . . . By contrast, America is today the leader of a
> worldwide anti-revolutionary movement in defense of vested in-
> terests. She now stands for what Rome stood for. Rome consis-
> tently supported the rich against the poor in all foreign communi-
> ties that fell under her sway; and . . . Rome's policy made for
> inequality, for injustice, and for the least happiness of the great-
> est number.[49]

It is not the argument of this essay that the United States

should not have engaged in foreign trade or foreign aid programs. The world needed American goods and aid desperately after the war; it was both humanitarian and realistic to offer destitute people the American economic hand. Rather, the central questions are: How and to whom did the United States extend its help? How did the United States use its economic power? What alternatives were available to American decision-makers trying to fulfill the concept of peace and prosperity?

NOTES

1. Truman is quoted respectively in Senate, Committee on Foreign Relations, *European Recovery Program: Basic Documents and Background Information,* 80th Cong., 1st sess., 1947, Doc. 111, p. 67; *Public Papers of the Presidents: Harry S. Truman, 1946* (Washington, D.C., 1962), p. 354, statement of July 23, 1946 (hereafter *Truman Papers*); *Department of State Bulletin,* XVI (March 16, 1947), 481 (hereafter *SDB*). Roosevelt in Samuel Rosenman, ed., *The Public Papers and Addresses of Franklin D. Roosevelt* (New York, 1950), XIII, 595, statement of March 26, 1945.

2. *New Republic,* CXII (April 9, 1945), 464; Curtis Calder in Senate, Committee on Foreign Relations, *European Recovery Program* (Hearings), (hereafter Senate, *ERP*), 80th Cong., 2nd sess., January 23, 1948, p. 806.

3. Quotations from Cleveland Trust Company, *Business Bulletin,* 28 (April 15, 1947); *SDB,* XIV (May 19, 1946), 831, statement of James A. Stilwell; Cohen in Department of State, *Development of the Foreign Reconstruction Policy of the United States, March–July, 1947* (Washington, D.C., 1947), p. 13; Heinz in Senate, *ERP,* January 23, 1948, p. 908; U.S. Economic Cooperation Administration, *European Recovery Program: Western Germany, Country Study* (Washington, D.C., 1949), p. 1. Also see Allen W. Dulles, "Responsibilities of Businessmen to the World," in Harwood F. Merrill, ed., *The Responsibilities of Business Leadership* (Cambridge, Mass., 1949), p. 80; and William Green's (President, American Federation of Labor) statement that "a hungry man does not stop to reason," in Senate, *ERP,* January 23, 1948, p. 841.

4. Harriman in Senate, *ERP,* January 12, 1948, p. 245; "First Staff Draft of the Council of Economic Advisers Report on the Foreign Aid Program," September 10, 1947, Scope of Recommendation Folder, President's Committee on Foreign Aid Records, Truman Library; Council of Economic Ad-

visers, *The Impact of the Foreign Aid Program upon the Domestic Economy* (Washington, D.C., 1947), p. 31; Samuel Rosenman to Leo T. Crowley, May 31, 1945, Export-Import Bank Folder, Rosenman Papers, Truman Library; Eugene P. Thomas to John Condliffe, June 11, 1945, Box 28, Condliffe Papers, Bancroft Library, University of California. When Truman signed the Truman Doctrine bill on May 22, 1947, he stated: "The conditions of peace include, among other things, the ability of nations to maintain order and independence, and to support themselves economically." *Truman Papers 1947* (Washington, D.C., 1963), p. 255 (also see pp. 256–257).

5. James H. McGraw in *Business Week*, May 24, 1947, p. 80; Meany in *American Federationist*, LV (January 1948), 6; "The Effects of the Marshall Plan on Our Foreign Trade," [n.d.], Subcommittee on Economic and Financial Analysis, President's Committee on Foreign Aid Records; staff memorandum in Harry B. Price, *The Marshall Plan and Its Meaning* (Ithaca, 1955), p. 22; Clayton in Ross J. Pritchard, "Will Clayton: A Study of Business-Statesmanship in the Formulation of United States Economic Foreign Policy" (unpublished Ph.D. dissertation, Fletcher School, 1956), p. 286; Marshall in *SDB*, XVI (June 15, 1947), 1160. Also see Senate, Committee on Foreign Relations, *Assistance to Greece and Turkey* (Hearings), 80th Cong., 1st sess., March 24 and 25, 1947, pp. 5 and 75, for statements by Dean Acheson and Clayton; *SDB*, XVII (November 2, 1947), 855; National Foreign Trade Council, *Report* of 35th National Convention (November 8, 1948), p. 94 (hereafter NFTC); *Nation's Business*, XXXIV (November 1946), 25.

6. House of Representatives, Special Committee on Post-War Economic Policy and Planning, *Post-War Foreign Economic Policy of the United States*, 6th Report, 79th Cong., 1st sess., May 8, 1945, p. 9; NFTC, *Report* of 33rd National Convention (November 1946), p. xiv; Committee on International Economic Policy in Senate, Committee on Banking and Currency, *Anglo-American Financial Agreement* (Hearings), 79th Cong., 2nd sess., March 13, 1946, p. 343.

7. Clayton in *SDB*, XII (May 27, 1945), 979; see Standard Oil president in Senate, Committee on the Judiciary, *Cartels* (Hearings), 78th Cong., 2nd sess., May 23, 1944, p. 7, and Heinz in Senate, *ERP*, January 23, 1948, p. 908; Paul G. Hoffman, "The Survival of Free Enterprise," *Harvard Business Review*, XXV (Autumn 1946), 24. See also *Steel*, CXXI (July 7, 1947), 68; House, *Post-War Foreign Economic Policy*, 6th Report, p. 3. For a discussion of the British Loan of 1946, see Thomas G. Paterson, "The Economic Cold War: American Business and Economic Foreign Policy, 1945–1950" (unpublished Ph.D. dissertation, University of California, Berkeley, 1968), ch. IV.

8. For the frequency of the expression "open door" and the prominence of its principles see: *Iron Age*, CLIX (January 2, 1947), 78; National Planning Association, "The Stakes of Bretton Woods" (mimeographed), April 23, 1945; Telephone Conversation, Senator Claude Pepper and James Forrestal, March 24, 1947, Box 91, Forrestal Papers, Princeton University Library; Herbert Feis, "Political Aspects of Foreign Loans," *Foreign Affairs*, XXIII (July 1945), 618–619; *Fortune*, XXXI (January 1945), 146; Henry L. Stimson, Diary, July 16, 1945, Vol. 51, Stimson Papers, Yale University Library; John K. Galbraith, *Recovery in Europe* (Washington, D.C., 1946);

Journal, July 23, 1945, Box 18, Joseph E. Davies Papers, Library of Congress; Senate, Committee on Foreign Relations, *Treaties of Peace with Italy, Bulgaria, and Hungary* (Hearings), 80th Cong., 1st sess., March 4, 1947, p. 8; Joseph Grew to John J. McCloy, May 21, 1945, Vol. 122, Grew Papers, Houghton Library, Harvard University; *SDB,* XII (May 27, 1945), 979, and XIX (September 12, 1948), 325; R. R. Hackford, "Our International Aviation Policy," *Harvard Business Review,* XXV (Summer 1947), 483–500; extensive citations in Paterson, "Economic Cold War," ch. II. Aldrich in *World Trade,* XII (July 1946), 2; Truman in *SDB,* XIII (October 28, 1945), 654–655; NFTC, *Report* of 35th National Convention (November 1948), p. xxii.

9. Quotations respectively from Allen J. Matusow, *Farm Policies and Politics in the Truman Years* (Cambridge, Mass., 1967), p. 91; *Fortune,* XXXII (August 1945), 115; Brown in Senate, Committee on Foreign Relations, *Proposed Treaty of Friendship, Commerce and Navigation Between the United States and the Italian Republic* (Hearings), 80th Cong., 2nd sess., April 30, 1948, p. 10. For some of the American violations of the Truman trade program, see C. Addison Hickman, *Our Farm Program and Foreign Trade* (New York, 1949); Raymond F. Mikesell, *United States Economic Policy and International Relations* (New York, 1952), p. 303; Senate, *Anglo-American Financial Agreement,* March 6, 1946, p. 124, and March 19, 1946, pp. 445–446, 456; George W. Stocking and Myron W. Watkins, *Cartels in Action* (New York, 1946); Gabriel Kolko, "American Business and Germany, 1930–1941," *Western Political Quarterly,* XV (September 1962), 713–728; and additional citations in Paterson, "Economic Cold War," ch. II.

10. For GATT see *Journal of Commerce,* March 15, 1947; Matusow, *Farm Policies,* pp. 95–97; Sumner Welles, "Pressure Groups and Foreign Policy," *Atlantic Monthly,* CLXXX (November 1947), 63–67; *Pravda* in *Soviet Press Translations,* I (November 1946); *Economist* in *Iron Age,* CLVIII (August 8, 1946), 146. Also see Richard Gardner, *Sterling-Dollar Diplomacy* (Oxford, 1956), p. 353, and Hans Heymann, *We Can Do Business with Russia* (Chicago, 1945), p. 153.

11. Fleming to John C. Whites, May 14, 1945, Clayton Papers, Truman Library; Black in David A. Baldwin, *Economic Development and American Foreign Policy, 1943–62* (Chicago, 1966), p. 99; Clayton in Gardner, *Sterling-Dollar Diplomacy,* p. 378.

12. *SDB,* XXII (April 3, 1950), 531; "Report of Special Committee on Point Four Program," Chamber of Commerce, October 1949, Foreign Aid Folder, Stephen Spingarn Papers, Truman Library. Also see *Journal of Commerce,* February 7 and 22, 1947, and *Business Week,* May 13, 1950, p. 120.

13. Clayton in Senate, *Anglo-American Financial Agreement,* March 6, 1946, p. 124; House, *Post-War Foreign Economic Policy,* p. 41.

14. Wallace in *Nation's Business,* XXXIII (August 1945), 50; Harriman in *Journal of Commerce,* February 24, 1947; *Iron Age,* CLIX (January 2, 1947), 77; Advertising Council, *Annual Report, 1946;* National Planning Association, *Public Policy Digest,* Nos. 74–76 (April–May–June 1947), p. 13; Kennan to the Secretary of State, February 22, 1946, Box 24, Forrestal Papers; Byrnes in *SDB,* XIII (August 26, 1945), 279; George Soule, "Will We Cooperate with Britain?" *New Republic,* CXII (April 2, 1945), 442. See also Alvin H. Hansen, *America's Role in the World Economy* (New York,

1945), pp. 8, 23–24; Acheson in Senate, Committee on Foreign Relations, *North Atlantic Treaty* (Hearings), 81st Cong., 1st sess., April 27, 1949, Part I, p. 53; NFTC, *Report* of 36th National Convention (November 2, 1949), p. 248.

15. Truman in Senate, *ERP: Basic Documents,* p. 67; Interior Secretary Julius Krug in Senate, *ERP,* January 18, 1948, p. 354; Council of Economic Advisers, *Impact,* pp. 58–59; Vinson in Senate, *Anglo-American Financial Agreement,* March 5, 1946, p. 3; *Business Week,* November 15, 1947, p. 116. For the opinion of GE's Philip Reed and other business and government leaders on this theme, see Paterson, "Economic Cold War," ch. II.

16. Department of Commerce, *Foreign Trade of the United States, 1936–49* (Washington, D.C., 1951), p. viii; *ibid., Foreign Investments of the United States* (Washington, D.C., 1953), p. 2.

17. *SDB,* XVI (March 23, 1947), 554–555 (oil); Mira Wilkins and Frank E. Hill, *American Business Abroad: Ford on Six Continents* (Detroit, 1964), p. 357, and Harry A. Bullis, *A Businessman Views a Changing World* (Minneapolis, 1952), p. 21 (autos); Department of Commerce, *Statistical Abstract. 1953* (Washington, D.C., 1953), p. 954 (merchant fleet); Wilson in B. C Forbes, ed., *America's Fifty Foremost Business Leaders* (New York, 1948), p. 447; David M. Potter, "The American Economic System," in Lyman Bryson, ed., *An Outline of Man's Knowledge of the Modern World* (New York, 1960), p. 456.

18. William K. Jackson in NFTC, *Report* of 33rd National Convention (November 13, 1946), p. 381; Marshall in Senate, *ERP,* January 8, 1948, p. 2; Truman in Department of State, *Peace, Freedom, and World Trade* (Washington, D.C., March 1947), p. 5. Also see General Electric's Philip Reed in New York State Chamber of Commerce, *Monthly Bulletin,* XXXVII (December 1945), 234; Walter Millis, ed., *The Forrestal Diaries* (New York, 1951), p. 268, entry for April 28, 1947; *Fortune,* XXXV (June 1947), 2; Otto H. Korican, "Aims of Our Foreign Investment Policy," *Harvard Business Review,* XXIV (Summer 1946), 498.

19. Thorp in Department of State, *Problems of United States Foreign Economic Policy* (Washington, D.C., September 1947), p. 3; Frank J. Taylor in *Journal of Commerce,* October 19, 1945, p. 4A. For other statements by both government and business people on the connection between American prosperity and foreign trade from 1944 to 1949, see Milo Perkins, "Can Our Foreign Customers Pay?," *Atlantic Monthly,* CLXXVI (September 1945), 49; *SDB,* XV (November 17, 1946), 916; Morris S. Rosenthal (Stein, Hall and Co.), "The Advantages of the International Trade Organization to American Business," Speech, June 28, 1949, Carton 8, Condliffe Papers; Department of State, *Foreign Relations of the United States: Conferences at Malta and Yalta, 1945* (Washington, D.C., 1955), pp. 325–327; and additional evidence in Paterson, "Economic Cold War," ch. II.

20. Senate, *ERP,* January 13, 1948, pp. 345–346; Matusow, *Farm Policies;* Department of Commerce, *Historical Statistics of the United States* (Washington, D.C., 1960), p. 542; *ibid., Statistical Abstract, 1948* (Washington, D.C., 1948), pp. 654, 662; Council of Economic Advisers, *Impact,* pp. 111–112.

21. Department of Interior, *Natural Resources and Foreign Aid* (Washington, D.C., October 1947), pp. 12–14, 70; Commerce, *Historical Statistics,* p. 542; *ibid., Foreign Trade, 1936–49,* pp. 55–56; Monsanto Chemical

Co., *Annual Report, 1947*, p. 14; General Motors, *Annual Report, 1948*, p. 13; James Parton (Time-Life) in *Journal of Commerce*, October 15, 1946.

22. Wallace to J. C. Coyle, April 9, 1945, Office of Secretary, GC95112, Box 797, Department of Commerce Records, National Archives; Johnston in Gardner, *Sterling-Dollar Diplomacy*, p. 242; Heinz in Senate, *ERP*, January 23, 1948, p. 908; Marvin Hoffenburg, "Employment Resulting from U.S. Exports," *Monthly Labor Review*, LXV (December 1947), 675–678.

23. Snyder to the President, "Comments on Draft of the Economic Report of the President," [n.d.], OF396, Truman Papers, Truman Library; Department of State, *World Trade and the United States* (Washington, D.C., 1949).

24. Theodore A. Sumberg, "The Government's Role in Export Trade," *Harvard Business Review*, XXIII (Winter 1945), 167; Committee for Economic Development, *International Trade, Foreign Investment, and Domestic Employment Including Bretton Woods* (New York, 1945), p. 10; Johnston quoted in Forbes, *America's*, p. 226; Draft, "Economic Consideration," by Harold Moulton, October 10, 1947, Subcommittee on Economic and Financial Analysis Folder, President's Committee on Foreign Aid Records.

25. In the first seven months of 1947, Europe acquired two-fifths of our total exports, and approximately one-third of American exports of industrial machinery went to Europe in the 1945–1947 period. Statistics from Department of Interior, *Natural Resources*, pp. 18, 70. Quotations from President's Committee on Foreign Aid, *European Recovery and American Aid* (Washington, D.C., November 1947), pp. 3, 18; Clayton, "Reminiscences," Columbia University Oral History, p. 198.

26. Director of Mines in Senate, *ERP*, January 13, 1948, p. 369; Truman in *SDB*, XXI (September 12, 1949), 401; Ickes in *Steel*, CXVIII (February 4, 1946), 97; *Steel*, CXXII (March 29, 1948), 38. For further discussion of the raw materials shortage, see Telephone Conversation, Julius Krug and Thomas J. Hargraves, April 28, 1948, Box 49, Krug Papers, Library of Congress; *Business Week*, April 20, 1946; William S. Paley, Chairman, to Joseph C. O'Mahoney, April 28, 1952, Box 1, President's Materials Policy Commission Records, Truman Library; Paterson, "Economic Cold War," ch. II.

27. Forrestal to Paul C. Smith (of *San Francisco Chronicle*), March 19, 1947, and Telephone Conversation, Forrestal and Paul Shields, March 20, 1947, Box 91, Forrestal Papers; "Draft of March 10, 1947," Greece Folder, Clark Clifford Papers (used when in his possession, now in Truman Library). Acheson asked for the deletion because he thought the statement placed too much emphasis on the strategic-economic question. See Joseph M. Jones, *The Fifteen Weeks* (New York, c. 1955; 1964), pp. 156–157. See also comments on raw materials and foreign aid in Millis, *Forrestal Diaries*, p. 410, entry for April 1, 1948, and Senate, Committee on Foreign Relations, *Interim Aid for Europe* (Hearings), 80th Cong., 1st sess., November 13, 1947, pp. 226–227. For a more recent connection between the location of raw materials and the positioning of American naval vessels, see Department of Navy, Office of Chief of Naval Operations, *U.S. Life Lines* (Washington, D.C., 1966).

28. Poll of September in Price, *Marshall Plan*, p. 85. For evidence that the Russians thought the United States wanted postwar economic collab-

oration with them to avoid a depression, see Department of State, *Foreign Relations of the United States* (hereafter *FR*), *1944*, IV, *Europe* (Washington, D.C., 1966), 1125; *ibid., 1945*, V, *Europe* (Washington, D.C., 1967), 942–943. For British concern, see Millis, *Forrestal Diaries*, p. 356, entry for January 6, 1948, and for that of Czechoslovakia, William Diamond, *Czechoslovakia Between East and West* (London, 1947), pp. 138–139. For Russian commentary, see *New Times* (Moscow), July 1, 1945, pp. 15–19, and Eugene Varga, "The Approach of an Economic Crisis in the Capitalist World," *Political Affairs*, XXVI (March 1947), 264–268.

29. Millis, *Forrestal Diaries*, p. 356, entry for January 6, 1948; Dulles to Thomas Dewey, September 24, 1948, Category II, Dulles Papers, Princeton University Library.

30. This question of a postwar depression and its relation to foreign policy is discussed with substantial evidence in Paterson, "Economic Cold War," ch. II. Committee for Economic Development, *Toward More Production, More Jobs, and More Freedom* (New York, 1945), p. 7; Snyder in *Journal of Commerce*, October 31, 1946. See also Everett E. Hagen and Nora Kirkpatrick, "Forecasting Gross National Product and Employment During the Transition Period," *Studies in Income and Wealth*, X (1947), 94–109; Michael Sapir, "Review of Economic Forecasts for the Transition Period," *ibid.*, XI (1949), 273–351; W. S. Woytinsky, "What Was Wrong in Forecasts of Postwar Depression?," *Journal of Political Economy*, LV (April 1947), 142–151.

31. Exports to Europe in 1947 showed the effects of economic distress there. From a peak of $565,180,000 in May 1947, they dropped to $470,-952,000 in July, to $404,312,000 in November, and to $400,892,000 in January 1948. In 1947 the United States exported approximately $15 billion worth of commodities. In 1948 the figure dropped about $3 billion, and in 1949 declined another half-billion dollars (*Survey of Current Business*, XXVIII [April 1948], S-21; Commerce, *Foreign Trade, 1936–49*, p. 42). *Journal of Commerce*, June 3, 1947; Truman in *ibid.*, June 17, 1947.

32. Council quoted in *SDB*, XVII (November 16, 1947), 933; figures from Council of Economic Advisers, *Impact*, p. 15.

33. *Iron Age*, CLXI (April 29, 1948), 144; *Fortune*, XXXVII (January 1948), 69; Memorandum, Turner to Steelman, March 5, 1948, OF396, Truman Papers.

34. Ilse Mintz, *American Exports During Business Cycles* (New York, 1961), p. 12; figure from Congressional Quarterly Service, *Evolution of Foreign Aid, 1945–1965* (Washington, D.C., 1966), p. 25. One study has concluded: "The increase in government expenditures on national defense and international affairs took place . . . at a critical stage in the development of the recession, namely the latter half of 1948 and the first half of 1949, and was therefore of considerable value in supporting the weakening economy during that period." M. I. Ghozlan, "The Recession of 1948–1949 in the United States" (unpublished Ph.D. dissertation, Yale University, 1954), p. 459, also pp. 494–495.

35. Between August 1945 and August 1948 the cost of living rose 35 per cent and wholesale prices 61 per cent. (Chandler, *Inflation*, p. 216.) In 1947 a wheat shortage, due to a poor European crop and bad weather in the United States, caused wheat prices to skyrocket. There were also shortages in coal, steel, some industrial equipment, and nitrogen fertilizers. (Department of Interior, *Natural Resources*, pp. 7–10; Chandler, *Inflation*, pp.

229–230; *Journal of Commerce,* September 2, 1947.) Republic Steel President in *Journal of Commerce,* September 2, 1947. For criticism of the Marshall Plan as inflationary, see evidence in Paterson, "Economic Cold War," p. 102.

36. *Journal of Commerce,* September 19, 1947; Truman in *SDB,* XVII (November 2, 1947), 854; for the political move on controls, see Senator Carl Hatch to Truman, October 16, 1947, Box 4, Clark Clifford Papers, Truman Library, and "The President's Price Dilemma," Box 12, Frank McNaughton Papers, Truman Library; Clifford in "Memorandum for President," October 3, 1947, Box 4, Clifford Papers; Marshall in Senate, *ERP,* January 8, 1948, p. 58; U.S. National Advisory Council on International Monetary and Financial Problems, *Statement of the Foreign Loan Policy of the United States Government,* 79th Cong., 2nd sess., March 1, 1946, House Doc. 489, p. 5. Also see the call for controls and foreign aid by: Philip Murray of CIO in Senate, *ERP,* February 3, 1948, p. 1300; Americans for Democratic Action, Press Release, October 2, 1947, Clifford Papers; Committee for the Marshall Plan, Executive Committee Minutes, January 16, 1948, Box 105, Winthrop Aldrich Papers, Baker Library, Harvard University.

37. American Institute of Public Opinion poll cited in Pritchard, "Clayton," p. 350; for the complete list of Marshall Plan Committee members, see Senate, *ERP,* pp. 747–753, and for the activities of the committee, consult the Records of the Committee, Truman Library.

38. For the support of the various interest groups, see the hearings, Senate, *ERP.* For Vandenberg, see H. Bradford Westerfield, *Foreign Policies and Party Politics: Pearl Harbor to Korea* (New Haven, 1955), pp. 278–279; Arthur H. Vandenberg, Jr., ed., *The Private Papers of Senator Vandenberg* (Boston, 1952), p. 383, quotation; Paterson, "Economic Cold War," pp. 25–26, 400–401. Forrestal in Millis, *Forrestal Diaries,* p. 268, entry for April 28, 1947. Opposition to the Marshall Plan came from those who thought the United States could not afford the program (Hearst press), that it would be inflationary (Illinois Manufacturers Association), that the ERP was socialistic (Henry Hazlitt and the National Economic Council), that Europe was beyond saving (Virgil Jordan of the National Industrial Conference Board), that it was a scheme of business trusts (American Labor party), that the United States should work through the United Nations (National Farmers Union), and that it divided Europe (Henry Wallace). See the Senate hearings, *ERP,* and "Chief Arguments Against the European Recovery Program," compiled by SD, [n.d.], Tray 18822, Committee on Foreign Affairs, House Records, National Archives.

39. For concern about the Italian elections, see "McNaughton Report," March 5, 1948, Box 13, McNaughton Papers; and Senator John D. Lodge to Truman, March 9, 1948, OF233-Misc., Truman Papers. Germany and the ERP are discussed in Paterson, "Economic Cold War," ch. VIII. Westerfield, *Foreign Policies,* p. 286, notes the crisis atmosphere. Also see Truman's speech in *Truman Papers, 1948,* pp. 182–186.

40. For the Paris meeting, see Walter LaFeber, *America, Russia, and the Cold War, 1945–1966* (New York, 1967), pp. 49–50; Kenneth Ingram, *History of the Cold War* (New York, 1955), pp. 60–63; Senate, *ERP: Basic Documents,* pp. 152–156; James P. Warburg, *Long Road Home* (Garden City, 1964), pp. 237–240; Howard K. Smith, *State of Europe* (New York, 1949), p. 98. Will Clayton, who attended the Paris conference, later dis-

cussed an episode which reveals the tenor of the meeting: "He [Molotov] tried to get Bevin [British Foreign Minister] to tell him what the U.S. and Britain had talked about. But Bevin would not tell him unless he was sure Molotov would come along." (Typescript, Clayton Interview, Marshall Plan Project, pp. 30–31, Ellen Garwood Papers, Truman Library.) For one Soviet statement against the ERP, read Walter Bedell Smith, *My Three Years in Moscow* (Philadelphia, 1950), pp. 198–200. George Kennan believed the *coup* was a "defensive reaction" to the ERP (*Memoirs* [Boston, 1967], p. 379).

41. Vera Micheles Dean, "Economic Trends in Eastern Europe—II," *Foreign Policy Reports*, XXIV (April 15, 1948), 38; Hugh Seton-Watson, *East European Revolution* (New York, 1956), p. 254; Kennan in Price, *Marshall Plan*, p. 24. Also consult Senate, *ERP*, January 8, 1948, p. 47, and *ERP: Basic Documents*, pp. 155–156.

42. *Pravda* in Wilfrid Knapp, *A History of War and Peace, 1939–1965* (New York, 1967), p. 114. Byrnes's "friends-enemies" dichotomy is clear in his September 24 cable to the State Department, quoted in James Riddleberger, SD, to Ambassador Laurence Steinhardt, October 3, 1946, Box 51, Steinhardt Papers, Library of Congress.

43. Kennan, *Memoirs*, pp. 338–341; Walt W. Rostow, "Machinery for Rebuilding the European Economy," I, "The Economic Commission for Europe," *International Organization*, III (May 1949), 254–268. Also see *SDB*, XVI (January 5, 1947), 4, and N.K., "East-West Trade in Europe," *World Today*, V (March 1949), 103.

44. Clayton and Kennan in "Meeting of May 23, 1947," Joseph Jones Papers, Truman Library; Kennan, *Memoirs*, p. 342; Pritchard, "Clayton," p. 293. On Wallace, see Joseph Jones to Dean Acheson, April 24, 1947, Jones Papers; Typescript, Douglas Interview, Garwood Papers; Henry Wallace, *Toward World Peace* (New York, 1958), pp. 11–12. The Marshall Plan Project interviews are in the Garwood Papers at the Truman Library.

45. Figures from Price, *Marshall Plan*, p. 162; for ECA activities, and results, see its *A Report on Recovery Progress and United States Aid* (Washington, D.C., 1949) and *Reports to Congress*; Kennan, *Memoirs*, pp. 362–363.

46. Kennan on NATO in *Memoirs*, pp. 406–410; Blaine in New York State Chamber of Commerce, *Monthly Bulletin*, XLI (May 1949), 36.

47. Wallace in *New York Times*, February 20, 1946; V. M. Molotov, "The Danube and Economic Problems," in *Problems of Foreign Policy: Speeches and Statements, April 1945–November 1948* (Moscow, 1949), pp. 209–214; Amery in *Journal of Commerce*, January 30, 1946; Taft in Henry W. Berger, "A Conservative Critique of Containment: Senator Taft on the Early Cold War Program," in David Horowitz, ed., *Containment and Revolution* (Boston, 1967), pp. 131–132; Arthur Besse (wool) in *Journal of Commerce*, March 12, 1947.

48. *Nation's Business*, XXXVII (June 1949), 25; "What About Business Conditions? Where Are We Heading? Digest of Business Letters," Confidential to the Committee for Economic Development Trustees, March 1949, Box 102, Ralph Flanders Papers, Syracuse University Library.

49. Arnold J. Toynbee, *America and the World Revolution* (New York, 1962), p. 92.

LLOYD C. GARDNER

America and the
German "Problem," 1945–1949

"THERE IS NO question in my mind whatever," Secretary of State
George C. Marshall advised Congress solemnly late in 1947, "that
the German economy is the heart of Europe, and if we do not
coordinate that in connection with the rest of Europe, certainly
western Europe, we [will] be in difficulties for an interminable
procession of years. . . ."[1] The time since V-E Day was still reck-
oned in months, yet already the German "problem" had been
turned upside down. Germany must be revived instead of re-
pressed. The thought of reworking Germany into European economic processes, of rebuilding the industrial might of the Ruhr,
even if it were to be done within the carefully planned structure
of the European Recovery Program (the Marshall Plan), dramatized the impact of the Cold War on foreign policy thinking.
Though the goal of German reintegration antedated the Cold
War, Marshall and his aides in the State Department now presented the nation with an unexpected choice: aid German recovery (with its risks) or face almost certain collapse in Western

Adapted from *Architects of Illusion: Men and Ideas in American Foreign
Policy, 1941–1949*, copyright © 1970 by Lloyd C. Gardner, by permission
of Quadrangle Books, Inc.

Europe. "If western Europe is overrun by communism," warned former Assistant Secretary of State Will Clayton, "I think the situation which we would face in this country would be a very grave one, even if we faced no great military danger—and we would. The economic consequences of such a disaster would be very, very great to us. We would have to reorder and readjust our whole economy in this country if we lost the whole European market."[2]

Upon Roosevelt's death in April 1945, American postwar planning for Germany was little more explicit than the Unconditional Surrender declaration the President had issued at Casablanca in 1943. Some months later at Teheran, Roosevelt had suggested that Germany be divided into several parts; but then at Yalta in February 1945, when Stalin proposed that they settle that issue at once, Roosevelt was evasive.[3]

The drift of Roosevelt's mind was already apparent as concrete war problems gave way to a new wave of issues. In this transition period, the process of solidification began with temporary occupation zones and was completed with the building of the Berlin Wall in August 1961.

Stalin's position on German dismemberment probably was not firm either. His planners had, however, worked out details for a German "land-reform" policy designed to create a new class dependent upon whatever government was installed in East Germany. It would also serve to change the social structure in the areas closest to Poland. This would harmonize with Russian plans to move Poland westward several hundred miles and secure Warsaw's allegiance to Moscow, regardless of the political form that finally evolved in the two countries. Stalin did not, therefore, need to "communize" either Poland or Germany to secure his central purposes, nor to engage in any further boundary redrawing—except for one thing. He badly needed German reparations to aid Russian recovery and to satisfy the "blood-debt" to his people.

Behind the rhetoric of the Unconditional Surrender declaration a bitter debate had taken place within Roosevelt's cabinet in 1944. The only document that survived that struggle was the much-amended Joint Chiefs of Staff Memorandum No. 1067. Because the reparations issue governed Russian-American relations over the German question—at least initially—the language of that memorandum concerning reparations is of some interest. JCS 1067 instructed whoever would be assigned to be the American military governor: "No action will be taken in execution of the reparations program or otherwise which would tend to support basic living conditions in Germany or in your zone on a higher level than that existing in any of the neighboring United Nations." Much of the American debate was over how to interpret that statement, or, some insisted, how to change it altogether.

On one side was Secretary of the Treasury Henry Morgenthau, who wanted to deny the American commander any authority to *re*-centralize Germany, even for the sake of providing large-scale reparations to the victors. Morgenthau had almost persuaded Roosevelt to his position at the time of the Quebec Conference with the British in the fall of 1944. Using the President's angry dissatisfaction with a "soft" army paper on postwar Germany as his opening, Morgenthau proposed a plan for de-industrializing Germany and redistributing its prewar foreign markets. When Prime Minister Winston Churchill first heard the plan, he objected violently. But two factors led him to change his mind: first, FDR and Morgenthau were insistent about it; second, Churchill had come to Quebec anxious to discuss transitional financial arrangements, and Morgenthau had offered the British a $6 billion credit as part of the bargain.

Morgenthau had a similar alternative for the Russians. To satisfy their need for German reparations, he would have offered Moscow an even larger credit, one which would also have had the advantage of tying the Soviets to American postwar economic planning.

After the Quebec Conference, however, word of the "Morgenthau Plan" was leaked to the press, and Roosevelt refused to go any further with German planning, regardless of what his advisers said or did. Morgenthau's arguments grew more strident, and he suspected his opponents of harboring secret desires to rebuild Germany as a bulwark against bolshevism. "This thing needs to be dragged out in the open," he wrote the President on January 10, 1945. "I feel so deeply about it that I speak strongly. If we don't face it I am just as sure as I can be that we are going to let a lot of hollow and hypocritical propaganda lead us into recreating a strong Germany and make a foe of Russia. I shudder for the sake of our children to think of what will follow."[4]

Morgenthau was also deeply disturbed when he learned a few weeks later that Roosevelt had agreed at Yalta to a figure of $20 billion—as a basis for discussion with Churchill and Stalin —for reparations from Germany. Such a figure could be achieved, thought Morgenthau, only if Germany were rebuilt to permit heavy extractions from current production; and in fact, the Yalta protocol specifically listed reparations from current production as one of three means for collecting Germany's obligations to the victors.

Morgenthau's opponents were equally upset about the $20 billion figure. In the first place many of them *were* concerned about the bolshevization of Germany, or, as James P. Warburg put it in 1950, of allowing Germany to work out its own long-deferred revolution.[5] But it was not, in 1945 at least, primarily because they wanted a bulwark against the Soviet Union; besides, the kind of nationalism needed to cement such a bulwark could too easily be turned against the West once again. Interested in reintegrating Germany into the world economy just as soon as possible, they feared the President's "generosity" presaged a return to the kind of patchwork financing of the 1920's when private and public loans to Germany blew up in the debacle of the Great Depression.

After Yalta a second divisive issue suddenly reappeared amidst the Allies. It had been lurking in the background since the Nazi-Soviet Pact, or, depending upon one's viewpoint, since Munich the year before. It was the question of East-West maneuvering to divert German nationalism and expansionism toward the other side, which, as the war came to an end, took the shape of a "surrender" race. Anglo-American negotiators in Berne had begun secret talks with SS General Karl Wolff concerning a surrender of all German forces in northern Italy. Moscow suspected the Western Allies were seeking a separate peace. Roosevelt's responses to Stalin's bitter messages on this subject did little to ease the situation—in large part, it is now apparent—because the President did not in fact have full information about OSS maneuvers, a preview of other crises to come in the Cold War. Stalin argued not that field commanders should refuse to accept a local surrender (his own had done so in Hungary), but that the West had gone ahead with a plan which, if carried out, would permit the transfer of several German divisions to the East.

"The Germans have 147 divisions on the Eastern Front," Stalin cabled Roosevelt on April 7, 1945. "They could safely withdraw from 15 to 20 divisions from the Eastern Front to aid their forces on the Western Front. Yet they have not done so, nor are they doing so." They were fighting for obscure places in Czechoslovakia which they needed "just as much as a dead man needs a poultice," Stalin asserted, and concluded: "You will admit that this behavior on the part of the Germans is more than strange and unaccountable."[6] The actual casualty figures supported Stalin's complaint about German resistance in the east, even if they did not support his conjecture about what was going on in Berne. In the ten days between April 11 and 20, 1945, 577 Germans died on the Western Front, and 7,587 perished in the east. 1,951 were wounded in the west, 35,414 in the east. But perhaps of even greater interest, 268,229 Germans were listed as missing in the west, but only 25,823 were so named in the east.[7]

"Despite military victories," the OSS chief in Berne, Allen Dulles, wrote privately, "I feel apprehensive as to what we will find in Europe for years to come. We are moving towards the dramatic finale which will leave a large part of Central Europe in chaos. If Hitler succeeds in nothing else, like Samson, he may pull down the pillars of the temple and leave a long and hard road of reconstruction."[8] Dulles has since written of the surrender negotiations that they were politically aimed at (1) preventing unnecessary destruction in that area where the partisans were strongest, and (2) permitting British and American troops to get to Trieste before "either Soviet troops coming across Hungary or Tito's followers reaching up out of Yugoslavia, supported by the pro-Communist partisans," could reach that city "and possibly west of there before we arrived."[9]

But from Moscow, the Berne negotiations seemed intended primarily to open the Western Front so that Anglo-American troops could drive on Berlin. On April 1, 1945, Stalin summoned two of his marshals, G. K. Zhukov and I. S. Konev, to the Kremlin where he read them a "telegram" which stated that the Anglo-American command was at that moment preparing such a thrust. "Well," said Stalin, "who is going to take Berlin, we or the Allies?"[10] Even though the Russian dictator had that same day informed Eisenhower that he regarded Berlin as strategically unimportant, this conference in the Kremlin signaled the beginning of the final Russian offensive in the east, designed frankly to beat the Western armies to the political center of the dying Third Reich. Stalin was furious, then, when the surrender was signed not in Berlin, where his soldiers had first raised Soviet banners, but in Reims, where the Russians were represented only by an undistinguished artillery general. So the war against Germany ended in secret suspicion and anxiety, even as public celebrations decorated Allied capitals.

JCS 1067, a presidential adviser told General Lucius Clay after FDR's death, "was assembled by economic idiots! It makes no sense to forbid the most skilled workers in Europe from producing as much as they can for a continent which is desperately short of everything."[11] As head of the American Military Government, General Clay became responsible for most American decisions in Germany from the beginning of the occupation through the Berlin blockade in 1948. His close relationship with James F. Byrnes, Truman's first Secretary of State, significantly enlarged his decision-making responsibilities in those crucial years. As Robert K. Murphy, Clay's political "commissar," wrote in his memoirs, the "Byrnes-Clay partnership not only changed the American conception of the German occupation, but affected the whole pattern of European events."[12] Given Roosevelt's ambiguous legacy, it is more accurate to say that this partnership clarified the conception of German policy, so that imperfect plans could be brought into line with overall American policy.

In a letter describing his initial impressions and activities, Clay warned the War Department that the whole question of eliminating German war potential had to be rethought. Industry that had not been destroyed was needed, even for a low standard of living. Hasty reparations removals could "make it impossible to bring order back to Germany."[13] But Clay's estimate of total German destruction was soon revised downward in General John Hilldring's congressional testimony. In the summer of 1945 in Cologne, for example, Hilldring said, first reports that the Ford plant had been completely destroyed proved erroneous when "closer inspection revealed that falling walls and roof had buried the heavy machinery with layers of bricks and mortar which had in fact served to protect against the weather." Within a short time that plant was producing five hundred trucks a month. Other witnesses estimated that I. G. Farben installations could, if the necessary input of raw materials were supplied, be brought back to 90 per cent of capacity within three months.[14] For American occupation officials, therefore, it was not so much a question of whether huge reparations could be extracted, but whether they *should* be taken at the expense of reestablishing the German economy.

Clay awaited the Potsdam Conference with considerable apprehension that the Big Three would reach reparations agreements that would make it impossible to integrate Germany into American policy, or, as one of his aides once put it, would turn Germany into a WPA project at considerable expense to the American taxpayer. Since the Russians demanded one-half of the proposed $20 billion as their share, if the United States did supply the capital for rebuilding the German economy, according to the Yalta protocol the Soviets could siphon off current production from the Western zones to meet their reconstruction needs. A huge reparations settlement would also, therefore, limit options for using economic levers against the Soviets in Eastern Europe.

Truman's chief representative to the Allied Reparations Com-

mission, Edwin Pauley, had been sparring with Russian negotiators for some time, trying not to make commitments until the
President and his advisers decided what to do about reparations
and reconstruction. At one point in these deliberations, the State
Department instructed the American chargé in Moscow, George
F. Kennan, to invite Russian reparations negotiators to accom-
pany their British and American counterparts on an inspection
tour of German industrial areas, before the Allied Reparations
Commission began its work in Moscow as per its Yalta directive.
Kennan misinterpreted the move; he protested it was a waste of
time to engage in such studies with the Russians. "In the end,"
Kennan insisted, "it will come down to a simple horse trade.
How much are we going to make available to the Russians from
our zones, and what price are we going to demand for it?" Ambassador Averell Harriman, who was in Washington helping to
make the policy, replied with a short lecture on the virtues of
postponement: "The principal point is that Mr. Pauley's instructions are very firm and while we may not reach any agreement
I have no fears about us giving in."[15]

Perturbed by Washington's tactics, the chief Russian reparations negotiator, Ivan Maisky, warned Kennan that both powers
would regret further delay. If it continued, Maisky said, "a number of countries interested in receiving reparations from Germany would take unilateral action to get what they could."

Yet Pauley went to Moscow not to clear up these matters
but in a mood to demand changes in the Yalta agreement on
reparations. He began the discussions with the blunt accusation
that the Russians were "looting" Germany; then he insisted there
could be no reparations out of current production until the
Germans could export enough to pay for "essential" imports.
He topped these statements by announcing that the United
States could no longer commit itself to *any* total reparations
figure.[16]

Although there were plenty of grounds for complaint that the
Russians had been carrying away German resources, as Maisky
said, such unilateral acts had already begun *on both sides*. With
advance units into Germany had gone American intelligence officers who gathered up German physicists and rocket experts to

prevent them from falling into Russian hands. Then on June 14, Secretary of the Interior Harold Ickes had informed Truman that northwest Europe would be desperately short of coal once cold weather began. Truman responded by directing General Eisenhower to make twenty-five million tons available for export from Western Germany over the next nine months. Moscow was sent only an "information copy" of the directive, "to avoid delay," as Truman put it.[17]

"I want to make it clear that not only the Russians have sinned," Stalin told Truman and Clement Attlee at Potsdam, and he handed them a report from General Zhukov estimating the number of railroad cars removed from the Russian zone by British and American authorities at over eleven thousand. Truman replied that if true it had not been an authorized act, and he would have General Eisenhower look into it at once. An American report on the Zhukov memorandum admitted that it was "probably largely correct," but it still insisted that the equipment described in the Russian report was not needed for a peacetime German economy, "whereas the Russian removals observed, such as agricultural equipment, sewing machines and textile machines, are certainly not war potentials."[18]

This term "war potentials" covered a multitude of sins for both sides, as we shall see, and was incapable of close definition. It was one more tangle in the whole reparations situation. Unless both sides were willing to be candid about their behavior, the outlook was not good for a big-power German settlement. Secretary of State Byrnes had opened the discussion of German reparations at Potsdam by asking—"not in any attitude of hostility"—if it was true that the Russians had taken large quantities of equipment and materials out of Germany. The answers he received from Foreign Minister V. M. Molotov were just a bit too candid for Byrnes's purposes in asking the question, because Molotov immediately offered to reduce the Soviets' claims by $300 million to pay for these removals, which he readily confessed. Byrnes asked if Molotov seriously thought $300 million would cover the removals. The Russian Foreign Minister offered to deduct $1 billion, "and thus dispose of the question." In a later conversation he even offered to drop claims to an additional billion dollars, provided Russia received a fixed amount of industrial equipment from the Ruhr, "say two billion."

Byrnes had had something very different in mind when he had asked the original question. He rejected the Russian offers and proposed instead that each nation take reparations from its own occupation zone. He was willing to agree not to $2 billion in reparations from the Ruhr, but to 25 per cent of the plants eventually declared available for reparations. But there was no way to determine what these would total in dollar value until there was some agreement on what level of industry would be permitted to the Germans. The lower such a level dipped, the more plants would be available as reparations. Byrnes's proposal, therefore, had a built-in incentive to the Russians to demand a low living standard for the Germans. When this is matched with the Secretary's desire that the Potsdam protocol read, "The proceeds of exports from current production and stocks shall be available in the first instance for payment . . . [of essential] imports"—the shift in American policy since Yalta becomes understandable only as a quest for an agreement which would require the least cooperation between East and West. If zonal commanders were to determine, in the final analysis, when "essential" imports had been paid for, all the king's horses and the commissar's men couldn't put Germany together again.

Molotov had seen the implications in Byrnes's proposal from the outset:

MR. MOLOTOV: said would not the Secretary's suggestion mean that each country would have a free hand in their own zone and would act entirely independently of the others?
THE SECRETARY: said that was true in substance . . .[19]

Against these divisive reparations proposals there was only the offer of 25 per cent of the factories in the West to assuage the angered Russians. Of the 25 per cent, only 10 per cent were to be shipped east without compensation; the remaining 15 per cent were to be in return for Russian food and coal shipments from their zone. All the plants were to be shipped within two years, while the raw materials were to be sent in agreed-upon lots over the following five years. (This became important later when U.S. officials in Germany charged the Russians had broken their promise to ship raw materials by May 1946.)

Stalin and Molotov did not readily accept these terms; they finally did so only when Byrnes told the Foreign Minister on July 31, 1945, that he and the President were leaving Potsdam the next day—whether or not the issue had been resolved. From an American point of view, the Potsdam agreement on reparations had three distinct advantages over Yalta: first, it eliminated references to any total figure and tied reparations to a level-of-industry agreement; second, it virtually eliminated the possibility that the Russians would get any reparations from current production in the West (and thus served larger policy purposes as well); third, it forced the Russians to continue looting East Germany if they expected to get anything like $10 billion in reparations. Of course, the more the Russians made their communist sycophants responsible for these acts, the less likelihood was there that Moscow could mount an ideological offensive against the West, or appeal to Germans to renounce ties to the West. (Relieved that the danger of the West's being made to pay for Russia's reparations had all but disappeared, General Clay was optimistic that new Big Four agreements could be negotiated within Germany, at least in regard to economic problems.)

On the other hand, the Potsdam agreement had certain unanticipated results less favorable to the West. In the first place, as Samuel Lubell observed in 1946, "The extent to which the handling of reparations . . . produced the effects of an economic iron curtain splitting Europe in two is not generally appreciated."[20] Even less expected was the rapid growth of interzonal boundaries *within* Western Germany: the real threat to American policy came, in the first instance, from that source; but the way in which General Clay and his aides handled the threat further exacerbated East-West relations.

"We are finally moving on quadri-partite control," Clay wrote privately on August 8, 1945, "and I am still an optimist with respect to its possibility of success. I have found our Russian colleagues, while fully realistic, desirous of a co-ordinated and co-operative treatment of Germany. They know what they *want* and it is always easy to do business with those who know their own desires. I think that we, too, know our objectives now, and that with patience and understanding much can be accomplished."[21]

No sooner did Clay finish this letter, however, than the French began obstructing the Allied Control Council, making it difficult, then impossible to carry out the Potsdam agreements on German economic unification. The French were angry with both East and West. They had been granted a seat on the Allied Control Council and a full share of those reparations that were to be made available after a big-power agreement on the level of industry. Like the Russians, with whom they ultimately forged an uneasy alliance on this question, the French wanted four-power control of the Ruhr. In Control Council meetings the French representative challenged the validity of all Big Three agreements, much to the embarrassment of Anglo-American members who had demanded that Paris be given its place on this body. At first Moscow suspected that France was being allowed to block the Potsdam agreements, but General Clay assured his colleagues that he was just as put out by French behavior as were the Soviets. Not only was France uncooperative in Berlin, but General de Gaulle had also set about incorporating the French zone into metropolitan France. On top of that, he publicly demanded the Saar and an equal share of the Ruhr. Cut off from expansionist possibilities in the east, de Gaulle asserted that German revenge-seekers would surely turn westward once again.

Great Britain's economic policies in the Ruhr and the remainder of its zone, while not deliberately disruptive, threatened to destroy the Potsdam agreements through slow disintegration. The Labour government was theoretically committed to socializing its own economy, but its military representatives in occupied Germany seemed anxious to implement a relatively conservative policy. Suspended between two economic policies, and American disapproval of "socialism" in any Western zone, London proved unable to carry out either plan. Instead, underpriced

British exports of timber and coal further reduced German capabilities for economic recovery. General Clay once charged that both the French and the British were carrying out a disguised reparations policy and calling it something else. Ruhr factories and coal mines failed to produce at anywhere near the prewar level. In 1945 they achieved only 25 per cent of that level, in 1946 only 40 per cent, in 1947, 50 per cent, and in 1948 still just 60 per cent.[22] While this could be accounted for partially by restrictions on German iron and steel production, it was clear to American policy-makers that the situation in the West called for much stronger pressure from Washington. Increasingly impatient with these Western failures, and the obvious danger they posed to the maintenance of order in all Western Europe, American officials developed a series of official excuses for the poor performance, including the specious argument that Russian reparations removals had drained the Western zones of economic strength.

Lewis H. Brown, chairman of the board of Johns-Manville, who was commissioned by Clay later to report to the American people on the German situation, once explained, "To the east of the line, the iron fist of the police state enforces the planned-economy concepts of Russia. To the west of the line, there is 'Schachtism,' control, and bureaucracy, but the philosophy of private enterprise is not yet without honor and there is still hope for its restoration."[23] Clay's first effort to restore private enterprise in the West, the introduction of the dollar trade system in the American zone in the fall of 1945, was almost completely undercut by the lack of coordination in the Western zones. The French were deliberately running their zone at a deficit—the highest in all Germany. And the British were bogged down in a "Papierkrieg."

These concerns were at the heart of the report Clay made to the Allied Control Council on American proposals concerning the negotiation of a German "level-of-industry" on September 10, 1945. It stated: ". . . The conflict between an extreme degree of industrial disarmament spread over a number of key industries and the goal of maintaining a minimum German standard of living according to the assumed formula while providing for the costs of occupying forces seems insoluble under conditions such as those brought about by losses of territory."

This report touched off the first serious U.S.-Russian disagreement in the Control Council. When the Russians objected, the State Department stepped into the dispute with both feet. In answer to a Soviet request to participate in the determination of what reparations properties could be made available in the west the Department responded that Russia would have to agree to treat Germany as an economic unit first. "This means that Soviet removals of industrial capital equipment from the Eastern Zone must be based on a plan arrived at among the four powers, which will treat each zone as a part of a unified Germany after reparation removals to subsist without external assistance." Otherwise, the Western zones would make their own computations. The Soviet Foreign Office replied that while it would allow inspection of the Russian zone by Western officials, it would not accept responsibility for a single four-power plan for reparations collections: "The Berlin Conference not only did not contemplate the drawing up of such a four-zone plan (it accepted the principle proposed by the American delegation of collection of reparations by zones—an Eastern Zone and Western Zones), but established one procedure of reparations collections in the Eastern Zone and another in the Western Zones."[24]

There was no denying that was the way the Potsdam protocol read—just as Byrnes had wanted it to. The West was saved only by other language in that document which provided, again according to American wishes, that reparations removals would be subject to final approval by the zone commander. At the London Foreign Ministers' Conference later that month, Foreign Minister Molotov formally served notice on his colleagues that since the Potsdam agreement had not been carried out, the Soviet Union was returning to its earlier demand that the Ruhr be internationalized. Franco-Russian unity on this issue very quickly became a wedge against American efforts to establish a unified policy in the west, and delayed the reintegration of West Ger-

many into the world economy to the dismay of Anglo-American
leaders.

Meanwhile, Robert Murphy, Clay's political adviser, wrote the
State Department:

> It is gradually being realized by officials here that any wholesale
> transfer of German plants to liberated areas will greatly disturb
> production generally for several years and is likely to drag down
> living standards for all concerned. In other words, it is becoming
> clearer that extreme, ill-considered de-industrialization of Ger-
> many may well have the effect of creating and extending chaos
> in Europe.[25]

Murphy's statement about the German situation, the impasse
at London, and the poor performance of Western Zone economies called for a policy review. In November 1945 Clay and
Murphy returned to Washington for extended consultations with
the War and State Departments. Clay reported that the French
had declared they would hold up the creation of centralized
agencies to facilitate interzonal travel and economic exchanges
until their proposals for internationalization of the Ruhr and the
Rhineland had been decided. It was simply impossible, therefore, for Clay's experts in Berlin to calculate the peacetime level
of industry. Had the State Department applied any diplomatic
pressure on the French to cooperate? he asked.

The answer was no. Then, Clay said, the Soviets could not be
expected to agree to central agencies either. To Clay's insistence
that the French be brought into line, State Department officers
countered that the Soviets had not demonstrated any intention
to carry out the political and economic principles of the Potsdam
agreements. Moreover, their control of the press in East Germany, support of favored political parties, and unilateral land
reform and nationalization policies demonstrated that they were
determined to do just the opposite. Somewhat annoyed, Clay retorted that the French had done some of the same things—as
indeed had all the zonal commanders.[26] Despite Clay's arguments, his listeners remained cool toward efforts to bring the
French into line. The State Department agreed with Clay, however, on the need to restate American reparations policy. In the

end this was far more important, for when the new statement
was released on December 11, 1945, it produced its own dynamic
within Big Four power relationships. American reparations policy, it said, aimed at a "balanced economic position," and did
not seek "to eliminate or weaken German industries of a peaceful character, in which Germany has produced effectively for
world markets." Although the surrounding paragraphs were
much the same as previous policy declarations in promising to
keep Germany demilitarized, the statement that Germany should
be allowed to resume its production for "world markets" raised
a whole series of new questions, especially as there still had been
no four-power agreement on what level of industry was to be
permitted that country. If German industries were to produce
effectively for world markets, didn't that mean enlarging support
industries like iron and steel? "Serious repercussions were inevitable," wrote two American reparations experts. "The Russians
would not take this lying down."[27] They reasoned that American
policy now foretold a unilateral effort to raise the level of industry, and the Soviets would object bitterly to losing the additional plants. Among American policy-makers the predominant
view was that the Soviet reaction had to be risked: Germany
was the "spark plug" of the whole European economy. If there
was to be an East-West struggle, it was imperative that the West
integrate Germany into the American-led political-economic system. If there was not to be an East-West struggle, others reasoned, it would only be because communism had been halted in
Germany, and Germany had been integrated successfully. And
if the American system were to function properly, concluded
Alfred P. Sloan, chairman of the board of General Motors, German living standards would have to be raised. General Motors,
he informed Bernard Baruch, had already spent over $600 mil-
lion getting ready to supply the pent-up demands of American
consumers. German industrial recovery would affect that demand—if not right away, then all the more ultimately.[28]

In addition, the success of American plans for postwar foreign
investment in Europe—at least so far as General Motors was concerned—turned on what happened in Germany. "Now I recog-

nize that if the production facilities formerly in Germany were eliminated," he wrote Baruch,

> it is bound to stimulate, in degree, the business opportunities of adjacent countries including England and incidentally ourselves. But I want to point out to you—and I say this from intimate experience . . . other countries . . . [in Western Europe] are just not comparable with Germany in their efficiency, their ability to work, and all the other things that form the foundation stones of an industrial development and production on the basis of efficiency. So far as we in General Motors are concerned, we were glad to have been able to operate in Germany, prewar, and it was frequently passed on to us by the German Economic Ministry that we had contributed much to the expansion of industry in Germany and to the advancement of their technological position in the areas in which we were operating.
>
> But, on the other hand, when it comes to operating in some of the countries . . . we would not be at all interested. For instance:— there is nothing that could convince us in General Motors that it was either sound or desirable or worthwhile to undertake an operation of any consequence in a country like France.[29]

Not all American businessmen shared Sloan's prejudices about France—as they would prove later—but among political and economic leaders the predominant view concerning Germany was just about as Sloan had put it. In February 1946, the State Department did exert pressure on France to cooperate in the establishment of Four Power economic agencies, but if a split did develop with Russia over reparations it was important to keep Britain and France in line with American policy. "My French colleague," Clay wrote in *Decision in Germany,* "later remarked that it had become obvious that early Soviet willingness to establish central administrative agencies was not sincere, and that fortunately the French veto had prevented us from creating agencies which would have been vehicles for Communist expansion." The fear that a centralized Germany would fall prey to the Soviets and international communism rose sharply in early 1946 when the Russians shifted their economic policy. Instead of opposing the new American reparations statement unequivocally, the Russians indicated a willingness to talk about raising the limits on German steel and other basic support industries—provided the Western powers first agreed to large-scale reparations from current production. The shift in Washington on France may well have come as a result of fears about the effectiveness of Russian progress in East Germany. Robert Murphy listed two considerations in a message to Secretary Byrnes. First, opposition to French demands for the Saar in East Germany "carry a powerful appeal for the support of the bulk of developing German opinion." Second, the "operation of German central agencies would have militated against zonal boundaries and served to break down exclusive Soviet control of one of the largest and most important German areas."

Those Soviet officials who had favored immediate dismantling of German industry in 1945 had persuaded Stalin with two arguments: the absolute need to make certain Germany would not rise again to dominate Central Europe, and the lack of alternate resources to rehabilitate the Soviet economy. When the rapid removals proved neither argument conclusively, opposition elements led by Anastas Mikoyan had a chance to offer counterproposals. They could cite, ironically, the recent American statement on reparations to discount the likelihood that there would ever be many plants made available from the West under any circumstances. Therefore, the best solution was a partial reestablishment of German industry in the Eastern Zone. Soviet-owned corporations, Mikoyan said, could produce for reparations and for German consumption.

Having received a green light in Moscow, Mikoyan hurried to Germany with the new orders. "Remember," he told Soviet officials there, "that economics determines politics. Speaking metaphorically, you are Soviet colonists. If it should happen that our government decides to withdraw its troops from Germany, you will be left alone there to face a bitter struggle with capitalist competitors. Remember that the most important thing is the solvency of the enterprise, its profits!" In 1946 more than three thousand industrial properties, comprising nearly 30 per cent of East Germany's industrial output, were converted into state-owned businesses.[30] At the same time the Russians forced the Social Democrats in East Germany to unite with the Communist party in an amalgam they called the Socialist Unity party.

On at least one occasion, Stalin did say publicly to East European Communists that he now expected all Germany would go communist.

Mikoyan's triumph had repercussions in the West, too. The more Clay feared the spread of Soviet-inspired subversion, the more he shut off even mild forms of socialism in West Germany. This made his tasks and those of his British and French colleagues even more difficult, since the mood in the West was clearly Social Democratic. Clay's exaggerated efforts to contain socialism made the American Military Government an exposed target to left political parties throughout the country, from the West's Social Democrats to the Socialist Unity party in the East. And, of course, the more the left parties attacked occupation policies, the greater effort the American Military Government made on behalf of the Christian Democrats, who were devoted to "free enterprise."

"Actually there has been little removal of reparations in the Western zones," a troubled Clay admitted privately, "and yet their economy is not on as substantial a basis as it is in the Soviet zone, where the removals have been heavy. The reason for this is quite simple. The Soviet zone is self-contained. The Western zones are not self-contained, and the existence of artificial boundaries and restrictions has retarded economic recovery until almost complete collapse threatens."[31]

The output of the Soviet plants in East Germany, Clay observed, was "proving an important contribution to a disrupted economy." During March and April the State Department received two messages from Moscow taking issue with Murphy's desire to put pressure on the French for Four Power economic agencies. Chargé George F. Kennan and the new ambassador, Walter Bedell Smith, concluded that the proper response to the "left" offensive would be to "adopt a line of action which, while proceeding in the direction of our ideal of a central government, will on the way produce a western Germany oriented toward western democracy." In April 1946 the United States demanded in the Allied Control Council that German exports be pooled, "with proceeds to go in the first place toward payment of essential imports." As might have been expected, this proposal met "with objection after objection from the Russians."[32] On his own initiative, Clay then suspended all reparations deliveries to the East, until the Russians agreed to a common pool of exports. As the general had noted, the real economic problem of the Western zones was *in* the West—the lack of coordination between the three zones, and the high boundaries which separated them—but American public relations handouts charged that the economic problem centered instead in the East, where the Russians were draining Germany's economic lifeblood by taking reparations from current production. To the Russians, American behavior must have seemed something like the following: The United States had gone back on its promise to ship industrial reparations to the East. That had been expected—if not welcome—but now it was also demanding access to the output of the Soviet zone by insisting that the Potsdam agreement meant that economic centralization took precedence over reparations in all zones. So long as the British and French continued to underprice exports from their zones, to support large military occupations from German funds, and to hold up economic centralization, Clay's proposal would drain the Russian zone interminably—and the situation the Americans complained about would be reversed with a vengeance.[33]

Clay's momentous decision set the stage for Secretary Byrnes's German policy in 1946. This policy was carried out in two phases: in the first step, Byrnes renewed an offer he had first made at the London Foreign Ministers conference the previous September as part of his general effort to persuade the Soviets to retire from Eastern Europe. Using a suggestion made originally by Senator Arthur Vandenberg in January 1945, Byrnes had asked Molotov in London if the Russians would be interested in a twenty-five-year four-power security treaty over Germany. He repeated this offer to Stalin personally in December 1945 at the Moscow Foreign Ministers conference. According to Byrnes's account of their conversation, the Soviet Premier had said that he could count on Russian support if he decided to fight for such a treaty. The treaty would have pledged each of the signatories to come to the aid of all if any were attacked by Germany. In addition, specific provisions for disarming Germany, and keeping it disarmed, were to be included. The final Potsdam agreement did call for guaranteed German disarmament, but, in the form it was first presented to the Russians, the draft security treaty was on the same model as the more positive guarantee Wilson had belatedly offered the French after World War I.

Byrnes had sent copies of the proposed pact to the British and Russians in February 1946. Molotov informed Byrnes just before the April session of the Paris Foreign Ministers conference that he objected to the American draft. When the meeting opened, Molotov asserted that the proposed treaty postponed German disarmament until after the occupation, would not take effect until after a German peace treaty was signed, and made no mention of Germany's responsibilities for reparations. Byrnes offered the Soviet Foreign Minister a quadri-partite inspection to confirm that the Western powers would in fact carry out all agreements on demilitarization. General Clay insisted, however, that if such an inspection were carried out it would have to include "the use of German industrial production for war purposes."[34] This move effectively stymied the Russians, because they knew very well (as they had insisted from the beginning) that production for war purposes and for peaceful purposes was difficult to separate. A public inspection of the Eastern Zone would give Clay an opportunity to demonstrate to the satisfaction of doubters in the West that the Russians were indeed exporting "excessive amounts" from industrial facilities—in supposed violation of the Potsdam agreement. Disagreement with the Russians was assumed in both phases of U.S. policy toward Germany in 1946; what Clay and Byrnes needed was leverage against Britain and France.

Less than a month after he halted reparations deliveries, Clay renewed earlier proposals he had made for merging the Western Zones. If some agreement were not soon reached, he warned, "we face a deteriorating German economy which will create a political unrest favorable to the development of communism in Germany."[35] On July 10, 1946, Molotov delivered a speech on Germany's future which handed Byrnes the crowbar he needed to pry open the Franco-Russian agreement on internationalizing the Ruhr. Attacking all plans for the so-called "agrarianization" of Germany—in line with the new Soviet policy of rebuilding German industry through state corporations—Molotov promised wide-scale development of its "peaceful" industries. At first American leaders were unsure how to deal with this new offensive, with its obvious bid for German support. "I realized at once the strength of this appeal," Byrnes recalled. Two days later the Secretary of State and British Foreign Minister Ernest Bevin announced their intention to merge their two zones. Bevin even told reporters that the Ruhr would soon be turning out a strong list of exportable commodities. But the Anglo-American declaration assumed the French had given up their claims to a share of the Ruhr, which they hadn't. Hence Byrnes wanted to deliver a speech that would embarrass the Russians, make it impossible for them to talk one way to the Germans and another to their clients in Warsaw, and somehow finesse the French all at once.

Just before Molotov's speech, elections in Hesse in the American Zone had given the Social Democrats forty-three seats and the Communists seven seats in a ninety-member constitutional assembly. The advocates of free enterprise were left in an uneasy minority. In the assembly's deliberations, the left pushed for—and got—a far-reaching program of nationalization embodied in Article 41 of the proposed draft constitution. Byrnes, therefore, was also interested in making a speech that would smite the socialist bogeyman directly. Clay encouraged Byrnes to combine all these concerns into a major address at a meeting of American occupation officials and local German officials— who very much needed encouragement against the left political offensive.

On his own, Clay suspended "for the time being" the operation of Article 41 in the Hesse constitution.[36] But it was Byrnes's "Stuttgart" speech which put the U.S. on the political and ideological offensive in Germany. International radio coverage was planned, and news reporters had been tipped off that the Secretary of State would make an important speech. "After studying the problem from every angle," Robert Murphy explained, "Byrnes's advisers came up with an adroit scheme." The Secretary would concede the French claim to the Saar but cast doubt on the finality of any other cessions, particularly the Russian-imposed Polish-German boundary.[37] By acknowledging the legitimacy of the French claim, Byrnes hoped to accomplish at least two things: cast additional French demands in a bad light and, by reopening the question of Germany's eastern boundaries, divide the French and the Russians. But there was more to the speech than narrow refencing, diplomatic or otherwise. Byrnes insisted that the four powers must now get on with the problem of an all-German political administration. Byrnes's suggestion for the composition of this new *all*-German government would only have confirmed the political process that had already taken place in the American Zone:

> It is the view of the American Government that the provisional government . . . should be a German national council composed of democratically responsible minister-presidents or other chief officials of the several states or provinces which have been established in each of the four zones.

This council would be charged with the development of a new German constitution.

Byrnes's speech forced Molotov to admit that the eastern boundary had not been finally fixed. But he asserted with a great show of confidence that this was only a formality, as the Western powers had already acquiesced in the decision to remove the populations from these areas. Russian policy in Germany did not reveal such confidence in everyday matters, however. Byrnes had specifically mentioned Silesia in his attack on the Russian boundary imposition, and, with all the publicity the speech received as a major policy address, seemed to suggest that America hoped to get back that military arsenal for "its" Germany. As the minister-president of Bavaria commented, "Mr. Byrnes did not speak as to a defeated nation, but as to a friend to whom he wanted to show the right way."

There were several ways the Russians could have interpreted that statement, none of them offering very attractive alternatives. Molotov's effort to "seduce" the Germans in the West had come back to haunt him; in the weeks after Byrnes's speech the Russians again reversed their reparations policy briefly, indulging in a new wave of industrial dismantling. But former Under Secretary of State Sumner Welles was fully as alarmed about the Stuttgart speech as the Soviets were. It demonstrated, he wrote in the *New York Herald-Tribune,* the disastrous results which the policy of postponement had brought on: "In a panic effort to circumvent Russia, whose increasing influence in Germany our own lack of foresight alone made possible, we have declared our intention of rebuilding a unified and strong Germany, under a central government. Such a Germany can once more bring ruin to the rest of the world."[38] If the American plan for unification were adopted and the minister-presidents were made equal in a national council, the preparation of a draft constitution would undoubtedly follow patterns approved in the West—by three-to-one votes.

Behind the furor raised by Byrnes's speech, American policy-makers quickly moved to insure German economic recovery in the British and American zones, now renamed, Orwell-like, "Bizonia." "If we delay," Allen Dulles admonished the 1946 National Foreign Trade Convention, "I rather fear we will play into the hands of those who favor a different kind of economy than our own. . . . Obviously failure by the Western powers to make the free economy system work in Germany is a strong argument for communism."[39]

On October 28, 1946, Stalin granted an interview to Hugh Baillie, president of the United Press, in which he affirmed that he thought it was not only possible but necessary to go ahead with German political unification. When the Moscow Foreign Ministers conference began in March 1947, Molotov submitted a lengthy proposal for achieving that unification, by moving almost at once to all-German elections. Molotov's proposal envisioned a German parliament with two chambers, a president elected by that parliament, and a constitution that would guarantee the same freedoms as the American Bill of Rights! Secretary of State Marshall's bipartisan adviser, John Foster Dulles, exclaimed in a letter to Senator Vandenberg back in the United States that the Russians were all for German unity because they felt that under present circumstances that would give them not only Germany but, for all practical purposes, the continent as well. Anglo-American proposals for German reunification were elaborations of proposals Byrnes had set forth originally at Stuttgart. When Molotov suggested that they settle the matter by a German plebiscite, Ernest Bevin snapped that he would not have European security determined by a German election.[40]

Even before the conference began, the American delegation had received a State Department memorandum which confirmed their worst fears: "Growing Communist control in the huge German trade union movement is a fact the importance of which can scarcely be overestimated. The recent Ruhr strikes, which are probably going to be repeated, are only an indication of what power such control gives the Communists and their Soviet masters." What made the situation so critical, however, was the posture of the Social Democrats who were pushing hard for what they called a co-determination policy: "This is probably the most important and universal demand of German trade unions today." Co-determination was simply another way to "socialize" major industries, or, at least, to achieve an equal voice in how they should be run. This had been the key issue in recent strikes; and the Communists would continue to exploit management-labor disputes on this issue with great hopes for ultimate control over the unions.

Vigorous countermeasures had to be taken immediately, especially all-out aid to non-communist trade unions. Even more important, in the context of the Moscow discussions, under no circumstances could the Russian proposal for all-German unions be accepted until it was certain that these unions would remain democratic.[41] Coincidental to the Moscow Conference, of course, was Truman's enunciation of the need to aid all countries threatened by communist subversion, the "Truman Doctrine" speech of March 12, 1947. But that speech was symptomatic, not causal —symptomatic of American concern about the whole state of Western Europe's ideological and political defenses. The State Department memorandum on the German labor movement was

also a product of this fear. It was further illustrated by the reaction to a proposal by Dulles for the internationalization of the
Ruhr. Dulles suggested to the American delegation that the
United States offer to neutralize the Ruhr under four-power
management after all foreign troops had been withdrawn. Dulles
thought that the vitally necessary Ruhr resources could thus be
used by all Europe, and any future German menace eliminated
at the same time; then the United States could begin rebuilding
Europe through France. Adamant against even discussing this
idea with the Russians, Clay argued (like Sloan before him)
that France was unstable, that the plan would allow the Russians to expand into the Ruhr, and that it would not lead to an
evacuation of their zone of Germany. "We had created a political vacuum in Central Europe," Clay insisted, and "unless we
could restore some sort of economic opportunity to the German
people, there was nothing we could do to prevent Communism
from taking over. Therefore, we had the problem of rebuilding
Germany."[42]

It was as simple as that—and just as final. The Moscow Conference ended in disagreement, with the Russians returning stubbornly to their old goal of $10 billion in reparations and the
Americans demanding that the German level-of-industry agreement be raised and that former German lands now in Poland be
exploited for raw materials so as to benefit all Germany. One
material result of the Moscow Conference was a fatal weakening
of the Franco-Russian entente. Any mention of a strong German
central government always stirred deep fears in the French delegation; Foreign Minister Bidault's private conversations with
Stalin on this point did not ease his mind. As Bidault confided
to American delegates, a communist government in Germany
would demand tight control of the Ruhr anyway, so the whole
issue might well become academic in a few months or years.
France could not change its public stance at once, however, for
fear of tipping the balance at home where the Communist party
currently had great strength. If further proof were needed by
the American delegation of the basic unity of communist aims,
Bidault's accusations (and fears) supplied it. After the Moscow
Conference, General Clay invited several groups of economic

leaders to visit Bizonia and report to the American people on what they found. Former President Hoover and a committee headed by Averell Harriman had already made full reports on the need to aid German recovery, but Clay wanted to validate their conclusions with more up-to-date evidence. The Moscow Conference, Clay's briefing officers told these visitors, proved that the Soviets would do all they could to obstruct German recovery.

In demanding $10 billion, the Russians failed to make the case effectively that reparations from current production could stimulate Germany's industrial output under a centralized political and economic system. "We did not want Germany quickly rebuilt as a great, modern industrial machine," Dulles said on an American radio broadcast after the conference. What he really meant to say was, as he wrote privately to Senator Vandenberg, that the present zonal system offered a shield and more time to build up the West against communist penetration; as for reconstruction in Bizonia, it was full speed ahead after Moscow. "It is too late," wrote one of Clay's guests, the editor of the *New York Journal of Commerce,* in one of his several articles from inside Germany. "It is too late . . . to wait longer to rectify the economic situation in the British and American zones." "I came away convinced," he wrote privately to Secretary of the Navy James Forrestal, "that we have got to put at least five billion dollars a year for five years into this situation if we do not want the Russians to take over all of Europe."[43] *Fortune's* editors effectively turned inside out discussion of "plans" for Germany: "In the case of Germany, the flow of private investment into the Rhine Valley is the only way of accomplishing that 'internationalization' of the powerhouse of Europe about which the planners are always talking. Here is the key not only to taking Europe off the taxpayers' shoulders, but to much more."[44]

But by far the fullest *Report on Germany* filed that summer was by Lewis H. Brown of Johns-Manville. Brown began his essay with a review of World War II military history which minimized the Russian role in Allied operations against Germany, and moved from that to a critique of unnecessary promises that had been made to Stalin by Roosevelt and Churchill.

Since Roosevelt's death and Churchill's retirement, Stalin had
been getting away with murder by claiming he had unfulfilled
"secret agreements" with them. As the Russian-American split
widened into full-scale Cold War, few were interested in check-
ing on any of Brown's historical facts or interpretations. Brown
demanded a policy to get Germany on its feet again: "The combination of the failure to get Germany on her feet, the retardance
of recovery in Europe, and the threat to Britain's dollar position
is threatening to curtail exports from America. As a consequence
we may be faced with a depression." Made up of one-fifth scare
tactics and four-fifths genuine concern for the American international economic system, Brown's "report" concluded with an
attack on further de-Nazification. Anglo-Saxon democratic beliefs could not be stuffed down already sore throats. To do so
would not produce effective leadership in Germany, only a bad
economic cold. "And it is high time we face the facts. It pro-
duces political leaders who ask the wishes of the people and
function as their elected representatives in a democratic assembly. But the German masses do not want to be asked, they want
to be told. They don't want to be represented. They want to be
directed." In Germany the truly effective leader has his mouth
to the people's ear. "He doesn't whisper, he yells like a drill ser-
geant." It was unfortunate that the Germans had this mentality;
nevertheless they were beginning to associate their hunger and
misery with the democracy we were trying to build for them.
"That way gives a Communist dictator his chance."[45]

In October 1947 Washington queried the American Military
Government to find out if Clay needed additional instructions
on the matter of "socialism." Clay replied that he did not because he had interpreted his general instructions to mean that
there must be political and economic stability in Germany before
the German people could be expected to make decisions freely.
"Time is on our side," Clay said. "If we can thus defer the issue
while free enterprise continues to operate and economic im-
provement results, it may never become an issue before the German people."[46]

The next month the Big Four Foreign Ministers made one

last try at the German problem in London. In Moscow each side had presented its case without vituperation, but now the gloves were off. In July and August, the new rulers of Bizonia had unilaterally raised the level-of-industry in their zones, jumping the quota on Ruhr steel production from 5.8 million tons per year to 10.7. On August 29, 1947, Generals Clay and Brian Robertson informed the Russians that as a result of these decisions the number of properties eligible for reparations would have to be reduced still further. The Russian representative on the Allied Control Council, Marshal Sokolovsky, charged immediately that the U.S. and British military administrations had broken completely with Potsdam. Clay replied that the record was plain: the Americans had tried to get economic unity for more than two and a half years. The invitation to join Bizonia (on Anglo-American terms of course) remained open.

Once again Sumner Welles raised a loud protest of his own, asserting in the *New York Herald-Tribune* that the move was favored by those who wanted to use Germany as a buffer against Russia, "and industrial interests that expect fat profits from a highly industrialized Germany."[47] Whether or not Welles was right, the atmosphere at London was charged with emotions which made rational discussion impossible. At one of the early sessions, Molotov brought forward a statement attributed to the deputy British commander in Germany to the effect that the London meeting was no more than a *pro forma* exercise to prepare the way for the creation of a West German republic. Molotov also accused the Western powers of wishing to exploit Germany for their own benefit, and of wishing to stifle German competition in world markets. It was a good demonstration of the weakness of Soviet Marxism, and how it was used to suit current belief about the other guy's proposals, or your own. As we have already seen, the "Morgenthau Plan," or anything like it, had been killed off long before; the problem, as Americans saw it, was now to fit Germany properly into the Marshall Plan. The Foreign Ministers made their speeches in the secret council sessions, then later the same afternoon released them to the press, a pretty certain sign that each side was writing its "white paper" in advance. Marshall insisted once again, as he had in

Moscow, that provisions must be made for insuring that key industrial resources in all Germany, including those in the lands ceded to Poland by the Soviet Union, would be made available to the whole German—and European—economy. The Secretary of State insisted upon a full accounting of all the Russians had taken from their zone—within three days. Molotov retorted that he would make such an accounting only when Britain and France were willing to state how much underpriced timber and coal they had sold out of Germany, and how much enterprise British and American capitalists had purchased in their zones. The Soviets, he added, would make such an accounting only in connection with a final reparations settlement.[48]

When the London meeting broke up without even an agreement to meet again, congressional hearings began in the United States on Representative Christian Herter's bill, H.R. 4579, designed to promote American private investment abroad by granting aid to those countries that were willing to use the funds to stabilize their currencies. Secretary of the Army Kenneth C. Royall testified that German currency reform was a key prerequisite to both German and European economic recovery.[49]

As Clay notes in *Decision in Germany,* printed currency for such a reform had actually been shipped to Germany by the time of the London Foreign Ministers meeting; he awaited only a go-ahead from Washington. Secretary Marshall advised Clay to make one more attempt at effective four-power currency reform in Germany and then to proceed with bizonal measures. At London the French had at last indicated a willingness to talk about trizonal fusion and other measures of Western economic unity.

The pace of events in early 1948, all stemming from the German question and the break-up of Big Four negotiations at London, accelerated and began to rumble ominously across the face of Europe. The British moved first, informing Washington that they planned to approach France and the Benelux countries with a proposal to undertake the formation of a "Western Union," with political and military connotations as well as economic goals. Actual talks were under way by mid-March, with strong

American encouragement. Next came the Russian-fomented Czech crisis and *coup d'état,* which ended the last unnatural projection on either side of the "Iron Curtain." In the midst of these events came General Clay's March 5, 1948, cable, which had its own special quality of moving things along rapidly. For many months, he said, logic had persuaded him that war with Russia was unlikely, at least for the next ten years. But within the last few weeks, "I have felt a subtle change in Soviet attitude which I cannot define but which now gives me a feeling that it may come with dramatic suddenness."[50] Washington overreacted, George F. Kennan asserted recently, "in the most deplorable way," and a real war scare ensued. In Berlin, Marshal Sokolovsky turned on his heel and walked out of an Allied Control Council meeting on March 20, after having demanded and been refused information on trizonal meetings held in London over the past two months. "The Allied Control Council was dead," Clay wrote. "The stage had been set for the imposition of the Soviet blockade against Berlin."[51]

Soviet traffic obstructions against the western sectors of Berlin began on March 31, and reached the point of total blockade on June 24, the day after the Western powers introduced currency reform into the trizonal area and their sectors of Berlin. "If we withdraw," Clay warned Washington even in April, "our position in Europe is threatened. If America does not understand this now, does not know that the issue is cast, then it never will and communism will run rampant."[52] Although Clay had earlier warned his superiors that the introduction of a currency reform might mean the need to resist force, he always insisted that the reform was not the cause of the Berlin blockade. But the reform *was* necessary to the economic rejuvenation of the Western Zones, in order that they might be integrated into ERP. On July 3, 1948, Clay and the other two Western military governors met with Sokolovsky. The Soviet commander told them bluntly that the "technical" difficulties barring West Berlin's transport links with West Germany would continue until the three gave up their intentions and plans for a West German government.[53]

Clay and Murphy recommended at one point that the block-

ade be smashed by sending an armored column across the Auto-
bahn straight into Berlin. Murphy even threatened to resign over
the issue, but he and Clay were overruled.

Instead, Western ambassadors had two meetings with Stalin
in the Kremlin during August in an effort to end the crisis. At
the first the Soviet Premier leaned back in his chair, and, after
lighting a cigarette, asked Ambassador Walter Bedell Smith,
"Would you like to settle the matter tonight?" Then he proposed
that the Russian mark be used in Berlin (at the second interview
he agreed to four-power controls over its issuance), that all the
transport restrictions (later amended to "lately imposed") be
removed by both sides, and that the insistent wish of the Soviet
government that trizonal unification be deferred be recorded in
the new agreement. Molotov then added another proposal in a
draft communiqué: that "consideration" had been given to the
Soviet "wish," and that the three Western powers had "stated"
they did not plan to go ahead with the formation of a West German government. The three Western ambassadors regarded Molotov's draft as an effort to maneuver them into accepting Stalin's
contention that the currency reform had invalidated all Big Four
agreements on Berlin. Whether or not that was the sole Russian
intention, the American ambassador and his colleagues did not
intend to sign any communiqué that would hinder "progress" in
the West, however defined.[54] So the blockade continued. At a
meeting in September of Clay, Secretary Marshall, Ambassador
Walter Bedell Smith, and several other American officials, it was
agreed that the Berlin crisis could be turned to great advantage
as a symbol of "all of those who wanted freedom, and especially
to offer hope and courage to the eastern European countries."
If "progress" in West Germany meant material gains for European recovery, "progress" in Berlin meant spiritual gains in the
world struggle with communism. Only Ambassador Smith dissented from this view, suggesting that the need to remain in
Berlin was only temporary, that in the long run it would prove
a liability. Clay rejected this at once: "Berlin had become a symbol of the firmness of the free countries of the world to retreat
no further in the face of Communist expansion." Clay's brilliant

improvisation of the airlift gave his words the added authority of one who could prove that he could "get the job done."[55]

From an American point of view, the Russian blockade completed Clay's work in bringing a forced harmony in the West under United States leadership. Marshall Plan aid to West Germany was channeled through the American Military Government. For some time the French fought a holding action against U.S. policies in Germany, particularly against the so-called "Ruhr Agreements" and the "Ruhr Authority," by which it had been agreed that the three occupying powers should allocate exports from the area in such a way as to promote the ERP goals, and that its industries should be held in international trusteeship. The United States had insisted upon a veto over these allocations while Washington was responsible for financial aid to Germany. The French, Clay informed Washington, "say that there are evidences of a tendency to make Germany the strongest economic power in Europe and the center of the continental economy. Unquestionably this comes about from the present upturn in the German economy which has made its recovery real and no longer academic."[56]

"The West will make Western Germany their own," Stalin told communist delegations from Eastern Europe, "and we shall turn Eastern Germany into our own state."[57] Unaware that negotiations were going on in the United Nations to end the blockade in the spring of 1949, Clay only knew that the State Department was increasingly anxious that the West German republic be brought into being as soon as possible. Clay had his own reasons for wanting to bring things to a speedy conclusion, and he was delighted when the new German constitution was ready for approval on May 12, 1949, "the same day that the blockade of Berlin was lifted."

Clay explained what had taken place since 1945 in a private letter to Bernard Baruch: The United States had recognized the various fears of Germany's neighbors. "However, their traditional and well justified fear of German aggression sometimes blinds them to the immediate and over-shadowing menace of the Red Army externally and planned revolution internally."[58] These two assumptions were the only justification Clay needed for American policy. What actually took place in Western Germany, however, was an American counterrevolution—against the policy of postponement, then against French obstructionism, German social democracy, and, finally, European radicalism.

NOTES

1. U.S. Senate, Committee on Foreign Relations, *Hearings: Interim Aid for Europe,* 80th Cong., 1st sess. (Washington, D.C., 1947), p. 47.

2. U.S. Senate, Committee on Foreign Relations, *Hearings: North Atlantic Treaty,* 81st Cong., 1st sess. (Washington, D.C., 1949), p. 405.

3. Bohlen Minutes, Second Plenary Meeting, February 5, 1945, Department of State, *Foreign Relations of the United States* (hereafter *FR*), *The Conferences at Malta and Yalta, 1945* (Washington, D.C., 1955), pp. 622–623.

4. Cited in Paul Y. Hammond, "Directives for the Occupation of Germany," in Harold Stein, ed., *American Civil-Military Decisions* (Birmingham, Ala., 1963), pp. 405–406.

5. James P. Warburg, "Germany and World Peace," in Hans J. Morgenthau, ed., *Germany and the Future of Europe* (Chicago, 1951), pp. 142–162.

6. Ministry of Foreign Affairs of the USSR, *Correspondence Between the Chairman of the Council of Ministers of the U.S.S.R. and the Presidents of the U.S.A. and the Prime Ministers of Great Britain During the Great Patriotic War of 1941–1945* (2 vols., Moscow, 1957), II, 208–210.

7. These figures are from Seweryn Bialer, ed., *Stalin and His Generals* (New York, 1969), p. 621.

8. Allen W. Dulles to John Foster Dulles, February 6, 1945, Papers of John Foster Dulles, Princeton University Library, Princeton, N. J., General Correspondence.

9. Allen Dulles, *The Secret Surrender* (New York, 1966), pp. 147, 161, 164–165.

10. Quoted in Bialer, *Stalin and His Generals,* pp. 516–517.

11. Robert K. Murphy, *Diplomat Among Warriors* (New York, 1964), p. 251.

12. *Ibid.*

13. John Gimbel, *The American Occupation of Germany: Politics and the Military, 1945–1949* (Palo Alto, Calif., 1968), p. 6.

14. U.S. Senate, Subcommittee of Committee on Military Affairs, *Hear-*

ings: Elimination of German Resources for War, 79th Cong., 1st sess. (Washington, D.C., 1946), pp. 621 and 1026.

15. Kennan to Harriman, May 14, 1945; Harriman to Kennan, May 20, 1945, *FR 1945* (Washington, D.C., 1968), III, 1213–1215.

16. "Summary of Procedure of Allied Commission on Reparations," undated, Summer 1945, Papers of Richard A. Scandrett, Cornell University Library, Ithaca, New York.

17. Gimbel, *American Occupation of Germany,* p. 9.

18. Cohen Notes, Eleventh Plenary Meeting, July 31, 1945; Zhukov to Stalin, undated; Pauley to Truman, July 29, 1945, *FR, The Conference of Berlin, 1945* (2 vols., Washington, D.C., 1960), II, 530, 903–905.

19. James F. Byrnes, *Speaking Frankly* (New York, 1947), pp. 83–85; Bohlen Minutes, Byrnes-Molotov Meeting, July 23, 1945; Bohlen Minutes, Byrnes-Molotov Meeting, July 27, 1945, Department of State Minutes, Eleventh Meeting of the Foreign Ministers, August 1, 1945, *Conference of Berlin,* II, 274–275, 450–451, 543–562; William Appleman Williams, *The Tragedy of American Diplomacy* (New York, 1962 ed.), pp. 250–251.

20. Quoted in Manuel Gottlieb, *The German Peace Settlement and the Berlin Crisis* (New York, 1960), p. 39.

21. Clay to Bernard Baruch, August 8, 1945, Papers of Bernard M. Baruch, Princeton University Library, Princeton, New Jersey.

22. See F. Roy Willis, *The French in Germany, 1945–1949* (Palo Alto, Calif., 1962), pp. 27–32; Gottlieb, *German Peace Settlement,* pp. 47–48, 78–79.

23. Lewis H. Brown, *Report on Germany* (New York, 1947), p. 31.

24. Reprinted in B. U. Ratchford and William D. Ross, *Berlin Reparations Assignment: Round One of the German Peace Settlement* (Chapel Hill, 1947), pp. 83, 89–92. *FR 1945,* III, 1283–1295.

25. Murphy to Secretary of State, September 30, 1945; *ibid.,* 1320–1321.

26. Gimbel, *American Occupation of Germany,* p. 27.

27. Ratchford and Ross, *Berlin Reparations Assignment,* pp. 174–176; see also Lucius D. Clay, *Decision in Germany* (New York, 1950), pp. 108–109.

28. Sloan to Baruch, November 9, 1945, Baruch Papers.

29. Sloan to Baruch, November 30, 1945, Baruch Papers.

30. Robert Slusser, ed., *Soviet Economic Policy in Postwar Germany: A Collection of Papers by Former Soviet Officials* (New York, 1953), pp. 52–53.

31. Clay to Baruch, April 22, 1946, Baruch Papers.

32. Kennan to Byrnes, March 6, 1946, Smith to Byrnes, April 2, 1946, *FR, 1946,* V, 516–520, 535–536; Clay, *Decision in Germany,* pp. 120–122.

33. *Ibid.,* pp. 120–125; Walter LaFeber, *America, Russia and the Cold War, 1945–1967* (New York, 1968), p. 32.

34. Clay, *Decision in Germany,* pp. 125–126; James Stuart Martin, *All Honorable Men* (Boston, 1950), p. 193; Byrnes, *Speaking Frankly,* pp. 174–175.

35. Gimbel, *American Occupation of Germany,* p. 55.

36. V. M. Molotov, *Problems of Foreign Policy* (Moscow, 1949), pp. 63–68; J. P. Nettl, *The Eastern Zone and Soviet Policy in Germany, 1945–*

1950 (New York, 1951), p. 51; Gimbel, *American Occupation of Germany,* p. 117.

37. Byrnes, *Speaking Frankly,* pp. 179–187; Murphy, *Diplomat Among Warriors,* pp. 302–303.

38. *New York Herald-Tribune,* September 11, 1946.

39. National Foreign Trade Council, *Proceedings of the National Foreign Trade Convention, 1946* (New York, 1947), p. 50.

40. Statement by Molotov, "Provisional Political Organization of Germany," March 22, 1947, Dulles Papers, Category IX; Dulles to Vandenberg, March 22, 1947, Dulles Papers.

41. Louis A. Weisner, "The Present Status of the German Trade Unions," April 17, 1947, Dulles Papers.

42. Interview with Lucius D. Clay, Dulles Oral History Project, Dulles Papers.

43. *New York Journal of Commerce,* June 17, 1947.

44. Editorial, "The United States in Europe," XXXVI (July 1947), 2–4.

45. Brown, *Report,* pp. 5–8, 15, 24–25, 38, 52–53.

46. Gimbel, *American Occupation of Germany,* p. 170.

47. September 16, 1947.

48. Press Release, November 27, 1947, Dulles Papers; Gottlieb, *German Peace Settlement,* p. 179.

49. U.S. House, Foreign Affairs Committee, *Hearings: Post-War Recovery Program,* 80th Cong., 1st and 2nd sess. (Washington, D.C., 1948), p. 357.

50. Walter Millis, ed., *The Forrestal Diaries* (New York, 1951), p. 387.

51. Clay, *Decision in Germany,* pp. 355–357.

52. *Ibid.,* p. 361.

53. *Ibid.,* p. 367.

54. Walter Bedell Smith, *My Three Years in Moscow* (New York, 1950), 245ff.; Department of State, *The "Berlin Crisis," A Report on the Moscow Discussions* (Washington, D.C., 1948).

55. Clay, *Decision in Germany,* pp. 375–377.

56. *Ibid.,* pp. 414–416.

57. Milovan Djilas, *Conversations with Stalin* (New York, 1962), p. 153.

58. Clay to Baruch, March 2, 1948, Baruch Papers.

DAVID GREEN

The Cold War
Comes to Latin America

WHEN HARRY TRUMAN became President of the United States
on April 12, 1945, the Big Three was not the only anti-Axis alliance experiencing internal stress. The new President also faced
serious problems in regard to America's key second-line alliance
—the Western Hemisphere anti-Axis All-American Front. Some
of these problems had fairly recent origins; they had developed
out of Latin American dissatisfaction with the announced postwar plans of the Roosevelt administration. Other problems were
of long-standing nature; they involved complex questions of inter-American economic relationships and reflected Latin American discontent with the results of inter-American economic "cooperation."

Despite a partial relaxation of tensions as a result of his Good
Neighbor policy, President Roosevelt did not bequeath to his
successor a harmonious relationship with Latin America. In order to understand the nature of the problems Truman faced and
his efforts to resolve them, it is necessary to begin with a brief
review of the inter-American situation in the months immediately preceding Roosevelt's death.

In an article published in January 1945, the distinguished

Peruvian educator Luís Alberto Sánchez summed up the war's
effect on Latin America:

> In Latin America, the war has further impoverished the poor and
> enriched the wealthy. It has increased the army's power, both
> politically and militarily. At most, salaries have doubled, while at
> the very least, the cost of living has tripled. . . . The large export-
> ing concerns of Latin America, generally financed with United
> States and British capital, are making fat profits. Meanwhile, the
> people, enthusiastically democratic, are doing without essentials.
> . . . Our average man has yet to see material or moral benefits
> from this war on which he staked his hopes long before his gov-
> ernment took a stand. . . . For us, the outcome of the war has
> been settled. Although "democracy" is clearly the winner, we fail
> to see any benefits.[1]

Sánchez' analysis was much more than a catalogue of economic
and political sacrifices which the Latin American peoples had
contributed to the war effort. It was also a bitter indictment of
the entire set of international economic and political relationships which had *forced* most of the Latin American nations to
make these sacrifices with no assurance of any rewards from
their ideological and substantive commitment to the side of the
United Nations.

From Sánchez' point of view, the fundamental trouble was
that Latin America had not developed economic independence
in the prewar period. All the Latin American nations relied
heavily upon exports of a few agricultural or mineral commodities to the United States and to the nations of Western and Central Europe. Having little industry of their own, the Latin Americans were also largely dependent upon these same nations for
industrial supplies and manufactured goods in general. The situation was not improved by the fact that large portions of Latin
America's export earnings ultimately reverted to foreign (particularly North American) owners of the raw materials.

Lack of economic independence left Latin America defense-
less when the war came in 1939. With the closing of continental
European markets, the Latin Americans were left with Britain
and the United States alone for export and import markets. Latin
American nations not only had to accept whatever prices they
could get for their exports, but also had to be content with what-

ever limited quantities of manufactured goods the two industrial
nations felt they could spare. U.S. Assistant Secretary of State
Nelson Rockefeller testified as to the results of the Latin American export dependency; he told a congressional committee in
1945 that the United States had obtained Latin American rubber for about one-fifth of what it would have cost under normal
market conditions. British and North American inability to deliver sufficient manufactured goods to Latin America caused
shortages which resulted in serious inflationary spirals (thus accounting for the increased living costs to which Sánchez referred). U.S. price control expert Seymour Harris summarized
inter-American wartime "cooperation" as follows:

> In short, in exchange for vitally necessary war materials we have
> provided these countries with paper credit, with dollars that are
> manufactured by our banking system, and with gold for which we
> have no use. In the postwar period it is hoped that they will obtain
> adequate compensation for their natural resources, for their addi-
> tional work, and for the reduced standard of living which they
> have encountered during the present war. . . . It does seem that
> on the whole the United States has had the better of the bargain.[2]

Though Sánchez was concerned with the short-run wartime
situation, in a broader sense he was also criticizing the U.S. and
Britain—and particularly the U.S. as the more powerful and influential of the two—for failing to act to promote Latin American
economic independence in the future. This criticism spoke to
the whole nature and purpose of Roosevelt's Good Neighbor
policy. What Sánchez was pointing to, and what many Latin
Americans were coming to realize by 1945, was that the Good
Neighbor policy *had never been intended* to end Latin America's
economic dependence upon the United States. On the contrary,
the Good Neighbor policy had been designed only to alleviate
some of the more politically abrasive features of the dependency
relationship, in order to undercut militant nationalist resentment
against the United States in Latin America.

President Roosevelt had enunciated the U.S. policy goal rather clearly in January 1940, when he told a group of reporters
about his "new approach" to Latin America. "Give them a share,"
the President had said. "They think they're just as good as we

are, and many of them are."[3] Behind the airily patronizing tone of his remark, Roosevelt's intention showed through clearly. It was to protect not only the United States' "share" of Latin America's wealth but to protect as well the United States' strategic control as giver, rather than receiver, of Latin America's own share.

Roosevelt's disavowal of military big-stick tactics had been designed to remove an irritation which was threatening the United States' traditional political influence in Latin America. In much the same way, the administration's use of economic aid programs after January 1940 was designed to protect, and reinforce, the United States' traditional economic leverage there. For example, the United States government, acting through the Export-Import Bank in Washington, loaned money to a number of Latin American nations to enable them to set up national development corporations (*fomentos*). As collateral for the loans, the Export-Import Bank retained as much as 50 per cent or more of the voting stock of the corporations, thus giving the United States a veto power over important development activities in these nations. In like manner, the United States took the lead in setting up the twenty-one-nation Inter-American Development Commission, an organization whose purpose was to help develop in Latin America new lines of production "not competitive" with existing lines of U.S. export products.[4] The emphasis on "noncompetitive" products was a way of insuring that Latin American economic development would not disturb the established place that U.S. exports held in Latin American markets.

The Roosevelt administration had also agreed to sponsor an Inter-American Bank, the purpose of which would be to channel public funds from all American nations into the economic development process in Latin America. The bank's charter, drafted in the spring of 1940, was written in such a way that the United States, by purchasing just over 20 per cent of the voting stock, could maintain a veto power over all the bank's important operations (an 80 per cent or four-fifths majority being required for most operating decisions). Ironically, U.S. ratification of the bank's charter was prevented by the opposition of certain key senators who felt that the bank could become an instrument for a wholesale "giveaway" of American public funds.[5]

At times administration officials were ahead not only of congressional leaders but of U.S. industrialists in the movement to promote U.S. economic influence in Latin America. In the spring of 1940, the Brazilian government requested United States assistance in the development of a Brazilian steel industry. The administration, not wishing to appear hostile to Latin American efforts to industrialize, agreed to do what it could to help the Brazilians. State Department officials at first tried to interest North American steel companies in making the necessary loans to the Brazilian government. But when one by one the steel companies refused—either because they saw no future in a Brazilian heavy industry market or, conversely, because they feared Brazilian competition in South America should the project succeed—the administration decided to extend a public loan through the Export-Import Bank. Administration thinking was not, however, merely negative in motivation. That is, the loan was not thought of simply as protection against Brazilian resentment should the project fail for lack of U.S. encouragement. Policymakers also saw the Brazil project as a powerful way to stimulate Latin American dependence upon a profitable southward flow of U.S. industrial exports. In building their steel industry, the Brazilians would need large quantities of sophisticated and expensive producer goods, as well as a great deal of technological know-how. "That," as one U.S. government economist noted, "is where we come in." U.S. Chamber of Commerce President Eric Johnston, who was also chairman of the United States subcommission of the Inter-American Development Commission, told a radio audience in May 1944:

> I am convinced that Brazil's increase in steel production will be a great benefit eventually to our workers. . . . During past years, Brazil has been importing many elementary steel products from abroad which she could better make herself. The increase in Brazil's productive capacity in steel will result in an increased earning power which the steel plants in the United States can enjoy by selling steel in Brazil in fabricated forms. In other words, Brazil will be able to buy more automobiles, refrigerators, railroad equip-

ment and other things. . . . I believe that you can increase the
purchasing power of a people better through industrialization than
through any other means.

Johnston summed up in succinct manner the economic aspects
of Roosevelt's Latin American strategies: "Just as the last century in Latin America was a 'British Century,'" Johnston noted,
"the next would be an American Century."[6]

By early 1945, the broad outlines of the administration's postwar Latin American policies were becoming clear. Those policies fitted very nicely with the President's overall plans for U.S.
policy in the postwar world. He hoped to maintain the general
economic health of the United States through the establishment
of an Open World, a world in which all regions would provide
markets for U.S. industrial exports, investments, and technological services. An Open World, of course, depended on the avoidance of closed regional or national economic systems anywhere
—not only Great Power spheres of influence but excesses of economic nationalism and state control of economic life in underdeveloped nations. Such economic nationalism and statism could
limit or even destroy possibilities for profitable interaction between the U.S. economy and that of the underdeveloped area.[7]

The Open World approach did not, to be sure, necessarily
imply conspiratorial or malevolent (i.e., exploitative) intentions
toward other countries. On the contrary, the approach was not
only rather frankly publicized; it could also be, and was, explained in terms of the most enlightened, even benevolent, self-
interest. As Assistant Secretary of State for Economic Affairs
Will Clayton put it: "The whole world is so closely knit together
now economically that it is not going to be possible for any one
area of the world to have prosperous conditions and a rising
standard of living if the rest of the world is on the downgrade;
it just cannot be done." At the same time, the Open World approach, having been defined as necessary for the continued internal health and stability of the United States, also implied
what Henry Luce in his earlier call for an "American Century"
had termed "a very tough attitude toward all hostile governments."[8]

At the Inter-American Conference on Problems of War and

Peace, held at Chapultepec Castle outside Mexico City less than two months before Roosevelt's death, U.S. plans for a postwar Open World collided with Latin American determination to use nationalist and statist techniques in promoting Latin American economic growth. Before the war, such countries as Bolivia and Mexico had expropriated U.S.-owned oil properties and used other nationalist policies to assert local control over local resources. Both countries had followed up with the establishment of state-controlled corporations to administer the newly acquired properties. Brazil had prohibited the incorporation of foreign-owned banks, while Mexico had enacted "51 per cent" laws insuring that certain Mexican industrial and commercial enterprises would always be controlled by at least a bare majority of Mexican-owned voting stock. During the war years, enforced hemispheric economic solidarity had generally halted the spread of such nationalist and statist maneuvers. The Latin American economies became closely tied to the war economy of the United States. At Chapultepec, however, a number of Latin American delegates talked of increasing the use of statist methods in the postwar era, in order to gain a greater measure of independence and control over Latin America's economic development.

Such talk was anathema to U.S. officials, but not because of any rigid opposition to state involvement in economic life. On the contrary, they knew perfectly well that the New Deal was itself an experiment in state intervention. And Roosevelt had in the past sanctioned a limited amount of government-to-government assistance between the United States and Latin America, in order to express concrete interest in Latin American economic development. The point, however, was precisely that such state involvement, both in the domestic New Deal and in the Good Neighbor policy, had been limited, and had been designed in both cases to strengthen private enterprise, not to replace it. The same was true of the whole Open World approach, in which the Bretton Woods proposals for a publicly financed International Monetary Fund and World Bank would provide what Treasury Secretary Morgenthau aptly referred to as a "New Deal in international economics." Thus at Chapultepec it became the business of the U.S. delegation to discourage statism *as an indiscrim-*

inate ideological trend, lest in the hands of *other* nations it get out of control and become a tool for challenging international private enterprise rather than strengthening it.[9]

Nationalism, as an ideology of economic anti-foreignism, was also anathema to Open World advocates; it might lead to repetitions of what presidential adviser Bernard Baruch had called the "Mexican stunt"—i.e., expropriation of U.S.-owned resources. Nationalism also pointed the way to other actions likely to challenge the U.S., for example in the field of tariff policy. The Colombian delegation at Chapultepec presented a draft resolution on tariffs which contained a clear reference to the unsatisfactory results of Latin America's wartime dependency on U.S. industrial exports. The resolution stated that the "common desire to abolish unnecessary trade barriers and to increase the volume of international interchange can and must be brought into harmony with the diversification of production in those American countries which are not sufficiently developed, and with their attainment of a higher degree of industrialization." A U.S. resolution on the same subject proposed that no industries be built up in Latin America which depended for their survival on government "subsidies," including protective tariffs.[10]

In response to Latin American talk about other nationalist and statist policies, such as import controls, currency manipulations, and so on, the U.S. delegation presented to the conference a broad proposal for an "Economic Charter of the Americas." The charter proposal stressed the "elimination of economic nationalism in all its forms" as well as avoidance of high tariffs and "private agreements" to restrict trade. One clause proposed that the Latin Americans not only "encourage private enterprise" as their dominant form of economic activity but also refrain from setting up any state-controlled trading enterprises. The U.S. also responded negatively to a Latin American attempt to revive the idea of an inter-American development bank; by 1945 President Roosevelt's emphasis on an Open World precluded the establishment of any such precedent-setting regional institution. Instead, United States spokesmen stressed the future importance of the World Bank as an alternative, and at the same time advised the Latin Americans to make their countries more attractive to private North American investors.[11]

In the end, North Americans and Latin Americans failed to agree at Chapultepec about the future of their economic relations. Many proposals put forward by both sides were either discarded or modified beyond recognition. The Economic Charter of the Americas was adopted, but much of its substantive anti-statist, anti-nationalist content was eliminated (though the clause attacking economic nationalism *per se* was left in). Very few concrete commitments of any kind emerged from the discussions.

Ironically, one point did emerge clearly from the Mexico City discussions. For all its insistence upon the need for low tariffs in Latin America, the United States would not be able in the immediate future to export to Latin America anything close to the amount of industrial and other manufactured goods that the Latin Americans *wanted* to purchase, both to relieve pent-up consumer demand and to equip Latin American industrial facilities. Assistant Secretary of State for Economic Affairs Will Clayton told the Latin Americans that the United States faced an "extremely difficult problem" in having to provide such goods to countries all over the world, particularly in war-torn Europe. The political primacy of European reconstruction came out clearly in Clayton's suggestion that the Latin Americans count the blessings that would accrue to them indirectly through early reconstruction of their traditional European markets. From the Latin American point of view, the major significance of this situation was that it further postponed the day when, in Sánchez' words, Latin America would "see any benefits" from her wartime commitment to the United Nations' cause.[12]

Quite as serious as the economic problems which faced the incoming Truman administration in early 1945 were the unresolved problems relating to political and military aspects of the inter-American alliance. It might have seemed paradoxical that, simultaneously with the Latin Americans' drive for more economic independence, they were also working toward a tighter, more powerful inter-American military and political defense system. The first goal implied distrust of the United States; the second seemed to imply a very great trust indeed.

There was no real paradox, however. Most Latin American governments viewed a formal inter-American military and political system as a way of at least limiting juridically the power of the United States in the hemisphere. A formal system would involve rules of procedure in case of disputes; presumably the United States could be counted upon to respect procedural safeguards when deploying its power. At best, such a system might become a means for harnessing a certain amount of U.S. military power on Latin American terms, inasmuch as the Latin Americans would always have a clear majority of voting strength (provided that they did not fragment permanently into U.S. "client" states vs. "non-client" states). An example of such thinking was provided in a resolution introduced by the Colombian delegation at the Chapultepec Conference. The resolution, if ratified, would bind all signatories to "defend by all means, including by arms, the territorial integrity and the political independence of all and each one of them, once it had been decided by the absolute majority of all the American states" that such action was necessary.[13]

This Colombian resolution also illustrated a third aspect of Latin American thinking about postwar regional and national security in the Western Hemisphere: the need for a strong, autonomous regional self-defense system, which could compel cooperation from all its members. The projected United Nations had not yet been set up, much less proved capable of maintaining peace in the postwar world. And Latin Americans were not inclined to trust their future to the hands of the U.N. Security Council, where only the Great Powers would be able to exercise a veto.

The United States opposed the creation of autonomous regional military and political systems as dangerous to the Open World ideal. Regional military alliances often degenerated into closed blocs dominated by the strongest member of the alliance. That member could then use the military and political power of the entire alliance for aggressive purposes. Closed political-military blocs could also lead to closed economic blocs, where the dominant nation could use its power to close off an entire region for its exclusive economic exploitation, contrary to Open World principles. At Chapultepec, therefore, the Roosevelt administration discouraged, as it had all through the war, the development of an autonomous Western Hemisphere military security system, so as not to give the Russians an excuse for establishing a closed system of their own in Eastern Europe.[14]

U.S. policy strategists felt that the Open World approach, upon which the Roosevelt administration's position at Chapultepec was based, provided the most effective lever for exercising U.S. influence in Latin America. With a world free of competing closed military and political blocs, superior competitive U.S. industrial, financial, and technological strength would easily carry the day in any international economic competition—not only in Latin America but in many other areas of the world as well. Shifting the competition into economic channels would also enable the United States to continue to adhere to the politically remunerative nonintervention program of the Good Neighbor policy. The United States opposed the Colombian proposal at the Chapultepec Conference, and succeeded in having it watered down to the point where it became nothing more than the innocuous "declaration of solidarity" embodied in the Final Act of the Conference.[15] Further discussion of the regional security problem was tabled, pending the convening of the United Nations organizing conference at San Francisco in April 1945.

The Latin Americans were not very happy with the outcome of the regional security debate at Mexico City. This problem, like the inter-American economic problems, remained unresolved during President Roosevelt's lifetime. Thus when Harry Truman succeeded to the presidency he inherited an inter-American situation full of unresolved tensions and disagreements. His predecessor was being universally eulogized in Latin America as the architect of the Good Neighbor policy. Nevertheless, as the Latin Americans also knew, the Good Neighbor policy had failed to solve the problems of inter-American economic relationships or the political and military problems of hemisphere security in the postwar world. The task of the new Truman administration was to resolve those conflicts left unresolved by the Roosevelt

approach, but presumably to do so without giving up President
Roosevelt's goal of maintaining the traditionally high degree of
U.S. power and influence in Latin America.

Within two months of assuming the presidency, Truman
agreed to a fundamental shift in political strategy toward Latin
America. At the United Nations organizing conference in San
Francisco, the United States delegation, with Truman's approval,
decided to support Latin America's demand for an autonomous
regional security system. There were three reasons for the
change in strategy.

In the first place, a majority of the United States delegates at
San Francisco came around to the view that the United States
had better support the "regionalist" position in order to remain
on good terms with the Latin Americans. Otherwise the United
States might stimulate an even more serious Latin American
movement toward anti-U.S. nationalism than had been observed
at Chapultepec. This theme was stressed constantly and with
great effectiveness by Nelson Rockefeller, Assistant Secretary of
State for Latin American Affairs, who was the delegation's chief
liaison with the Latin American delegations. Rockefeller's success in convincing Senator Arthur Vandenberg of the seriousness
of the situation was of domestic political significance as well.
Vandenberg, a key member of the U.S. delegation, was also the
ranking Republican on the Senate Foreign Relations Committee; as such, he was in a position to swing a lot of votes for or
against confirmation of the U.N. Charter in the Senate. At a
crucial moment in the conference proceedings, Vandenberg and
Rockefeller wrote a letter to Secretary of State Stettinius, over
Vandenberg's signature, warning that a failure to honor either
the United States' "Pan American obligations" or the United
States' "rights" under the Monroe Doctrine would constitute "a
threat to confirmation of the entire San Francisco charter by the
Senate of the United States." This thinly veiled threat made the
Vandenberg letter a key document in ultimately swinging U.S.
support behind the regionalist position; that position was written into the Charter as Articles 51 and 52, which guaranteed to
all nations the right of "individual and collective" self-defense.[16]

The decision to support the Latin American position did not, to be sure, indicate that the United States was now prepared to allow a strong inter-American alliance to circumscribe United States power. Discussions in the United States delegation brought out clearly the fact that the United States would expect to dominate the alliance. As Assistant Secretary of War John McCloy put it, the arrangement would "protect our concept of preclusive rights in this hemisphere." War Department adviser General Stanley Embick was more blunt. It was essential, he noted, for the United States to maintain "our preclusive control over this hemisphere." Vandenberg preferred to speak in terms of protecting the Monroe Doctrine. The point was nevertheless the same.[17]

The second reason for the change in strategy had more to do with United States–Russian relations than with inter-American relations. Roosevelt's main reason for downgrading the military and political aspects of the inter-American alliance had been to avoid giving Russia a pretext for dangerous parallel action in Eastern Europe. By the time the regional arrangements question came up at San Francisco, however, President Truman had already decided that, pretext or no pretext, the Russians were not to be permitted to establish exclusive control over Eastern Europe. Even before the San Francisco Conference, Truman had dressed down Soviet Foreign Minister Molotov in rather blunt language because of alleged Soviet violations of the Yalta agreement on Poland. Immediately after V-E Day, which by coincidence occurred during the same week that the regional problem was in its most intense stages of discussion at San Francisco, President Truman canceled all further Lend-Lease aid to Russia, a move which Stalin later correctly interpreted to Harry Hopkins as a warning signal to the Russians on the Polish situation. By the time of the Potsdam Conference in late July, Truman began pressuring Stalin to open up Bulgaria and Rumania to free elections.

During the San Francisco Conference, Secretary of War Stimson provided the rationale for the United States' new position on the regional question. Russia's position in Eastern Europe was *not* really parallel to the United States' position in the Western Hemisphere, Stimson noted.

> She's not such an overwhelmingly gigantic power from the ones which she's probably going to make a row about as we are here and on the other hand our fussing around among those little fellows [in Latin America] doesn't upset any balance in Europe at all. That's the main answer. . . .[18]

Ironically, while Stimson was not nearly as militant as Truman in his approach to the Russians, he was quite frank in his views on U.S. prerogatives in Latin America. "I am very much disturbed," the Secretary of War noted in his diary during the San Francisco Conference, "at what I find has been the course of the various conferences with [the] South American republics under the Roosevelt Administration during the past twelve years. I am afraid that the Good Neighbor Policy has put serious obstacles in the path of the exercise of the Monroe Doctrine." All the United States really wanted on this score, Stimson told John McCloy, was "a freer hand as a policeman in this hemisphere" plus a "little freer hand in defending the hemisphere against any outside power other even than the Axis." Articles 51 and 52 would give the United States both.[19]

Finally, the Truman administration reversed Roosevelt's strategy on regionalism because of a third consideration which seemed to unite and yet transcend the first two. Senator Vandenberg stated it most clearly, though later events indicated that it may also have been on Truman's mind at the time. As early as April 1945, Vandenberg was evidently thinking very explicitly of replacing the wartime anti-Axis All-American Front with a postwar anti-communist All-American Front. Such a front, he noted, would be useful both during and after the San Francisco Conference as a tool in rolling back the expansion of the Soviet-led world communist movement. Needless to add, it would also weaken Soviet efforts to "subvert" Latin America through local Communist parties. Vandenberg's position crystallized very early in the San Francisco proceedings.

Even before the regional security question came up at the conference, a crisis had arisen over the question of whether or not to invite Argentina. Because of her refusal to break diplo-

matic relations with the Axis powers, and because of her failure
to cooperate fully in the anti-Axis war effort, Argentina had
been excluded by the Big Three at Yalta from the list of nations
to be invited to the U.N. conference. Argentina had also been
excluded from the Chapultepec Conference of February 1945.
That conference had produced a formula under which Argentina
would be invited to rejoin the inter-American "family of nations" if she (a) declared war on the Axis powers, and (b)
eliminated all Axis political, economic, and social influences
from within her borders. Argentina had accordingly declared
war on Germany and Japan on March 27, 1945, and had *announced* a policy of internal anti-Axis "housecleaning." She was
invited to sign the Final Act of the Chapultepec Conference, and
did so, on April 4, 1945. This, however, did not remove big-
power opposition to her participation in the San Francisco Conference. President Truman was himself still strongly opposed to
Argentine participation; he explicitly instructed the U.S. delegation to the conference *not* to support Argentine admission until the anti-Axis "housecleaning" had been proved successful to
the satisfaction of all the U.N. conferees.[20]

The question of Argentine participation arose almost inevitably once the conference was under way, and a crisis was in
the making. Because of Argentina's post-Chapultepec performance, her admission was favored by the Latin Americans. It
was strongly opposed by the Soviet Union. A number of liberal
anti-communist newspapers in the United States, particularly
the *New York Times* and the *Washington Post,* also opposed
U.S. sponsorship of Argentine admission, precisely because it
would give the Russians grist for their anti-American propaganda mill.

Senator Vandenberg was unconcerned about newspaper opposition. On the other hand, he was delighted by the Soviet
position. After a four-day diplomatic crisis, Argentina was admitted to the conference over the loud and bitter protests of
Soviet Foreign Minister Molotov. Vandenberg gleefully noted
in his diary, on the day Argentina was voted in, that Molotov's
conduct in the crisis had "done more in four days to solidify
Pan America against Russia than anything that ever happened."

Then, in a passage omitted from the posthumously published portions of Vandenberg's diary, the Senator summed up the immediate significance of the victory: "He [Molotov] has done more to put the two Americas into a solid bloc than anything that ever happened heretofore. We shall see the results in subsequent events in this Conference."[21]

The results did not always completely justify Vandenberg's expectations. At one point in the conference, a member of the U.S. delegation brusquely told Nelson Rockefeller: "Your goddam peanut nations aren't voting right. Go line them up." In general, however, the Latin Americans did vote with the United States. At the end of the conference, Vandenberg summed up both the significance of the new inter-American position of the United States and Rockefeller's contribution to it:

> I want to add a word about the work of Assistant Secretary Nelson Rockefeller [Vandenberg wrote in his diary]. He has been responsible for our Pan-American contacts. I never realized before how important the work of his department is in keeping our "good neighbors" united with us.
>
> *Now that we are going into an international organization where, as a practical matter, we shall* NEED VOTES *from time to time in the General Assembly, as well as for other reasons, I think Rockefeller's work is indispensable.* I do not see how anyone could be more efficient.[22]

Rockefeller himself provided the U.S. delegation with an insightful commentary on the relationship between U.S. power in the Western Hemisphere and U.S. ambitions in the world at large. Unless the United States "operated with a solid group in this hemisphere," Rockefeller warned, it "could not do what we wanted to do on the world front." With a solid group, the worldwide tasks would fall into place much more easily. Delegation advisers Hamilton Fish Armstrong, John Foster Dulles, and Isaiah Bowman agreed with Vandenberg on the importance of having maximal support in the United Nations. Vandenberg approvingly quoted Armstrong as saying that "no matter how bad" the U.N. might be, it was "better than nothing," and that "*if* we are headed for trouble with Russia, it is better to have a mechanism that can mobilize the world against her."[23]

President Truman made one final move regarding the inter-

American alliance during the San Francisco Conference. He gave U.S. approval to a proposal for a full-fledged conference on inter-American military organization, to be held at Rio de Janeiro in October 1945. The purpose of the conference would be to draft a treaty to put teeth into the Mexico City "declaration of solidarity" (also known as the Act of Chapultepec).

Truman's new Latin American policy did not mean that the United States was retreating from its goal of creating an Open World. On the contrary, Truman was already moving to gain Russian acceptance of the goal in a much more militant, less conciliatory way than had President Roosevelt. Roosevelt had declined to build a strong inter-American military and political system in order to set a "good example" for the Russians. Truman was going ahead to organize the Western Hemisphere militarily while defying the Russians to do likewise in Eastern Europe. As John McCloy put it, "We ought to have our cake and eat it too; . . . we ought to be free to operate under this regional arrangement in South America, and at the same time intervene promptly in Europe; . . . we oughtn't to give away either asset, we oughtn't be forced to take a Hopkins [sic] choice on this matter."[24] Reduced to basic terms, the Truman administration was moving toward a Closed Hemisphere in an Open World.

It was not entirely clear, to be sure, precisely how much a Closed Hemisphere was really needed to protect Latin America against the dangers of communist "subversion" or "infiltration." Latin America's various Communist parties were indeed at peak strength in 1945, owing largely to the prestige which the Russians had gained by their military successes against the Nazi invaders. There could be little question, moreover, as to the loyalty of the Latin American Communist parties to Moscow. On the other hand, it was at precisely this same time that a resurgent nationalism in Latin America was bringing to power such popularly based, noncommunist movements as the *Auténticos* in Cuba, *Acción Democrática* in Venezuela, *Apra* in Peru, and the Peronists in Argentina. Communists might sometimes encourage such nationalist groups in order to weaken U.S. prestige; but in no instance during the Truman era were communists able to dominate such nationalist movements. Informed U.S.

observers in Latin America realized the extent of communist
weakness, and reported their observations to Washington. From
Caracas, U.S. Ambassador Frank Corrigan described the Venezuelan Communists as "nonrevolutionary," noting their insistence that "further capitalistic development in Venezuela" was
a necessary prerequisite to a revolutionary situation. During the
summer of 1945, U.S. Ambassador to Brazil Adolf Berle noted
the political weakness, indeed irrelevance, of the Brazilian Communists. "Their economic program," he told President Truman,
"is about that of Theodore Roosevelt in 1904."[25]

Nonetheless, to men like Truman and Vandenberg the potential threat was as important as the real one when it came to
dangers of this type. Moreover, as we have seen, both Truman
and Vandenberg had plenty of other reasons for going ahead
with the Closed Hemisphere approach. By August 1945, Vandenberg was already hard at work drafting proposals to formalize the Closed Hemisphere approach through the mechanism of the proposed Rio defense pact. In a letter to Truman's
new Secretary of State, James F. Byrnes, Vandenberg explained
how the Rio meeting might be used to harmonize the Closed
Hemisphere approach with the United Nations' goal of world
peace:

> We might well accept, in connection with our inter-American al-
> lies and pursuant to the Treaty which will soon implement the
> Act of Chapultepec, the exclusive responsibility for any armed
> forces required to maintain peace and security in the Western
> Hemisphere. I doubt whether we shall ever want *any other* armed
> forces to enter this area.[26]

Because of domestic political problems in connection with the
Argentine situation, Truman had to arrange postponement of
the Rio Conference. He continued to move ahead vigorously,
however, with his program of organizing Latin America politically and militarily. In May 1946 the President sent to Congress
a proposal for an Inter-American Military Cooperation Act. If
he could not move ahead directly with inter-American consultations, he could at least begin to line up the necessary legislative
authority at home.

The draft bill which Truman sent to Congress gave the administration wide authority to build up Latin American military establishments, pursuant to the anticipated inter-American treaty of "reciprocal military assistance." The bill's major function was to promote the development of "standardization" procedures in the hemisphere; all Latin American nations were to accept standardized U.S.-type military equipment and military training procedures. Fleet Admiral Chester Nimitz, Chief of Naval Operations, told the House Foreign Affairs Committee that the bill would establish a military supply system which would free the Latin Americans entirely from any dependence on European or other foreign suppliers. General of the Army Dwight D. Eisenhower, Army Chief of Staff, added that the bill would "tend to improve the security of the United States by securing within the vital areas of South America a structure that is oriented toward us militarily."[27] At a second round of hearings in 1947, Secretary of War Robert Patterson stressed the importance of excluding all non-American military participation from the Western Hemisphere.

> We learned from World War II that the introduction of foreign equipment, foreign training methods, are a hazard, a definite hazard to the security of the United States, a definite hazard to the security of the Panama Canal. If we do not furnish them, someone else will, and I think that it is wise policy to remove the existing impediments.

General Eisenhower added that the State Department was expected to establish a "gentlemen's agreement" with the Latin American nations confirming the United States' position as sole supplier of military goods for the inter-American system. A U.S. military supply monopoly would thus complement the alliance's monopoly control of military personnel movements in the hemisphere.[28]

Before the arrangements for a militarily Closed Hemisphere could be formalized in the Rio Treaty, however, one further problem had to be solved: Argentina. During the San Francisco Conference, largely as a result of the skillful maneuvering of Assistant Secretary of State Nelson Rockefeller, Truman had reluctantly agreed to support Argentine admission to the conference as a step toward inter-American unity. Rockefeller's statements and actions during the conference suggest that his reasoning on the Argentine question was somewhat as follows. He realized, first of all, that Argentina's wartime "pro-fascist" neutrality was more a manifestation of traditional Argentine anti-U.S. nationalism than of anything else. Argentina had not, in fact, been economically pro-Axis. Her only substantive commitment during the war had been in the form of large exports of beef to the Allied side.

Likewise, Rockefeller saw an element of the same anti-U.S. nationalism, mixed with fear of resurgent North American big stickism, in the demand of the other Latin American countries that the United States support Argentine admission to the U.N. conference. Rockefeller evidently reasoned that a more conciliatory U.S. approach to the Argentine government, dominated at the time by Colonel Juan Perón, would undercut the nationalist hostility of both the Argentines and the other Latin Americans, thus smoothing the way for the construction of a strong hemispheric alliance under U.S. leadership. Even before the San Francisco Conference, Rockefeller had quietly sent State Department official Avra Warren down to Buenos Aires, with General George Brett, to discuss reestablishment of close economic and military relations between the Argentine and North American governments. Warren and Brett had a series of promising talks about U.S. military aid to Argentina and the reopening of Argentine markets for U.S. industrial exports.[29]

Truman's decision to support Argentina at San Francisco aroused severe public criticism in the United States from anti-Axis liberals who felt that the Argentine regime was not making satisfactory progress in its announced drive to "clean out" Axis influences. Public criticism of both Rockefeller and Secretary of State Stettinius increased when, after the conference had ratified Argentine admission, news reports began to filter back to the United States indicating that the Perón regime had further slackened the pace of its domestic anti-Axis campaign. A series of well-publicized clashes between Perón and the militantly anti-fascist U.S. Ambassador to Argentina, Spruille Braden, underscored the seriousness of the situation. Just before his resignation at the close of the San Francisco Conference, Stettinius himself delivered a strong blast against the Perón regime, castigating it for abandoning its anti-Axis commitments.[30]

The public criticism, and particularly the attacks of eastern liberal newspapers on Rockefeller and the State Department's "pro-Perónist" policy, continued, however. By late August 1945, Truman decided that the situation demanded some clearly visible response. He thereupon fired Rockefeller from his post as Assistant Secretary of State for Latin American Affairs, and replaced him with the militantly anti-Perónist Braden. Braden returned to the United States in late September and began a successful public campaign to force postponement of the impending Rio Conference until a satisfactory "solution" to the Argentine problem could be found. At the same time, Braden initiated another campaign, this one unsuccessful, to rally anti-Perónists in Argentina so as to prevent Perón's winning the Argentine presidential election scheduled for February 1946.

There was an irony in the situation, for Braden was evidently not supposed to carry his anti-Perónism to such extremes *after* he had been promoted. On the contrary, the real purpose of the Braden-for-Rockefeller exchange, though it could not be admitted at the time, was to *expedite* the policy of Argentine-American rapprochement, not to halt or reverse it. By August 1945 Truman had become thoroughly committed to the rapprochement policy. Because of the public criticism, however, he needed to do something which would give the *appearance* of a policy change. Firing Rockefeller, who was publicly identified with a conciliatory approach, and replacing him with Braden, who was publicly known as a "hard-liner" vis-à-vis Perón, was the perfect public relations move. In actuality, removing Braden from the center of events in Buenos Aires would weaken rather than strengthen his anti-Perónist leverage.[31]

Braden knew this at the time and was disturbed by it. Publicly, he told reporters that he would use the "wider authority" of his new post for a stronger and more effective campaign against "fascism" in Argentina. Privately, he attempted to get Truman and Secretary of State Byrnes to let him delay his departure as long as possible, knowing that his leaving Buenos Aires would weaken the anti-Perónists there.[32] Braden had been

"kicked upstairs" in the classic manner. His continued anti-Perónist militance upon his return to Washington therefore came
as something of an embarrassment to the administration. Senator
Vandenberg, who evidently was not aware of the real motivation
behind the Braden promotion, complained vehemently about
the "showdown between the country and the State Department"
which Braden's actions seemed to symbolize. Always quick to
point out the possibilities of Russian successes growing out of
American distresses, Vandenberg noted that Braden's unexpected and unwanted interruption of the trend toward Argentine-
American rapprochement involved "a potential Communist menace throughout Central and South America which *could* be far
more dangerous than the Fascist problem in the Argentine."
Vandenberg wrote to newspaperman Roy Howard warning that
"if our Pan American neighbors get it into their heads that the
'colossus of the North' has again 'gone imperialistic' on a big
stick basis our Inter-American system will blow up higher than
a kite."[33]

Ultimately, Braden's promotion did undercut his power in the
fight against Perón. Once away from the center of events, Braden was deprived of his only effective point of leverage, while
the anti-Perónists were deprived of his day-to-day working assistance. Braden's opposition quickly degenerated into a simple
propaganda offensive, which Perón cleverly turned against him
by campaigning on the theme of defense of Argentine national
sovereignty. "Braden or Perón" was the astute colonel's victory
slogan in the presidential election campaign that followed. Braden's last-minute publication of the famous "Blue Book" on fascist influences in Argentina, misleadingly labeled a *Consultation Among the American Republics with Respect to the
Argentine Situation,* only validated Perón's claim of *yanqui* intervention in Argentine internal affairs. "As an Argentine," Perón remarked some time after his election victory, "I must resent
Mr. Braden's intervention in our internal affairs and in the election; as Juan Perón, I am deeply grateful to him."[34]

Shortly before Perón's inauguration as President of Argentina
in June 1946, Truman appointed George Messersmith to be the
new U.S. Ambassador to Argentina. Messersmith went to Buenos

Aires with explicit instructions to take a conciliatory attitude
toward Perón, and thereby to persuade the new president to
complete the anti-Axis "housecleaning" so that the Rio Conference could proceed.[35] Messersmith followed his instructions to
the letter. For about a year he and Braden worked at cross purposes, Messersmith constantly cajoling and persuading Perón
while Braden continued to issue public broadsides attacking the
"neurotic nationalism" of the Argentine government.

By early 1947 Braden began rapidly losing ground. In a well-
publicized speech in Cleveland, Vandenberg (who was now
chairman of the Republican-controlled Senate Foreign Relations
Committee as well as president *pro tem* of the Senate) called
for early convening of the Rio Conference, and, by implication,
for Braden's resignation. At first the new Secretary of State,
General George C. Marshall, was preoccupied with European
problems. By the late spring of that year, however, Marshall and
President Truman decided that the conference had been postponed long enough. Braden was quietly informed that his services would no longer be needed. He agreed to resign "voluntarily" on condition that Messersmith also be recalled.[36]

Accordingly, the "resignations" of both officials were announced early in June 1947. The Rio Conference was held during late August of that year. During a House Foreign Affairs
Committee hearing on the proposed Inter-American Military
Cooperation Act (which was finally abandoned by the Truman
administration because of congressional opposition), Secretary
Marshall was asked by Representative Jacob Javits of New York
if Argentina's anti-fascist commitments were now considered to
have been satisfactorily fulfilled. Marshall replied in the affirmative. The Rio Treaty went forward.[37]

Because of Braden's energetic delaying tactics, it had taken
the Truman administration more than two years from the time
of the San Francisco Conference to finish building the military
alliance that would close the Western Hemisphere in an otherwise open world. Having been defeated in their bid for a full-
fledged Inter-American Military Cooperation Act, administration
officials now moved to implement the *substance* of the act's
provisions anyway; this they did by concluding a series of bi-

lateral military assistance agreements with individual Latin American governments. After 1947, with the United States government controlling equipment supplies to Latin America, assisting in the training of Latin American military officers, and dominating the strategically vital Panama Canal, there was little doubt that, just as War Department advisers had advocated in 1945, the United States would maintain "preclusive control" over Western Hemisphere military policy.[38]

On the other hand, Truman and his advisers never did find an alternative to President Roosevelt's economic approach to Latin America. Despite clear evidences of Latin American hostility to the Roosevelt approach at the Mexico City Conference, the Truman administration continued and intensified that approach in all of its anti-nationalist, anti-statist emphasis. One reason for this was that in the early postwar years, with the overwhelming bulk of U.S. public assistance programs being concentrated in Western Europe, the administration simply could not afford to encourage Latin American hopes for large-scale U.S. aid. Administration officials rationalized this attitude as part of a general disapproval of state intervention in Latin American economic life. A second reason for Truman's continuation of the Mexico City approach was that most U.S. policy advisers felt it was best calculated to preserve U.S. economic power in Latin America, Latin American hostility notwithstanding. Truman and his major advisers evidently thought the United States did have sufficient economic power to brave the tide of Latin American nationalist hostility and to pressure the Latin Americans into accepting the United States' version of preferred inter-American economic relationships.

One of the most consistent militants in promoting the anti-statist, anti-nationalist economic approach to Latin America was Assistant Secretary of State Braden. His anti-fascism was only one aspect of his philosophy of international relations, for he was just as vigorously anti-communist. And since both communism and fascism represented alternative logical developments of extreme nationalist or statist positions, Braden was just as strongly anti-nationalist and anti-statist. Even in 1945, Braden had opposed Perón *not* merely because he thought of Perón as a fascist but because he thought Perón's policies might ultimately benefit the forces of communism in South America. Sir David Kelly, the British Ambassador in Buenos Aires, wanted to take a conciliatory approach to Perón, hoping thereby to extract an Argentine commitment to protect British investments. Braden thought the risk was a bad one. He told reporters:

> Sir David keeps coming back to the point that British investments are so much more important than American. My reply has been No matter—[sic] if this guy keeps on your investments will be worth nothing either through him or by a reaction to communism.[39]

All through 1946, Braden continued to attack Perón's "neurotic nationalism" as a threat to long-range U.S. interests in Latin America. Nationalism, statism, fascism, and communism were to Braden fundamentally kindred evils in that they all challenged the dominance of international free enterprise, which the United States hoped to promote in Latin America and around the world. In September 1946, in a speech reprinted as an official State Department policy release, Braden summed up the Truman administration's postwar economic approach to Latin America:

> I wish to emphasize that private enterprise is the best and in most circumstances the only really sound means to develop the known or unknown resources of a new country, because there has appeared a school of thought which, when considering United States cooperation in the development of Latin America, overlooks or even in a few cases condemns the use of private capital. Instead it advocates that the requisite financing be done by our government, either in the form of loans at low rates of interest or of what is tantamount to outright grants, in the case of certain public health, nutrition, and educational projects. . . .
>
> The institution of private property ranks with those of religion and the family as a bulwark of civilization. To tamper with private enterprise, except to apply well-conceived, legal, and essential controls, will precipitate a disintegration of life and liberty as we conceive and treasure them.

"The time has come," Braden added, "to realize that the United States Treasury is not an inexhaustible reservoir."[40]

Braden's reference to the Treasury's limited capacity underscored Truman's general concern to avoid committing large-scale

economic aid outside of Western Europe. Illustrating the point
that the administration had, for political reasons, raised this general concern to the level of ideology, Braden summed up the
"legitimate" channels through which the U.S. could use public
resources in international economic life. The channels included
long-term government loans, such as the postwar American loans
to Britain and France, to "prevent world-wide economic chaos";
donations in war-ravaged areas; and short-term credits to promote U.S. exports and imports. "Self-evidently," Braden noted,
"our Government should undertake no financial operation when
the effect will be to harm American investments or foreign
trade." Nor should it "compete with commercial banks or private
investors."[41] Braden was simply rationalizing the administration's policy of extending large reconstruction loans to Europe
while hedging on development loans to Latin America. Nevertheless, the policy was now part of official administration ideology. For the remainder of Truman's tenure in office, the overwhelming bulk of U.S. aid went to Western Europe rather than
to the Western Hemisphere.

The Republican party's foreign policy adviser, John Foster
Dulles, agreed with Braden and other administration officials
as to the need for relying on Western-style private enterprise in
developing Latin America. Communist ideology, Dulles warned
early in 1947, posed a serious challenge to U.S. influence in the
hemisphere. "There is a highly organized effort," Dulles told the
Inland Daily Press Association in Chicago, "to extend to the
South American countries the Soviet system of proletariat dic-
tatorship. It ignores the declaration of President Monroe, made
to Russia and others in 1823, that 'to extend their system to any
portions of this Hemisphere is dangerous to our peace and security.'" Dulles advocated an active expansion of U.S. private
enterprise into Latin America in order to "help the countries of
South America to get more vigorous and healthy economies
which will end the masses of discontent which too widely prevail." What Dulles was saying was that North American private
entrepreneurs should become the postwar guardians of Franklin
Roosevelt's prewar New Deal program of "giving Latin America
a share" of its own developing wealth. Dulles noted the poten-

tial profitability of such a program for U.S. investors, even without the stimulus of U.S. government aid. The development of Latin America, he noted, would "not require any vast outpouring of our money. Rather, it requires an intelligent comprehension of the possibilities of these naturally rich lands."[42] Such an approach would combat not only communism but all other potentially dangerous statist and nationalist ideologies in Latin America.

At the Havana Conference of 1947, the Truman administration took the lead in pushing for a strong International Trade Organization. Such an organization would aid in the expansion of U.S. private enterprise abroad by providing a favorable tariff structure in Latin America and other developing areas. While the Havana Conference was in progress, Treasury Secretary John W. Snyder went to Houston to tell Texan businessmen of the importance of the ITO in encouraging the growth of U.S. private enterprise abroad. "Your city and your state," Snyder told the Houston Chamber of Commerce, "with their far-flung trading activities, have a real stake in these efforts to substitute a rule of reason and common interest for cut-throat competitive economic nationalism in the trade relations between countries." State Department spokesman Paul Nitze assured a group of New England businessmen that the United States' point of view would prevail in the ITO. "I have been asked," Nitze stated, "whether the United States, with only one vote, will not be outnumbered in the ITO by the many smaller countries and forced to accept all kinds of things that it does not like. I do not think," he noted, "we need be afraid. Such a thing has not yet happened in any international agency with which we work. Such a fear leaves out of account the strategic position of leadership that the United States enjoys in the world."[43]

At the Bogotá Conference of 1948, the administration made clear its insistence upon a formal Latin American commitment to respect private enterprise rather than statism—and to protect international private enterprise against the depredations of economic nationalism—in developing the economies of Latin America. Just as the Rio Conference had produced a treaty which formalized Truman's military approach in Latin America, so did the Bogotá Conference formalize inter-American political and economic relations by establishing the Organization of American States and the Economic Agreement of Bogotá.

At the conference, Secretary of State Marshall, heading the U.S. delegation, stressed as the "dominant theme" of United States policy the "role which private capital might play in the economic development of Latin America." Throughout the discussions, as the delegation's report of the conference meetings indicated, the United States' position was that "private capital, whether domestic or foreign, would have to be counted upon and should be allowed to do the main part of the job." According to the delegation report, the United States maintained this stand despite the fact that the Latin Americans strongly favored giving their own economic development its "principal" impetus

> not by private initiative as it is known in the United States, but through governmental development corporations financed by foreign and local government capital, or, at the most, mixed governmental and private financing, with a considerable degree of government influence and control in planning and operations.[44]

During the conference, President Truman did announce that he would ask Congress to increase the lending authority of the Export-Import Bank by $500 million, the increased funds to be used primarily for loans to Latin America.[45] But this was a comparatively small sum considering the magnitude of the job to be done in Latin America; and, as the Latin Americans well knew, the main purpose of Export-Import Bank loans was to promote U.S. exports to Latin America.

At Bogotá, North Americans and Latin Americans clashed over the question of the inviolability of private property—particularly foreign-owned property—in Latin America. The United States attempted to force the inclusion of a sentence in the economic agreement stating that "any expropriation shall be accompanied by payment of fair compensation in a prompt, adequate, and effective manner." Seven Latin American delegations appended specific reservations to their ratification agreements, noting the primacy of their respective constitutions over the language of the economic agreement. The Latin Americans threw out entirely a U.S.-sponsored draft proposal limiting such expropriations to "clearly defined public purposes."

At Bogotá, as at Mexico City, the Latin Americans pressed for increased U.S. aid and for the establishment of an inter-American development bank. At Bogotá, as at Mexico City, the U.S. delegation vetoed the inter-American bank proposal while admitting that the United States "was not in a position" to offer the Latin Americans "the amounts of financial and other economic assistance" which they were seeking through intergovernmental arrangements.[46]

The two sides also clashed again on the question of political organization of the hemisphere. The Latin Americans attempted, as they had at Mexico City, to secure United States acceptance of a Latin American concept of hemispheric political security. They managed to secure the insertion into the OAS Charter of Articles 15, 16, and 17, prohibiting political, military, or economic intervention in the affairs of any state by any other state or group of states. But the United States actually carried the day by securing the inclusion of a special resolution condemning "international communism or any other totalitarian doctrine" as being "incompatible with the concept of American freedom." Years later, through its intervention in the Dominican Republic in 1965, the United States was to demonstrate forcefully (and forcibly) just how strongly this Resolution 32 on "Preservation and Defense of Democracy in America" took precedence over Articles 15, 16, and especially 17, which prohibited even temporary military occupation of another state "on any grounds whatever." At the time, Resolution 32 could be seen as a potential escape clause, through which the U.S. might use the OAS as a means of protecting the concept of the Closed Hemisphere in an Open World.

By the end of May 1948, the Closed Hemisphere was complete as a formal system. The Rio Treaty provided the military framework for the system, while the OAS Charter and the Economic Agreement of Bogotá provided the political and economic framework. All non-American military and political power had been successfully excluded from the hemisphere. With respect to the economic situation, the U.S. had apparently gotten the Latin Americans to accept, with some reservations, an approach to Latin American development that would protect U.S. dominance of the development process. There was only one problem with the system: it failed to help the Latin Americans treat the *causes* of their political and economic difficulties. In the long run, the Truman policies only intensified the inter-American conflicts that President Roosevelt had bequeathed to Truman in 1945.

In the first place, military security against outside attack was not one of Latin America's prime needs. The anti-communist All-American Front, insofar as it sought to meet the danger of Soviet invasion, was, as one respected North American historian later pointed out, a response to an "illusory" threat. There never was any real danger of such invasion either before or after World War II; had there been, the United States would undoubtedly have met it directly, unilaterally, and without waiting for formal authorization from the Latin Americans.[47] Thus the Rio Treaty was in this respect unnecessary.

As for intra-hemispheric military threats to the peace, the Rio Treaty and the OAS machinery rarely functioned effectively in times of major crisis. When they did, as in the dispute between Nicaragua and Costa Rica in 1948, it was only because United States interests were not directly involved. When U.S. interests were involved, as in the Honduras-based Guatemalan exile invasion of 1954, the Bay of Pigs invasion of 1961, and the Dominican Republic crisis of 1965, military maneuvers were launched outside the framework of both the Rio Pact and the OAS. If the OAS was called in at all, it was summoned after the fact, as in 1965, to legitimize a military *fait accompli* on the part of the United States. After 1948, the U.S. attitude toward intra-hemispheric disputes seemed consistent with the pre-1948 statements of those policy advisers who had predicted that U.S. participation in a hemispheric security system would not interfere with its "preclusive rights" in the hemisphere.

The primary political problem in Latin America after 1948 continued to be internal instability within the various nations;

this was generally more closely related to internal socio-economic conditions than to externally sponsored plottings. To the degree that the United States shared responsibility for these conditions, the problem lay with the fundamental ineffectiveness of the administration's approach to Latin American economic development.

The Economic Agreement of Bogotá remained a dead letter. Only three Latin American states ratified it, at which point the administration gave up and quietly laid it aside without so much as a formal ratification by the United States. President Truman continued to use the Export-Import Bank to provide some loans to Latin American governments, thus showing that he, like President Roosevelt, was not rigidly opposed to state involvement in Latin American economic development. But Export-Import Bank loans were not significantly larger after 1948 than they were in the 1945–1948 period, and such loans as were forthcoming were clearly not designed to promote economic independence for Latin America. The April 1948 announcement of a $500 million increase in Eximbank lending authority, designed to coincide with the holding of the Bogotá Conference, had been an effort to neutralize Latin American opposition to the rest of the administration's economic program at the conference. The announcement, as Ambassador William Pawley suggested to Truman (with calculated understatement), "would go a long way in creating a much more favorable climate for the negotiations at Bogotá." A $125 million credit to the Perón regime, made in the spring of 1950 for the announced purpose of increasing U.S. exports to Argentina, was avowedly both a reward for Perón's retreat from militant economic nationalism and an inducement to further retreat. In discussing the proposed credit with New York exporters, a State Department spokesman cited a number of specific instances to show that Perón was abandoning his "erratic" nationalist policies and was now "facing realistically [Argentina's] foreign and domestic problems." Referring to recent discussions between U.S. and Argentine officials, the spokesman remarked: "All of us in Washington who have taken part in many, if not all, of these discussions, whether directly or indirectly, are highly encouraged. And, I feel safe in saying that the individual [U.S.] businessmen affected by the actions taken are also encouraged."[48]

The Point Four technical assistance program, announced in Truman's January 1949 inaugural address, was no more than a well-publicized and slightly updated version of programs which Roosevelt's Office of the Coordinator of Inter-American Affairs (OCIAA), headed by Nelson Rockefeller, had worked on from 1941 to 1945. The Point Four program had very limited developmental value without the large amounts of capital needed to translate technical aid into large-scale development projects. For Latin America, such capital was not forthcoming from any U.S. source in the late 1940's or early 1950's. Nor was Point Four *designed* to diminish Latin American dependence on the industrial exports of the United States. Presidential Assistant John R. Steelman reassured a group of Chicago businessmen in May 1949 that the Point Four program would not create Latin American industries to compete with those of the United States. "I think we have only to look back upon the history of our trade with Europe and Latin America to see the folly of such fears," Steelman noted. "Certainly, for the foreseeable future, the economic development of other areas will require capital goods from the United States." Said Technical Cooperation Administrator Henry Bennett: "The Point Four Program of economic development is, in the truest and broadest sense, good business for Americans."[49]

Primary reliance upon private U.S. capital as the source of funds for Latin American development turned out to be a dead end during the remainder of the Truman years. The statistics tell the story. There was a very large influx of U.S. capital into one clearly profitable activity—Venezuelan oil development. Net foreign investments in Venezuelan oil, of which U.S. investments were the vast majority, increased by $957 million between 1946 and 1949 alone. On the other hand, total net U.S. investments (including reinvested profits) in Latin American manufacturing in the years 1946–1953 were not even as great as net investments in Venezuelan oil in the years 1946–1949. Total U.S. investments in Latin American agriculture, including reinvested profits, were not quite one-eighth as large as total oil investments in the same period, 1946–1953.[50]

With regard to bonds and other portfolio investments, there was a distinct trend toward *disinvestment* during this period. An International Monetary Fund study estimated that actual net payments from Latin America to the United States for repatriation of dollar bonds and other long-term assets totaled as high as $361 million during the 1946–1953 period. Most important, in the period 1946–1951, investment income paid out to U.S. investors by Latin American concerns totaled $3,078 million, exclusive of reinvested profits, while net U.S. investment inflows into Latin America, including reinvested profits, totaled $2,549 million. In other words, during these six years almost 20 per cent more working capital left Latin America than went into it because of these very U.S. investments.[51] Such investments, to be sure, aided the Latin Americans significantly in those instances where they left behind improved plant facilities and increased production for commercial interchange. But the rate of profit and repatriation of funds was so high that one could not fairly speak in this period of an expanding Latin American capital market, at least not on the basis of tabulated U.S. capital movements. Moreover, the improvements financed by such foreign investments were often made in foreign-owned enterprises; in such cases, the net financial benefits from the improvements were largely reserved to the foreign owners rather than to the Latin American host countries.

As early as 1949, Alberto Lleras Camargo, Secretary-General of the newly formed OAS, pointed out the significance of the capital investment situation in Latin America. Truman administration policies, he noted, coupled with general distrust of Latin American nationalism on the part of private U.S. investors, had resulted in a contracting rather than an expanding Latin American capital market.

We are now going through the Latin-American depression caused by that fact. Those who are thoroughly familiar with that subtle economic machinery know very well that all that would be necessary to produce a depression in the United States would be the adoption of a policy of restricted credits. What is so extraordinary, then, in the fact that Latin America has suffered so cruelly from the suspension of foreign credits?[52]

The Latin American nations were indeed in a dilemma. Dissatisfaction with the results of wartime inter-American economic "cooperation" had led them toward a more nationalistic approach to development; but this move toward nationalism caused the United States government, as well as private U.S. investors, to adopt even more closed-handed, restrictive investment and loan policies in Latin America. North Americans were simply not about to underwrite Latin American economic nationalism or statism. Truman's goal was, on the contrary, to make Latin America secure against external attack and internal disorder so that economic development could go forward along lines consonant with U.S. interests.

The administration's policies, however, ultimately proved as ineffective in preventing internal disorder as they were unnecessary in meeting the "threat" of external attack. In a strikingly incisive book, published posthumously in 1949, former State Department political adviser Laurence Duggan warned of the futility of attempts to solve Latin America's social crises through political and military organization.

> At the risk of becoming tiresome, I repeat that United States aid in developing the resources of Latin America and thereby raising the standard of living will be much more potent in creating an environment in which democracy can flourish than anything we can do directly to encourage political democracy while present economic conditions continue.[53]

In 1948, during the Bogotá Conference itself, an event had occurred which demonstrated graphically the validity of Duggan's point. On April 9, 1948, Jorge Eliécer Gaitán, demagogic leader of the left wing of the Colombian Liberal party and popular symbol of the rising power of Colombia's urban masses, was assassinated in the streets of Bogotá. The assassination touched off rioting and street fighting so serious that the conference was temporarily recessed and moved to safer quarters outside the city. But the *Bogotazo*, as the rioting was called, was much more than a series of street riots. It was the manifestation of a tremendous undercurrent of economic and social unrest which had been building ever since the end of the war; the riots only exposed to plain view the social and economic bankruptcy of the policies that Colombian administrations had been pursuing for years. In a larger sense, the *Bogotazo* was striking testimony to the fundamental social irrelevance of the entire security-oriented approach of the United States.[54]

In the years after the Bogotá Conference, Truman's policies did have one important effect upon internal Latin American developments. From 1945 to 1948, U.S. ambitions in Latin America had run up against nationalist opposition from both inside and outside various Latin American governments. After 1948, the balance of power within a number of countries began to shift away from the nationalists and toward groups who preferred to cooperate with the military and political security program of the United States. U.S. military aid became a highly successful device for buying the allegiance of otherwise potentially hostile governments (the Perón regime in Argentina, for example). And it was often easier for Latin American governments to accept U.S. military aid, and use it as an instrument of internal social *control*, than to face up to the difficult problems of internal social *reform*.

As economic stagnation continued to produce social discontent in the form of urban riots, strikes, and street demonstrations, more and more Latin American governments replied to the unrest by using military force. Some even used equipment supplied by the United States. In more than one country, military groups which the Truman policies helped to build used U.S.-supplied equipment to take political and economic power directly, and to hold that power in defiance of popular disapproval.[55] This result was not something which Truman or his advisers had particularly hoped for—at least there is no evidence available to indicate that they did. As early as 1949 the President expressed opposition to the idea of military takeovers of political authority. As early as 1946, however, the administration had been challenged with the possibility that such results might follow military build-ups in Latin America. During the first round of hearings on the Inter-American Military Cooperation Act, Secretary of State Byrnes was asked whether or not the proposed U.S. military aid program might give certain governments the military leverage to "stay in power over the desires of any other faction or group within" their countries. Byrnes replied that such a result "would be entirely in conflict with our policy." But he did not, and very possibly could not, indicate how the program could be designed to prevent it.[56] At the second round of hearings in 1947, former Pan American Union official Ernesto Galarza told the House Foreign Affairs Committee that in a number of Latin American countries, parades and peaceful demonstrations against economic privation were already being broken up by government troops using weapons obtained from the United States under the lend-lease program. The proposed armaments program would only intensify such developments, Galarza warned. Though the Act itself was finally abandoned, the bilateral treaties later used to implement the military build-up encouraged by the Rio Pact did have much the same effects forecast by Galarza.[57]

Caught in an attempt to use stability-oriented political, military, and economic policies to solve deep-rooted social problems, the Truman administration could not admit the fundamental ineffectiveness of its solutions. Administration officials therefore could not admit that continued signs of social instability in Latin America were understandable responses to the failure of the inter-American system to develop viable programs for promoting balanced, independent Latin American economic development. Instead, the administration, acting in concert with those Latin American governments in whose countries embarrassing outbursts occurred, quickly developed a policy of defining such outbursts as illegitimate, subversive, and probably externally directed. Social instability, under this definition, became associated with (and to many U.S. and Latin American officials, equivalent to) communist subversion, because even if communists did not start the riots or strikes, they always profited by them and encouraged them.

Official reaction to the *Bogotazo* provided an early example of this kind of administration thinking. The Colombian government, in order to save face, could not and did not admit the presence of deep-rooted *internal* causes behind the rioting. Instead, it stressed the presence of communist elements in the affair. The Truman administration faithfully echoed this line. In a radio address delivered in Washington, Assistant Secretary of State Norman Armour remarked: "The reality of international Communism's opposition to all that the American states stand for was thrust forcibly upon the consciousness of the delegates at Bogotá by the obvious efforts of Communist adherents to sabotage the Conference."[58]

Interestingly, at least one ranking U.S. official saw other reasons for the outburst. World Bank President John McCloy wrote to his old War Department boss, Henry L. Stimson, noting that "general social conditions not only in Colombia but in other countries [were] such as to make possible, even without communist inspiration, flash powder explosions such as the Bogotá affair." For political reasons, however, the official administration interpretation remained unchanged, and, significantly, was passed down to future generations of students by respectable academic historians who could explain the *Bogotazo* by stating, as one did: "International Communism had resorted to direct action in Bogotá to break up and discredit the great conference of American states."[59]

For the remainder of his term, Truman stuck to this explanation of Latin American instability in general. During the Korean War, the administration seized upon the new "world-wide" communist threat to sponsor a further tightening of internal political and military controls in Latin America. In a press release of December 16, 1950, Secretary of State Dean Acheson called for a meeting of the Foreign Ministers of the OAS nations. "The aggressive policy of international communism, carried out through its satellites," Acheson stated, "has brought about a situation in which the entire free world is threatened." The United States, he noted, wished to "consult its fellow members in the inter-American community with respect to the situation which we all face and on the coordination of the common effort required to meet it."[60]

President Truman opened this Foreign Ministers Conference in Washington the following March by calling upon the Latin

Americans to join the anti-communist crusade being waged by
the United States and its allies in Korea. "The issue in Korea,"
the President stated, "is the survival of the principles on which
we have built our countries. . . . If justice and order do not prevail in Korea, they will be in danger everywhere." At the same
time, Truman called for a general tightening of *internal* political
controls in Latin America. A U.S.-sponsored draft "Project on
Internal Security," submitted to the conference on March 27,
1951, contained an extremely broad proposal that the American
republics adopt,

> in accordance with their respective constitutional provisions, the
> measures necessary to eradicate and prevent activities directed,
> assisted, or instigated by foreign governments, organizations or
> individuals tending to overthrow their institutions by violence, to
> foment disorder in their domestic political life, or to disturb, by
> means of pressure, subversive propaganda, threats or by any other
> means, the free and sovereign right of their peoples to govern
> themselves in accordance with their democratic aspirations.[61]

Since virtually any social unrest could be attributed to foreign-
based elements, this resolution could be easily used as an excuse to stamp out any social unrest through repressive, though
perfectly legal, political and military measures. Resolution 8 of
the Final Act of the Conference reflected the strong influence
of the U.S. proposal. It recommended that "each American Republic examine its respective laws and regulations and adopt
such changes as it considers necessary to ensure that subversive
activities of the agents of international Communism, directed
against any of them, may be adequately forestalled and pe-
nalized."[62]

Ironically, the one result which did not emerge from the
Washington Conference was a Latin American commitment to
participate in the anti-communist struggle world-wide. The Latin American governments were willing to pass an anti-subversion resolution designed to strengthen their own political power
at home; but of the twenty Latin American republics, only one
actually became militarily involved in Korea. The one was Colombia, a country where the authoritarian regime of President
Laureano Gomez was so inept, and so incapable of dealing with

the social violence that had convulsed Colombia since 1948, that when the military finally stepped in and took power in 1953 it was to the general relief of the populace at large.

Except for Colombia, which sent only a token contribution of men and material to Korea anyway, the overwhelming Latin American reaction to the Korean War was a distinct preference for noninvolvement. Six years after its inception, Truman's hemispheric anti-communist All-American Front met to face its first "foreign policy" test, and promptly responded by writing its own epitaph—in a word, irrelevance.

Yet the effects of the Truman policies *within* Latin America were real enough. Militarily imposed political stability did become the primary means in many countries of dealing with socio-economic difficulties. A number of Latin American nations —Peru, Venezuela, Cuba, and the Dominican Republic, for example—were thereby subjected to the continued stress of stability-oriented military dictatorships which far outlasted the Truman presidency. As a result of the passage of the Mutual Security Act of 1951, the Truman administration further escalated its military assistance to Latin America by inaugurating a new series of bilateral "defense" agreements, under the terms of which the United States sent military missions to all signatory countries. U.S. military aid grants quickly increased from $200,-000 in fiscal year 1952 to several millions in fiscal year 1953. Interestingly, each bilateral agreement also committed the Latin American signatory to limit its trade with Soviet bloc nations. Once again, U.S. military policy was designed to have both military-political and economic consequences.[63]

A year after Truman left the White House, Secretary of State John Foster Dulles carried the Truman approach to its logical conclusion in dealing with a particularly threatening situation in Guatemala. In 1953, a militantly nationalistic government had expropriated 400,000 acres of agricultural land owned by the United Fruit Company, a large U.S. corporation with considerable Latin American property holdings. The Guatemalan government offered compensation of approximately $600,000, the figure at which United Fruit had evaluated the land for tax purposes. United Fruit now insisted the land was worth $15

million, and, in the resulting impasse, sought State Department
assistance. Secretary Dulles feared that the Guatemalan action
might set a dangerous precedent throughout Latin America.
Therefore he and his brother Allen (chief of the U.S. Central
Intelligence Agency) worked with exiled Guatemalan military
leaders in a successful effort to overthrow the Guatemalan nationalists and replace them with military leaders committed to
the restoration and protection of U.S. property rights. While not
publicly acknowledging U.S. ties with the invading rebels, Dulles made sure to "legitimize" the coup in advance by pushing
through the Inter-American Conference at Caracas a resolution
condemning the provocations of "international communism" in
Guatemala.[64]

In a curious sort of way, even the Guatemalan episode had
been previsaged by U.S. policy analysts as early as 1947. During
the second round of hearings on the Inter-American Military
Cooperation Act, House Foreign Affairs Committee chairman
Charles Eaton asked Secretary of State Marshall if the Congress
could be "sure that thought will be given under this legislation,
and arrangements made, to protect the national interests of the
United States by putting into the bargain 'secure access to and
protection to and protection of United States property, rights,
or its citizens' rights, in strategic minerals or materials in Latin
America.'" "My answer to that," Marshall had replied, "is in the
affirmative."[65]

Neither Marshall nor Eaton appears to have had in mind the
kind of connection which the Dulles brothers made between
U.S. military aid and protection of U.S. property rights. Marshall
and Eaton were thinking only of legal guarantees to be written
into the aid agreements (such as *were* eventually enacted in the
Hickenlooper Amendment of 1962). But in developing primary
reliance upon a military solution to Latin America's social problems, by justifying that solution in terms of Cold War necessity,
and, above all, by incorporating into the rhetoric of justification
a firm commitment to the inviolability of U.S.-owned private
enterprise in Latin America, Truman's policy-makers had provided a ready-made rationale for the Dulles version of the "guarantee" program. It had been Truman and his advisers, not Dul-

les, who had first developed a postwar policy approach that equated nationalism with communism and instability with subversion in Latin America. Dulles became, up to 1961, the most spectacular practitioner of this approach. But the Truman administration had already set the ideological tone for United States policy in Latin America during the 1950's—and after.

To sum up:

1. The Truman administration accepted Roosevelt's dream of a postwar Open World and sought to realize it through a continuing assault on economic nationalism and state intervention in Latin American economic development. Such public economic aid as Truman offered Latin America was designed, just as Roosevelt's aid had been, to protect and promote U.S. economic influence. Meanwhile, U.S. private investments contributed to a net loss of working capital (decapitalization) in Latin America.

2. As a concomitant of its developing Cold War position vis-à-vis the Soviet Union, the Truman administration committed itself to a policy of vigorous military and political organization of the hemisphere along militantly anti-communist lines. But in the absence of a real Soviet threat to Latin America, U.S. military aid became useful primarily as a vehicle for increasing the domestic political power of the Latin American military. Administration officials did not necessarily approve of such a result, but they were warned in advance that it might occur, and their policy contained no safeguards against this eventuality.

3. As the lack of meaningful economic progress in Latin America resulted in continued social unrest, the administration's response was to deemphasize the socio-economic origins of such unrest, and to define it instead as part of an externally sponsored, "subversive" challenge to "free world" security. Under this definition, both social disruptions and nationalist impulses became equivalent to communist subversion, though in actuality nationalist groups were far more powerful than the communists, were often hostile to communists, and in any event pursued goals and ideals which had a life of their own, independent of any communist doctrine. By adopting its own definition of social unrest, however, the Truman administration was able to rationalize its program of military assistance to repressive, dictatorial

regimes in a number of countries. During the Korean War years, Truman's policies increasingly emphasized military protection of Latin American governments against social unrest, now redefined as subversion. Military aid to Latin America increased markedly during Truman's last year in office. The administration also used its military aid program as a vehicle to limit Latin American trade with socialist bloc nations, and thereby to tie Latin America even closer to the U.S. economically.

4. In short, while Truman's overall commitment was to the maintenance of an Open World, and thus to the prevention of closed Great Power spheres of influence, U.S. military, political, and economic policies in Latin America actually worked to secure a U.S. sphere of influence by eliminating both competing foreign powers and competing economic and political ideologies. Under the Truman administration, the United States worked to secure a Closed Hemisphere in an otherwise Open World.

NOTES

1. Luís Alberto Sánchez, "What's Left of Inter-Americanism?," in *Inter-American*, January 1945, pp. 13–14.

2. For Rockefeller's statement, see U.S. Congress, House Ways and Means Committee, *Hearings on the Extension of the Reciprocal Trade Act, 1945* (Washington, D.C., 1945), p. 377. See also Seymour Harris, ed., *Economic Problems of Latin America* (New York, 1944), p. 37.

3. Quoted in Bryce Wood, *The Making of the Good Neighbor Policy* (New York, 1961), p. 359.

4. The Export-Import Bank held 50 per cent of the voting stock of the Ecuadorean and Bolivian *fomentos*, and 100 per cent of the stock of the Haitian Development Corporation. See discussion of this practice in George Soule, David Efron, and Norman Ness, *Latin America in the Future World* (New York, 1945), pp. 273ff. On the establishment of the Inter-American Development Commission, see File 710.Dev.Com., Document No. 1 (hereafter cited as 710.Dev.Com./1), Record Group 59, Department of State Archives, Washington, D.C. (hereafter DSA).

5. The Roosevelt administration's efforts to set up an Inter-American Bank can be traced in 710.Bank/1-255, DSA.

6. On the Brazilian loan, see memo by Simon G. Hanson, October 21, 1940, in Records of the Office of Inter-American Affairs, Entry No. 17, File entitled "Brazil—Steel," RG229, National Archives, Washington, D.C. (hereafter OIAA:17:Brazil—Steel). Text of Johnston's radio address is in OIAA:24:Conference, National Commissions, IADC. His remark on the "American Century" is quoted in the *South American Journal* (London), March 11, 1944, p. 150.

7. Some New Dealers were even talking about opening up the Soviet economy to an invasion by U.S. exports. See Lloyd Gardner, *Economic Aspects of New Deal Diplomacy* (Madison, Wisc., 1964), pp. 314–315. Imbued with such global ambitions, U.S. policy-makers naturally assumed that Latin America, the traditional "back yard" of U.S. foreign policy, would be easily integrated into the Open World economy.

8. Statement by Hon. William L. Clayton, in U.S. Congress, Senate, Committee on Foreign Relations, *Hearings on the Nominations of Joseph C. Grew, Nelson A. Rockefeller, W. L. Clayton, Archibald MacLeish, Brig. Gen. Julius C. Holmes, and James C. Dunn, December 12, 13, 1944* (Washington, D.C., 1944), p. 67. Also see Henry R. Luce, *The American Century* (New York, 1941), p. 38.

9. For Morgenthau's comment, see Morgenthau to President Roosevelt, May 16, 1942, in Official File 229, Franklin D. Roosevelt Library, Hyde Park, New York.

10. See the texts of the Colombian and North American resolutions in U.S. Department of State, Conference Series No. 85, *Report of the Delegation of the United States of America to the Inter-American Conference on Problems of War and Peace, Mexico City, February 21–March 8, 1945* (Washington, D.C., 1946), pp. 216–217, 275–276.

11. *Ibid.,* pp. 277–280.

12. See text of Clayton's speech in *Department of State Bulletin* (hereafter *SDB*), XII (March 4, 1945), 334–338.

13. See discussion of the Colombian proposal in Ruth Russell, *A History of the United Nations Charter* (Washington, D.C., 1958), p. 561.

14. For a specific commentary on the question of Russian behavior in Eastern Europe, see memo prepared for the Council on Foreign Relations in November 1944 by Columbia University political scientist Grayson Kirk, in Council on Foreign Relations, *Studies of American Interests in the War and the Peace* (New York, 1945), Armaments Series, No. A-B 119, November 28, 1944, p. 6.

15. The text of the declaration is in *SDB*, XII (March 4, 1945), 339–340.

16. Rockefeller's active involvement in the deliberations of the U.S. delegation can be seen clearly in the minutes of the delegation meetings, published in U.S. Department of State, *Foreign Relations of the United States* (hereafter *FR*), *1945* (Washington, D.C., 1967), I, 385ff. The Vandenberg letter is dated May 5, 1945, and is available in the Correspondence File, Arthur H. Vandenberg Papers, William L. Clements Library, Ann Arbor, Michigan. For further discussion of the Vandenberg letter, see *FR, 1945*, I, 617ff; Arthur H. Vandenberg, Jr., ed., *The Private Papers of Senator Vandenberg* (Boston, 1952), pp. 186ff; and Joe Alex Morris, *Nelson Rockefeller* (New York, 1960), pp. 218–220.

17. *FR, 1945,* I, 591, 594.

18. See transcript of telephone conversation between Stimson in Washington and John McCloy in San Francisco, May 8, 1945, in Henry L. Stimson Manuscripts, Yale University Library, New Haven, Connecticut.

19. Stimson Diary, May 2, 1945, and Stimson-McCloy transcript, both in Stimson MSS.

20. For background material on the Argentine question, including Truman's views, see Russell, *U.N. Charter,* pp. 571–572, 632.

21. See *New York Times,* May 1, 1945, and *Washington Post,* May 1, 1945. Also see Vandenberg's unpublished San Francisco Diary, April 30, 1945, in Vandenberg MSS.

22. For the comment on the "peanut nations," see Donald M. Dozer, *Are We Good Neighbors?* (Gainesville, Fla., 1961), p. 200. Also see Vandenberg Diary, June 23, 1945, Vandenberg MSS.

23. *FR, 1945,* I, 722. Also Vandenberg Diary, May 19, 1945, Vandenberg MSS.

24. Stimson-McCloy transcript, May 8, 1945, Stimson MSS.

25. Corrigan to Secretary of State Hull, Caracas, March 31, 1944, in 831.504/132, DSA; also Berle to President Truman, Rio de Janeiro, August 13, 1945, in Official File 606, Harry S. Truman Manuscripts, Harry S. Truman Library, Independence, Missouri (hereafter OF 606, HST MSS).

26. Vandenberg to Byrnes, August 3, 1945, Correspondence File, Vandenberg MSS.

27. U.S. Congress, House Foreign Affairs Committee, *Hearings on Inter-American Military Cooperation Act, 1946* (Washington, D.C., 1946), pp. 3, 17.

28. U.S. Congress, House Foreign Affairs Committee, *Hearings on Inter-American Military Cooperation Act, 1947* (Washington, D.C., 1947), pp. 26, 43–44.

29. For comments on Rockefeller and the Warren-Brett mission, see *Inter-American,* May 1945, "News Survey of the Month."

30. See text of Stettinius' statement in *New York Times,* May 29, 1945, p. 8.

31. One State Department official commented privately that Rockefeller had been "blown through the roof" of the State Department by the attacks of the *New York Times* and the *Washington Post.* See memo of a conversation between Carl Spaeth and Charles Burrows of the Buenos Aires Embassy staff, in Washington, June 24, 1946, in George S. Messersmith Papers, University of Delaware Library, Newark, Delaware. The public relations explanation of the Braden-for-Rockefeller exchange was confirmed for me by former Assistant Secretary of State Adolf Berle in an interview in New York City, March 28, 1967.

32. For Braden's public statement, see *New York Times,* August 26, 1945. The information on Braden's private efforts was supplied to me by Mr. Braden in an interview in New York City, March 28, 1967.

33. Vandenberg to Howard, October 12, 1945, in Correspondence File, Vandenberg MSS. Also see *Congressional Record,* XCI, Part 8, 9899–9908.

34. Quoted in George Messersmith to William Pawley, February 26, 1947, in Messersmith MSS.

35. A full discussion of the Messersmith appointment and its political significance can be found in Messersmith's unpublished manuscript of his Memoirs, Vol. II, No. 20, in Messersmith MSS.

36. See account of Vandenberg's speech in *New York World-Telegram*, January 12, 1947. The information on Braden's resignation is from Braden interview, March 28, 1967.

37. For the Javits-Marshall exchange, see *Hearings on Inter-American Military Cooperation Act, 1947*, p. 17. The Act evidently died in committee because many committee members were not yet ready to approve the kind of vague authority and loose controls provided in the draft bill. Some also objected to the increased militarization of Latin America which the bill portended. See, for example, statement by Rep. Helen Gahagan Douglas of California, *ibid.*, p. 49. For details of the Rio negotiations, see U.S. Department of State, *Report of the Delegation of the United States of America to the Inter-American Conference for the Maintenance of Continental Peace and Security, Quitandinha, Brazil, August 15–September 2, 1947* (Washington, D.C., 1947).

38. See announcements of military assistance agreements with Brazil, Argentina, Colombia, and Peru, respectively, in *SDB*, XIX (August 15, October 17, 1948), 211–212, 494; *ibid.*, XX (March 6, 1949), 303; and *ibid.*, XXI (July 11, 1949), 38.

39. Notes by Collins of UPI, of Braden's press conference of September 18, 1945, Buenos Aires, in Messersmith MSS. In an interview with me, Braden recalled that he had sent two long dispatches to the State Department warning that Perón was working with the Argentine communists. These dispatches never reached Secretary Byrnes, however; Braden noted that they had probably been intercepted by communists in the State Department. Braden interview, March 28, 1967.

40. U.S. Department of State, Inter-American Series No. 32, *Private Enterprise in the Development of the Americas,* An Address by Assistant Secretary Braden before the Executives' Club of Chicago, September 13, 1946 (Washington, D.C., 1946), pp. 2–3, 5. See also Braden's article, "Latin American Industrialization and Foreign Trade," in Lloyd J. Hughlett, ed., *Industrialization of Latin America* (New York, 1946), pp. 486–493. "Either the exaggerated nationalisms now so prevalent everywhere must be completely extirpated from relations between peoples," Braden wrote, "or those nationalisms will prevent reconstruction, destroy trade and investment, lower living standards, and again imperil civilization."

41. *Private Enterprise in the Development of the Americas,* pp. 7–9. Export-Import Bank loans to Latin America for development projects totaled less than $600 million in the nine years from fiscal 1946 through fiscal 1954, inclusive. See Raymond Mikesell, *Foreign Investments in Latin America* (Washington, D.C., 1955), pp. 21–22. In contrast, the 1946 U.S. loan to Britain amounted to over $3 billion.

42. The text of the Dulles speech is enclosed in Dulles to Vandenberg, January 29, 1947, in Correspondence File, Vandenberg MSS. Quotes are from pp. 12 and 15 of text.

43. Text of Snyder's speech, dated December 6, 1947, is in Box 24 (Snyder Correspondence), Jesse Jones Papers, Library of Congress, Washington,

D.C. Also see Address by Paul H. Nitze, Deputy Assistant Secretary of State for Economic Affairs, to Boston Conference on Distribution, October 25, 1948, in *SDB*, XIX (November 7, 1948), 579.

44. U.S. Department of State, *Ninth International Conference of American States, Report of the Delegation of the United States of America* (Washington, D.C., 1948), pp. 64, 239. See text of Marshall's speech to the full conference, *ibid.*, pp. 309–317.

45. *SDB*, XVIII (April 25, 1948), 548–549.

46. *Ninth International Conference of American States, Report . . . ,* pp. 64, 66, 209, 215–216, 239.

47. See Edwin Lieuwen, *Arms and Politics in Latin America* (New York, 1961), pp. 208–209, for comment on the Soviet military "threat."

48. For statistics on total Export-Import Bank loans, see n. 41 above; also Pawley to President Truman, Rio de Janeiro, February 17, 1948, in OF27-B, "Export-Import Bank (1945–1949)," HST MSS. On the $125 million credit to the Perón regime, see address by Rollin S. Atwood, Director, Office of North and West Coast Affairs, American Republics Area, Department of State, before Export Managers' Club, New York City, May 2, 1950, in *SDB*, XXII (May 22, 1950), 801–803; see also State Department press release of May 17, 1950, on "Factors in Economic Relations with Argentina," *ibid.*, pp. 860–861.

49. *Ibid.*, XX (June 12, 1949), 761, and XXIII (December 25, 1950), 1017.

50. United Nations, Department of Economic and Social Affairs, *Foreign Capital in Latin America* (United Nations, N.Y., 1955), pp. 145–146. Also Mikesell, *Foreign Investments*, p. 16.

51. IMF study cited in *Foreign Capital in Latin America*, p. 11. For income and investment figures, see *ibid.*, Tables XVII, XXVIII, pp. 160, 164. The total income figure is given in Table XXVIII, while the total investment figure is obtained by adding the figure given in Table XXVIII, which excludes reinvested earnings of subsidiaries, to the figures in Table XVII, which give such reinvestments for the years 1946 to 1951, inclusive.

52. Organization of American States, *Annals*, I, No. 1 (1949), 58–59.

53. Laurence Duggan, *The Americas: The Search for Hemisphere Security* (New York, 1949), p. 214.

54. For an excellent discussion of the social and economic conditions underlying the *Bogotazo*, see Vernon Lee Fluharty, *Dance of the Millions: Military Rule and the Social Revolution in Colombia, 1930–1956* (Pittsburgh, 1957), pp. 91ff.

55. See, for example, discussion of events in Brazil and Colombia in Lieuwen, *Arms and Politics*, pp. 230–231.

56. For Truman's statement of opposition to military coups, see *ibid.*, p. 234. Also see *Hearings on Inter-American Military Cooperation Act, 1946*, p. 34.

57. *Ibid.*, 1947, p. 113. Note also the opposition to the program expressed by Latin American civilian leaders who feared "political adventurism by the military," cited in Lieuwen, *Arms and Politics*, pp. 236–237.

58. *SDB*, XVIII (May 30, 1948), 715.

59. McCloy to Stimson, May 14, 1948, Stimson MSS; also J. Lloyd Mecham, *The United States and Inter-American Security, 1889–1960* (Aus-

tin, Tex., 1961), p. 301. After 1948 the "communist threat" became an increasingly convenient explanation for the internal problems that beset Latin American nations. In April 1950, Assistant Secretary of State Edward Miller told the Pan American Society of New England: "The basic situation in the hemisphere today is this. The 21 American states together face the challenge of Communist political aggression against the hemisphere." *SDB*, XXII (May 15, 1950), 770. Miller gave no examples in support of his assertion.

60. *Ibid.*, XXIV (January 1, 1951), 8.
61. *Ibid.*, XXIV (April 9, 1951), 567, 573.
62. *Ibid.*, XXIV (April 16, 1951), 608–609.
63. Different sources give different figures for U.S. military aid to Latin America in fiscal year 1953. Harold A. Hovey, *United States Military Assistance* (New York, 1965), p. 51, gives a figure of $11.2 million; Lieuwen, *Arms and Politics*, p. 202, gives a figure of $65.2 million. The higher figure apparently includes shipments of surplus stocks. On limiting trade with the Soviet bloc, see *ibid.*, p. 201.
64. For full details of the Guatemalan invasion, see Thomas Wise and David Ross, *The Invisible Government* (New York, 1964); also see John Gerassi, *The Great Fear in Latin America* (New York, 1965), pp. 181–183, 240–242.
65. *Hearings on Inter-American Military Cooperation Act, 1947*, p. 6.

ATHAN THEOHARIS

The Rhetoric of Politics: Foreign Policy, Internal Security, and Domestic Politics in the Truman Era, 1945–1950

AMERICAN POLITICS after World War II poses an intriguing problem for the historian of the Cold War: the emergence of McCarthyism and the effectiveness after 1950 of the senator and his cohorts, the McCarthyites.[1] How does one explain the different political objectives of McCarthy's principal exponents (political conservatives) and a major source of his popular support (small businessmen, professionals, urban workers, and members of ethnic groups)? While the exponents of McCarthyism were anti-progressive and sought to undercut reform, these other supporters rejected attacks that simply disparaged the New

I wish to express my appreciation to the Truman Institute for National and International Affairs and to Wayne State University for their support of my research, and to the University of Iowa, particularly Mrs. Emily Hartnell, for assistance in typing the manuscript. I am grateful for the editorial assistance and criticisms of Stanley Shapiro, Walter LaFeber, Richard Kirkendall, David Shannon, Otis Graham, Michael Rogin, and Ivan Dee.

Deal. Furthermore, each group had very different reasons for supporting the senator's concern with national security.

How did McCarthy successfully exploit tactics which earlier had failed for other conservatives? Since 1934 conservative congressmen (primarily Republicans) had accused the New Deal of being alien, subversive, and communistic. During World War II, and more openly from 1945 through 1948, these congressmen had extended their assault to the foreign policy decisions of the Roosevelt–Truman administrations.[2] But their charges of "softness toward communism," whether aimed at domestic or international policy, were not credible to a public that had come to revere the New Deal and support internationalism.

The success of the McCarthyites' attacks after 1950 poses another paradox in view of their earlier opposition to the Truman administration's foreign policy. Although their rhetoric was militantly anti-communist, most McCarthyites from 1946 through 1949 denounced such containment policies as foreign aid, the Truman Doctrine, the commitment of U.S. troops overseas, and NATO. They considered these military-economic responses too aggressive, an unwarranted overextension of American commitments. They saw the "communist threat" as primarily domestic, not international. After World War II they pressed for retrenchment; their conception of the proper national defense was not collective security but unilateral preparedness. Despite their militant posture, in their position on legislation the McCarthyites were cautious and restrained. They opposed the administration's policy of confrontation, preferring to conserve national resources and to deal with internal problems of subversion (by which they meant the New Deal outlook).[3]

The Truman administration's militant anti-Soviet policy from 1945 through 1950 (including the loyalty program, prosecution of the American Communist party leadership, and development of the containment policy) contrasted sharply with the McCarthyites' negativism. One might have expected the Truman administration, because it pursued an anti-communist course (in both international and internal security), to have been invulnerable to charges of vacillation, indecisiveness, laxity, or "soft-

ness toward communism." And one might have expected that,
when confronted by the McCarthyite assault, the Truman administration could have reviewed the McCarthyites' own record
on foreign policy from 1945 to 1950 to discredit such accusations.
In fact, the administration adopted this tactic. Its failure poses
the paradox in explaining the effectiveness of McCarthyism.[4]

Another problem for the historian lies in the conflicting positions of liberals (whether inside the Truman administration or
among its supporters) and conservative McCarthyites on democratic procedures and the right to dissent. More often after 1948
the liberals, not the McCarthyites, sought to restrict the political
dialogue, to define certain subjects as beyond the pale of responsible discussion. Asserting that they were protecting the national
security, administration supporters dismissed criticism as dangerous and subversive. They based their position on the separation
of powers and the need to protect individual rights, and affirmed
the President's right to refuse congressional requests for confidential information (loyalty reports or international agreements).
In contrast, the McCarthyites demanded an open, searching appraisal of foreign policy decisions and the internal security program. Their democratic posture, limited to national security
considerations, did not imply a tolerance of all dissent but was
restricted to legislative-executive relations. Thus they demanded
an end to executive secrecy, affirmed Congress' right of access
to all privileged information secured by the administration, and
asserted their right to share in decision-making, to review administration policy decisions, and to investigate federal personnel. Formally, the McCarthyites adopted a democratic stance
and rejected the doctrine of executive privilege or expertise.[5]

These contradictions and apparent inconsistencies make it
difficult to explain even the phenomenon of McCarthy, much
less his impact. The negative, irresponsible nature of the Mc-
Carthyite critique and the hysterical, conspiratorial tone of the
post-1950 policy debate have provided the basis for the currently accepted view, advanced by Daniel Bell, Richard Hof-
stader, *et al.*, of "status politics."[6] The "status" theorists see Mc-
Carthyism as an emotional, demagogic, backward-looking movement. According to this view, the McCarthyites, by resorting to

conspiratorial explanations, were able to capitalize on the disaffection of those Americans who were frustrated over their loss of status and incapable of understanding the complexities of the modern world.

Undeniably, popular anti-communism was often emotional, oversimplified, and took the conspiratorial view. But these features were not unique or consistent. More important, a shifting, aimless, nonideological quality characterized popular anticommunism. The shifts reflect not a definite set of principles but a response to specific events—or to the public perception of the meaning of those events. Americans in the immediate postwar period were, for the most part, anti-communist and anti-Soviet, despite memories of the wartime alliance. Postwar international developments and domestic differences, such as the conflict between communists and noncommunists within the labor and progressive movements, added to this distrust. Anti-communism did assume an ideological form among many American Catholics, a phenomenon due in great part to the Vatican's reaction to the atheistic materialism of communism and to communist restrictions on the Catholic Church in postwar Eastern Europe. But the emotional 'anti-communism of most Catholics and non-Catholics resulted from the tensions of the Cold War.

In 1945 and 1946 there had been distinct tolerance toward the Soviet Union and American Communists, a tolerance that was not to last in succeeding years. In March (55 per cent to 31 per cent) and September (54 per cent to 30 per cent) 1945, the public remained confident that U.S.-Soviet cooperation could be sustained. This trust fluctuated in 1946 and 1947 but remained, as did public support for summit diplomacy or the United Nations as instruments for preserving the peace. Even the initial public assessment of the Truman Doctrine (March 1947) focused on nonmilitary (economic or political) policy options. Most Americans approved of the Truman Doctrine (57 per cent to 32 per cent, 12 per cent no opinion), supported sending civilian experts to Greece to supervise the handling of aid (83 per cent to 14 per cent, 3 per cent no opinion), yet opposed sending military experts to assist the Greek armed forces (54 per cent to 37 per cent, 9 per cent no opinion). Similarly, while suspicious of American Communists, the public was less rigid than in later years: in 1945 it advocated surveillance or was either indifferent or tolerant. Moreover, the public distinguished between communists and radicals. As late as October 1947, 36 per cent supported and 41 per cent opposed legislation prohibiting communist sympathizers from holding public office.[7]

This ambivalence reflects the pragmatic character of popular anti-communism as it was shaped by certain crises. From 1945 through 1947 the tone of presidential statements and news stories about U.S.-Soviet relations was conciliatory and reasonably tolerant. The Yalta, Potsdam, and Moscow conferences and the Sino-Soviet treaty of August 1945 were reported with great enthusiasm. Even *Time* magazine extolled Yalta as "the most important conference of the century," praised its spirit of co-operation as providing the basis for a lasting peace, and claimed that no citizen of the United States, the Soviet Union, or Great Britain could charge that his nation's interests had been "sold down the river."[8]

This tolerance was an early victim of the Cold War. The information presented to the public after 1947, which in turn shaped the public's perception of the Soviet Union and American Communists, became increasingly anti-communist. This shift in perception and the dominant anti-communist rhetoric contributed to the McCarthyite impact after 1950.

The Bell-Hofstadter analysis is deficient, on the one hand, because it is ahistorical in ignoring the peculiar characteristics of the McCarthyites (the timing of their impact) and, on the other, because it fails to examine the direction of the postwar policy debate. The aim of this essay is to offer another evaluation, to view McCarthyism not as an aberration but as a development consistent with the rhetoric of the postwar political debate.

One of my basic assumptions is that President Truman's manner of defining the objectives of American policy radically altered the rhetoric of American politics; that Truman's statements and decisions structured the national security debate, affecting the understanding of the American public and thus their expectations and fears. It is true that public attitudes, already anti-communist, were altered by the events around which controversy sharpened—Soviet foreign policy and subversion. But the emotional anti-communism of the postwar years was shaped by Truman's depiction of Soviet motives and U.S. policy options, his portrayal of U.S. actions as wholly altruistic, and his preference for military power over accommodation.

Second, I contend that McCarthyism was made possible by the intensification of the Cold War. A heightened concern over national security matters transformed domestic priorities and radically changed many of the basic tenets of American politics. And McCarthyism derived its impact from these new tenets—which provided the rationale for containment and the loyalty program. The nature of these policies—because they conceived of radicalism, whether at home or abroad, as potentially subversive, because they denied the legitimacy of Soviet power and strategic objectives, and because they saw communism as monolithic, alien, and unpopular—served to legitimize conservative, status quo politics.

Third, McCarthyism was consistent with this new Cold War rhetoric. Administration policy, both domestic and foreign, reacted against disruptive change. Administration policy statements sought scapegoats, not solutions, attempted to preclude, not adapt to, change, and were vague in defining terms like "subversion," "disloyalty," and "aggression." Moreover, the *ad hoc* nature of administration policy responses, and the reversal of Franklin Roosevelt's priorities, demanded that public support be secured. To arouse the public to accept a more interventionist role in the immediate postwar years required that the administration resort to the use of anti-communist symbols in almost a reflex fashion. At the same time, the administration failed to delineate the limits of American power or the specific nature of the communist threat.

As one result, the interests of the American public gradually shifted during the postwar years from a concern over socio-economic reform to an obsession with the communist threat to national security. With the passage of time, and the fears of a catastrophic nuclear war or an endless Cold War, rigidity and intolerance became characteristic of the American polity. A policy of firmness, of seeking to negotiate from positions of strength, may have been at first restrained and realistic, but it was soon transformed into a rhetoric wherein all disagreements became tests of American will or courage. Self-esteem became self-righteous arrogance. And political conservatives, by centering their protest on the administration's inability to safeguard national security (instead of attacking New Deal reforms), acquired new respectability and influence.

Finally, the timing of McCarthy's attack was propitious—immediately after the trials of Alger Hiss and Judith Coplon, the Soviet explosion of an atomic bomb, the success of the Chinese Communists, the arrest of the Rosenbergs, and the outbreak of the Korean War. These events seemingly confirmed the existence of an internal security threat. Through misleading specific charges, McCarthy was able to capitalize on this malaise and concern.

I

President Truman's leadership marked a sharp break from that of Franklin Roosevelt and altered the focus of the domestic political debate. Involved principally in domestic affairs as a senator and as Vice-President, Truman had a limited understanding of the complexities of international politics. He had not participated in the formulation or development of Roosevelt's foreign policy. Nor, as President, did Truman seem to understand Roosevelt's attempts at cooperation with the Soviet Union. Clearly anti-Soviet and a "hard-liner" diplomatically, Truman initially was a dependent President, often relying unquestioningly on his advisers. Because of the new President's proclivities and suspicions, the hard-liners in the State Department and in the cabinet (men such as Averell Harriman, James Forrestal, and William Leahy, who opposed Roosevelt's conciliatory approach to the Soviet Union) found a receptive ear for their espousal of confrontation rather than concession. Though Truman publicly expressed allegiance to Roosevelt's diplomacy and agreements, his priorities differed, and his administration's conception of Roosevelt's policy—for example, the meaning of the Yalta agreements—changed significantly. Instead of quiet, flexible diplomacy, Truman emphasized military strength and adopted a rigid interpretation of past U.S.-Soviet agreements.

The first instance of this shift occurred in April 1945, when Truman admonished Soviet Foreign Minister Molotov that the Soviet Union had violated the Yalta provisions concerning Poland.[9] Less obvious to the Soviet Union and to the American public, on May 12—four days after the German surrender—administration personnel began a reappraisal of the United States commitment to the Yalta Far Eastern agreements.[10] And in a December 19, 1945, special message to Congress, Truman recommended the enactment (to "preserve" the peace) of universal military training and the development of strong military forces.[11]

In this message the President spelled out the grave dangers of disarmament. Noting that 1.5 million veterans were being discharged each month, Truman called for the establishment of universal military training

> at the *earliest possible moment* to provide a reserve upon which we can draw if, unhappily, it should become necessary. A grave responsibility will rest upon the Congress if it continues to delay this *most important and urgent measure.* . . . Unification . . . along with universal training—[is essential to] the development of a comprehensive and continuous program for our future safety and for the peace and security of the world.[12]

Recalling the recent war experience, Truman further argued that

> the desire for peace is futile unless there is enough *strength* ready and willing to *enforce* that desire in *any* emergency. Among the things that have *encouraged aggression* and the spread of war in the past have been the unwillingness of the United States realistically to face the fact, and her refusal to fortify her *arms of peace before* the forces of aggression could gather in strength. [The future of world peace] will depend upon whether or not the United States is willing to maintain the *physical* strength necessary to act as *a safeguard against any future aggressor.*[13]

The administration, aware of public pressures for demobilization and fears that a policy based on military strength might frustrate a lasting settlement and lead only to a new arms race, sought to persuade the public to accept the need for a strengthened military. It had to convince the American people that the Soviet Union was untrustworthy and that only a policy based on firmness, not international cooperation or diplomatic compromise, could effectively preserve the peace. Simultaneously, the administration had to assure the people that its approach was consistent with Roosevelt's policies. These conflicting objectives contributed to a vacillating diplomacy.

Thus, when seeking public and congressional support in 1945, Truman claimed that his foreign policy was liberal, internationalist, and anti-totalitarian (by implication only, anti-Soviet). While he was reluctant after Potsdam to meet with Stalin, he publicly emphasized the importance of mutual cooperation and understanding for the attainment of a "just" peace. Economic and social injustice, the President said, were the causes of war and to attain peace trade and political barriers must be broken.[14]

Increasingly during 1946 and 1947—particularly after the 1946 congressional election—the themes of liberalism and internationalism faded into the background. After the election the administration confronted a hostile, Republican-dominated Congress, whose leadership bitterly opposed the New Deal and had grave doubts about Roosevelt's international commitments and conciliatory policy toward the Soviets. Thereafter, Truman emphasized the national interest, not simply internationalism, adopted a more openly anti-communist stance, and no longer defended his policies as a continuation of Roosevelt's but as a response to specific contemporary crises. He stressed the need to "win the peace" (not negotiate a compromise peace) and the importance of strength for the attainment of a "just" peace (never defined).

In contrast to later years, Truman in 1946–1947 defined economic problems, such as trade barriers and underdevelopment, as the major obstacles to a lasting peace—not ideological differences between nations. When he delineated the guidelines for the administration's China policy, the President said the United States had no intention of interfering in the "internal" conflict between the Nationalists and Communists.[15]

This emphasis on economic priorities was forcefully affirmed by the President in a special message to Congress on May 6, 1946 (reiterated on May 26, 1947), concerning military cooperation with other American states. This aid, Truman asserted, was intended only to maintain peace and security. The United States would not participate in programs of indiscriminate military aid, contribute to an arms race, or help those who might use weapons of war "to oppose the peaceful and democratic principles to which the United States and other American nations have so often subscribed." He added:

> In executing this program it will be borne in mind, moreover, that it is the policy of this Government to encourage the establishment of sound economic conditions in the other American republics. . . . Operations under the proposed legislation will be conducted with full and constant awareness that no encouragement should be given to the imposition upon other people of any useless burden of armaments which would handicap the economic improvement which all countries so strongly desire.[16]

Seeking support in 1946 for the British loan[17] and in 1947 for the Truman Doctrine[18] and the Marshall Plan,[19] the President stressed the economic aspects of his policy proposals. Indeed, the Truman Doctrine was first presented as a program intended to insure economic aid for reconstruction and development. Truman never discounted the effect of military conflict in frustrating economic recovery, but he nonetheless defined the major objective of his program for Greece as the resolution of economic chaos and underdevelopment.* He pointedly emphasized this priority when responding to a question posed during a special conference on May 13, 1947, with the Association of Radio News Analysts. Asked whether the military or economic aspect of the Greco-Turkish aid proposal was "most important at the present moment," the President replied that

> the internal construction and the restoration to a peacetime economy is what we principally are interested in, on a free basis. . . . My idea is the restoration of a peacetime economy in these

*Most people believed this to be the purpose of U.S. aid, despite criticisms of the military character of the doctrine voiced by liberals and many commentators. See the poll cited on page 199.

countries, with the hope that they will themselves inaugurate a free government that will be for the benefit of the people.[20]

The Truman Doctrine marked a major shift in the administration's explanation of its policy objectives. First, the doctrine dramatically established active American involvement in postwar international affairs and extended the definition of events affecting the national security to include peacetime political developments outside the Western Hemisphere. By this definition, changes in Europe or Asia that altered American or Soviet influence came to be represented in national security terms (the "domino theory"). The United States, because it was *in* the world, had to act to insure that international change was "favorable" (never explicitly defined) to its interests. Second, the doctrine marked the explicit repudiation of Roosevelt's tactics of accommodation. Truman continued publicly to emphasize the importance of cooperation, understanding, and the United Nations; but his actions were unilateral and intended to preserve order and stability through a military-based policy.

In soliciting congressional and public support for the doctrine, Truman structured the future political debate. The urgent tone of his covertly anti-Soviet message to the joint session of Congress on March 12, 1947, was intended to silence criticisms either that the policy was unduly aggressive or that it was unnecessary. In effect, Truman's message heightened public fears about the nature of the Soviet threat to the national security and contributed to a parochial, self-righteous nationalism. Vague and sweeping in tone, the message to Congress provided an American definition of peace, aggression, and internationalism: American military aid was peaceful; American unilateral action was consistent with the United Nations Charter; American support of the monarchy in the Greek civil war was not interventionist.

By 1948, Truman, when defining administration policy objectives, had shifted to emphasize the importance of military strength for the attainment of peace, warning: "We must not fall victim to the insidious propaganda that peace can be obtained solely by wanting peace." In contrast to previous allusions to the Soviet Union, he singled out the Soviets as the real obstacle to peace.* He charged that the Soviets' objective, reflected in their actions in Eastern Europe, was to subjugate all of Europe. Truman confidently predicted that the combination of the European Recovery Program and military rearmament would achieve peace and that the United States "would raise the Iron Curtain by peaceable means."[21]

By 1948 the emphasis of the administration's policy toward Greece had also changed dramatically. "Owing to Communist obstruction," Truman contended, measures intended to promote Greece's economic recovery would have to be postponed until internal security had been established. The primary policy objective was now to aid the Greek government against an armed, foreign-supported "minority." Policy rhetoric assumed a militaristic form; gone was the earlier emphasis on removing the causes of poverty and revolutionary sentiment.[22]

Western European political-economic problems in 1948, particularly the prospect of a communist electoral success in Italy,

*Until 1948 Truman had not adopted a public posture of hostility toward the Soviet Union but had counseled patience and good faith. Not all administration spokesmen preserved the same silence. Many (Forrestal, James F. Byrnes, Harriman, Will Clayton, Dean Acheson, and Tom Clark), in public speeches or congressional and press briefings, were openly anti-Soviet. Thus Truman's 1948 reference to the Soviet Union marked a rhetorical and not a policy shift. Correspondingly, this shift was related to a change in public attitudes toward Soviet intentions. Whereas in 1945 only a slim majority felt that the Soviet Union was a peace-loving nation interested in defense (38.6 per cent to 37.8 per cent, 8.4 per cent no opinion), this sentiment had radically changed by September 1947 (12 per cent to 66 per cent). Although more suspicious, the public's assessment of Truman's Soviet policy remained ambivalent, confused, and contradictory. Responding to polls conducted in 1947 and 1948, 73 per cent thought this policy was too soft, 3 per cent too tough, and 11 per cent about right, with 13 per cent expressing no opinion. At the same time, only 17 per cent felt that Truman was giving in to the Russians, 53 per cent that he was against giving in, 4 per cent had no position, and 26 per cent didn't know (*Public Opinion Quarterly* [hereafter *POQ*], IX, 386-388; X, 665-667; XII, 159, 354, 359). In these and other public opinion data cited in this essay, the percentages sometimes do not add up to 100 because I have chosen to eliminate miscellaneous responses ("don't know," "undecided," and so forth) where they do not bear directly on the significance of the public response.

were similarly depicted. Truman affirmed that the main threat to Western Europe was internal subversion, defined as the political attempt of Soviet "agents" (the Communist party) to dominate Western Europe by exploiting the misery, devastation, and chaos caused by World War II. This subversive effort, Truman claimed, affected the national security of the United States directly.

At the same time, the President sought to force Congress to support military aid by emphasizing Western Europe's critical importance for the national security. His statements were open-ended, lacking in a sense of limits to American power, and loaded with emotive adjectives. Thus, in a special message to Congress on March 17, 1948, after the Czechoslovakian crisis (an event that had a dramatic impact on the public's and the administration's perceptions of Soviet intent*), Truman argued:

> I am here today to report to you on the *critical* nature of the situation in Europe and to recommend action for your consideration.
>
> Rapid changes are taking place in Europe which *affect* our foreign and our national security. There is an *increasing threat* to nations which are striving to maintain a form of government which grants freedom to its citizens. The United States is deeply concerned with the survival of freedom in those nations. It is of *vital importance* that we act *now*. . . .
>
> While economic recovery in Europe is essential, measures for economic rehabilitation are not enough. The free nations of Europe realize that economic recovery, if it is to succeed, must be afforded *some* measure of protection against *internal* and external *aggression*.[23]

---

*The public response was more emotional shock than a demand for U.S. action. In a February poll (before the crisis), when questioned whether the United States should intervene militarily to prevent a takeover by Italian Communists, 28.3 per cent supported military intervention, 52.2 per cent did not (*POQ*, XII, 537). The very framing of this question might have programmed a sharper anti-communist response. By July public fears had sharpened considerably: 54 per cent said yes, 39 per cent said no, and 7 per cent were undecided as to whether the United States should attempt to stop any Russian effort to control bordering territory in Europe or Asia (*POQ*, XII, 577). Again the question programmed an anti-communist response. In contrast to the February poll, however, Russian and not Italian communism had been identified.

This new approach interpreted revolutionary or political change (potentially violent, radical in effect, and using subversive means) as inspired and directed by alien minorities; further, any disruptive change, political or military, threatened the security of both that nation *and* the United States. National security thus came to depend on preserving the status quo, without distinction between political pressure and overt aggression. The administration emphasized the need for order and stability, for nonviolent political change within Western-style democratic institutions (constitutionalism and safeguards for individual liberties and private property). This inherently conservative, status-quo-oriented assessment of proper international change, moreover, implied that an effective counterrevolutionary or counter-subversive policy could be devised with active American support. A policy of firmness could avert change, and communization could be defeated because communist subversive "agents" lacked a popular, national base. Truman's depiction of revolutionary change as endangering American security provided a model that predetermined the American response. Using the "appeasement" imagery of Munich, he sought to capitalize on the very real, if simplistic, public concern over the causes of international conflict.*

Shifting its policy emphasis sharply from the earlier focus on economic aid, beginning in 1949 the administration stressed the need for strengthening Western military defenses. In justifying the formation of NATO, however, the administration did not con-

---

*A June 1948 poll captured this concern. A definite sentiment in favor of a firmer policy toward the Soviet Union emerged, though the public preferred diplomatic to military means. Questioned about U.S. policy toward the Soviets, 10 per cent thought the administration should be more willing to compromise, 26 per cent considered policy about right, 53 per cent supported a firmer policy, while 11 per cent were undecided. Of those who advocated a firmer policy, only 6 per cent supported strengthening the armed forces, 13 per cent a stronger diplomatic posture, and 12 per cent the use of economic pressure. Despite this apparent militancy in May, 63 per cent supported, 28 per cent opposed, and 9 per cent had no opinion on the desirability of a conference between the United States and the Soviet Union to work out terms for peace (*POQ*, XII, 761–762; XIII, 163–164).

tend that it would enable the United States to wage war more effectively. Rather, it depicted NATO as a diplomatic deterrent to Soviet expansion; through military cooperation the alliance would restrain possible Soviet aggression and thus avert a military or political move that might lead to war.* War could only be prevented, Truman argued, by providing enough warning signals to insure that would-be aggressors would not misinterpret concession as weakness. Seeking to document this position, he maintained that American resolve and involvement could have prevented World Wars I and II. The President further charged that diplomatic means alone could not prevent aggression because Soviet compliance with formal agreements was based simply on expediency. In the absence of countervailing power, a Soviet promise was not worth the paper it was written on. In contrast to his earlier reticence, Truman openly disparaged the suggestion for another Big Three conference.[24]

In Europe the policy of confronting revolution or radicalism with economic aid and military-diplomatic support succeeded. The crisis in Europe, with the prospect of communist electoral success in Italy and France, or revolutionary success in Greece, resulted primarily from the devastating impact of World War II. U.S. aid was thus the determining factor in preserving the status quo. The success of the containment policy in averting the communization of Europe (whether "expansion" or "subversion"), in the absence of presidential leadership which noted the uniqueness of the European situation or the limits of American influence, created for the American public distinct expectations about American foreign policy. The European experience

*In testimony before the Senate on the NATO treaty, both Secretary of State Dean Acheson and Army Chief of Staff Omar Bradley stressed this political aspect. See U.S., Senate Committee on Foreign Relations, *Hearings on the North Atlantic Treaty*, 81st Cong., 1st sess., 1949, pp. 47, 292. In May 1949, 27 per cent thought NATO increased the chances of war with the Soviet Union, 43 per cent that it decreased them, 11 per cent that it would make no difference, and 23 per cent had no opinion. In addition, 53 per cent conceived of NATO as a defensive pact, only 5 per cent as an alliance for an attack on the Soviet Union, 7 per cent had no opinion, while 35 per cent were unfamiliar with the alliance (*POQ*, XIII, 548–550).

thereby established the standards by which the administration's Far Eastern policy came to be judged.

America's Far Eastern policy before 1948, in contrast to its European policy, had not been a major public concern. Nonetheless, the rationale for that policy remained the same: to avert revolution or the extension of Soviet influence. The administration had relied primarily on political and diplomatic means during this period. By 1948 that policy had failed in China, and in Korea occupation zones had become political boundaries. Truman was not resigned to these developments and, emphasizing the same containment objectives, stressed the strategic importance of the Far East for the national security. Specifically, in a special message to Congress on June 7, 1949, requesting continued economic aid for South Korea, Truman represented that nation as a "testing ground" for communism and democracy. He argued:

> The survival and progress of the Republic [of South Korea] toward a self-supporting, stable economy . . . will encourage the people of southern and southeastern Asia and the islands of the Pacific to resist and reject the communist propaganda with which they are besieged. Moreover, the Korean Republic, by demonstrating the success and tenacity of democracy in resisting communism, will stand as a beacon to the people of northern Asia in resisting the control of the communist forces which have overrun them.[25]

After the defeat in the House of the Korean Aid Bill in January 1950, the administration warned that failure to help Korea would inevitably lead the United States into a future war in less advantageous circumstances. In a letter to the President (made public by the White House), Secretary of State Dean Acheson called the House action "disastrous for the foreign policy of the United States," and argued:

> This action, if not quickly repaired, will have *the most far-reaching effects* upon our foreign policy, *not only in Korea but in many other areas of the world.* . . .
> We are concerned not only about the consequences of this *abrupt about-face* in Korea, whose government and people have made valiant efforts to win their independence and establish free institutions under the most difficult circumstances, but we are also

deeply concerned by the *effect* which would be created in other parts of the world where *our encouragement is a major element in the struggle for freedom.*[26]

By 1950, this emphasis constituted the main thrust of administration policy rhetoric. Committed to a course of military deterrence, Truman sought to allay doubts or criticisms about the military character of his policy responses. Thus, he depicted the decision to develop a thermonuclear bomb as a defensive measure neither aggressive nor provocative but a positive step toward securing peace. In addition, Truman affirmed that the Cold War could have been avoided had Congress earlier acceded to his request for universal military training.[27] The President specifically sought to discredit right-wing critics of the administration's military-oriented internationalist policies by representing their position as "isolationist." The effect of their efforts to limit American overseas commitments, the President argued, would simply encourage aggression and subversion and thereby further Soviet objectives and undermine the national security.[28]

A note of confident optimism underlay early 1950 administration foreign policy pronouncements. The President predicted that relations with the Soviet Union would be normalized and that, with patience and firmness, the United States would successfully preserve the peace.* Truman explicitly asserted that as United States resolve and leadership was made clear,

---

*Although formally the administration proclaimed the inevitability of American success, there were real doubts about the immediate solution behind the scenes, as the debate over N.S.C. 68 illustrated. (N.S.C. 68 was a highly secret document prepared by the National Security Council in early 1950 which recommended a "bold and massive program" of military preparedness to insure U.S. military superiority over the Soviet Union.) Truman thought that superior military strength, not yet achieved, was essential to a lasting peace, and this emphasis became the basis for U.S. policy in the 1950's. Coral Bell, in an insightful book, *Negotiation from Strength* (New York, 1962), traces the evolution of the idea. Basic to this policy position of Secretary of State Dean Acheson, expressed with more sophistication than the popular espousal by Truman, was a particular view of what constituted realistic and successful diplomacy. Placing primacy on power, it implied that time and patience would ultimately insure success. For a dissenting view of a position rejected within the administration, see the *Memoirs* of George Kennan (Boston, 1967).

and as the people "who stood in doubt" turned to democracy, the "danger of communist domination will dwindle and it will finally disappear."[29] Speaking at Gonzaga University, the President belittled the Soviet Union as a "modern tyranny led by a small group who have abandoned their faith in God." At Glen Falls, Idaho, he pledged that a peace consistent with American ideals and objectives would be attained. "We are on the right track," he observed, "and we will win—because God is with us in that enterprise."[30]

Administration rhetoric increasingly emphasized these crusading themes; ultimately this served to limit its options. Because Americans were encouraged to expect victory as inevitable, owing to American purity, to Providence, and to Soviet perfidy and atheism, they were led to reject a policy of compromise and concession. The administration effectively equated restraint with appeasement and thereby discredited suggestions that a proper policy should rely on conciliation and not military strength.* Because the Soviet Union was also portrayed as the Anti-Christ, Truman's moralistic tone obviated a policy course that sought to reach some form of accommodation. Negotiation would involve compromise with principle and complicity with evil. This portrayal, coupled with the administration's oversimplified description of communist influence (nonindigenous

---

*The public was not, however, committed simply to military means. Thus, although in August 1949 (before the announcement of the Soviet atomic explosion) most Americans opposed (70 per cent to 20 per cent) a formal declaration that the U.S. would not use the atomic bomb unless it was used by another nation first, at the same time the public did not unquestioningly support aid to beleaguered countries if it might involve the United States in armed conflict. Only 8 per cent supported general aid by the U.S., 7 per cent military aid, 4 per cent economic aid, and 2 per cent propaganda support, while 36 per cent opposed any aid and 45 per cent expressed no opinion on what the United States should do to prevent China from going communist. Similarly, 35 per cent supported U.S. military aid to Western Europe, 18 per cent opposed it, 7 per cent had no opinion, and 42 per cent expressed unfamiliarity with NATO. Forty-two per cent supported U.S. military or economic aid to those countries seeking to build up their military defenses against the Soviet Union, 40 per cent disapproved, and 14 per cent had no opinion (*POQ*, XIII, 710, 721-722, 725). Public militancy was more emotional than substantive; the people were reluctant to become involved, yet buffeted by pressures implying that noninvolvement was dangerous or beneficial to communism.

and unpopular), increased public expectations that the U.S. inevitably could and should repulse communism.*

In speeches around the country in 1949 and 1950, Attorney General J. Howard McGrath developed these themes.† McGrath specifically emphasized the critical threat posed by communism to American security. To counter that threat he stressed the importance of public awareness of and vigilance against the communist menace. Those who believed "with us in God's law and the dignity of human personality," McGrath argued, must take up the "modern struggle against pagan communist philosophies that seek to enslave mankind." He warned against the subtle subversion of students' minds by their teachers and

---

*In August 1949 the public was skeptical about the prospects for a long-term peace—50 per cent expected a war in the next twenty-five years, while 41 per cent felt war could be averted, and 9 per cent had no opinion. At the same time the public distrusted Soviet intentions. A December poll on the likelihood of war because the Soviets had the atomic bomb revealed this fear: 45 per cent felt Soviet possession made war more likely, 28 per cent less likely, 17 per cent no difference, 10 per cent no opinion. Only 22 per cent thought the Soviet Union wanted peace, 60 per cent disagreed, 18 per cent had no opinion. Contrary to Truman's confident assurances, in March 1950 only 16 per cent thought the U.S. was winning the Cold War, 23 per cent the Soviet Union, 5 per cent neither nation, 14 per cent didn't know, and 42 per cent expressed ignorance of the term Cold War. Administration optimism had not convinced the public; nor was its militancy shared. A definite malaise, a sense of confusion and insecurity, dominated the body politic. Thus 68 per cent thought the administration should first attempt to reach agreement on atomic control before developing the hydrogen bomb, 23 per cent opposed such an effort, and 9 per cent expressed no opinion (POQ, XIII, 728; XIV, 182, 192, 372, 609).

†McGrath's speech-making was not unusual; it was an administration tactic. When the President sought to rebut his critics, he did so indirectly by assigning the task to cabinet members. McGrath's predecessor as Attorney General, Tom Clark, and other representatives of the Justice, State, and Defense departments had publicly expressed the same themes. What was significant about McGrath's effort was his shrill tone and the number of speeches he made. His qualifications were his religion (Roman Catholic) and his position as Attorney General. His protestations presumably would be more credible and his defense of the administration's anti-communism more effective. McGrath spoke primarily to anti-communist or patriotic groups, such as national meetings of college fraternities, police or law enforcement associations, Catholic lay groups, and Irish-American and veterans' organizations. See J. Howard McGrath Papers, Speech Files 1949–1952, Truman Library. See also Democratic National Committee Files for the years 1947–1952, Truman Library, for a sample of other administration statements, interviews, and press comments.

asserted that anti-communist speakers should be invited to the campus, and anti-communist books promoted in the bookstores. Linking foreign policy and internal security, McGrath charged that "Communism today represents a vital danger to America."

> There are today many Communists in America. They are everywhere—in factories, offices, butcher stores, on street corners, in private businesses. And each carries in himself the germ of death for society.[31]

This rhetoric provided the framework for the McCarthyites' bitter assault on the Truman administration's China policy and their contention that Far Eastern developments confirmed either the weakness of that policy or successful subversion by "communist" policy-makers. If revolutions were foreign-inspired and directed by an armed, anti-Christian, subversive minority, and if American purposes were noble and attainable through a policy of firmness and strength, then the Chinese Nationalist defeat was a result of the administration's failure to act vigorously, a failure due perhaps to betrayal or indifference because it was "soft toward communism."

The invasion of South Korea in 1950 lent new force to this view. In responding, the Truman administration called the attack a major threat to the national security. The conflict was presented as international aggression, not civil war. Moreover, the administration charged that the crisis had been precipitated by an alien (non-Korean) minority. Truman's conception of Soviet direction, reflected in his responses involving Taiwan, the Philippines, and Indochina, was underscored in what was later described as a slip during a June 29, 1950, press conference Explaining why a formal declaration of war had not been made, Truman noted that the legally recognized Republic of Korea had been attacked "by a bunch of bandits which are neighbors of North Korea."*

The President, moreover, sought to capitalize on the Korean situation to press for congressional approval of extensive foreign

---

*The initial public view of the conflict agreed with this assessment. In an August 1950 poll, 57 per cent thought the United States was involved in World War III, 28 per cent that the Korean War could be localized short of world war, while 15 per cent expressed no opinion (*POQ*, XIV, 811).

aid. To disarm criticisms that earlier aid policies had failed to
secure peace or deter the Soviet Union, Truman described the
outbreak of the Korean War as in fact a confirmation of the
success of American aid policy—because it forced the Soviet
Union to shift from subversion to overt aggression. Korea, Truman argued, because it symbolized this shift in Soviet policy,
must be defended so that future potential aggressors would be
forewarned that direct aggression would not pay. The next
greatest threat to American security, Truman added, came from
the "isolationists." National unity and support, the President
argued, were necessary in this period of crisis. Accordingly, he
urged the public to support his policies without question and
to reject the criticisms of administration opponents.[32]

After Chinese Communist intervention in the Korean War,
the administration elaborated upon these themes. It specifically
denied that China's interests or security were in any way
threatened by U.S. actions. Emphasizing our peaceful, altruistic
intentions, Truman regretted that the Chinese had allowed themselves to be manipulated by Moscow.*[33]

Truman expressed this view in a statement he read at a November 30, 1950, press conference:

Recent developments in Korea confront the world with a serious
crisis. The Chinese Communist *leaders* have sent their troops from
Manchuria to launch a strong and well-organized attack against
the United Nations from North Korea. This has been done despite
prolonged and earnest efforts to bring home to the communist
leaders of China the plain fact that neither the United Nations nor
the United States has *any aggressive* intentions toward China. . . .

If the United Nations *yields* to the forces of aggression, *no nation* will be safe or secure. *If aggression is successful in Korea, we
can expect it to spread throughout Asia and Europe to this hemisphere. We are fighting in Korea for our own national security
and survival.* . . . We hope that the Chinese *people* will not continue to be *forced or deceived* into serving the ends of *Russian
colonial policy* in Asia.

I am certain that, if the Chinese people *now* under the *control*

*The American public assessed Chinese intervention similarly. In a
December 1950 poll, 81 per cent thought the Chinese entered the Korean
War on orders from Moscow, 5 per cent disagreed, while 14 per cent
expressed no opinion (*POQ,* XV, 170–171).

of the Communists were free to speak for themselves, they would denounce this *aggression* against the United Nations.[34]

This conspiratorial view of revolution and conflict shaped the political debate. It placed a premium on deterring revolutions (whether in Taiwan, Korea, or Indochina) and insured a reliance on military power and preparedness. Thus, when confronted by Chinese intervention the administration refused to reject the possibility that the United States would not either attack the Chinese mainland or abstain from the use of atomic weapons. Administration policy, as enunciated publicly by the President, came to rely on the effective use of overwhelming military strength. Diplomacy, whether in the sense of accommodation, acceptance of legitimate spheres of influence, or the limits of national power, ceased to be a part of administration policy rhetoric.[35]

This threat of force carried maximal risks, of course, particularly if the U.S. bluff were called. The refusal to disavow the use of atomic weapons later contributed to a public sense that the nation's resources had not been fully applied. Domestically, the resort to verbal militancy—but a restrained use of power— contributed to a credibility crisis. On the one hand, administration actions were not consistent with its rhetoric. On the other hand, its rhetoric added credence, even legitimacy, to what became the McCarthyites' central demand for a policy based on victory, one which set no limits on American military power.*

By 1950 the Truman administration's policy pronouncements were distinctly alarmist. They heightened insecurity and tension rather than encouraged dispassion, reason, and confidence. The administration continued to try to evoke an aura of crisis to

---

*Events during late 1950 and early 1951 contributed to the intensification of an already ambivalent, tense public mood. In December 1950, 46 per cent thought that if Chinese Communist troops intervened in Korea, the U.S. military effort should still be confined to Korea, 39 per cent supported crossing the border into China, 15 per cent didn't know. At the same time, when questioned whether the U.S. should support a U.N. decision to admit China in return for the end of Chinese involvement in Korea, 57 per cent agreed, 28 per cent disagreed, and 15 per cent had no opinion. By February 1951 a mood of public disenchantment had emerged: 68 per cent supported a U.S. pullout, only 28 per cent supported staying in Korea after Chinese intervention. In addition, 50 per cent thought the

secure support for possibly controversial policies, as in its November 1950 request for aid to Yugoslavia.

Yugoslavia was an anomaly in the Cold War: a communist state that had broken from the Soviet bloc but had been able to sustain a quasi-neutrality. Having suffered a serious agricultural crisis (the result of drought and bad harvests), Yugoslavia gravely needed economic aid. Administration policy had been pointedly anti-communist, so that aid to a communist state was a clear contradiction. Truman's problem in securing aid was further accentuated by the fiscal conservatism of the congressional leadership and its indifference to foreign economic aid, and to the heightened influence of the McCarthyites, partly because of the militant anti-communist public mood and partly because of the McCarthyites' striking successes in the 1950 congressional elections. The President tried to undercut criticisms in letters to Senators Tom Connally (chairman of the Foreign Relations Committee) and Millard Tydings (chairman of the Armed Services Committee), and to Representatives John Kee (chairman of the Foreign Affairs Committee) and Carl Vinson (chairman of the Armed Services Committee). Truman warned:

> The drought, the consequent crop failure and the imminence of famine in Yugoslavia is a development which seriously affects the security of the North Atlantic area. These events dangerously weaken the ability of Yugoslavia to defend itself against aggression, for, among other circumstances, it imperils the combat effectiveness of the Yugoslav armed forces.

U.S. had made a mistake in entering the Korean War, 39 per cent disagreed, and 11 per cent expressed no opinion (*POQ*, XV, 170–171, 386–387). Despite considerable effort, the administration had not convinced the public of Korea's strategic importance. It had created a crisis of ambivalence between support for American troops and doubts about the war, between a militant anti-communism and a sense of caution based upon a fear of escalation. At the same time, while the majority of the public thought the U.S. should use atomic weapons first in the event of war (66 per cent to 19 per cent, 15 per cent no opinion), there was a sharp increase in expectations about the likelihood of a U.S.-Soviet shooting war within a year (40 per cent to 45 per cent, 15 per cent undecided) and who was winning the Cold War (by February 1951, 30 per cent thought it was the Soviet Union, 9 per cent the U.S., 12 per cent neither, 4 per cent no opinion, and 45 per cent expressed ignorance about the term Cold War) (*POQ*, XV, 381, 393, 399).

Yugoslavia, moreover, is a nation whose strategic location makes it of direct importance to the defense of the North Atlantic area. . . .

As a result of these factors, an immediate increase in Yugoslavia's ability to defend itself over that which would exist if no assistance were supplied will contribute to the peace and security of the North Atlantic area. . . . It is a settled premise of our foreign policy that the peace and security of the North Atlantic area is vital to the security of the United States.[36]

II

As with its foreign policy, the Truman administration's manner of defining, as well as its response to criticisms of, its internal security policy contributed to the development of a distinctly repressive domestic climate. In 1947 Truman had instituted a federal employee loyalty program, ostensibly for national security reasons. At that time and subsequently he did not clearly define the program's limited objectives. Specifically, he did not distinguish between individual disloyalty and political radicalism (whether belief or act). This imprecision, by blurring distinctions, helped reshape the public view about political activism and its conception that past or current radicalism confirmed an individual's subversive proclivities.* Investigations

*A distinct shift in the public view about the rights of U.S. Communists occurred. The President's decisions and statements provided no effective counterweight to this concern, which the McCarthyites capitalized on. Thus, whereas in early 1946 most Americans thought that Communists should be allowed to speak on the radio (49 per cent to 39 per cent, 12 per cent undecided), doubted that Communists were loyal to the U.S. (23 per cent to 48 per cent, 29 per cent no opinion), opposed allowing Communists to hold office (7 per cent supported with surveillance, 16 per cent advocated doing nothing, 36 per cent advocated strong measures, 28 per cent no opinion), and opposed allowing Communists to retain civil service jobs (17 per cent to 69 per cent, 14 per cent no opinion), even this strained tolerance was later repudiated (*POQ*, X, 409, 436, 608). In April 1947 (after the President's inauguration of a loyalty program for federal employees), 61 per cent supported legislation prohibiting membership in the Communist party, 26 per cent opposed, 13 per cent had no opinion. Sixty-seven per cent thought Communists should be forbidden to hold government jobs, while 19 per cent believed Communists to have the same rights as other citizens, and 14 per cent had no opinion (*POQ*, X, 281). In succeeding years this suspicion increased. The announcement of the loyalty program tended to stigmatize Communists as disloyal.

of the political activities and beliefs of government personnel
became justified as a legitimate security concern and eventually
led to a shift in the standard for dismissal. Presumption of doubt
as to the loyalty of a prospective or incumbent employee became sufficient justification for a denial of clearance.

The administration had defined the loyalty program's principal objective as the exclusion of *all* potentially disloyal individuals from federal employment. The program's rationale was
outlined in the recommendations of a Temporary Commission
(established by the President in November 1946 to determine
the adequacy of existing loyalty procedures). The commission
agreed that a loyalty program was needed, and noted:

> The *presence* within the government of *any* disloyal or subversive
> persons, or the attempt by *any* such persons to *obtain* government
> employment, presents a problem of *such importance* that it must
> be dealt with *vigorously and effectively.*

This was a grave "threat" to the national security, the commission said, though it did not enumerate, document, or specifically
define its nature. Concerned with insuring effective surveillance
procedures, vague in its standards and fears, the commission
argued:

> While the Commission believes that the employment of disloyal
> or subversive persons presents *more than a speculative* threat to
> our system of government, it is *unable,* based on the *facts* pre-
> sented to it, to state with any degree of certainty *how far reaching*
> that threat is. Certainly, the recent Canadian Espionage exposé,
> the *Communist Party line activities* of *some* of the members of a
> government employee organization, and current disclosures of
> disloyal employees provide *sufficient* evidence to convince a fair-
> minded person that a threat exists.[37]

The attempt to achieve absolute security by averting potential subversion implied that security could not be achieved by
traditional surveillance methods or by dismissing an employee
after proving his disloyalty. Suspect persons, who might engage
in "subversive" activities, were security risks. The program therefore rested on the premise that disloyalty and subversive tendencies must be determined in advance to preclude a threat to
the national security. By this standard, subsequent disclosures

of "spying" activities (Alger Hiss, Judith Coplon, Ethel and Julius Rosenberg, John Stewart Service, William Remington) highlighted the inadequacies of the President's loyalty program. The administration's subsequent denial that any threat existed, following these developments and contradicting its earlier rhetoric, pointed apparently to negligence or culpability. To have suggested, moreover, that "even one disloyal person constitutes [a serious threat] to the security" of the United States served to strengthen Joe McCarthy's numbers charges. If one disloyal person was a serious threat, didn't 205, 81, 57, or 3 demand urgent action, not apology?

In another sense, the Truman administration's response to Henry Wallace's presidential candidacy also contributed to the development of a more intolerant political climate. In the 1948 presidential campaign, Truman, the Democratic National Committee, and the Americans for Democratic Action resorted to red-baiting in order to discredit Wallace. In an address on St. Patrick's Day, Truman rejected the support of "Wallace and his communists." The President further emphasized the "communists'" efforts to defeat him by supporting a third party. And the Democratic National Committee published a series of pamphlets and advertisements labeling the Progressive party as communist-influenced. Both Truman and the National Committee stressed the administration's anti-communist foreign policy and internal security record. They contrasted this record to Republican obstructionism and the GOP's seeming indifference to the communist threat posed by the Progressive party at home (as reflected in its complicity with Progressive efforts to get on the ballot) and Soviet expansionism abroad (its opposition to foreign aid policies).[38]

To discredit the Progressive party, the ADA paid for advertisements in major urban newspapers, listing the names of the party's principal contributors and the organizations on the Attorney General's list to which these contributors belonged or had belonged.[39] Ironically, the McCarthyites later resorted to this same presumption of guilt by association when attacking personnel of the Truman administration and the ADA. (During the 1950 congressional campaign the Democratic State Central

Committee of Pennsylvania sought to use this tactic against certain Republican congressional incumbents. The committee contrasted the similarity of these Republicans' voting records on key foreign policy issues to that of Congressman Vito Marcantonio.)[40]

This rhetoric heightened public fears about communism. The administration's attempt to impugn the motives of its right-wing critics added another aspect—a loss of credibility. The partisan, anti-congressional manner of Truman's response to the House Committee on Un-American Activities allowed the McCarthyites to adopt an anti-executive stance. In the form of congressional authority, on the premise of the need for restraints on executive powers, and in the guise of a national security concern, the McCarthyites were able to capitalize on Truman's resort to censorship of the investigative records of loyalty proceedings. Moreover, the President's tactic of dismissing criticisms of the loyalty program as partisan in motivation increased public doubts about his priorities. The public came to interpret administration prosecution of "disloyal" federal employees as evidence not of administration vigilance but as a partisan response to pressure from the McCarthyites.

This view of administration priorities became the norm in 1950 but had not been the original basis for the Truman-McCarthyite confrontation. In 1945–1948 Truman could conveniently ignore or dismiss right-wing accusations that a serious communist threat existed. In part the administration's tactic succeeded because the public viewed the charges of the House Committee on Un-American Activities as having a specific conservative purpose, directed less at internal subversion than against the New Deal. And during this period the public was relatively unconcerned about internal security matters.*

*The public neither wholly rejected nor accepted the committee's charges. In a September 1948 poll (after Truman's "red herring" remark), of those who had heard about the "communist spy hearings," 74 per cent thought the committee was "proving something," 17 per cent that the hearings were "purely politics," while 9 per cent had no opinion (*POQ*, XII, 781). The loaded reference of the poll to "communist spy hearings" and the unqualified references to "purely politics" and "proving some-

In 1947 and 1948 HUAC's investigation had concentrated on domestic attitudes, specifically whether communists had infiltrated the New Deal and the motion picture industry.[41] These initial investigations were concerned not so much with "espionage" in the sense of sabotage or foreign subversion, but with ideas and associations. The implication was that communists, by infiltrating the Roosevelt administration, or Hollywood, had created an un-American climate (reformist New Deal or sympathetic to the Soviet Union). Only after the disclosure of the "pumpkin papers" by Whittaker Chambers in December 1948 did the committee emphasize espionage activities.[42] And Chambers, during this preliminary phase, had echoed the charge that communists, by infiltrating the New Deal, had successfully influenced policy-making. In testimony and public statements prior to November, Chambers had denied that Alger Hiss had engaged in espionage and insisted that Hiss's sole activity as a Communist party member had been to promote communist infiltration of the New Deal.[43]

In view of the obvious partisanship of the House Committee and the still tolerant public attitude toward radicalism—distinguishing between radicalism and communism in 1947 and 1948—Truman then had the opportunity to develop a climate conducive

---

thing" reduce the impact of this response. In August 1948, 63 per cent favored passage of the Mundt-Nixon bill (providing for the registration of the Communist party and front organizations), 22 per cent opposed it, and 15 per cent expressed no opinion. But in a January 1948 poll, 40 per cent felt that the U.S. Communist party posed *no* threat to the U.S., while 45 per cent felt that the party was strong or posed a potential threat (*POQ*, XII, 350–351). This response was made after the formation of the Progressive party, when the Communist party was a cohesive national force, having openly contested for control of the labor and other progressive movements.

From 1946 through 1948 the public was principally concerned about domestic reform issues and secondly about foreign policy. See *POQ*, X, 128, 133; XI, 292, 300; XII, 557. Domestic communism was a peripheral issue. Reflecting the confidence Truman then commanded, in March 1947 only 20 per cent thought a Democratic electoral victory would allow communists to increase their influence, 54 per cent that it would not, 20 per cent had no opinion (*POQ*, XI, 300). When polled in September 1948 about Truman's and Dewey's qualifications, the public's response centered on domestic and administrative considerations, not foreign policy or internal security (*POQ*, XII, 772–776).

to civil liberties.* Instead, he only emphasized the committee's excessive, publicity-seeking procedures. His partisan responses were effective, not because they were articulate and well-reasoned but primarily because the committee had overreacted and had not been able to prove its grave accusations.† When faced with the committee's "communists-in-government" charges, Truman dismissed them as a "red herring" devised by anti–New Deal Republicans to cover up for the 80th Congress' reactionary record. He challenged the committee to turn over to the Attorney General evidence of wrongdoing. At the same time the President and his Attorney General, Tom Clark, cited the administration's effective anti-communist record and particularly its actions dismissing disloyal federal employees and prosecuting the leaders of the U.S. Communist party.[44] Clark contrasted this "positive" record to that of the 80th Congress, expressing his frustration over Congress' indifference to legislation proposed by the Justice Department that had been designed to "strengthen" existing security procedures (authorizing wiretapping, extending registration requirements, and increasing surveillance).[45]

In response to a subpoena of the House Committee for the loyalty records of certain federal employees, Truman on March 14, 1948, directed federal agencies to ignore future congressional requests or subpoenas for confidential information without his express approval. This reversed earlier procedures and widened the rift between Congress and the President. Truman justified his

*Thus, whereas in September–October 1947 most Americans favored (64 per cent to 17 per cent, 19 per cent no opinion) legislation preventing communists from holding public office, they distinguished between communists and radicals. Accordingly, they supported allowing "communist sympathizers" to hold public office (41 per cent to 36 per cent, 23 per cent no opinion) and permitting an individual whose loyalty was questioned to present his side (68 per cent to 24 per cent, 8 per cent no opinion) (POQ, X, 641–642).

†Indeed, in 1948 (as cited in the footnote on page 222), the public was willing to believe that there was some substance to the committee's charges, that it was "proving something," and that its objectives were not "purely partisan." The public attitude lay between the formal position of both the committee and the President, convinced by neither but concerned about "communist spy" activities.

refusal by citing three arguments: (1) the constitutional separation of the executive and legislative branches; (2) the importance of secrecy to protect innocent employees from publicity
of unfounded charges; and (3) the need to preserve the confidentiality of FBI sources to expedite future investigations.[46]

But Truman did not use this opportunity to explain that much
of the information contained in these reports was clearly unreliable and unsubstantiated. He made no distinction between
researched and confirmed information of FBI agents, on the
one hand, and the hearsay testimony of paid informants, personal interviews, or unsolicited letters, on the other. By failing
to make this distinction, Truman helped to create the impression
that all the information in these reports had been secured
through accurate, thorough investigations. Later, McCarthy
would cite excerpts from these reports as "evidence" that security risks were still found in the federal service, thereby confirming the need for further exposure. And McCarthy could say
that administration censorship was designed to cover up its
laxity, and thus endangered the national security.

The decision (in March 1948) to bar HUAC from access to the
loyalty reports was surprising. Just two months earlier, the House
Appropriations Committee had secured permission to examine
the State Department loyalty reports. The committee's access to
these reports had hardly undermined the national security. And,
considering McCarthy's principal sources of information—State
and Justice Department personnel—the administration's reitera-
tion of the argument that disclosure to Congress would cripple
the FBI's investigations had little impact. Instead, it appeared
to the public that this administration decision was less a concern
for the national interest than a desire to cover up administration
culpability.* McCarthy could adopt the posture of a disinter-

---

*In May and July 1950 polls, the public accepted the thrust of Mc-
Carthy's critique. Questioned in May about Truman's contention that
McCarthy was "the best asset the Kremlin has," 29 per cent thought Mc-
Carthy's charges were harmful, 39 per cent beneficial, 16 per cent were
unfamiliar with them, and 16 per cent had no opinion about their effect.
When this question was posed less negatively in July, 22 per cent ex-
pressed ignorance, 31 per cent approved or believed, 10 per cent expressed

ested, loyal public servant deeply concerned about the national security and desiring solely to inform the public of the real internal security problem covered up by the administration.

As a pronounced anti-communist, Truman did not, in 1948, 1949, or early 1950, take these charges seriously. Indeed, he called the 1948 election results a confirmation of public support for his handling of internal security, and a repudiation of the charges and tactics of the House Committee on Un-American Activities.[47] Because he had been able during the 1948 campaign to dismiss the HUAC members as partisan publicity seekers, Truman maintained this stance and relied on the belief that he had public support. Thus, when charges of an internal security problem were repeated in 1949, Truman simply castigated these congressmen and other critics of his loyalty program as headline hunters.[48]

At the same time Truman asserted that no one "who believes in the destruction of our form of government" should teach children.[49] This kind of vague, emotion-laden statement contributed to insecurity and fear and precluded a realistic understanding of what constituted a threat to the national security. Truman never clearly defined the nature of this threat or what constituted "destruction of our form of government." This vagueness created a tension which the administration intensified by its earlier uncritical commitment to instituting more "effective" internal security procedures.

Indeed, from 1946 through 1948 the Department of Justice had operated with few executive restraints in its efforts to insure the passage of internal security legislation. Specifically, in 1946 Attorney General Clark had successfully secured additional in-

qualified approval, 20 per cent disapproved or disbelieved, and 6 per cent thought that McCarthy's charges were sometimes right and sometimes wrong, while 11 per cent had no opinion (POQ, XIV, 596, 801). McCarthy's impact was not dramatic. He struck home to the already convinced, but with the distinct security obsession that had developed since 1947 the public was not ready to dismiss McCarthyism summarily. Truman's approach was wide of the mark, for the concern was not effectiveness in the sense of the adequacy of existing safguards (Truman's justification of confidentiality), but whether further changes ought to be imposed from outside the executive branch.

vestigative authority for the FBI by capitalizing on Truman's distress over the Canadian Royal Commission's disclosure of Soviet wartime espionage. By distorting an earlier (1940) Roosevelt directive authorizing the FBI to wiretap in well-defined circumstances, Clark obtained Truman's assent to a new directive extending the authorization to include investigations of "subversion" and "criminal activities."[50] Concurrently, in 1947 and 1948, Justice (unsuccessfully) pressed the Congress to enact legislation broadly extending its authority in matters affecting the "national security." The effect of these actions was to heighten public fears about the communist threat and contribute to a vastly changed climate in which McCarthyism flourished.

In addition, the excessive independence of the department during these earlier years served to distinguish its actions in the public mind from those of the President. This distinction was strengthened as the result of efforts by White House staff members after 1949 to curb the department's legislative efforts. In effect, this rift tended to contradict administration protestations of anti-communism: it was seemingly less concerned about the communist threat than the department. White House efforts to restrain Justice failed because of the outbreak of the Korean War.[51]

The Korean War made internal security legislation politically popular. And whereas earlier measures (Mundt-Nixon, Ferguson-Johnston) had been stymied, by 1950 the combination of the war and public obsession with "subversion" increased the prospect that some form of "internal security" legislation would be enacted.* Although Truman acted to avert the passage of repressive legislation and accordingly introduced a measure far

---

*An August 1950 poll (at the time the Senate was considering internal security legislation) revealed the extent of the public's concern, though the phrasing of the question elicited maximal fears. Asked what policy the government should adopt toward U.S. Communists in the event of war with the Soviet Union, 28 per cent favored internment of Communists, 18 per cent favored imprisonment, 15 per cent favored exile, 13 per cent favored deportation to the Soviet Union, 13 per cent favored execution, 4 per cent favored registration, 1 per cent thought nothing should be done (freedom of thought), 10 per cent had no opinion, and there were 9 per cent miscellaneous responses (*POQ*, XIV, 801–802).

less restrictive of civil liberties, the nature and quality of the
administration's leadership against Senator McCarran's proposed
bill was neither principled nor courageous. In fact, the administration's equivocation served only to increase public fears.

In its proposal the administration had accepted the premise
that the American Communist party posed a serious threat to
the national security, requiring that its activities and those of
its alleged fronts should be curbed, and that existing security
procedures were inadequate to deal with the threat. In essence
this position provided the rationale for Senator McCarran's bill,
a bill that was more restrictive of civil liberties and vaguer in
its definition of subversive activities. The administration thereby
lost whatever leverage it might have commanded to defeat the
McCarran bill. It could not simultaneously argue that the national security was seriously threatened and that civil liberties
should not be transgressed. Traditionally, in times of serious
crisis or war, individual liberties had been sacrificed (suspension of the writ of habeas corpus, internment of the Japanese).
The administration's protests against excessive restrictions on
civil liberties appeared less than realistic.[52]

Truman's strategy of stopping the McCarthyites by proposing
an alternate bill failed. The President's decision to veto the
omnibus measure introduced by Senator McCarran did not contribute to a more tolerant political climate, but, like his proposed
measure, intensified the public obsession with communism. In
his veto message, Truman said:

> It has been claimed over and over again that this [the McCarran
> bill] is an "anti-communist" bill—a "communist control" bill. But
> in actual operation the bill would . . . actually weaken our existing
> internal security measures and would seriously hamper the Federal
> Bureau of Investigation and other security agencies. . . .
>
> No consideration of expediency can justify the enactment of
> such a bill as this, a bill which would so greatly weaken our lib-
> erties and give aid and comfort to those who would destroy us.[53]

Truman's denunciation, on anti-communist grounds, of the Mc-
Carran bill changed the mind of no one who felt that the nation
needed more effective internal security legislation. The act might
be unconstitutional (subsequent Supreme Court decisions con-

firmed this), and it did circumscribe individual liberties. But its purpose was to hamper recruitment and the secrecy of the Communist party and communist-front organizations. Conceding the gravity of the threat, that effort was desirable and realistic. To suggest, as Truman did, that the measure would aid the communists was incredible and reflected on the administration's partisanship or "softness toward communism."

Truman's primary concern was not to safeguard civil liberties but to establish his anti-communist credentials and thus refute his critics. This commitment is revealed in the timing and nature of the President's reaction to McCarthy's charges of communist infiltration of the State Department. When the Senate decided to investigate these charges, Truman seemed indifferent. Confident that the public was convinced of the effectiveness of his internal security program, Truman, in a March 30, 1950, press conference, summarily dismissed McCarthy as "the greatest asset that the Kremlin has." In support of his own solid anti-communist credentials, Truman cited his policy decisions—the loyalty program and various military-economic policies to contain Soviet expansion. Focusing on McCarthy's motives, Truman argued that

> there are a certain number of members of the Republican Party who are trying to dig up that old malodorous horse called "isolationism." And in order to do that, they are perfectly willing to sabotage the bipartisan foreign policy of the United States. And this fiasco which has been going on in the Senate is the very best asset that the Kremlin could have in the operation of the cold war.

As in his earlier response to the House Committee, Truman again challenged his critics to turn over any evidence they had to the proper authorities so that prosecution could be initiated. This criticism was not only groundless but treasonous, Truman implied, and he denounced criticisms of his foreign policy decisions as an effort to "sabotage the foreign policy of the United States [which] is just as bad in this cold war as it would be to shoot our soldiers in the back in a hot war."[54]

In two major responses to McCarthyism, Truman revealed his estimate of the senator's political effectiveness and underscored his own ambivalent commitment to civil liberties. Specifically,

Truman failed to take an unequivocal stand on the question of the confidentiality of loyalty records; instead he vacillated, responding to public pressure. At first he agreed to cooperate fully with the Tydings Committee which was investigating McCarthy's charges. At the same time he refused, on national security grounds, to permit committee access to State Department files; instead he offered to have the Loyalty Review Board examine the cases under investigation and submit its recommendations to the President. Then Truman reversed himself and ordered the board to report directly to the committee. And, in a still more dramatic reversal, he later agreed to release the loyalty files of the State Department, but not those of the FBI, to the Tydings Committee. Truman's indecision and vacillation reflected the partisan priorities underlying his decisions—when a principled stand became unpopular, pressure was relieved by gradual concessions.[55]

Because he did not at first view McCarthyism—at least the senator's charges of February–April 1950—as a major political threat, Truman rejected proposals by White House staff members and Democratic congressmen (such as Representative Helen Douglas and Senators Tydings and McMahon) that might have restored public confidence in the administration's loyalty program and procedures. Again, in May 1950, these staff members and congressmen urged Truman to reestablish this confidence by appointing a special presidential commission to investigate the loyalty program. It would determine what procedures might be needed to protect the national security yet provide safeguards to individual rights.* These advocates argued

*The original suggestion of a special presidential commission had been made for different reasons. In late 1948 and early 1949, liberals, concerned over the loyalty program's abuses of individual rights and heartened by Truman's electoral victory, had urged the President to initiate a review of the program with the purpose of correcting these abuses and thus safeguarding individual rights. The proponents saw an expert commission as legitimizing civil liberties concerns and denying the claims of the Loyalty Review Board and the Justice Department to disinterested expertise. Truman essentially ignored these suggestions. Both the Department of Justice and the Loyalty Review Board claimed that an investigation was not warranted and defended the correctness of existing procedures

that the Tydings Committee had failed to rebut McCarthy's
charges because the American public considered the committee's
report incómplete, partisan, or biased. In contrast, a bipartisan
blue-ribbon commission, they maintained, could effectively re-
pudiate McCarthy's charges. This proposal was seriously considered in early June 1950 but was temporarily sidetracked with
the outbreak of the Korean War.[56]

Members of the White House staff, nonetheless, continued to
press for a commission. The Korean War, they argued, created
a climate that made possible the enactment of proposed internal
security bills (by Senators Karl Mundt, Homer Ferguson, and
Pat McCarran, and Representatives John Wood and Richard
Nixon) that threatened civil liberties. Staff members doubted
that the President could exercise the impartial leadership necessary to defeat these measures but thought a presidential commission could.[57] After the enactment of the McCarran Act and
McCarthyism's demonstrated effectiveness in the 1950 congressional elections—and only then—Truman reconsidered the proposal and in January 1951 formally appointed a special commission headed by Admiral Chester Nimitz.[58]

Ostensibly, the commission was established to review existing
internal security procedures. Based on that investigation, the
commission was to recommend improvements to protect individual rights and the national security. This balanced objective
did not constitute the basic thrust of the commission's operation
or concern. When it did function, the commission at first did
nothing more than consider a proposed amendment of the
loyalty program's standard for dismissal. Suggested by the De-

and administration of the program. See Leon Henderson (Chairman, ADA)
to Truman, September 27, 1948; and Walter White (Executive-Secretary,
NAACP) to Truman, November 26, 1948, OF252-K. Morris Ernst (ACLU)
to Matthew Connelly, April 28, 1949; Stephen Spingarn to Clark Clifford,
May 5, 1949; Spingarn to Donald Dawson, June 17, 1949; all in Spingarn
Papers, Loyalty Program. McGrath to Dawson, December 23, 1949; and
L. A. Moyers (Executive Director and Chief Examiner, Loyalty Review
Board) to Civil Service Commission, February 2, 1949, OF252-K. Charles
Murphy to Truman, February 1, 1950, Spingarn Papers, Loyalty Program.
Joseph Rauh (Chairman, ADA), Washington, D.C., February 24, 1950,
Spingarn Papers, National Defense.

partment of Justice and the Loyalty Review Board as early as 1949, the revision was seriously considered within the administration in early 1951. The appointment of the Nimitz Commission only delayed presidential action on this recommendation.[59] Because the effective operation of the commission was stymied, Truman decided to act without awaiting the commission's decision. On April 21, 1951, he issued Executive Order 10241, implementing this new standard.[60]

The new standard for dismissal impinged upon individual rights and indirectly affirmed McCarthyite charges that the existing loyalty program had been ineffective. As one result, cases once cleared—the most notable being that of John Stewart Service—were reviewed again. Under the new provision, Service was denied loyalty clearance in 1951. This reversal of earlier departmental and board decisions clearing him was not based on evidence of Service's disloyalty but on his former personal associations and some of the reports he had made criticizing Chiang Kai-shek's Nationalist government while stationed in China as a foreign service officer during the war.[61]

III

Although he differed in both principle and objective from Senator McCarthy, Truman in his own right was a militant anti-communist. Initially confident that his internal security and foreign policy record rendered him invulnerable to charges of "softness toward communism," Truman dismissed the McCarthyite attacks as partisan while he reiterated his own anti-communism. When he was confronted by a loss of public confidence, Truman essentially complied with the McCarthyites' demands while simultaneously denying that existing loyalty procedures were inadequate. In addition, he sought to discredit the McCarthyites by suggesting that their attack undermined the national security. These tactics—self-righteous anti-communism and attempts to discredit dissent—were ineffective, primarily because of the crisis in public confidence created by the Korean War and the "spy" scandals of 1949–1950. The partisan nature of Truman's response to attacks on his internal security program and his conduct of foreign policy, moreover, increased this loss of public confidence.

The Korean War and the communist victory in China, following the Soviet explosion of an atomic bomb and the Hiss, Coplon, and Rosenberg "espionage" cases, increased public demands for effective internal security safeguards. The Cold War threatened imminently to become a hot war; it seemed that a real internal threat to the national security existed. Particularly after 1950, the Soviet threat, both external and internal, became a major and frightening concern to the American public. In addition, the administration had earlier oversold its policies. Hoping to undermine prevailing fears of war, the administration prior to 1950 had adopted a confident, predictive tone over the prospects for success. Truman then sought to quiet public fears about containment by proclaiming boldly that his policies would avert war and insure an American peace. The Korean War thus had a psychologically devastating impact upon the public by undercutting these hopes. At the same time, by contradicting earlier administration assurances, the war undermined Truman's credibility.

Judged in light of the kind of leadership Truman offered, and the options and rhetoric he presented, the public response to McCarthyism was neither irrational nor frenzied. McCarthy's slogans and solutions might seem simplistic, but since 1945 Truman had defined foreign and domestic issues in equally simplistic terms. Not only the issues, but the solutions to foreign policy and internal security problems were presented as obvious and clear-cut. International change and revolution were simply Soviet subversion which threatened the national security. Each crisis was a confrontation, or potential one, with the Soviet Union. Revolutionary movements were foreign subversion, not national radicalism. With these definitions, the Truman administration failed to provide a realistic assessment of the nature of the Cold War conflict. Confrontation was described in moralistic terms; there was no concession that Soviet actions were strategic or the result of power-political or geographic factors. Instead, the administration usually described the Soviets as not worthy of diplomatic concession, as a numerically small leadership group without popular support (thus politically fragile), and as untrustworthy except if confronted by superior power. This exaggerated, moralistic description ignored the limits of American influence, the international political situation, legitimate Soviet security fears, and the inevitable counter-response inherent in confrontation. Truman's overreliance on power, the confident predictions of containment, and the premises of the "domino theory" strengthened a peculiar perception of national security.

Given this definition of United States altruism and omnipotence, the American people might well ask why our postwar foreign policy had failed to secure the peace, failed to "liberate" Eastern Europe, failed to "save" China or preclude the Korean War and Chinese Communist intervention in that war. How had the Soviet Union acquired knowledge to produce the atomic bomb and thus directly threaten American security? A ready explanation to these questions was subversion—for the existence of "even one" disloyal person in the administration posed a grave threat to the national security. It was in this context that the public came to see the major threat to the national security as "communists in government." Had not Alger Hiss attended the Yalta Conference where China and Eastern Europe were "lost"? Had not the Rosenbergs passed on *the* "secret" of the atomic bomb to Soviet agents? Were not these cases symptomatic? And had not the McCarthyites consistently warned the public about the political unreliability of the New Dealers and about the naiveté or stupidity of Roosevelt's Soviet policy, as at Yalta?

The Korean War contributed to this reassessment and directed public attention to the primacy of internal security and domestic subversion. An effective loyalty-security program was needed; a strong military already existed but had not been effectively used by the Truman administration. If the public sought scapegoats and easy answers to complex problems, its response was consistent with the prevailing rhetoric which the President had used to define international and domestic security problems since 1945. Necessarily, this rhetoric and Truman's policies affected the domestic political climate. In creating new standards

for judgment and response, President Truman unwittingly created the basis for McCarthyism's later effectiveness—a repressive
political climate and an erroneous conception of Soviet weakness,
the nature of subversion, and American omnipotence.

NOTES

1. There has been no satisfactory definition of the McCarthyite movement. Although individual McCarthyites can be readily identified, their
motives and philosophy were not necessarily consistent or identical. Some
were conservatives whose principal motivation was to discredit the New
Deal, others were motivated primarily by simple partisan (anti-Democratic)
considerations. This distinction is central to reconciling the diverse ends
sought by the McCarthyites. I would list as McCarthyites Senators Kenneth Wherry, Hugh Butler, George Malone, Everett Dirksen, James Kem,
Harry Cain, William Knowland, Richard Nixon, Karl Mundt, Homer
Capehart, Pat McCarran, Homer Ferguson, Arthur Watkins, Robert Taft,
William Langer, William Jenner, and Bourke Hickenlooper; and Repre-
sentatives Clare Hoffman, Lawrence Smith, Paul Shafer, J. Parnell Thomas,
Daniel Reed, Carl Curtis, Charles Vursell, William Lemke, Howard Buf-
fett, Noah Mason, George Dondero, John Taber, John Rankin, John Wood,
Timothy Sheehan, Charles Kersten, Charles Halleck, Joseph Martin, and
Alvin Bentley. For a more intensive analysis of the McCarthyites and
their political objectives and outlook, see my book *The Yalta Myths: An
Issue in American Politics, 1945–1955* (Columbia, Mo., 1969).
2. From 1945 through 1952 the McCarthyites assailed New Deal–Fair
Deal domestic policies as being essentially communistic. In assessing administration foreign policy they charged either that communists or communist sympathizers had infiltrated the Roosevelt-Truman administrations
and were thus able to influence policy, or that these administrations were
pro-Soviet in outlook and sympathy. For a selected, but not comprehen-
sive, list of these attacks, see *Congressional Record* (hereafter *CR*), 79th
Cong., 1st sess., 1945, pp. 1425, 1700–1702, A66–67, A605–606, A679–680,
A696, A730–731, A737, A912–913 A938, A965, A977, A5159, A5175; *ibid.*,
79th Cong., 2nd sess., 1946, pp. 1182–1183 1949, 2052–2054; *ibid.*, 80th
Cong., 1st sess., 1947, pp. 1620, 1649–1650, 2215–2217, 2292, 2627, 2784–
2785, 2833, 4589–4599, 9890–9892, A766, A838, A4801; *ibid.*, 81st Cong.,
1st sess., 1949, pp. 3266–3267, 3827 5237–5241, 6390–6391, 9553–9561,
10941–10942, 10958, 10961–10962, 11810–11813, 13158, 13264–13267,

14341, A158, A174, A458, A1129, A1344–1345, A2187–2189, A2871, A3108, A5456, A5704. U.S. Congress, House Committee on Un-American Activities, *Hearings Regarding Communist Espionage in the United States Government*, 80th Cong., 2nd sess., 1948, pp. 4–8, 11, 14.

3. *CR*, 79th Cong., 1st sess., 1945, pp. 1425, 1700–1702, 1769–1770, 4093, 4128, 5040, 5845, A65, A605–606, A666–667, A678–680, A696, A730–731, A737, A912–913, A938, A977, A1569–1570, A1684, A2413, A3144–3145, A4083, A4731–4733, A4776–4777; *ibid.*, 79th Cong., 2nd sess., 1946, pp. 1970–1971, 1974, 3066–3067; *ibid.*, 80th Cong., 1st sess., 1947, pp. 2215–2217, 2335–2337, 2460, 2784–2785, 2833, 2849, 3369–3370, 4598–4599, 4600, 4606, 4611, 4621, 4628, 4685–4686, 4731–4732, 4798; *ibid.*, 80th Cong., 2nd sess., 1948, pp. 2549, 3241, 3626, 3659–3661, A55, A933–934, A2105; *ibid.*, 81st Cong., 1st sess., 1949, pp. 3266–3267, 3767–3771, 5029–5034, 9092–9094, 9106, 9553–9561, 11662–11663, 13158, 13160–13161; *ibid.*, 81st Cong., 2nd sess., 1950, pp. 572, 635, 656, 16478–16479, 16513, 16553–16559, 16874–16875.

4. Secretary of State Stettinius to Secretary of War Stimson, May 12, 1945, Stettinius Papers, University of Virginia. Harry S. Truman, *Memoirs: Year of Decisions*, I (Garden City, 1955), 315–319, provides insights into the administration's changed commitment to the Yalta Far Eastern agreements. Executive Order 9835, issued on March 22, 1947, Truman Papers, OF252-K, Truman Library, provides insights into the administration's concerns when instituting the Federal Employee Loyalty Program. (All OF citations refer to the Truman Papers, Truman Library.) Moreover, despite McCarthyite charges, Truman's Secretary of State, Dean Acheson, was a hard-liner diplomatically and a conservative in economic policy. Indeed, Acheson broke with Roosevelt over his early economic policies and in the 1930's flirted with the Liberty League. See George Wolfskill, *The Revolt of the Conservatives: A History of the Liberty League, 1934–1940* (Boston, 1962), p. 150.

5. *CR*, 82nd Cong., 1st sess., 1951, pp. 320–325, 485–486, 1719–1721, 2653, 2907, 2957–2959, 3015, 3272–3273, 3282. See also Directive on the Need for Maintaining the Confidential Status of Employee Loyalty Records, March 15, 1948, OF41. Truman's Executive Order 10290, issued September 24, 1951, extended security classification to all federal agencies. *Washington Daily News*, September 26, 1951, p. 62.

6. See Daniel Bell, ed., *The Radical Right* (Garden City, 1964). Cf. Nelson Polsby, "Towards an Explanation of McCarthyism," *Political Studies*, VIII (October 1960), 250–271; Martin Trow, "Small Businessmen, Political Tolerance and Support for McCarthy," *American Journal of Sociology*, LXIV (November 1958), 270–281; Edward Shils, *The Torment of Secrecy* (Glencoe, Ill., 1956). For a critique of this view, see Michael Rogin, *The Intellectuals and McCarthy: The Radical Specter* (Cambridge, Mass., 1967).

7. *Public Opinion Quarterly* (hereafter *POQ*), IX, 91–95, 101–103, 252, 386–388, 533; X, 105, 115, 263–264, 409, 416–417, 436, 608, 618–619; XI, 147–150, 281, 285–286, 290, 315, 497, 641–642, 650. Truman's public correspondence files reveal a similar preference for accommodation and political tolerance during the early 1940's. Admittedly selective because written by those most concerned, these letters reveal a striking change in tone and emphasis between 1945 and 1950 on the part of both adminis-

tration supporters and critics. See Truman Papers, Personal Files, correspondence. A persistent question by reporters at Truman's early press conferences was whether and when another Big Three conference might be held to iron out differences between the United States and the Soviet Union. Among the general public, as late as May 1948, interest in summit diplomacy remained dominant with 63 per cent favoring, 28 per cent opposing, and 9 per cent having no opinion. At the same time, the public was pessimistic about its results, 34 per cent expecting success, 5 per cent a qualified success, 35 per cent a failure, and 26 per cent having no opinion. *POQ,* XII, 559.

8. *Time,* February 19, 1945, pp. 15, 23; February 26, 1945, pp. 15, 23–24; July 16, 1945, pp. 13–15; July 23, 1945, pp. 40–42; August 20, 1945, p. 13. *Saturday Evening Post,* February 3, 1945, p. 100. *New York Times,* February 3, 1945, p. 10; February 13, 1945, p. 22; February 14, 1945, p. 18; February 15, 1945, p. 18; February 16, 1945, p. 22; March 1, 1945, p. 20; March 2, 1945, p. 18; March 4, 1945, p. 3E; May 25, 1945, p. 18; June 30, 1945, p. 16; July 29, 1945, p. 10E; August 3, 1945, p. 16; August 9, 1945, p. 20; August 13, 1945, p. 18; September 9, 1945, p. 8E. *Newsweek,* February 5, 1945, p. 108; February 12, 1945, p. 30; February 26, 1945, pp. 24, 40–42, 44, 50, 68; July 23, 1945, p. 96; August 20, 1945, p. 56. *U.S. News,* February 23, 1945, pp. 11–12, 27, 32; March 2, 1945, p. 14; April 27, 1945, pp. 13–14; May 25, 1945, pp. 13–14, 28–29.

9. Truman, *Memoirs,* I, 75–82.

10. *Ibid.,* pp. 315–319. Stettinius to Stimson, May 12, 1945, Stettinius Papers. For further insights into the factors leading to the administration's decision not to publish the text of the Yalta Far Eastern agreements until February 1946, see my article "James F. Byrnes: Unwitting Yalta Myth-Maker," *Political Science Quarterly,* December 1966.

11. *Public Papers of the Presidents of the United States: Harry S. Truman, 1945* (Washington, D.C., 1961), pp. 546–560 (hereafter *Truman Papers*).

12. *Ibid.,* p. 547, my italics.

13. *Ibid.,* pp. 548–549, my italics.

14. *Ibid.,* pp. 1–6, 20–23, 25–26, 48–50, 118–127, 138–144, 203–214, 254–257, 359–366, 381–388, 404–413, 428–430, 431–438, 491–497, 504–514, 543–545. Significantly, Truman emphasized the importance of Allied unity, expressed pleasure over Russia's "yielding" on some matters of interest to the United States, and argued that the "Russians are just as anxious to get along with us as we are with them." *Ibid.,* pp. 118–127. Moreover, Truman stressed the importance for world peace and security of a united, democratic China and hoped that China's "internal differences" would be peacefully resolved. The United States, he said, would not interfere with or attempt to influence the course of any Chinese "internal strife." *Ibid.,* pp. 543–545.

15. *Truman Papers 1946,* pp. 38–47, 76, 87, 96–100, 144–148, 155–159, 185–190, 233–235, 346–349, 457–463, 477–480, 499–505; *Truman Papers 1947,* pp. 1–12, 113–117, 149–150, 176–180, 192–196, 207–216, 238–241, 254–257, 268–272, 449–450, 469–473, 515–529.

16. *Truman Papers 1946,* pp. 233–235; *Truman Papers 1947,* pp. 255–257.

17. *Truman Papers 1946,* pp. 346–347.

18. *Truman Papers 1947*, pp. 176–180, 211–216, 238–241, 254–255.
19. *Ibid.*, pp. 515–519.
20. *Ibid.*, p. 238.
21. *Truman Papers 1948*, pp. 182–189, 200–203, 231–235, 287–290, 336–340, 482–485, 815–818.
22. *Ibid.*, pp. 140–141, 144–146, 336–340.
23. *Ibid.*, pp. 182–186, my italics.
24. *Truman Papers 1949*, pp. 1–7, 44–97, 112–116, 196–198, 206–207, 230–232, 241–244, 277–279, 286–291, 395–400, 438, 455–459, 501–505, 517–525, 582–583.
25. *Ibid.*, p. 279.
26. *Truman Papers 1950*, pp. 120, 228–229, my italics.
27. *Ibid.*, pp. 138, 149–153, 159–163, 177–180.
28. *Ibid.*, pp. 2–11, 44–106, 131–132, 238–240, 423–425, 445–449, 473–477.
29. *Ibid.*, pp. 2–11, 238–240, 250–256, 284–288, 333–338, 342–344, 423–425, 449–452.
30. *Ibid.*, pp. 342–344, 374–377.
31. J. Howard McGrath, District of Columbia AMVETS Convention, April 8, 1949, McGrath Papers, Truman Library. The following references are to McGrath's speeches on deposit in the McGrath Papers: Pensacola, Fla., July 16, 1949; Boston, Mass., October 4, 1949; Hartford, Conn., October 10, 1949; Press Club, October 20, 1949; Troy, N.Y., October 28, 1949; Washington, D.C., November 25, 1949; Palm Beach, Fla., January 22, January 28, 1950; Atlantic City, N.J., February 7, 1950; Amherst, Mass., March 1, 1950; New York, N.Y., March 17, 1950; Boston, Mass., March 30, 1950; Charleston, W. Va., March 31, 1950; New York, N.Y., April 19, 1950; Omaha, Nebr., May 27, 1950; Philadelphia, Pa., June 18, 1950; Washington, D.C., September 20, 1950; St. Louis, Mo., October 5, 1950; Colorado Springs, Colo., October 11, 1950; Long Beach, Calif., October 17, October 28, 1950; Westminster, Md., November 18, 1950.
32. *Truman Papers 1950*, pp. 491–492, 498–506, 522–524, 527–537, 564–566, 599–600, 626–631, 687–689, 697–703, 719–720, 728–731, 741–746.
33. *Ibid.*, pp. 711–716, 724–731, 741–746.
34. *Ibid.*, pp. 724–725, my italics.
35. *Ibid.*, pp. 502–506, 522–524, 599–600, 643–645, 711–716, 724–728.
36. *Ibid.*, pp. 718–719.
37. See Report of the President's Temporary Commission on Employee Loyalty, Charles Murphy Papers, Truman Library, my italics. The reference to "Communist Party line activities" of government employees was to attempts to form a union of federal employees and to the radical political views of the members of that union organization on foreign and domestic policy questions.
38. William Batt, Jr. (Director, Research Division, Democratic National Committee) to Charles Murphy, September 13, 1948, Spingarn Papers, White House Assignment. Truman, Oklahoma City, Okla., September 28, 1948, PPF200. Press Release, Democratic National Committee (DNC), March 11, 1948; Files of the Facts, DNC, 1948; McGrath (Chairman, DNC), April 7, 1948; McGrath, February 18, 1948; File No. 5: The Democratic Record, DNC, 1948; all above in McGrath Papers, DNC Files.

Truman Papers 1948, pp. 186–190, 555, 801–806, 844–845, 882–886. Resolution, Adopted by the National Board of ADA, August 29, 1948, DNC Library Clipping File, Truman Library.

39. Karl Schmidt, *Henry A. Wallace: Quixotic Crusade, 1948* (Syracuse, 1960), pp. 159, 252–253, 261–262.

40. "Fellow Traveling Pa. GOP Congressmen Follow Red Party Line," Democratic State Committee of Pennsylvania, 1950, Theodore Tannenwald Papers, Truman Library.

41. U.S. House of Representatives, *Interim Report on Hearings Regarding Espionage in the United States Government*, 80th Cong., 2nd sess., 1948. In this August report the title of the hearings did not include the term "communism," an omission capsulizing the earlier anti–New Deal emphasis of the committee.

42. See the pre-November testimony and questioning of the committee members and compare it with their emphasis after the release of the "pumpkin papers." House Committee on Un-American Activities, *Hearings*, 1948.

43. *Ibid.*, p. 1202. Chambers also had repeatedly denied that Hiss had ever engaged in espionage activities, whether in testimony before the federal grand jury, in pre-trial proceedings, or on the national radio program "Meet the Press." See Alger Hiss, *In the Court of Public Opinion* (New York, 1957), pp. 153–155, 158–159, 170–171. After December, Chambers repudiated his earlier testimony, describing Hiss then as one of the "most zealous" Russian spies in Washington. *Chicago Tribune*, December 5, 1948, p. 1; November 22, 1949, p. 1.

44. *Truman Papers 1948*, pp. 186–190, 431–435, 457–461, 844–845, 882–888, 925–930, 959–962, 963–966. File No. 3: The Democratic Record, DNC, 1948; McGrath, September 7, 1948; and Files of the Facts, DNC, 1948; all above in McGrath Papers, DNC Files. *Washington Post*, August 31, 1948. Secretary of Commerce Charles Sawyer, St. Louis, Mo., August 31, 1948; Presidential Platform Material, prepared by Spingarn, October 13, 1948; and Department of Justice Press Release, September 29, 1949; all above in Spingarn Papers, White House Assignment. *New York Times*, September 18, 1948, p. 8.

45. Clark, French Lick Springs, Ind., August 21, 1948, McGrath Papers, DNC File. Clark, Des Moines, Iowa, September 6, 1948; and Spingarn, September 21, 1948; Spingarn Papers, White House Assignment.

46. Truman to All Agency and Department Heads, March 13, 1948, OF252-K. *Truman Papers 1948*, pp. 181–182.

47. *Ibid.*, pp. 959–966.

48. *Truman Papers 1949*, pp. 280–283, 292–296.

49. *Ibid.*, pp. 280–283.

50. Cf. Roosevelt's original directive of May 1940, compared with Clark's altered version of that directive. Roosevelt to Attorney General Jackson, May 21, 1940; Attorney General Clark to Truman, July 17, 1946, Spingarn Papers, Truman Library. For a discussion of the significance of this deletion, see my article "Attorney General Tom Clark, Internal Security and the Truman Administration," *New University Thought* (Spring 1968).

51. Spingarn to Clark Clifford, February 1, 1949, Spingarn Papers, White House Assignment. Murphy to Clark, February 4, 1949, Murphy

Files, Internal Security. Spingarn to Lynch, January 26, 1949; Spingarn for the Files, August 23, 1949; Assistant Attorney General Peyton Ford to Frank Pace (Director, Bureau of the Budget), August 20, 1949; Spingarn to Murphy, February 1, 1950; George Elsey to Truman, February 2, 1950; Spingarn for the Files, May 6, 1950; Spingarn and Murphy to Truman, May 16, 1950; and Spingarn for the Record, July 17, 1950; all in Spingarn Papers, National Defense. Truman to McGrath, May 19, 1950; and Spingarn for the Files, May 20, 1950, OF2750. Spingarn to Clifford, December 30, 1949, Spingarn Papers, Chronological File.

52. *Truman Papers 1950*, pp. 560–564, 571–576, 619–622. Spingarn to Truman, July 14, 1950; Spingarn to White House Staff, August 1, 1950; Spingarn for the Files, August 9, 1950; David Lloyd for the Files, August 12, 1950; Spingarn to Murphy, August 15, 1950; Spingarn to Senators Tydings, Myers, Kefauver, O'Mahoney, and Hill, August 16, 1950; Justice Explanation of Substitute Bill, July 26, 1950; Spingarn to Philip Dreyer (Democratic National Committee), August 17, 1950; Richard Neustadt on Pros and Cons on Signature or Veto of the McCarran Bill, August 18, 1950; William Boyle (Chairman, Democratic National Committee), September 5, 1950; Spingarn for the White House Staff, September 6, 1950; all in Spingarn Papers, National Defense. Spingarn for the Files, August 11, 1950, Murphy Files, Internal Security.

53. *Truman Papers 1950*, pp. 645–653, 679–682, 697–703. Memo for the Files, September 4, 1950; Spingarn to White House Staff, September 20, 1950; Spingarn to Roger Jones (Bureau of the Budget), September 29, 1950; all in Spingarn Papers, National Defense.

54. *Truman Papers 1950*, pp. 159–163, 177–185, 229–238, 240–241, 250–256, 267–272, 284–288, 418–423. Donald Dawson, May 8, 1950, OF419-K.

55. *Truman Papers 1950*, pp. 177–185, 229–232, 240–241, 267–272. Memo to Adrian Fisher (Legal Adviser, State Department), March 9, 1950; Murphy to Elsey, March 27, 1950; Murphy and Spingarn to Truman, May 24, 1950; all in Murphy Files, Loyalty. Senator Tydings to Secretary of State Acheson, March 22, 1950; Seth Richardson (Chairman, Loyalty Review Board) to Dawson, June 26, 1950; Tydings to Truman, April 12, 1950; all in OF419-K. Spingarn, May 22, 1950, Spingarn Papers, National Defense. *Washington Post*, May 5, 1950, p. 1. *New York Times*, April 4, 1950.

56. Spingarn to Dawson, May 20, 1950; Representative Helen Douglas, June 1, 1950; Spingarn, May 22, 1950; all in Spingarn Papers, National Defense. Charles Maylon to Murphy, March 28, 1950; Meeting (John Peurifoy, Adrian Fisher, Samuel Boykin, Peyton Ford, Donald Dawson, George Elsey, Franklin Pailis, Charles Murphy), May 23, 1950; Murphy and Spingarn to Truman, May 24, 1950; Draft Executive Order to establish President's Commission on Internal Security and Individual Rights, June 1, 1950; Murphy to Truman, June 5, 1950; Spingarn to Murphy, June 19, 1950; Spingarn for the Files, June 23, 1950; Spingarn on Pros and Cons of Establishment of Presidential Commission, June 26, 1950; all in Murphy Files, Loyalty. Richardson to Dawson, June 26, 1950, OF419-K. Tydings to Truman, July 24, 1950, OF252-K. *Washington Post*, June 16, 1950, p. 1.

57. Spingarn for the Files, August 15, 1950; Spingarn to Dawson, September 30, 1950; Spingarn for the Record, July 21, 1950; Murphy, Elsey, and Spingarn, July 11, 1950; all in Spingarn Papers, National Defense. Spingarn to Murphy, July 20, 1950, Murphy Files, Loyalty. Draft Executive Order for President's Commission on Internal Security and Individual Rights, July 25, 1950, Murphy Files, Internal Security. Theodore Tannenwald to W. Averell Harriman, July 27, 1950, Tannenwald Papers, Chronological File. Spingarn for the Files, September 19, 1950, Philleo Nash Files, Truman Library.

58. David Bell to Murphy, November 14, 1950; and Murphy to Truman, November 15, 1950; Murphy Files, Internal Security. Max Kampleman (Legislative Counsel, Senator Humphrey) to Murphy, November 20, 1950, Murphy Papers. Truman to Herbert Hoover, November 25, 1950, and reply, November 26, 1950; Truman to Hoover, December 7, 1950; Truman to Admiral Chester Nimitz, January 4, 1951, and reply, January 9, 1951; all in OF2750-A. Truman, January 23, 1951, President's Commission . . ., RG220, Truman Library. (All RG220 citations refer to the files of the President's Commission on Internal Security and Individual Rights, Truman Library.) Executive Order 10207, January 23, 1951; and Truman, February 12, 1951; RG220.

59. Meeting of the President's Commission, February 12 through 15, 1951; Nimitz to Hiram Bingham (Chairman, Loyalty Review Board), February 16, 1951; Bingham to Nimitz, February 16, 1951; Bingham to John Danaher (commission member), February 19, 1951; Matthew Connelly to Nimitz, February 21, 1951; R. C. Leffingwell (commission member) to Nimitz, February 23, 1951; Charles Silver (commission member) to Nimitz, February 26, 1951; Harvey Firestone (commission member) to Nimitz, February 26, 1951; Emmet Walsh (commission member) to Nimitz, February 27, 1951; Danaher to Nimitz, February 27, 1951; Karl Block (commission member) to Harold Benson (Administrative Assistant to the Commission), February 28, 1951; Danaher to Nimitz, March 2, 1951; Nimitz to Benson, March 6, 1951; Benson to Danaher, March 9, 1951; Anna Strauss (commission member) to Nimitz, March 9, 1951; Bingham to Nimitz, March 16, 1951; all in RG220. L. A. Moyer (Executive Director, Civil Service Loyalty Board) to Civil Service Commission, February 2, 1949; Bingham to Harry Mitchell (Chairman, Civil Service Commission), February 15, 1951; Assistant Attorney General Peyton Ford to Murphy, April 20, 1951; Robert Ramspeck (Chairman, Civil Service Commission) to Truman, April 16, 1951; all in OF252-K.

60. Nimitz to Truman, April 4, 1951; Truman to Nimitz, April 27, 1951; Press Release, April 28, 1951; all in RG220. Bingham to all heads of departments and agencies, May 23, 1951, OF252-K.

61. *Washington Post*, March 17, 1950. Donald Hansen, January 3, 1952, Spingarn Papers, Loyalty. Bingham to all executive departments and agencies, December 21, 1951, OF252-K.

ATHAN THEOHARIS

The Escalation of
the Loyalty Program

WITH THE EMERGENCE of the Cold War, the Truman administration sought to protect the nation from what the President
defined as the serious menace of subversion. To achieve that
objective, his administration developed procedures intended to
avert an internal security threat, whether in the form of sabotage,
espionage, or "subversive" political activities. The goal was absolute security: the operational premise was preventative, not
corrective—i.e., to avert any possible (and not necessarily imminent) threat of subversion. These priorities were basic to
what became a permanent federal employee loyalty program
directed to prevent "communist" infiltration of the federal
government.

In establishing the program, a second and no less important
motivation was President Truman's interest in foreclosing Republican use of the issue of anti-communism, either criticizing

The author wishes to express his appreciation to the Truman Institute
for National and International Affairs and to Wayne State University for
their support of his research, and to the University of Iowa, particularly
Mrs. Emily Hartnell, for assistance in typing the manuscript. He further
acknowledges the editorial assistance and criticisms of Barton Bernstein,
Lynn Parsons, and Ivan Dee.

242

his administration's surveillance of communist activities or charging that previous Democratic administrations (the New Deal) had "coddled" communists or were sympathetic to communism. Truman in his own right was a militant anti-communist and he distrusted political radicalism, specifically the American Communist party. His commitment was intensified by the criticisms of former New Dealers (particularly Harold Ickes, Henry Wallace, and Rexford Guy Tugwell) that the Truman administration had repudiated or betrayed the principles of Roosevelt's foreign and domestic policies, and by the 1948 Progressive party campaign aimed at denying Truman and the Democrats electoral success.

These factors explain Truman's support for a federal employee loyalty program. Initially he sought to balance anti-subversive procedures with safeguards to minimize the effect of the program on individual liberties. But this balancing act failed. Instead, the administration established a far-ranging loyalty program which extended beyond simple considerations of national security. Intended safeguards for individual rights were subverted or abandoned. And the federal program served to legitimize state and private loyalty investigations. The nature of the administration's leadership and policy priorities, moreover, intensified public fears, contributed to a more repressive political atmosphere, and eventually led to a real obsession with loyalty that culminated in the rise of Senator Joseph McCarthy and "McCarthyism."

The loyalty program, moreover, altered national politics by redefining national priorities and recasting the domestic political debate. At the same time, the bureaucracy that was established to administer the program, because it was committed to establishing its expertise and perpetuation, insured a preference for administrative efficiency over individual rights.

With the passage of time, procedures which in 1945 would have been bitterly renounced on constitutional or civil libertarian grounds were accepted because they appeared to advance the loyalty program's objectives. These procedures, by further altering the program's priorities, in turn served to support demands for additional, essentially repressive "corrective" revisions. The movement was gradual, but the shift away from individual liberties was significant.

The groundwork for the loyalty program had been laid even before World War II—a fear that the United States might suffer the same fascist and communist subversion that plagued Europe in the 1930's, as dramatized in Czechoslovakia, Austria, and France. Congress assumed a central role in establishing safeguards against such activities, at times independent of or in opposition to Roosevelt's efforts. Only over the question of wiretapping did Congress, both in 1940 and 1941, reject Roosevelt's request for legislative authority in cases affecting the national security. Otherwise, in 1939, Congress forbade federal employment to any member of an organization advocating the overthrow of "our constitutional government." In 1940 it ceded to the armed services the right of summary dismissal of "suspect" employees, and during World War II it significantly extended this authority by empowering the Civil Service Commission to dismiss suspect employees in either the civil or military services. In 1941 special appropriations of $100,000 authorized the Department of Justice to investigate federal employees suspected of belonging to "subversive organizations." Subsequently Congress voted an additional $200,000 for these investigations. And in 1943 congressional conservatives sought to force the dismissal of certain "suspect" individuals already in government employ. The House, in fact, designated a subcommittee of the Appropriations Committee, the Kerr Committee, to investigate all charges of "subversive tendencies" of federal employees. This committee recommended and the House formally stipulated that no money be spent for the salaries of three particular employees.[1]

World War II provided the impetus for these congressional actions. Although their stated purpose was anti-subversion, they were frequently applied to political radicalism. Cognizant of this possibility and of conservative attempts to hamstring the New Deal, President Roosevelt, in establishing guidelines for a wartime anti-espionage program, tried to insure that investigatory procedures would distinguish between radical politics and espionage. The President imposed definite restraints and required proof of overt action as the basis for dismissing a federal employee for security reasons.

In an August 1940 order, Roosevelt stipulated that the FBI could initiate investigations of incumbent employees only upon the request of the individual's department head. By placing responsibility and initiative within the department, Roosevelt's order limited the FBI's investigatory role. A year later, on October 22, 1941, Attorney General Francis Biddle countermanded this protection when he authorized the FBI to investigate "subversive" activities of federal employees. Biddle directed the FBI, however, to submit its findings to the head of the appropriate department, and he did not require the head to act on the report.

This procedure created administrative problems, complicated by the heightened security concern which came with American involvement in World War II. In response to the situation, the President, on the advice of the Attorney General, established a special Interdepartmental Committee. This committee was intended to provide an expert, independent service to inexperienced department heads who lacked competence or confidence in their ability to evaluate the FBI reports. Again, the department head was not required to act on the committee's recommendation. And the committee's actions were limited to the "credible evidence" standards established by the Hatch Act (party membership or present advocacy of revolution) and not mere suspicion.[2]

Thus Roosevelt's internal security program restricted the scope of FBI investigations and insured that dismissals would be based on documented charges. Inevitably, violations of individual rights occurred, but they were limited by the program's temporary duration, the emphasis on departmental responsibility, the refusal to delegate authority to investigating agencies, and the fact that a permanent loyalty bureaucracy had not been established. Because of its war orientation, the program presumably would end with the surrender of Germany and Japan.

The limited character of this program was affirmed by Roosevelt's Attorney General Biddle. Shortly before the end of the

war (March 19, 1945) he introduced and recommended congressional action on legislation dealing with sabotage. Biddle
specifically warned against repression, declaring that "the crime
of sabotage should be comprehensively defined and should
include conspiracies to commit the offense." Seeking to limit
legislative restrictions on civil liberties, the Attorney General
stressed the effectiveness of the administration's wartime internal security program with its commitment to civil liberties.[3]

No action was taken on Biddle's proposals, for a new administration under Harry S. Truman was soon inaugurated. Truman
responded to the tensions in U.S.-Soviet relations and continued
the wartime program. A marked change in focus now occurred,
however: the Truman administration's program was directed
not only at the activities of "subversive" agents who might be
spies but also at the open political activism and involvement of
the American Communist party in the labor and civil rights
(anti-segregation) movements. Truman's priorities increased the
influence of hard-liners in the Congress and in the Justice
Department, particularly that of his appointee as Attorney General, Tom Clark.[4]

Clark had a broader view than Biddle of what constituted
threats to internal security. Specifically, by relying on postwar
developments Clark pressed Truman to revise existing procedures and allow the FBI greater investigative leeway. Soon
after acceding to the Attorney Generalship, Clark urged the
President to order the repatriation of "alien enemies" who
seriously endangered the safety of the United States because
of their adherence to foreign governments or to the "principles"
of such governments.[5]

At the same time Clark enhanced the FBI's investigatory
authority. Despite the formal restrictions of Roosevelt's directives, during the war the FBI had exceeded those limits and
had even acted contrary to constitutional safeguards. In fact,
FBI agents had, as the *Amerasia* case subsequently disclosed,
resorted to wiretapping and had unlawfully entered and searched
private offices and homes of suspect individuals.[6] Although its
investigations did not result in conviction (for procedural reasons), the FBI did uncover evidence confirming that foreign

service personnel had pilfered government documents for the use of *Amerasia* editors. The *Amerasia* case, although technically not involving espionage (the documents were published and not passed on to foreign agents), contributed to a heightened concern over subversion. A Royal Canadian Commission report of 1946, disclosing Soviet atomic espionage efforts during the war, added to this fear and provided important leverage for congressional internal security proponents. These congressmen pressed the administration for action in the internal security field. Related to this purpose, during late 1945 and 1946 a subcommittee of the House Committee on Civil Service conducted hearings investigating federal employee loyalty. After these hearings, the subcommittee recommended that Congress establish a special commission composed exclusively of individuals having an investigative background, to study existing laws, standards, and procedures and ascertain whether the government was effectively protected from individuals not "primarily loyal" to the United States. The subcommittee further recommended that the Congress appropriate sufficient funds to fingerprint all federal employees.[7]

Truman encountered relentless 'pressure from the chairman of the parent committee, Jennings Randolph, from Civil Service Commissioner Arthur Flemming (and his successor Harry Mitchell), and from Attorney General Tom Clark, to establish the proposed commission. Though he never expressed opposition to the commission and investigation, Truman did not act immediately upon the suggestion. Until the November 1946 congressional elections, the President simply kept the proposal under study.[8]

The Republicans' dramatic victory in the 1946 elections forced Truman to act. After November he could no longer ignore the possibility that a congressional loyalty investigation, relying on the impact of the Canadian Royal Commission disclosure of Soviet espionage, would institute a conservative investigation of the entire New Deal. On November 25 the President established by executive order a Temporary Commission on Employee Loyalty to review existing programs, standards, and procedures. Composed of representatives of executive departments involved in investigative activities, the commission was directed to evaluate the adequacy of existing security measures in protecting the government from "disloyal or subversive" employees. The commission was further directed to report back to the President no later than February 1, 1947, and to recommend specifically whether any agency (or agencies) should be given responsibility for prescribing and supervising the implementation of security procedures.[9]

The wording of the executive order, the composition of the Temporary Commission (solely of individuals with investigative experience), and the letters of the commission chairman (A. Devitt Vanech of the Justice Department) to department heads and intelligence agencies, asking their recommendations and advice, reflected the predilections of the investigation. Truman had decided that unquestionably a loyalty program and more effective safeguards were needed to protect the national security. Through the commission he intended to establish the limits and requirements for an effective but fairly administered program.[10]

The timing of the order, as well as the stipulation that the commission report back no later than February 1, also reflected Truman's desire to avert congressional action and preclude Republican efforts to monopolize the anti-communist issue. In part his haste was laudable, for Truman sought to remove loyalty from partisan politics and protect individual rights against the danger of loyalty investigations. Nonetheless, the haste and sense of expediency that led to the establishment of the program, in addition to the priorities basic to the approach, effectively outweighed this limited gain. By his action Truman in effect bowed to the pressures of conservative, anti–New Dealers in Congress and indirectly legitimized their concerns and procedures.

The commission witnesses* generally emphasized that in the

---

*They included FBI Director J. Edgar Hoover, Attorney General Tom Clark, Thomas Inglis (Office of Naval Intelligence), S. J. Chamberlin (Director of Intelligence of the War Department), and Herbert Gaston (Chairman, Wartime Interdepartmental Committee on Employee Investigations). Gaston alone did not believe the nation confronted a serious loyalty problem.

absence of a loyalty program the national security was gravely threatened. Stressing the need for loyalty safeguards, they affirmed that "even one" disloyal federal employee was a "serious" threat to the national security. Ostensibly their testimony emphasized the need for safeguards against sabotage or espionage. Their concern centered, however, not only on overt acts but on potential "subversion" as reflected in an individual's political radicalism. Distinctly conservative, the witnesses maintained that only individuals with correct and patriotic ideas should obtain federal employment, for it offered the opportunity to shape domestic and foreign policy.[11]

The testimony of FBI Director Hoover dramatized the main priorities. He listed espionage as one of five potential dangers that the employment of *a* "subversive or disloyal person" posed for the federal government. He then enumerated the other four dangers, indicating his anti-reformist concern:

b. Influencing the formation of policies of the United States Government either domestic or foreign so that those policies will either favor the foreign country of their ideological choice or will weaken the United States Government domestically or abroad to the ultimate advantage of the above indicated foreign power.

c. Influencing the execution of the foreign or domestic policies of the United States Government or the policies of the Federal agency with which the employee is connected . . .

d. The spreading by the employee within his particular agency of the Federal service of propaganda favorable to the foreign country of his ideological choice in such a way as to influence other personnel of the agency and the expression of such propaganda to non-employees in such a way as to create an impression of official sanction to such propaganda.

e. Recruiting of other individuals, either federal workers or non-Government employees, for membership in the subversive or disloyal group which the employee represents.[12]

The conclusions of the commission's final report were shaped by the emphasis of Hoover's testimony (as that of the other witnesses), the investigatory orientation of commission members, and the President's initial directive. The commission concluded that existing standards and procedures would not effectively safeguard the national security from internal threats, and that a loyalty program, administered by the executive branch and requiring the screening and surveillance of federal employees, was needed. The commission admitted, however, that it had not uncovered conclusive evidence to support these recommendations.

In an executive order of March 22, 1947, President Truman adopted these recommendations and established a Federal Employee Loyalty Program. The President's order sought to balance internal security and civil libertarian considerations. The procedures outlined were designed to insure the government against the employment of disloyal individuals without violating due process of law or individual rights, or simply dismissing an individual because of his political ideas or activities. Loyalty procedures, accordingly, were standardized; a hierarchical system of review boards in each department, under the supervision of a Loyalty Review Board, was established to conduct investigations and hearings. The order, like the commission's report, was inadvertently vague in defining "loyalty," "disloyalty," "serious" threats, or "subversion." And the thrust of the program was that dismissal or denial of clearance need not be limited to overt acts confirming disloyalty or treason but included a review of the employee's subversive proclivities, hence his ideas and associations.

To limit abuses, the order established two standards. First, it provided that past political associations (particularly membership in organizations listed by the Attorney General as subversive) would not *ipso facto* justify an adverse loyalty decision. The standard for dismissal stipulated that "on all the evidence, reasonable grounds exist for the belief that the person involved is disloyal to the Government of the United States." This standard, though vague, required proof, not mere suspicion, of disloyalty. In addition, the order, by establishing a hierarchical review procedure, enabled the accused employee to appeal an adverse ruling and to refute unsubstantiated charges.

As a second safeguard, Truman limited the investigatory roles of the FBI and the Loyalty Review Board (established to coordinate and provide an impartial overview for an agency-centered program). The FBI was strictly limited to gathering information about incumbent employees; agencies were not required to use its investigative services. The commission had intentionally recommended restricting the role of the FBI in order to allay suspicions of a program based on the Bureau's investigations. Truman's executive order, moreover, delegated to the Civil Service Commission supervisory responsibility over both the investigative and review (through the Loyalty Review Board) phases of the program. At the same time, agency heads were designated as the final authority for dismissing an employee and developing procedures for the operation of the program. (The Loyalty Review Board's decisions were to be only advisory, not binding, recommendations.) If an agency lacked investigative means, its director could rely either on the services of the Civil Service Commission or on the FBI.[13]

These intended safeguards did not work. Instead, the desire for efficiency in administering the program superseded the concern for individual rights; investigation and prosecution objectives became primary considerations. The independence of departments, the standard for dismissal, and the functions of the FBI and the Loyalty Review Board were subsequently altered to reflect this desire. Operating on the premise that federal employment was a privilege and not a right, the program subordinated individual rights to the quest for absolute security against potential subversion.

The first major shift, in essence contradicting the provisions of the President's executive order, concerned the FBI's investigatory role. Whereas the order stringently restricted the functions of the FBI to securing information when requested by the Civil Service, the Bureau, aided by Attorney General Clark, pressed for unlimited jurisdiction over investigations. The shift was related to budgetary considerations. Existing budgeted appropriations for 1947 did not cover expenses for administering loyalty investigations of present or potential employees. The proposed special supplemental appropriations, which the administration requested, provided for a substantial increase only for the FBI and thus insured its sway over investigations.

The Civil Service protested this budgetary decision and shift in priority. Appealing to the President and the White House staff, Harry Mitchell, the chairman of the Civil Service Commission, contended that FBI investigations had been confined to the incumbent employee phase of the program in order to insure administrative efficiency. The Civil Service Commission, Mitchell argued, should properly conduct investigations of all future applicants or of employees whose applications were being processed (and thus were classified as "temporary").

Attorney General Clark convinced President Truman that Civil Service's position had neither "legal" nor "practical" merit and that the President should reaffirm his "previous decision to the effect that all investigations of employees whether permanent or temporary . . . be conducted by the Federal Bureau of Investigation." Civil Service's procedure, Clark pointedly argued, would undermine the program's effectiveness. "Temporary employees," Clark added, "sometimes work for a year or more. As soon as the agencies find out about it [that these investigations would be conducted by the Civil Service Commission and not by the FBI] they may try to avoid investigation by appointing people on a temporary basis."[14]

This preference for effective prosecution underlay a related decision by the Truman administration to insure the confidentiality of FBI investigative reports. The March executive order had directed investigating agencies to make available to department heads "all investigative material and information" concerning the designated employee. The investigating agency was allowed to refuse to disclose the names of confidential informants if it provided sufficient backround information about such informants to permit an adequate evaluation of the charges, and if it established "in writing" the necessity of confidentiality for "the protection of the informants or . . . the investigation of other cases." The order further stipulated that "Investigating agencies shall not use this discretion to decline to reveal sources of information where such action is not essential."[15] The intent was to insure maximum information, to protect the accused employee from unfounded charges, and to avert the possibility that resort to confidentiality might become a ruse for refusing disclosure. The investigating agency would have to justify its resort to confidentiality, and this action was clearly to be the exception.

After 1947, however, a procedure evolved to insure the complete confidentiality of the FBI investigative reports. This development resulted from the administration's partisanship and commitment to expediting prosecution and aiding the FBI. Initially (as in the 1947–1948 House Appropriations Subcommittee investigation of the State Department) the administration had cooperated with Congress to permit committee access to departmental loyalty files. Truman, in March 1948, reversed this procedure to require prior presidential approval of all nonexecutive requests for loyalty records. By this order the President sought to thwart Republican attempts to discredit the Roosevelt-Truman administrations and to deny the Congress, particularly the Republican leadership, access to the FBI's investigatory record. In 1950 Truman reaffirmed this order, rejecting demands raised by Senator McCarthy and other conservatives for the end of this executive restriction. Confidentiality, Truman then asserted, was essential to insure the effective operation of FBI investigations (safeguarding potential and actual sources) and to protect innocent employees from the publicity of unfounded accusations.[16]

Earlier, in 1947, confidentiality had also been applied to deny departmental access to the FBI reports. Certain executive departments, primarily Interior, had then attempted, when devising loyalty procedures under the newly established program, to secure the total report, including information about FBI investigative procedures. This attempt resulted in a confrontation with the Department of Justice. At issue was the question of priorities: the FBI's quest for secrecy *versus* the departmental concern that anonymity not preclude an accused employee from developing an effective defense. Basically, the conflict revolved around the leeway which confidential testimony permitted an employee—whether it would elicit fairer or more dishonest testimony against his co-workers.

As early as July 8, 1947, Attorney General Tom Clark had restricted information obtained from FBI informants. Clark denied such information to other departments without his approval. In December 1947 the Department of the Interior contested this decision. As basic guidelines for the operation of the loyalty program, Interior specified that an accused employee should receive a list of charges and an opportunity to cross-examine his accusers. In this conflict between Interior and Justice, President Truman upheld the Department of Justice on the grounds that Interior's procedures would cripple FBI investigations. Subsequently (1953), the definition of a "confidential informant" was extended to include all informers who requested that their identity not be disclosed. The "not essential" aspect of the original order (prohibiting the confidentiality of informants where not necessary) had by then been rendered inoperative.[17]

The same subordination of individual rights to administrative requirements evolved from the operational role of the Loyalty Review Board. Initially it had been given limited review responsibility over adverse (dismissal) decisions of department loyalty boards. Its recommendations were advisory, intended to safeguard the individual employee from unfair departmental investigators. In time, however, the board's presumably advisory recommendations became binding on agency heads. In December 1951 the Loyalty Review Board assumed the right to review *any* decision of a lower review board, even in cases where the individual had been cleared, if the board felt that the case might affect the national security. Thereby the board attempted to impose on other federal agencies its definition of what constituted loyalty or threats to the national security. A procedure originally intended to preclude departmental abuses of individual rights and to insure uniformity and fairness in the operation of the loyalty program, had resulted in the emergence of a self-appointed, all-encompassing central authority.[18]

The Loyalty Review Board consistently sought to avert any civil-libertarian criticisms of the loyalty program and, at the same time, to insure the program's continuance. The original loyalty program, as established in 1947, had not been considered permanent or perfect. The Temporary Commission and the White House staff had recognized that the operation of the program might disclose the need for minor or radical revisions, or even that time would diminish the need for such a program. Once established, however, the program was accepted as a permanent and necessary protection. More significantly, after 1947 the only changes seriously considered by the administration were intended to insure efficiency or prosecution. The Loyalty Review Board thereby assumed a central role. From 1948 through 1950 the board publicly denounced protests by civil-libertarians, whether Congresswoman Helen Douglas, the Americans for Democratic Action, the American Civil Liberties Union, the NAACP, or the White House staff, that the program violated individual rights. These protests, the board affirmed, were unwarranted; the demands for an impartial review of loyalty procedures were unnecessary and harmful.

The Loyalty Review Board defined its objective as insuring the "unswerving loyalty" of all federal employees. The board then rhetorically defended an employee's right to belong to radical political organizations and affirmed that membership should not affect his employment status. Only overt actions, not suspicions based upon radical associations, the board contended, should constitute grounds for a disloyalty dismissal. But the board objected to the proposal that an accused employee be given a written list of charges in advance of his hearing. The board also discounted suggestions either providing for an independent review of the Attorney General's list of subversive organizations or stipulating the time when an organization was determined to be communist-controlled. At the same time, the board recommended extending the coverage and investigative authority of the loyalty program.

In 1950 the operation of the program was again challenged. Senator McCarthy's charges of "communists in government," and the Tydings Committee's unconvincing rebuttal of his "81 cases," provided the opportunity for liberals to pressure the President to appoint an impartial commission to review existing loyalty procedures. In discussions on this proposal, the Loyalty Review Board and the Justice Department, joined by Democratic congressional leaders, opposed an independent review of the program. The congressional leaders questioned the efficacy of

an outside investigation and feared that it might simply tend
to support McCarthy. The board and the Justice Department
opposed any interference with existing arrangements. Defending
existing procedures and denying that the McCarthyites' criticisms were justified, the board chairman, Seth Richardson,
impugned the patriotism of those demanding a review. He suggested that only individuals who opposed a loyalty program
would support a review of existing procedures. The independent
administration of the program and the continued confidentiality
of the loyalty records, Richardson affirmed, were necessary to
safeguard the national security and the reputations of unfairly
accused employees. The Justice Department's and the board's
concern for civil liberties was more rhetorical than central: by
this time both were pressing for approval of a proposed bill
providing for the summary dismissal of "suspect" civilian employees.[19]

While the Loyalty Review Board and the Justice Department
opposed suggestions that restricted the operation of the program, they argued for administrative reforms which would close
loopholes and prevent the employment of individuals of "doubtful" loyalty "potentially" dangerous to the national security. The
implication was that existing procedures reflected an excessive
concern with individual rights. Attorney General J. Howard
McGrath, Clark's successor, forthrightly expressed this view in
averring that

> the Basic Loyalty Program . . . is quite satisfactory . . . there are
> no sound grounds for criticizing its findings. Therefore, I believe
> the question as to whether the basic program should be re-exam-
> ined at this time should be answered in the negative. However,
> experience gained in operating the program through the past two
> and one-half years has demonstrated . . . the desirability of an
> administrative review of the organizational structure . . . as well
> as some of the regulations and procedures which have been adopt-
> ed. . . . I believe that such review should be made by you in
> consultation with persons in this Department and the Civil Service
> Commission who have been connected directly with the Loyalty
> Program.[20]

In a 1949 report on the operation of the loyalty program, the board urged revision of the standard for dismissal. The board objected to the requirement that loyalty officers interpret this standard—namely, "on all the evidence, reasonable *grounds* exist for the belief that the person involved is *disloyal* to the Government of the United States"—to mean that an incumbent employee "is at present disloyal." Individuals "who are *potentially* disloyal or who are bad security risks," the board protested, had thus been able to secure clearance. The board recommended instead that clearance be denied "if there is a reasonable *doubt* as to their [the applicants'] *loyalty* to the Government of the United States."[21]

Although the board's recommendation originally was to be limited to applicants for federal employment, by 1950 it sought to secure adoption of this standard for the loyalty program as a whole. Senator McCarthy's dramatic accusations, the crisis of the Korean War, the resulting public concern over administration priorities, and the passage (in 1950) of the McCarran Internal Security Act provided new impetus for a more "effective" program. These developments enabled the board in early 1951 to renew pressure on the administration for a revised standard. The board wanted to replace "reasonable *grounds* exist for the belief that the person involved is *disloyal*" with "reasonable *doubt* exists as to the *loyalty* of the person involved."[22]

The proposed change was a complete reversal of the burden of proof. Sweeping in scope and intent, this standard resolved doubts about an individual's loyalty in favor of the loyalty officers, thereby expediting dismissal or the denial of clearance. Mere suspicion, as opposed to tangible evidence, became enough for a dismissal or refusal to grant clearance. Inevitably, this revised standard placed greater emphasis on the individual's political beliefs and associations, for it involved a judgment of his proclivities for subversion.

The original standard had prevented the board from approving the dismissal of suspect employees, such as John Stewart Service, whose former associations and opinions had made them controversial and the focus for McCarthyite attacks. The con-

tinued employment of these individuals seemingly confirmed
the McCarthyites' charges and served to undermine public confidence in the administration and in even the adequacy of the
loyalty program. A revised standard, by expediting dismissal
of suspect employees, would presumably restore public confidence in the board's vigilance and the program's effectiveness.

Hiram Bingham, chairman of the board, offered his recommendation at a time when Truman had established a special
commission to investigate the adequacy of existing loyalty procedures and legislation. Truman directed the commission to
settle on procedures for an effective loyalty program to protect
the national security without transgressing individual rights.

Bingham immediately pressured the new commission, headed
by former Admiral Chester Nimitz, to consider the recommended revision of the standard for dismissal. Emphasizing the
board's heavy work load and the perils of delay, Bingham (with
support from the Department of Justice) urged the commission
to render an "early" decision approving the new standard. The
commission, however, was then unprepared to act, having as yet
not resolved organizational or operational problems. It was waiting for Congress to approve special enabling legislation waiving
the conflict-of-interest requirement for commission employees.
Despite Senator Pat McCarran's opposition, it appeared that
the commission might gain congressional approval of this legislation. Given the situation, the President required the Loyalty
Review Board to defer any changes in the operation of the
loyalty program unless approved or considered by the commission.[23]

As congressional opposition to waiving the conflict of interest
requirement hardened, the commission was not able to organize
itself. President Truman was soon faced with the decision either
to await congressional approval of special legislation, with the
prospect of a long delay, or to bypass the commission and
implement the board's request. At issue was a choice between
administrative expediency and individual rights. Ostensibly,
Truman had appointed the Nimitz Commission to insure an
impartial judgment of existing procedures and legislation, in-

tended to strengthen both security safeguards and individual liberties. That impartial judgment was never made. In April 1951 Truman, unwilling to wait until the commission became operative, approved the new standard.[24]

The Loyalty Review Board and the Department of Justice immediately sought to exploit this executive decision. In May the board ordered all department loyalty boards to apply the new standard to the 565 cases then under consideration and, in addition, to review the cases of those federal employees who had been dismissed but later cleared on appeal to a higher loyalty board. Agency heads were further directed to review any case (even if the individual in question had previously been cleared) if there was reasonable doubt as to the employee's loyalty, and then to inform the Loyalty Review Board of all favorable decisions so that these cases could be post-audited. Extending the procedure in December, the board announced its intention to review periodically "as it deems necessary" any agency decision, even in cases where no appeal had been made.

In substance the board assumed ultimate jurisdiction over the loyalty program and attempted to achieve absolute security. The board viewed its recommendations as binding, not advisory, and sought to remove any doubt concerning the program's efficacy in confronting the "communist menace." Thus the board recommended and secured the dismissal of John Stewart Service (who earlier had been thrice reviewed and cleared). The government, board chairman Bingham noted, could not take "unnecessary chances" with federal employees of "doubtful loyalty" and, regardless of outside protests, ought to be the "sole" judge of employee loyalty. At the same time, Bingham warned against the "potential danger" of an undue concern over laxity. An effective program could not simply be judged by the number of dismissals, he said, because communists would be discouraged from seeking federal employment.[25]

The board was not alone in seeking to exploit the opportunities offered by the heightened concern for security. The Department of Justice similarly attempted to press Congress to enact legislation designed to expedite the prosecution or dismissal of alleged subversives. First, reversing an earlier (1947) recommendation, the department proposed transferring the responsibility for conducting continuing loyalty investigations from the FBI to the Civil Service Commission. This transfer, the department explained, was intended simply to free the FBI for more urgent and dramatic work and would not circumvent the Bureau's primary responsibility for internal security. Second, the Justice Department's internal security division was expanded and Roy Cohn (later of McCarthy fame) appointed to head it. Third, the department introduced legislation increasing penalties for perjury and authorizing the Attorney General to grant immunity from prosecution to witnesses testifying on internal security matters before federal grand juries or congressional committees.

In effect, the department sought to revise traditional safeguards for civil liberties which were designed to protect the individual from government prosecution. The provision for immunity for witnesses was the most controversial of these recommendations. In justification of this measure, Attorney General McGrath warned Congress that the self-incrimination "loophole" posed "an ever-present danger" to the national security. He conceded that freedom from self-incrimination was a fundamental right, but emphasized the equally fundamental need to facilitate federal law enforcement. If the Attorney General were allowed to waive prosecution by granting immunity to a witness, McGrath argued, information vitally necessary to the national defense could be secured. "The right against self-incrimination would be maintained in its full vigor," McGrath affirmed, "but it could no longer be utilized to thwart the disclosure of conspiracies and group efforts to violate the law." Perjury penalties must also be extended, McGrath argued, to include those persons who willfully gave contradictory statements when under oath. He also recommended eliminating the requirement that the prosecution prove "which of the inconsistent statements made under oath is false."[26]

On a different plane, the Truman administration acted to extend the scope of the loyalty program. In part the administration hoped to establish its unquestioned anti-communism, the vigilance of its methods, and the correctness of its approach, thereby discrediting McCarthyite attacks. The new procedures instituted in 1951 were not simply intended to deal with new contingencies or threats. Rather, they reflected a cautious policy designed to avoid cases which the McCarthyites might exploit.

The original review procedure of the loyalty program had not covered presidential appointments to advisory or consultative commissions. In 1952, at the behest of the loyalty agencies, the question of such exclusion came under White House review. The White House staff supported only a limited investigative program (simply to be on the same side), consisting of a pre-appointment check. In contrast, the Civil Service Commission, the Loyalty Review Board, the Department of Justice, and the FBI recommended doing away with this exclusion so that all federal employees and applicants would be covered by the loyalty program (the Civil Service Commissioner even insisted that ambassadorial appointments be included). Hiram Bingham, chairman of the Loyalty Review Board, pointedly asserted that

consultants who have any contact with policy-making or with scientific or technical studies having any relationship to the national defense should not be excluded from the investigative requirements of the Loyalty program.[27]

The proponents of extended coverage won. The priorities basic to this new procedure effectively stifled dissent. As one result, simple opposition to existing "national security" policies (whether the loyalty program's procedures or the containment of communism throughout the world) raised doubts about an individual employee's loyalty; the individual's policy recommendations became one basis for a denial of clearance.

This obsession similarly lent support to demands for restrictions on the news media's access to federal information. In 1951 the White House, after reviewing existing policy, extended classified or security coverage (formerly confined to defense and foreign policy agencies) to civilian agencies of the federal government. Truman defended this extension on national security grounds, arguing that it had become necessary to "strengthen our safeguards against divulging to potential enemies information harmful to the security of the United States." The President denied that this decision would result in censorship, the concealing of mistakes, or the denial of legitimate information to the public. He emphasized that departmental restrictions would require affirmative proof that divulgence of information would harm the national security. Although the new restrictions applied only to public employees, Truman appealed to the patriotic responsibilities of the general public and of newspapermen not to divulge information (of "great value to the Soviet Union") which they might uncover from private sources.

Despite the President's denial, his order did impose definite restrictions on the divulgence of information. A federal employee naturally would hesitate to release information that had a possible bearing on national security. Inevitably the news media protested the order, arguing that it unduly restricted access to necessary information. Specifically, the Associated Press Managing Editors' Association assailed the standard's vagueness, its lack of clear-cut definitions of security-related information, and its failure to provide a review procedure concerning classification. The editors also denied any immediate necessity for the issuance of the order. Accordingly, they urged the President to rescind it and instead establish an impartial (non-administration) commission to review the operations of civilian agencies and determine the need for new security safeguards consistent with the public's right to full information about the government.

In reply, administration spokesmen reaffirmed the need for the order and disparaged these criticisms as irresponsible. Too much security information, Secretary of Commerce Charles Sawyer noted, had already been released. The Secretary argued that "Our object should be not only the utmost freedom consistent with safety, but the utmost safety consistent with freedom." And the President admonished the newspaper editors for standing "on the outside and carp[ing] and criticiz[ing] without being at all helpful." The editors, Truman observed, had not taken up his offer of cooperation to improve the order but had "passed up this opportunity to serve the cause of freedom of information in the dangerous days ahead when the safety of our country and the freedom for which it stands are in peril. . . . We can only win in the present struggle if we all work together."[28]

This portrayal of opposition to "national security" restrictions as unpatriotic had by this time become the norm for the administration's defense of the loyalty program. The administration demanded an unquestioned acceptance of existing procedures and dismissed criticisms of the program (whether protesting excess or adequacy) as somehow disloyal, partisan, or unpatriotic. As defined by the government, legitimate and responsible criticisms were limited to positive suggestions that "perfected" existing procedures. Robert Ramspeck, the chairman of the Civil Service Commission, summed up this reasoning. Responding to the Department of the Interior's recommendation that investigations of incumbent employees be discontinued, Ramspeck doubted that this phase of the program would ever be completed. The FBI, Ramspeck declared, often secured additional information after clearance that required another field investigation and security review. Ramspeck argued that experience showed the need for a "continuing program."[29]

By 1952 the earlier (whether in 1945 or 1947) concern over the effect of administrative procedures on civil liberties had been subordinated to the goal of insuring potential loyalty or expediting prosecution of "suspect" employees. At the same time, the administration, by releasing for publication the number of suspect employees denied clearance or dismissed, sought to dramatize its vigilant anti-communism.[30] By 1952 the administration supported the loyalty program in part to preclude disloyal acts, in part to undercut the McCarthyite protest and to legitimize an anti-communist policy. The process, not policy or principle, had become controlling.

In essence, the establishment of the loyalty program altered national priorities. First, a review of the political beliefs and associations of federal employees (and indirectly of private citizens) had been legitimized. A program ostensibly aimed at safeguarding the national security from subversive threats established standards that reviewed individual loyalty not on the basis of overt actions or proven offenses but on the basis of suspicions and doubts. Standards that would have been rejected in 1945 or 1947 as repressive and unfair—reasonable doubt as to loyalty, or restrictions on civilian agency information—were accepted by 1951.

Second, the establishment of the Loyalty Review Board, intended originally to coordinate matters and insure fairness to the individual, actually increased pressures to extend the program. The board used its supervisory status to insure its dominance over, and the continued existence of, the program. The duration of the program established, at least in the public mind, the "expertise" of board members. Their parochial view of loyalty became the program's operational norm. At the same time, this direction effectively discounted civil libertarian protests over administrative procedures or recommendations. As a result, the Loyalty Review Board successfully monopolized control over, while extending the scope of, the program by: (1) revising the loyalty standard to permit the dismissal of suspicious employees without having to secure documented evidence; (2) assuming determinative, not advisory, jurisdiction over the program; and (3) identifying criticisms of the program as irresponsible if not treasonous.

Finally, the loyalty program legitimized the tactics of McCarthy and similar procedures by state and local governments and private industry. The result was a plethora of loyalty oath crusades, loyalty programs, loyalty investigations—all seeking the total, unremitting loyalty of the individual. Emotional patriotism displaced critical reasoning; an assessment of issues became secondary to proven anti-communism; dissent and criticism were discredited. The climate and tone of the American political debate were significantly altered. A conservative concern for order and conformity was sustained. And the Attorney General's list, established without due process or the right to review, and based on the political biases of FBI agents or Attorneys General Tom Clark and J. Howard McGrath, became the litmus test for distinguishing between loyal and disloyal organizations and individuals. These consequences were neither inherent in nor intended by the original loyalty program. But the very establishment of the program and the Truman administration's hesitant, appeasing responses contributed to an escalatory process which could not be reversed.

NOTES

1. See U.S. Congress, *House Report No. 2574,* 76th Cong., 3rd sess.; *House Report No. 2048,* 77th Cong., 2nd sess.; *Senate Report No. 1304,* 76th Cong., 3rd sess. Senate Committee on Interstate Commerce, *Hearings Investigating Wiretapping,* 76th Cong., 3rd sess. Eleanor Bontecou, *The Federal Loyalty-Security Program* (Ithaca, 1953), pp. 10–11. Walter Goodman, *The Committee* (New York, 1968), pp. 135, 136, 140–151.

2. Bontecou, *Loyalty-Security Program,* pp. 12–20.

3. Press Release, Department of Justice (hereafter DJ), March 19, 1945, DJ Library (source of all DJ press releases).

4. For an example of Clark's concern, see his June 21, 1946, address to the Chicago Bar Association. In it the Attorney General identified the recent "strikes and dissension" as part of a "communist conspiracy to achieve final power." Clark also dismissed protests over the Department of Justice's failure to act in civil rights incidents in the South as simply protests of "outside ideologists." Address, June 21, 1946, Truman Papers, OF10-Misc. (1945–1946), Truman Library. (All OF references are to Truman Papers on deposit in the Truman Library.)

5. Press Release, DJ, July 19, 1945.

6. For a more detailed discussion of the *Amerasia* case, see Earl Latham, *The Communist Controversy in Washington* (Cambridge, Mass., 1966), pp. 203–216.

7. Jennings Randolph to Truman, July 25, 1946, OF252-I.

8. Arthur Flemming (Civil Service Commission) to Clark, July 22, 1946, OF252-I. George Elsey to Clark Clifford, August 16, 1946, OF252-I. John Steelman to Latta, August 21, 1946, OF252-I. Harry Mitchell (Civil Service Commission) to Truman, September 9, 1946, OF2 (1945–1946). John Collet to Steelman, September 18, 1946, OF252-I. Memo, Matthew Connelly, October 1, 1946, OF482.

9. James Webb (Director, Bureau of the Budget) to Clark, November 20, 1946, OF252-I. Executive Order 9806, establishing the Temporary Commission, November 25, 1946, is in OF252-I.

10. Members of the commission included A. Devitt Vanech (Justice), John Peurifoy (State), Edward Foley (Treasury), Kenneth Royall (War), John L. Sullivan (Navy), and Harry Mitchell (Civil Service). Letters, Vanech to all agency and department heads and to the FBI Military Intelligence Division and the Office of Naval Intelligence, December 26, 1946, OF252-I.

11. J. Edgar Hoover to Vanech, January 3, 1947, OF252-I. Thomas Inglis to Vanech, January 8, 1947, OF252-I. S. J. Chamberlin to Vanech, February 11, 1947, OF252-I. Clark to Vanech, February 14, 1947, OF252-I. In contrast to these other witnesses, Herbert Gaston warned against an

266 ATHAN THEOHARIS

overzealous obsession with loyalty-security. He stressed the need for extreme caution and care in conducting loyalty investigations to insure that individuals were not dismissed or denied clearance because of their political beliefs. "The past several years," Gaston noted, "has seen a determined effort to confuse these matters and to attempt to coerce agencies of the government into enforcing unlawful standards of employment based on condemnation of political ideas." Statement, Gaston, January, 1947, in OF252-I.

12. Hoover to Vanech, January 3, 1947, OF252-I.

13. Webb to Clark, March 21, 1947, OF252-K. Executive Order 9835, March 22, 1947, is in OF252-K. Report of the President's Temporary Commission on Employee Loyalty is in Charles Murphy Files, Loyalty, Truman Library.

14. Memo for President, April 7, 1947, OF252-I. Stephen Spingarn to Foley (Treasury Department), April 9, 1947, Spingarn Papers, General Loyalty Files, Truman Library. Telephone Memo, April 10, 1947, OF252-I. Harry Mitchell and Francis Perkins to Truman, April 25, 1947, OF252-K. Webb to Truman, April 30, 1947, OF252-K. Clark to Truman, May 1, 1947, OF252-K. Clifford to Truman, May 7 and 9, 1947, OF252-K. Truman to Mitchell, May 9, 1947, OF252-K. Press Release, May 9, 1947, OF2 (1947). Clifford to Truman, May 23, 1947, OF252-K. Donald Dawson to Truman, October 24, 1947, OF252-K. Elmer Staats (Acting Personnel Officer, Bureau of the Budget) to all employees of the Bureau of the Budget, September 24, 1947, Webb Papers, Truman Library.

15. See Part IV, Executive Order 9835.

16. *Washington Star,* October 9, 1947, p. 1. Clare Hoffman to Truman, October 8, 1947, and reply of October 21, 1947, OF2 (1947). Truman to J. Parnell Thomas, May 16, 1947, Spingarn Papers, General Government-Congressional Investigations. U.S. Congress, House Subcommittee of the Committee on Appropriations, *Hearings on Department of State Appropriation Bill for 1949,* 80th Cong., 2nd sess., 1948. Truman to all agency and department heads, March 13, 1948, OF252-K. Presidential Directive, March 14, 1948, OF41. Mitchell to Dawson, June 15, 1948, OF252-K. Dawson to all agency and department heads, August 5, 1948, OF252-K. President's news conference, August 5, 1948, *Public Papers of the Presidents: Harry S. Truman, 1948,* pp. 431–435 (hereafter *Truman Papers*). John Taber to Webb, August 6, 1948, OF252-K. Dawson to Truman, August 12, 1948, OF252-K. Spingarn to Charles Ross, March 4, 1950, Spingarn Papers, Federal Loyalty Program. Charles Murphy to Elsey, March 27, 1950, Murphy Files, Loyalty. Letters regarding disclosure of confidential files on employee loyalty, March 28, 1950, *Truman Papers 1950,* pp. 229–232. J. Howard McGrath to Truman, March 17, 1950, OF.

17. Order N. 3464, Supplement No. 4, Office of the Attorney General, July 8, 1947, OF285-M (November 1951–June 10, 1952). C. Girard Davidson (Assistant Secretary of the Interior) to Clifford, December 29, 1947, Murphy Files, Loyalty. *Washington Post,* January 8, 1948, p. 2. Dawson to Clifford, January 7, 1948, OF252-K. Bontecou, *Loyalty-Security Program,* p. 246.

18. Bontecou, *Loyalty-Security Program,* pp. 54, 56, 72. Ralph S. Brown,

Loyalty and Security: Employment Tests in the United States (New Haven, 1958), p. 46.

19. Loyalty Review Board, December 17, 1947, OF252-K. John Snyder (Secretary of the Treasury) to Seth Richardson (Chairman, Loyalty Review Board), April 15, 1948, Snyder Papers, Personnel 1946–1952, Truman Library. Spingarn to Clark, September 9, 1948, Spingarn Papers, White House Assignment. Leon Henderson (Americans for Democratic Action) to Truman, September 9, 1948, OF252-K. Spingarn to Truman, October 15, 1948, Spingarn Papers, National Defense. Walter White (NAACP) to Truman, November 26, 1948, OF252-K. Clark to Truman, December 21, 1948, Clifford Files, Truman Library. L. A. Moyer (Executive Director and Chief Examiner, Loyalty Review Board) to Civil Service Commission, February 2, 1949, OF252-K. Spingarn to Clifford, December 30, 1949, Spingarn Papers, Chronological Files. Hoover to McGrath, February 24, 1950, Murphy Files, Loyalty. President's news conference, March 2, 1950, *Truman Papers 1950,* pp. 181–185. Murphy and Spingarn to Truman, May 24, 1950, Murphy Files, Loyalty. Spingarn, June 20, 1950, Spingarn Papers, Loyalty. Spingarn for the Files, June 23, 1950, Murphy Files, Loyalty. Richardson to Dawson, June 26, 1950, OF419-K. Donald MacPhail (Assistant Director, Legislative Reference, Bureau of the Budget) to Hopkins, August 25, 1950, Truman Papers, Bill File. Murphy to Truman, November 15, 1950, Murphy Files, Internal Security.

20. McGrath to Dawson, December 23, 1949, OF252-I.

21. Moyer to Civil Service Commission, February 2, 1949, OF252-K, emphasis added.

22. Hiram Bingham to Mitchell, February 15, 1951, OF252-K, emphasis added.

23. Truman to Admiral Chester Nimitz, January 4, 1951, OF2750-A. Statement upon establishing Nimitz Commission, January 23, 1951, *Truman Papers 1951,* pp. 119–121. Remarks at swearing-in of President's Commission on Internal Security and Individual Rights, February 12, 1951, *ibid.,* pp. 152–153. Meeting of the Commission, February 12–15, 1951; Bingham to Nimitz, February 16, 1951, and reply, February 16, 1951; Connelly to Nimitz, February 21, 1951; John Danaher (commission member) to Nimitz, March 2, 1951; Nimitz to Harold Benson (Administrative Assistant for the Commission), March 6, 1951; Bingham to Nimitz, March 12, 1951; Nimitz to Bingham, March 16, 1951; Meeting of the President's Commission, April 3–4, 1951; Nimitz to Truman, April 4, 1951, all in President's Commission, RG220, Truman Library. (All RG220 references are to President's Commission files on deposit at the Truman Library.) Peyton Ford (Department of Justice) to Murphy, April 20, 1951, OF252-K. Robert Ramspeck (Civil Service Commission) to Truman, April 16, 1951, OF252-K.

24. Truman to Nimitz, April 27, 1951; Press Release, April 28, 1951, both in RG220.

25. Harold Chase, *Security and Liberty: The Problem of Native Communists* (Garden City, 1955), p. 42. Bingham to all heads of departments and agencies, May 23, 1951, OF252-K. Bingham to all executive departments and agencies, December 21, 1951, OF252-K. *New York Times,* April 4, 1952. Bingham, address in New York City, September 18, 1951,

RG220. Bingham to Truman, June 16, 1952, Martin Friedman Papers, Loyalty-Security Program, Truman Library.

26. Press Releases, DJ, August 24, 1951; September 4, 1951, DJ Library. Roger Jones (Bureau of the Budget) to Dawson, September 11, 1951, OF-252-K. McGrath to the Judiciary Conference of the United States, September 24, 1951, McGrath Papers, Speeches, Attorney General 1949–1952, Truman Library. McGrath, Cleveland (Ohio) Bar Association, November 15, 1951, McGrath Papers, Speeches, Attorney General 1949–1952. McGrath to Truman, November 19, 1951, Philleo Nash Files, Department of Justice, Truman Library. In 1952 McGrath's efforts failed. Ultimately, in 1954, a Republican administration and Congress enacted these proposals into law. Press Releases, DJ, May 8, 1953; January 18, 1954; January 26, 1954; February 5, 1954; May 10, 1954; July 30, 1954, DJ Library.

27. Dawson to Murphy, April 8, 1952, Murphy Papers, Dawson Donald. Donald Hansen to Murphy, April 14, 1952, Murphy Papers, Dawson Donald. Murphy to Dawson, April 16, 1952, Murphy Papers, Chronological File. Bingham to Dawson, November 28, 1952, OF252-K. Dawson to Bingham, December 8, 1952, Friedman Papers, Loyalty-Security Program. Dawson to Ramspeck, September 17, 1952, Friedman Papers, Loyalty Review Board.

28. Roger Jones to Murphy, May 7, 1951, Murphy Files, National Security Council. Statement by Truman, September 29, 1951, *Truman Papers 1951*, pp. 535–536. Text of Editors' Resolutions, September 29, 1951, Democratic National Committee Clipping File, Truman Library. President's news conference and statement, October 4, 1951, *Truman Papers 1951*, pp. 554–563. *Washington Post*, October 10, 1951. Truman to President of Associated Press Managing Editors Association, December 18, 1951, *Truman Papers 1951*, pp. 648–649. Press Release, January 12, 1952, OF1290-C. Raymond Whearty (Chairman, Interdepartmental Committee on Internal Security) for the Files, June 17, 1952, OF285-M.

29. Ramspeck to Dawson, June 16, 1952, Friedman Papers, Loyalty-Security Program.

30. In effect, a "numbers game" had been instituted. The effectiveness of the President's loyalty program was defended by administration spokesmen by citing the number of "suspect" employees who had been dismissed. But the administration did not provide similar statistics on the number of individuals who had been denied clearance. From 1947 through 1956, 3,150 civilian employees and 750 military personnel were dismissed on loyalty grounds. And in the non-federal sector over the same period, roughly 5,400 individuals were denied clearance or dismissed by private industry and 1,000 state and local employees were dismissed on loyalty grounds. Brown, *Loyalty and Security*, pp. 487–488. Moreover, Truman periodically cited the number of employees dismissed in his reports on the progress of the loyalty program. For the most part the President minimized the number of "disloyal" employees as an infinitesimal percentage of the total employed. He emphasized, however, the importance of insuring a totally loyal federal service as one means of establishing his commitment and concern. See, for example, *Truman Papers 1950*, pp. 267–272, 571–576; *ibid., 1951*, pp. 119–121, 152–153; *ibid., 1952*, pp. 35, 235–236, 310–315.

BARTON J. BERNSTEIN

The Ambiguous Legacy: The Truman Administration and Civil Rights

---

"I have received a great heritage from my lamented predecessor. I shall strive to attain the ideals for which he fought and am strengthened by the assurance of your support in that effort."

—Harry S. Truman to Walter White,
April 26, 1945

"See, the Negro is very pragmatic. He isn't worried particularly about whether the bread comes from the devil or from heaven, as long as it's there, and doesn't have too big a price tag."

—Roy Wilkins

"I assure you, people are sick and tired of your empty pronouncements regarding civil rights. The nation has made itself ridiculous long enough by meddling in foreign countries while callously disregarding its manifest duty at home."

—A citizen to Harry S. Truman,
November 26, 1951

HARRY S. TRUMAN, unexpectedly thrust into the presidency, was the heir of an ambiguous legacy in civil rights. As the successor to Franklin D. Roosevelt, he inherited some of the Negro's loyalty and the torn Democratic coalition as well. The party, rent by factionalism between liberals and conservatives, was a product of history and not logic. Its strong Southern wing opposed Negro rights while the national party relied upon the Negro vote for biennial electoral success. Despite the power of Southern Democrats within Congress, Negroes had slowly abandoned the Republican party to become Roosevelt's staunch supporters. His New Deal had rescued them from starvation and desperation. Though never receiving their fair share, they were grateful to their benefactor in the White House. His government had bestowed benefits upon them as poor, not as Negroes, but its reasons and motives were not important to the majority of black men, who had never before received much assistance from any government. And the Roosevelt administration had done more: it had recognized them. Courted by Northern Democrats, flattered by the much-heralded invitation of their leaders to the White House and the appointment of some of their race to prominent federal offices, Negroes had achieved belatedly some gains which the society and earlier governments had denied them. Yet, despite the changes, their advance during the depression had been marked more by promise than by substance.[1]

Negroes were still unprotected from lynching and were often victims of violence, and they received only faltering aid from the federal government in their lonely quest for equal protection of the laws. Roosevelt, generally assured of their support, was not prepared to risk his popularity or power by aiding the

The author wishes to express his gratitude to Oscar Handlin, David M. Potter, Hugh D. Graham, Richard S. Kirkendall, Allen J. Matusow, Alonzo Hamby, Athan Theoharis, and Tamara Hareven for their criticisms. Research on this subject was initiated under a grant from the Harry S. Truman Library Institute, and continued with assistance from the Samuel S. Fels Fund, the American Philosophical Society, the Rabinowitz Foundation, the American Council of Learned Societies, and the Institute of American History (Stanford). A more heavily documented copy of an earlier version of this paper (presented at the American Historical Association meeting in 1966) is available at the Truman Library.

struggle for equality. Nor did he move far even to protect their economic interests. Not until they threatened a march on Washington were they able even to wring from the government a federal Fair Employment Practice Committee (FEPC) and a significant share of the jobs and prosperity generated by a war economy. Nor would Roosevelt yield further and desegregate the armed forces. Yet Negroes achieved new dignity as some fought for the nation and others worked in defense production. They flocked into Northern cities and discovered new opportunities, new possibilities, new freedoms—and new and more subtle forms of discrimination. Freed of Southern oppression, many were still thwarted, still denied equality in neighborhoods, schools, unions, factories, and offices. Negroes, as the Urban League emphasized, did "not enjoy equal opportunities and services in the fields of employment, education, health, housing, and civil liberties." They encountered lingering and deep-rooted prejudices, but also they found reason for hope, and their expectations rose. Struggling for advantages, gaining new political power, they became a more important force in urban politics and hence in American political life. They constituted a political and moral challenge which neither the government nor the nation could ultimately deny. ("The Negro problem," wrote Gunnar Myrdal in 1944, "is not only America's greatest failure but also America's incomparably great opportunity for the future. . . . America can demonstrate that justice, equality and cooperation are possible between white and colored people.")[2]

I

Harry S. Truman, a border-state senator and a moderate on racial and economic issues, had been the compromise candidate in 1944 for the vice-presidency. Selected partly because he had offended no one, he seemed ill equipped to face this new challenge. He was a man of great decency and of limited education. His uncle had served in the Confederate Army, his mother still condemned Republicans as abolitionists. Only slowly and falteringly did he move beyond the racial prejudices of his section. Before the war he had (reluctantly) endorsed an anti-lynching bill, probably because he was dependent on the Negro vote of Kansas City and St. Louis. In his later years as senator, when his nation struggled against Nazi racism, political necessity may have begun to fuse into a new moral conviction for Harry S. Truman. During the war he voted for FEPC, signed an unsuccessful petition to end a filibuster on an anti–poll tax measure, and agreed to investigations of racial discrimination on war contracts and in the armed services. But he was never severely tested and surely not sympathetic to demands for bold social reform; he was not deeply troubled by the plight of American Negroes, and he did not oppose racial segregation. Like many Americans, he believed that Negroes did not want to end segregation, only inequality. He failed to acknowledge that in many ways America denigrated her black citizens and condemned them to define their quest for dignity as a denial of their color and a plea for color-blindness. He shared the views of many decent men of his generation and thought that equality before the law could be achieved within the framework of "separate but equal." ("I am not appealing for social equality of the Negro," he had said. "The Negro himself knows better than that. . . . Negroes want justice, not social relations.") His vision was parochial and his bias clear. Like many Americans, he found racial matters peripheral to his interests and considered the problem only when it was thrust upon him.[3]

The issue which Truman and his generation had largely avoided forced its way into the national forum during his presidency, and disrupted American politics. Shortly after entering the White House, when asked about his plans to advance the rights of Negroes and his attitude toward FEPC and the poll tax, he sidestepped the question. "All you need to do is read the Senate record of one Harry S. Truman," he replied. Soon he would struggle briefly before acquiescing while Congress killed FEPC. Roosevelt, just before his death, had sought a large appropriation for the temporary FEPC, but a subcommittee cut the request in half and then the House Appropriations Committee eliminated all funds. Truman, though apparently unwilling to expend much effort or risk much prestige, tried to reverse the committee's action. Defeated in the House, he let the proponents of FEPC battle without his support in the Senate. Indeed, when they seemed near victory, a compromise by Senator Alben Barkley, the Majority Leader, allowed their enemies to settle on a small appropriation, and the House ultimately agreed. The committee, left without sufficient funds, cut its staff, closed offices, and quickly declined, as FEPC officials had predicted.[4]

Truman, while unable to stop Congress from strangling the *temporary* wartime agency, did publicly endorse a *permanent* FEPC. His support was cautious, and again he was careful not to invest much political capital. He pleased both wings of the party and avoided fragmenting the crumbling Democratic coalition. Probably fearing the antagonism of Southern Democrats, he refused even to meet with A. Philip Randolph, determined Negro leader of the Brotherhood of Sleeping Car Porters and organizer of the threatened march on Washington in 1941 which had led to FEPC, and others who urged the President to prod the Congress. He was unwilling to take a politically unnecessary risk in a cause which did not enlist great sympathy, although he mildly endorsed FEPC in his twenty-one-point speech of September 6, 1945, which ended his honeymoon with Congress.[5]

His "declaration of independence" from congressional conservatives, as he privately described this liberal speech, promised to continue and extend the New Deal; his requests for such welfare measures as a full employment act, increased unemployment compensation, and a higher minimum wage were valued by civil rights leaders who believed this legislation would be particularly useful to Negroes during the anticipated postwar depression. Indeed, the NAACP was so fearful of a depression that it placed the full employment bill first on its list of priorities, and FEPC second. But Truman's commitment to the employment bill and other welfare measures seemed halfhearted, and his efforts specifically on behalf of the Negro were occasional and usually ambiguous. Like Roosevelt, he did not emphasize the nation's obligation to the Negro.[6]

(Nor did Truman's wife, unlike Eleanor Roosevelt, ever champion the Negro. Indeed, when the Daughters of the American Revolution refused to rent Constitution Hall to Hazel Scott, the Negro pianist, Bess Truman, departing from her predecessor's response to a similar provocation, refused even to stay away from a DAR tea given in her honor. Miss Scott's husband, a Negro congressman, Adam Clayton Powell, scorned the First Lady as "the last lady.")[7]

Late in the fall of 1945, Truman dealt the already weakened FEPC another blow. When the government seized the strike-bound Capital Transit Company and the FEPC decided to order the company to end discriminatory hiring, the President halted the directive and then ignored the committee's request for a conference. One member resigned in protest, charging that the government "is not only empowered to, but must enforce the national policy of non-discrimination in employment." He emphasized that Truman was condoning racial discrimination and repudiating the committee. Truman, defending his action, explained that the law empowering seizure required him to maintain the term of employment during government operation.[8]

Meanwhile, the President continued to appeal publicly for a *permanent* FEPC. On January 3, 1946, he complained to the nation that congressmen were blocking his reform program, and he lashed out at "a small handful of Congressmen in the Rules Committee" who had prevented a number of measures, including the FEPC bill, from reaching the House floor. Truman continued to give FEPC some support, but his efforts did not seem designed to spur Congress. He ultimately acquiesced in the refusal of the Rules Committee to release the measure, and he never openly criticized a Senate filibuster against FEPC in January and February, nor rallied support for cloture. After some sparring, when cloture failed, the advocates of FEPC abandoned their attempt. To many observers, the struggle of the civil rights advocates appeared halfhearted, their efforts "a sham if not a fraud." They did not press for extra sessions or harass those filibustering, as parliamentary rules permitted. Instead, meeting largely during banking hours, the Senate appeared to follow an expected routine. Civil rights measures, including federal anti-lynching and anti–poll tax laws, did not receive support from either the Democratic or Republican leadership in Congress, although both parties had pledged support for FEPC. And with the President on the sidelines, hopes for reform crumbled.[9]

By the middle of 1946 it was clear that Truman's government, despite his words, was not as active in the struggle for civil rights as Roosevelt's had been during the war. When FEPC expired at the end of June, for example, a presidential assistant drafted a directive "to insure compliance with . . . [the] policy of nondiscrimination in Federal service and by government contractors," but apparently the President rejected the measure and discrimination as well as segregation continued. While Truman had expressed "friendship for the Negro people" (according to the largest Negro paper), he had not acted significantly to advance their welfare. Yet, when violence against Negroes erupted, Truman's words were important. When advances made by minorities during the New Deal and the war seemed in doubt, his public commitment was important. By appointing a few Negroes to office, he reaffirmed racial equality in symbolic form and recognized the Negro's political power. His efforts also generated mild sympathy among Northern liberals, although he sidestepped conflict and avoided a direct clash with Southern interests.[10]

Truman's occasional support of FEPC and abolition of the poll tax kept these issues alive. By his words he even encouraged the hopes of civil rights advocates. "The right to use [the ballot] must be protected," he wrote to the NAACP national convention in June 1946. He condemned the upsurge of violence, the outbreak of racial lynchings and assaults upon Negroes. Every citizen, he declared, "must be protected from all forms of organized terrorism." Yet, earlier in the year, when law enforcement officers in Columbia, Tennessee, had attacked Negroes, he had been silent; when a returning Negro veteran was removed from a bus in South Carolina, and beaten and blinded, he had been silent. Even shortly after his message to the NAACP, he waited a few days, until angry protests reached his office, before condemning an unmasked white mob in Georgia which had seized two Negro couples in broad daylight and murdered them. ("Three volleys of shots," later reported an investigating committee, "were fired as if by a squad of professional executioners." "Speak! Speak! Mr. President, where is Democracy?" asked angry pickets at the White House.) Spurred on by national shame, troubled that racial violence was providing ammunition for Russian propaganda,

Truman directed the Justice Department to investigate whether a federal crime had been committed. But he did not use the opportunity to launch protective legislation. He was already scrapping with Congress and unwilling to antagonize the South or move ahead of national sentiment. Though the liberalism of the postwar years was slowly finding a central place in its "ideology" for a crusade against racial injustice and inequality, and even the national conscience was growing more sensitive to racial violence, only a few white reformers and a handful of Negro leaders were pushing Truman to move beyond the occasional rhetoric of condemnation. They were too few and too weak, without great prestige or substantial power, to be effective.[11]

But events were conspiring to move Truman. In mid-September 1946 the National Emergency Committee Against Mob Violence sent a delegation, including, among others, Walter White, Negro executive secretary of the NAACP, Channing Tobias, Negro executive of the Phelps-Stokes Fund, James Carey, secretary-treasurer of the CIO, and Boris Shiskin, AFL economist, to confer with the President. They told him grimly of lynchings of Negroes in Georgia and Louisiana, and asked him to use the authority of his office to halt the terror. What they hoped for was not action but, as Walter White confided, "so strong a statement in denunciation of lynchings and the Ku Klux Klan that it will make real news." (Actually, Truman had already prepared a formal message for the annual meeting of the Urban League in which he declared that America "must not . . . and shall not remain indifferent in the face of acts of intimidation and violence in our . . . communities.") While Truman replied that he "had no idea it was as terrible as all that," it is clear that he had known of the terror and had already formulated a plan. Like Roosevelt, he was distressed when the nation fell so far short of its pledge of law and order. He lacked his predecessor's political capital among white liberals and black men, and there were political and moral reasons for doing more about civil rights. It was not just to appease his visitors and the groups they represented (to which he attributed more power than they really had) that he promised to create a civil rights committee. White and his colleagues had no guarantee that Truman's proposed committee was not simply a tactic of delay, but they could do little other than accept the gesture and regard it publicly as a minor triumph. Committed to working through the political process and the Democratic party, they had nowhere else to go for help. They had to rely upon the man in the White House.[12]

It is true that Truman could have used the promise to gain time and avoid a decision before the autumn election and perhaps even afterward. The appointment of a committee entailed some risks, but they could be minimized: the President had the power to select members, shape the investigations, influence conclusions, and perhaps even prevent publication of the ensuing report. Rather than creating unwanted pressures and nurturing uncontrollable aspirations, he might, through a committee, stall and restrain disruptive demands for reform. In government, where studies are designed more frequently to divert energies and impede action than to promote reform, appointment of another panel can be a clever maneuver, not evidence of concern or promise of remedy. But by promising to act, by creating a committee, Truman could temporarily affirm his commitment to legal equality without antagonizing the South. If he appointed prominent men of liberal faith, however, the committee could be a political danger and commit him to a course of action, and cost him more than he cared to spend. These, then, were some of the influences shaping his decision.

On October 11 Attorney General Tom Clark privately urged Truman to establish the committee, for it "would be of the utmost value in the task of preserving civil rights." Within ten days Truman's assistant for civil rights, David K. Niles, began selecting members for the special investigation, and he secured commitments from Franklin D. Roosevelt, Jr., who served as vice-chairman; Reverend Francis J. Haas, Bishop of Grand Rapids and former chairman of the FEPC; Francis Matthews, former executive of the Chamber of Commerce and head of the Knights of Columbus; and apparently Charles E. Wilson, the president of General Electric who served as chairman. In the short time before the election in early November, the administration probably was not able to find willing, suitable candidates for many of the other positions, and perhaps the quest continued well after the voters' overwhelming repudiation of the Democrats. Whatever the reasons for delay, not until December 5 did the President announce the appointment of his Committee on Civil Rights, and by the standards of the forties it was a group of liberal, prominent citizens. Within the administration it was described as "Noah's Ark" because it included two Negroes, two women, two Catholics, two Jews, two businessmen, two Southerners, two labor leaders, and two college presidents. Chaired by Wilson, the committee also included: Sadie T. Alexander, Philadelphia city solicitor and a Negro; James B. Carey, secretary-treasurer of the CIO and a member of the National Emergency Committee Against Mob Violence; John S. Dickey, president of Dartmouth College; Charles Luckman, president of Lever Brothers; Morris Ernst, prominent New York attorney and an active member of the ACLU; Rabbi Roland B. Gittelson of Rockville Center, New York; Frank Graham, liberal president of the University of North Carolina; Henry Knox Sherrill, Presiding Bishop of the Episcopal Church; Boris Shiskin, AFL economist and a member of the National Emergency Committee Against Mob Violence; Mrs. M. E. Tilly, a prominent Methodist and Southern friend of the Negro; and Channing Tobias, Negro executive of the Phelps-Stokes Fund and a member of the National Emergency Committee Against Mob Violence. Robert K. Carr, a political scientist at Dartmouth and a liberal student of civil rights, became the executive secretary and guiding spirit of the committee.[13]

In publicly establishing the committee, Truman's executive order declared that democratic institutions could not survive "where law and order have broken down and individuals . . . have been killed, maimed or intimidated." He concluded that inadequate civil rights statutes hampered the federal government in discharging its constitutional obligations, and called upon the committee to recommend whatever legislation and administrative actions were necessary for protecting civil rights. Significantly, his action provoked little interest among Southerners. There were no dramatic outbursts, no threats or warnings, no expressed fears of betrayal; nor did his State of the Union message, which included a section on civil rights, alarm the South.[14]

Despite Truman's expressed concern about restrictions of the franchise and racial bars to employment, his own government continued to discriminate against Negroes. In part, the government was too large, the system too intractable, to reverse direction abruptly; in part, the President was not *committed* to ending discrimination in federal employment. But by the summer of 1947, as he despaired of compromise with Congress and struggled to mend the tattered Democratic coalition, he spoke more vigorously on civil rights and courted more energetically the Negro vote. Agreeing to address an NAACP rally in June, he rejected an assistant's cautious advice that he limit civil rights to the last paragraph, "not to exceed a minute"; instead he asked two staff members of the civil rights committee to draft his speech. In his address, at the Lincoln Memorial, he openly acknowledged some of the shortcomings of American society and affirmed the need for federal remedies ("vigilant defender of the rights and equalities of all Americans")—but he omitted specific proposals.[15]

Without seriously antagonizing the South, Truman had won the praise of much of the Negro press, the NAACP, and other white liberals. But some Negro leaders were eager to push him from rhetoric to action. Encouraged to seek a better life for their people, they were guided by vocal support for racial equality from prominent social scientists. These Negro leaders were aware of Truman's political weakness at home and were able to exploit his fear that mistreatment of Negroes could mean Russian propaganda victories abroad. Moreover, they knew that Truman was not as insulated from their pressures as was his predecessor, whose popularity with the mass of Negroes sometimes inhibited Negro leaders in pressing their demands. Perhaps to spur Truman to action, the NAACP in October petitioned the United Nations, outlining the plight of the American Negro and pleading with "the nations of the world to persuade . . . [America] to be just to its people."[16]

Six days after this petition, by releasing the long-awaited

study of the Committee on Civil Rights, Truman publicized charges that America treated its Negroes as second-class citizens. In nearly every sector of American life, concluded the report, practice violated traditional ideals. Negroes were subject to lynchings and police brutality. They were frequently denied equal protection of the law. In the armed services they were segregated and restricted mostly to menial tasks. They were also effectively barred from many professions and denied equality in education, housing, medical care, and in the allocation of government assistance and services. They were, the committee concluded, victims of the "separate-but-equal" doctrine, virtually abandoned by the society. By attacking Jim Crow, the committee moved beyond the issue of federal protection of civil rights (for example, the right to life which lynching threatened) to a redefinition of the conditions for equality.[17]

The federal government must act to *secure* civil rights, asserted the committee. Left unprotected and sometimes persecuted by local and state officials, Negroes needed federal safeguards. "By mobilizing the idealism and prestige of our whole people," the committee reasoned, the government could "check the wayward tendencies of part of them," for the nation could not afford to delay "until the most backward country has learned to prize civil liberty." Nor could America neglect the "growing international implications" of civil rights violations. While admitting that legislation might not eliminate prejudice and intolerance, the committee avoided the trap of conservative thought —that change must *await* education and conversion—and concluded that the government should move to abolish discriminatory practices.[18]

To protect civil rights, the committee unanimously recommended federal machinery: expansion of the Civil Rights Section of the Department of Justice to a division; creation of a permanent commission on civil rights in the Executive and a joint committee on civil rights in Congress. The committee also proposed national legislation: increasing penalties and revising the requirements of evidence in cases of violation of federal civil rights statutes by private individuals or public officials; outlawing police brutality; barring segregation in interstate transportation; making lynching a federal crime; abolishing the poll tax; protecting participants in federal elections and primaries; ending (also by administrative action) discrimination and segregation in the military; eliminating public discrimination against members of the armed forces; establishing FEPC; and terminating federal discrimination and segregation in public schools and other publicly supported institutions in the District of Columbia. The committee looked forward to the end of racial segregation in American life, and a majority advised Congress to bar financial aid to any government agency (even in the states and communities) guilty of racial discrimination. Tilly and Graham, both Southerners, would not endorse compulsory FEPC or the cutting off of federal aid to government agencies which discriminated. At first the committee had split almost evenly on the latter issue, but by limiting the recommendation to discrimination and excluding segregation, the other members of the committee were able to reach agreement.[19]

Truman, in appointing liberals, had established a committee likely to recommend *some* federal legislation to protect the rights of black citizens. By selecting prominent men the President had forfeited the option of shaping their recommendations or quashing their report. It was not a committee he could control or silence. During its ten months of meetings, neither Truman nor his assistants,, surprisingly, sought to influence the report. Cynics may attribute the choice of a liberal commission to sloppy staff work in the White House or to the excessive influence of liberal assistants, and cynics may attribute the failure to keep the commission within safe channels to assistants pushing the President beyond his desires, but it seems more likely that Truman wanted a report urging *some* action. Such a report from respected Americans could serve as a partial mandate and make his political course easier. Be that as it may, the extent of the committee's recommendations surprised many citizens, including Truman's assistant on civil rights and presumably the President himself. Yet he should have known what was coming. Already, in May, the Compton Commission on Universal Military Training had condemned segregation in the military, and in December the President's Commission on Higher Education would assail the "separate-but-equal doctrine" and would recommend abolishing segregation in higher education.[20]

Truman, while offering the report of his Committee on Civil Rights as "an American charter of human freedom . . . [and] a guide for action," claimed publicly that he had not read the brief study. (One member of the committee, Channing Tobias, reported to the NAACP that the President, upon being presented with the report, privately told the committee, "I have already read the report and I want you to know that . . . you have done what I wanted you to do.") He was still cautious. He seemed sympathetic but promised nothing. Soon, though, he would have to choose. Compelled by the report to take a position, he might have to request vigorous legislation or risk losing pivotal Negro votes. He found his alternatives narrowed, his room for maneuvering limited. No longer could he easily remain an ally of Southern Democrats and maintain the wary allegiance of Negro leaders and urban liberals. Forced to yield to demands for the advancement of the Negro—pressures which he did not wish fully to resist—Truman had encouraged these forces which were now moving beyond his control. His political future might rest precariously on his decision.[21]

For a few months he seemed to hesitate. The issue was not whether he would do nothing—the hour was far too late for inaction—but how much of the report he would endorse. In large measure Truman's decision was influenced by the prospect of a new third party led by Henry Wallace, Roosevelt's vice-president whom Truman had dismissed as Secretary of Commerce. Estimates of Wallace's likely support in 1948 were mixtures of conjecture and anxiety, but early polls suggested that he might capture about 10 per cent of the vote. Wallace's candidacy compelled the President to take a stronger position on civil rights. Only by moving to the left could Truman prevent a bolt of important numbers of urban Negroes and some white liberals from the uneasy Democratic coalition; without their substantial support, he and many urban Democrats were doomed to defeat.

Though Wallace's candidacy would spur the administration to greater liberalism, the new threat did not alter the basic form of that liberalism. Ever since the Democrats suffered defeat in

the 1946 elections, advisers had been pressing Truman to reshape
the coalition by courting labor and minority groups. Analyzing
the situation after the committee's report, Clark Clifford, probably the President's closest and wisest political counselor, recommended that the administration move to the left to pick up
disgruntled New Dealers, and build the party on Western farmers, urban workers, and Negroes. Truman, by picking his issues
carefully, could avoid clashes between these groups. The administration might antagonize Southern voters, Clifford reasoned, but he foresaw no risk of losing Southern Democrats, no
possibility of a bolt by dissidents. The mild Southern response
to the civil rights report seemed to confirm his judgment. There
was no torrent of protest, and many Southerners who objected
to the report restricted their objections to the committee's attack
upon segregation.[22]

Clifford sketched the strategy which Truman would follow in
his uphill battle for re-election:

> Insofar as it has control of the situation, the Administration should
> select the issues upon which there will be conflict with the ma-
> jority in Congress. It can assume that it will get no major part of
> its own program approved. Its tactics must, therefore, be entirely
> different than if there were any real point to bargaining and com-
> promise. Its recommendations—in the State of the Union message
> and elsewhere—must be tailored for the voter, not the Congress-
> man; they must display a label which reads "no compromise."
> [That strategy worked with Taft-Hartley and] should be expanded
> in the next session to include all the *domestic* issues.[23]

II

Truman launched his campaign in 1948 with his message on
the State of the Union. He reaffirmed the reform program Congress had thwarted, added a few more items, and promised a
special message on civil rights. Though liberals greeted his
speech with cynicism and conservatives with hostility, prominent
Southern politicians paid little attention to the statement about
civil rights. On both sides, in the Executive and among Dixie's
responsible leaders, there was some misreading of intention and
perhaps of sentiment.[24]

Within a few weeks the President surprised the South. On February 2, shortly after two hundred Negro ministers had prayed publicly at the Capitol for the end of Jim Crow, Truman asked Congress to enact most of the recommendations offered by his Civil Rights Committee (except most of those attacking segregation). His boldness won praise from friends of the Negro and provoked attacks by Southerners, although most did not notice that, with the exception of opposing segregation in interstate transportation, he had barely challenged Jim Crow. Despite his executive power and the recommendation of the Civil Rights Committee, he did not even act to wipe out segregation in federal employment or within the military. Instead, he announced that he had instructed the Secretary of Defense to end discrimination (but not specifically Jim Crow) in the armed services "as rapidly as possible," and he *promised* to issue an order restating and enforcing Roosevelt's policy of nondiscrimination (but not nonsegregation) in federal employment. (Truman had also requested expansion of the Civil Rights Section into a division in the Justice Department, but an Assistant Attorney General, T. Vincent Quinn, was opposing the reorganization, and the Bureau of the Budget even reduced the appropriations for civil rights attorneys.) The strategy seemed to be one of reasonably bold requests in the legislative arena, where they could not succeed, and more cautious proposals in the executive arena, where the President had greater power.[25]

Undeterred by threats of a Southern rebellion, Truman and his advisers undoubtedly anticipated the brief flurry of loud Southern protests that occurred well before the Democratic national convention. Of course, some intransigent Southerners such as Senator James Eastland of Mississippi and Representative Eugene Cox of Georgia would continue to denounce the report and Truman's endorsement of it. But they were simply racists, full of hatred, and with constituencies admiring their pyrotechnics; he could discount their wrath and their threats. Others, however, were more moderate: to strengthen their bargaining position with the administration and the liberal wing of the party, they would threaten; to persuade their constituents of their devotion to the Southern heritage, they would protest. But they, as well as the administration, knew that Truman's legislative program did not endanger the Southern way of life, for they could block civil rights legislation by filibustering in the Senate. As long as passions did not blind men, as long as substance remained more important than symbols, Truman could count upon Southern leaders to support the party.[26]

Briefly, the counsel of moderation seemed to prevail. Senator Barkley, who had not been consulted about the proposed legislation, decided not to risk a party rift and estrange the South: he refused to sponsor the measure. In turn, Southern governors, at a long-scheduled conference, overrode a few extremists and endorsed the mechanics of compromise. They appointed a committee to confer with the Democratic national chairman, Senator J. Howard McGrath. Though Truman's press secretary announced that the President would not retreat on any point, McGrath at first seemed conciliatory; but a few days later he appeared less willing to compromise. In the interim, a Wallace candidate had won a surprising victory in a special congressional election in New York City, and the Progressive party loomed as an increasingly powerful threat, likely to gain as much as 7 per cent of the vote. McGrath, fearful of Wallace, rebuffed Southern demands that Truman withdraw his civil rights measures. Nevertheless, the national chairman did emphasize the moderation of the President's program, which would leave segregation largely intact, and he suggested a concession—the mild Democratic plank of 1944 as the model for the 1948 platform. The governors, refusing publicly to be mollified, warned that "the South is no longer 'in the bag.'" Sharpening the threat, Governor Ben Laney of Arkansas warned, "The Democratic Party doesn't want to run the race with a politically dead Missouri mule."[27]

Southern politicians began girding for battle. Most were still maneuvering to improve their leverage within the party; only a few were planning rebellion. In seven Southern states, governors recommended that presidential electors not vote for a candidate favoring civil rights and that delegates to the national convention be instructed to oppose Truman's position. In two states, Mississippi and Alabama, the party's executive committees threatened to bolt if the convention endorsed a civil rights

plank. Though no one in the administration expected a rebellion, many advised moderation.[28]

Truman, now an avowed candidate for re-election, was reluctant to press his program. He was unwilling to risk schism or
even bad feelings and tried to rest on his laurels and let passions
cool. ("The strategy," an assistant later explained, "was to start
with a bold measure and then temporize to pick up the right-
wing forces. Simply stated, backtrack after the bang.") Explaining that Congress would reject legislation recommended by his
office, the President admitted that he did not plan to submit a
civil rights bill. But A. Philip Randolph, with the Reverend
Grant Reynolds, director of the five-month-old Committee
Against Jim Crow in Military Service and Training, tried to upset the presidential strategy of conciliation. They were persuaded that Truman was primarily a politician eager to avoid conflict
and to escape moral and political challenges, and so they continued to threaten him, and with him, white America. On March
22 at the White House they informed Truman that unless he
ended Jim Crow in the military they would lead a massive campaign of civil disobedience; Negroes would not shoulder "a gun
to fight for democracy abroad" while they were denied democracy here, Randolph declared. A week later, Reynolds and Randolph delivered the same message to the Senate Armed Services
Committee, and Randolph pledged "to openly counsel, aid, and
abet youth . . . to quarantine any Jim Crow conscription system." Negroes, they warned, were prepared for sacrifices, suffering, terrorism, even concentration camps, in order to achieve
their rights. A poll of Negro college students (mostly veterans)
concluded that 71 per cent supported the campaign. Leaders of
the Urban League and the NAACP, while abhorring the tactics
of disobedience and preferring to work within the political system, gave the movement mild and indirect support.[29]

The administration arranged for moderate Negro leaders to
confer with the military and to serve as consultants to the services, but the session ended in disaster for the President. While
the Navy promised to improve its program and the Air Force
agreed to reexamine its policies of discrimination and segregation, the Secretary of the Army, Kenneth Royall, from North

Carolina, refused to revise the Army's policy of segregation. Enraged by Royall, these prominent Negroes refused the offer of consultantships, and they publicly renewed the challenge: they wanted both segregation and discrimination eliminated in the military, for "segregation is a form of discrimination." Without naming Royall, the Negro leaders of twenty organizations, including the Urban League and the NAACP, demanded the removal of public officials who would not end segregation and discrimination in the federal government. "Our nation, to its shame," they declared, "is condemned throughout the world for speaking of freedom while continuing to permit the perpetuation of gross discrimination against its own minorities."[30]

Despite these demands, Truman remained cautious and still did nothing about civil rights. Obviously delaying and perhaps intending to abandon the promised directive ending discrimination in federal agencies, he was moving toward a compromise with the South. In May, apparently with Royall's approval, the keynote speaker told the Democratic convention in North Carolina, "The Republican Party has gone much, much further in its advocacy of Federal interference in racial adjustments than has the Democratic Party," and he implied that the administration would not alter racial policies in the military. Truman apparently found this speech useful, for he did not dissent privately or publicly. The President retreated further from the boldness of February and sought to ease Southern doubts by inserting in the 1948 platform the party's moderate 1944 plank on civil rights. It was a mild statement, declaring simply that Congress should "exert its full constitutional powers to protect . . . the right [of minorities] to live, develop and vote equally with all citizens and share the rights that are guaranteed by our Constitution."[31]

This plank was not strong enough to keep some Negroes from moving into the camps of Henry Wallace or Thomas Dewey, the Republican standard bearer. Dewey, as governor of New York, had won acclaim for securing a state FEPC and appointing a few Negroes to prominent office. By pledging in the Republican platform support of an anti-lynching bill, equality of opportunity in employment, abolition of the poll tax, and elimination of segregation in the military, the GOP threatened to cut into Democratic strength in Negro ghettos. In addition, Dewey, according to the pundits, would receive indirect aid from Wallace. Charges of communist domination were weakening the Progressive party, but Truman faced in Wallace a foe whose strength in traditional Democratic urban areas could throw the election to the Republicans. Wallace's earlier concern with civil rights had been questionable, but in 1948 he wore the mantle of a crusader for Negro rights. By condemning segregation and discrimination "in all forms and in all places," and thereby drawing curses and taunts, and some rotten fruit, Wallace courted the Negro vote and castigated Truman for his hypocrisy. So great was the feared defection of Negro voters from the Democratic party that two of the best ward leaders in Brooklyn and Harlem expected that about 75 per cent of the voters in their wards might support Wallace.[32]

In the NAACP, also, local support for Wallace was developing. In Indiana the state president was supporting Wallace, and in many of the large cities, including San Francisco and Philadelphia, local officials were backing the third-party ticket. Unlike these local leaders and the black people trapped in the ghettos, most prominent Negro civil rights leaders feared the taint of Wallace. And they were unwilling to return to the Republican party. They knew that the GOP, through its congressional party's involvement in the conservative coalition, was closely tied to the Southern Democrats and could not be depended upon to support the quest for equality. So Negro leaders stayed with the Democrats and Truman. They might press him to act with more boldness, they might demand that he fire subordinates who supported segregation, but most would not abandon him at the convention, for his advocacy of rights for the Negroes was unmatched by any twentieth-century President. To turn their backs on him in his time of need, most Negro leaders feared, would be injuring their own cause: no President might ever again risk supporting civil rights.[33]

While the national officials of the NAACP and most prominent Negro leaders were prepared to support the President, others in the party were ready for revolt. Urban bosses, persuaded that Truman would lose, hoped to save their local tickets, and prom-

inent white Northern liberals sought power and principle. Their
desperate boom for Dwight D. Eisenhower had collapsed when
the general refused to run, but they battled at the convention
to pledge the wavering President and the party to the civil
rights recommendations he had submitted to Congress in February. They were unwilling to let Truman placate the Southern
Democrats with the 1944 plank. Even though the platform committee had approved his compromise, the liberals and the bosses,
supported by Negro leaders, pressed their case on the convention floor. Theirs was a struggle not for legislation but at best for
technical commitment; for them the plank was an expression of
considerable political value as well as a symbol of great moral
importance. Spurred on by the Americans for Democratic Action, galvanized by one of that liberal organization's leaders,
Hubert Humphrey, then mayor of Minneapolis, the convention
endorsed a firm civil rights plank. It praised Truman for his
courageous vision and called for federal laws guaranteeing political participation, equal opportunity in employment, security
of person, and equal treatment in the services. Despite the
drama and the passion, the convention did not directly attack
Jim Crow: it did not promise social equality. By offering equality when it was still regarded as compatible with segregation,
the convention was offering far less than the "walk forthrightly
into the bright sunshine of human rights" which Humphrey had
pledged.[34]

Nonetheless, the civil rights plank split the convention. The
Mississippi delegation and about half of the Alabama delegates
walked out. Convening at Birmingham a few days later, the
states righters, according to V. O. Key, were composed of "the
big brass" of the Mississippi and Alabama parties, Governor J.
Strom Thurmond of South Carolina and his entourage, and "a
miscellaneous assortment of persons of no particular importance."
These disgruntled Democrats briefly challenged the existing
party framework and struck fear in the ranks of many organization regulars by forming the States Rights party.[35]

The addition of the popular Alben Barkley of Kentucky to
the national Democratic ticket helped to salve some wounds. A
loyal New Dealer, a moderate on racial matters, and a skilled

tactician of compromise, he was an ideal candidate as a native of a border state. But even Barkley failed to lift the convention out of the clutches of despair; the party was convinced it could not win in November. Truman, facing challenges from the left and right, acted to puncture the gloom and in his acceptance speech hammered at the Republican-dominated Congress. The "Do-Nothing Congress," as he castigated it, would be called into special session to accomplish unfinished business, to test the promises of the Republican platform. By necessity, Truman had taken the bold approach.[36]

In 1948 there was no white backlash to fear in urban America outside the South, and a Democratic politician could court the Negro vote without risking the estrangement of Northern white voters. To most of the nation, America's racial problem was a Southern problem, and that conception shaped Truman's tactics. No longer in bondage to the South, he could follow but one political path. He had to capture the urban vote outside the South, for his chances of success rested heavily upon the cities. Without further stalling, Truman acted: on July 26 he barred discrimination in federal employment and created a board to consider complaints, and he declared a policy of equality of opportunity in the armed forces and established a committee (with members to be designated) to advise on the implementation of this vaguely formulated policy. In his executive orders the President still avoided an open legal assault on Jim Crow, promising only to end federal discrimination, not segregation. In the armed services the process would prove to be slow. But when General Omar Bradley, Army Chief of Staff, declared that the Army "is not out to make any social reform" and would continue segregation until the nation revised its racial policies, Truman publicly rebuked him and acknowledged that he wanted segregation ended. Within the week, McGrath conferred with Negro leaders, promising that the President was committed to the elimination of segregation in the armed forces and that he would soon appoint the committee to advise the military in its revision of race policies. On September 18, without fanfare, Truman appointed the seven-man committee, which was liberal and included two Negroes.[37]

Truman, though eager to win Negro votes, was careful not to emphasize the differences on civil rights between the party's sectional wings or to antagonize loyal Southerners. When he addressed the special session of Congress in late July, he carefully tucked civil rights into a single paragraph. So close to the election, he was eager to prevent further disputes within the party over civil rights and unwilling to risk a Southern filibuster. To dramatize the failure of the Republican Congress, particularly its responsibility for inflation, he had asked for price controls which he did not want, and shifted attention from civil rights. His strategy almost miscarried in the Senate when a Southern filibuster against an anti–poll tax bill dragged on for nearly a week and blocked other legislation. Truman predictably was rebuffed by the Congress, which rejected price controls. He was also denied other requests—a housing program, aid to education, a higher minimum wage, relaxed immigration policies, and the civil rights program of February—on which he planned to conduct his campaign.

During the campaign, Truman played politics carefully and generally stayed away from civil rights. Following Clifford's strategy, the President concentrated on the Western farm states, where he talked primarily about public power and farm problems, and the Eastern and Midwestern industrial centers, where he spoke mostly of inflation, public housing, and the Taft-Hartley law. A campaign adviser urged the President to mention his accomplishments in civil rights "to prove that he acts as well as talks civil rights. The Negro votes in the crucial states will more than cancel out any votes he may lose in the South." Toward the end of his campaign Truman openly courted the Negro. He became the first President to speak in Negro Harlem.

An aggressive campaigner, a master of invective, Truman lusted for combat and gleefully condemned the GOP-dominated "Do-Nothing Congress." In a story generally familiar to Americans, he refuted the pollsters and won a close election. Battling the silent, evasive, seemingly smug Dewey, who avoided the issues, he "gave 'em hell." At least briefly, he had reshaped the Democratic coalition. It is easy in such tight races to demonstrate that the votes of any one group were critical: without the upsurge of farm support, Truman would have lost; without strong labor support, he would have lost. The NAACP concluded that 69 per cent of the Negro vote in twenty-seven major cities supported the President. The election revealed that the urban Negro vote, in a close election, could be more important than Southern solidarity and even suggested that Southern loyalty to the party could survive the struggle over civil rights.[38]

III

Truman, the confident recipient of a mandate, had great expectations as he awaited the new Congress. He did not disappoint Negro leaders, who were encouraged by the election and anticipated that the government would move closer toward advancing equality for their race. The President, promising the nation a "fair deal" (largely the policies he had urged during his first term), asked the Eighty-First Congress for the civil rights legislation its predecessor had refused. To secure these statutes, Democrats had to cut a path through the legislative bramble bush. In the House they weakened the Rules Committee, long an impediment to civil rights. But in the Senate liberal Democrats struggled without success.[39]

Their aim was liberalization of Senate rules to halt filibusters on motions (procedural issues) and measures; but poor strategy and party defections contributed to a serious defeat. To cut off unlimited debate, a bipartisan group proposed that two-thirds of the senators *present* could invoke cloture on motions. By choosing two-thirds, rather than a simple majority, they were offering the Southern Democrats a compromise, which was rejected. Democratic leaders, fearing a party split which could block Truman's other domestic legislation, moved cautiously. When the Senate bogged down in a filibuster preventing consideration of a rules change, Truman suggested a simple majority for cloture, thereby upsetting all hopes for the two-thirds compromise. Ultimately a coalition of Northern Republicans and Southern Democrats, joined by many Northern Democrats, triumphed and wrote an even tougher cloture rule, which required two-thirds of the *entire* membership.[40]

Defeated on procedures, the administration soon failed in its quest for civil rights legislation outlawing the poll tax, making lynching a federal crime, establishing FEPC, and prohibiting segregation and discrimination in interstate transportation. Truman, though blocked by the Southern Democrat–Republican coalition, rejected a compromise—a voluntary FEPC, a constitutional amendment eliminating the poll tax, and an anti-lynching bill resting on state action—offered by Senator Richard Russell, the coalition's leader.[41]

Perhaps the President still believed he could marshal enough votes for a victory on civil rights; certainly some of his assistants still hoped for success. But Truman's action was also influenced, and perhaps even shaped, by the demands and expectations of white liberals and Negro leaders. To them the compromise would have seemed a "sell-out," for the states might never pass the amendment outlawing the poll tax, and the anti-lynching bill might suffer a similar fate. The President could not risk estranging the advocates of civil rights, for, without their support, this settlement would be of no political value. They, in turn, were apparently still optimistic that Congress would grant much of the civil rights legislation, and they certainly would not settle for a voluntary FEPC, much less *only* a voluntary FEPC. On that they were probably wrong, for the Congress would not grant more, and experience with the wartime FEPC suggested that negotiations and education by FEPC were more important than a sanction because they were more likely to be tried.[42]

The advocates of civil rights would not compromise and accept Russell's proposal, and they could not win on their own terms. Yet at times many of them would compromise, as for example in the spring of 1949, when they confronted the choice of an expanded, but segregated, public-housing program or no new program at all. (Presumably they also did not realize that slum clearance meant "Negro clearance.") Though the NAACP voted to "withhold active support from any federal legislation in . . . housing, health or education which does not expressly forbid segregation," the organization was unwilling to oppose such laws, and its liberal friends in Congress generally voted for such legislation. By the standards of these years, they were frequently practical liberals willing to sacrifice the goal of integration to meet what seemed to be some of the more immediate needs of the poor and disadvantaged. With liberal support, Congress also passed some of Truman's other Fair Deal proposals—public power, expanded social security, and higher minimum wages.[43]

Most liberals did not realize that these welfare measures did not effectively help the neglected millions suffering in poverty. Ironically, while the liberals chafed at Truman's limitations and believed that another President might lead Congress effectively and rally the nation to a crusade, they frequently failed to recognize the shallowness of the Fair Deal proposals. White liberals and black leaders were effectively isolated from the poor and the slums, and in the absence of militancy among lower-class blacks, there was little recognition of their needs—almost no communication from the bottom to the top. Like the President and his advisers, most liberals were unaware of the extent of poverty in America, or of the economic plight of many Negroes; they did not urge special programs to assist Negroes left unemployed (at roughly double the white rate) in the mild recession of 1949–1950. Concentrating on limited measures to restore a modicum of human dignity, the liberals and their allies emphasized legislation, primarily FEPC, which could not solve the deeper problems they failed to understand. To some, of course, FEPC itself had become a rallying ground for civil rights, an issue to dramatize the quest. Yet, not only was it an unsatisfactory issue, but civil rights leaders, because of their loose alliance with some labor leaders, were unwilling to acknowledge the discriminatory practices of many unions and the deep hatred of Negroes upon which these practices often rested. At least eighteen unions—eleven in the AFL and seven others, including four major railway brotherhoods—barred Negroes. Nor were white liberals generally concerned to seek social equality for the Negro. Perhaps it is an added irony that such liberals as Henry Wallace, Max Ascoli, Isador Lubin, and Oswald Garrison Villard could comfortably be members of the Cosmos Club, which excluded Negroes.[44]

If faulty or limited vision was one of the obvious defects of

American liberalism in these years, perhaps its greatest flaw was a heavy emphasis on change through legislation and judicial decisions affirming equality or outlawing segregation. In a sense, the proponents of civil rights allowed their means to be shaped partly by their conservative opponents, who favored old laws and older social patterns and denied the capacity of new laws to alter social behavior. The liberal way was the legal way, and it was seldom measured against radical demands, never against bold new tactics. Only occasionally—in some ride-ins in 1947 and in the campaign of civil disobedience against the draft in 1948—had there been bolder means. Nor was the organized left—the Communists, the Socialists, and the Progressives—more profound in its analysis, more visionary in the choice of tactics; it was only more demanding in the egalitarian legislation it sought. The point is not to judge the liberalism of those years anachronistically by current standards, nor to expect techniques which would probably have failed, but rather to emphasize from the perspective of our own time how little the liberals asked and how little their success would have accomplished in structural terms.[45]

They continued to struggle for the shallow reforms that Truman had requested. Despite some achievements in the new Congress, by late summer the President's hopes faded for even a piece of his civil rights program. He acknowledged defeat in October and agreed to postpone civil rights until the next session. Soon Negro leaders began to organize a mass lobby for civil rights legislation, and particularly for FEPC. At a publicized White House meeting with the leaders in January 1950, Truman promised that FEPC would reach a vote "if it takes all summer." Despite his pledge, Truman "was reluctant to invest much executive capital in a legislative enterprise that could bankrupt the rest of his program." When Speaker Sam Rayburn blocked FEPC in the House, the President did not prod him, but friends of the legislation managed to pry the bill loose. A few weeks later its foes cut out the provision for enforcement, and the House passed the measure.[46]

It expired in a filibuster in the Senate. The proceedings were a "parliamentary sham," concluded Arthur Krock. "Leaders of the Democratic party, boasting a majority in the Senate, were bold and vigorous in their public affirmations of support for FEPC, but singularly weak, hesitant, and inactive on the Senate floor." Rather than waging a determined battle against the fili-buster, as the new Majority Leader, Senator Scott Lucas, had promised, FEPC's friends participated in what the *Times* derided as a "rocking-chair affair . . . no all night sessions . . . no laryn-gitis or body strain." (A. Philip Randolph criticized Lucas for "transparent, hypocritical tactics.") After this mild setback, Tru-man in July endorsed a second attempt to secure FEPC, but again his efforts were inadequate to rally his own party.[47]

By the summer of 1950 the administration's response to the challenge of civil rights was becoming clear. Truman would go on record in support of civil rights, but he could not press his program on a recalcitrant Congress and a torn party which he sought to patch. As a legislative leader on domestic issues he was a failure, unable to get Congress to do his bidding. He gave priority to foreign policy and had to temper his domestic pro-gram and offer concessions to Southern Democrats who en-dorsed his conduct of foreign affairs. As a moral leader he was limited. His sense of indignation was restricted, his voice muted. In his demands and actions he did seek to end Jim Crow in interstate transportation and in the military, but he avoided op-portunities to condemn segregation or to lead a crusade. When, for example, Negroes were attacked at an integrated swimming pool in the nation's capital, the White House did not protest or even publicly express sympathy. Political wisdom dictated cau-tion and frequently silence, but the recognition of these political necessities revealed the shortcomings of Truman's administra-tion and of liberal democracy in America.[48]

Despite these equivocations and neglected opportunities, the administration was not without its achievements on behalf of civil rights. During these years of legislative stalemate, Truman's Department of Justice, despite his apparent indifference, was an active warrior in the battle against Jim Crow. It entered cases as an *amicus curiae* and submitted briefs arguing the unconsti-tutionality of enforcing restrictive covenants and of requiring separate-but-equal facilities in interstate transportation and in higher education. Prodded by Justice, and particularly the Solicitor General's office, the Supreme Court continued to chip away at racial discrimination. It struck down state laws requiring segregation in interstate travel and declared enforcement of restrictive covenants unconstitutional. (Two years after the court's decision, and after pressure from members of the administration and civil rights groups, the Federal Housing Administration finally declared it would not issue mortgages on property with restrictive covenants. But it continued, by its policies, to protect residential segregation.)[49]

Perhaps most important, Truman had moved to integrate the armed services. On September 18, 1948, he had initiated this program by appointing a committee of Charles Fahy, former Solicitor General; Lester Granger, Negro executive secretary of the Urban League; John Sengstacke, Negro editor of the *Chicago Defender*; Dwight Palmer, president of General Cable Corporation and member of the Urban League; and William Stevenson, president of Oberlin College. At their first meeting, Truman declared he wanted desegregation accomplished "in such a way that it is not a publicity stunt." For nearly two years the committee investigated the military and quietly sought cooperation for racial integration. From the beginning the members emphasized that racial segregation denied equal opportunity, and they found ample evidence that segregation used personnel inefficiently and injured morale. Backed by the President, the committee slowly made headway toward equal opportunity and integration. The Navy, which had few Negroes and did not officially segregate, agreed to seek more Negroes. The Marine Corps abolished segregated basic training but still retained some all-Negro units. The Air Force, while retaining a racial quota for some units and keeping some all-Negro forces, agreed to end most segregation and to open opportunities to both races. The Army lagged behind the other services, partly because it relied upon the draft and had more Negroes. After first seeking to deceive the committee, it moved slowly toward integration. Even then, however, Truman had to promise the Secretary secretly that the Army could restore its restrictive Negro quota if it received a disproportionately high number of

Negroes. Well into the Korean War the Army retained many segregated units, and integration in Europe did not even begin until April 1952, more than four years after Truman had promised to issue his executive order.[50]

Negro leaders recognized the government's efforts in their behalf, but they and their white allies realized sadly that Truman's efforts were not enlisted fully in the struggle for equality. When the Korean War erupted in June 1950, Negro leaders and white liberals urged Truman to emulate Roosevelt and create an FEPC "as an integral factor in mobilization of manpower . . . against . . . aggression." But Truman was blocked from establishing an FEPC by a legislative rider (which barred funds for an FEPC without explicit congressional approval), and he never explained the statutory impediment, never acted to inform the nation, and failed to create an FEPC-type agency which would be legal. Perhaps the civil rights groups knew of the statutory restriction to an executive-created FEPC, but probably they did not. That the President did not explain his position to them indicates the widening gap between him and the liberals. And it is symptomatic of Truman's conception of his office that he did not regard educating the people as part of the responsibility of presidential leadership.[51]

While urging Congress to approve FEPC legislation, Truman still did not act for months in this area where he had some effective power. On February 2, 1951, the third anniversary of his original civil rights message and after nearly seven months of war, the President moved only part way. Reaffirming Roosevelt's executive order, Truman authorized the Secretaries of Defense and Commerce to require and enforce non-discriminatory clauses in their government contracts. Proponents of FEPC were still dissatisfied. They suspected that federal agencies would continue to countenance discrimination by contractors, and they organized a vigorous campaign to spur the President to greater activity. On June 25, the tenth anniversary of Roosevelt's creation of FEPC, seven governors and eight mayors proclaimed "Fair Employment Practice Day," and Mrs. Roosevelt supported the effort by commemorating FEPC in a ceremony at the grave of her husband. Only after vigorous liberal demands continued for another six

months did Truman create a Committee on Government Contracts Compliance (from funds of participating federal agencies) to review adherence to the non-discriminatory provisions
required in government contracts. The committee found that the
clause was "almost forgotten," that most contractors "made little, if any attempt to adhere to its standards," and that officials
of many federal agencies lacked "even the will" to enforce the
requirement. With a small budget and few personnel, without
power of enforcement or the right to hold public hearings, in
effect without presidential support, the committee was not very
effective in halting discrimination.[52]

In this area of executive action, as in others, Truman was
never as bold as Negro leaders or staunch proponents of civil
rights desired. A decade had passed in the assault upon discrimination, but the Democratic administration remained a cautious friend of civil rights. The President would not use his great
powers fully even in his last years in the White House; yet he
continued to ask Congress to pass the legislation he had recommended in 1948. The Democratic Congress, dominated on
domestic issues by the bipartisan conservative alliance, was unwilling to cooperate with the President and blocked most of the
Fair Deal. After the Korean War began, Congress balked at all
social reform. The Democratic defeats in the congressional races
of 1950 made Truman and the legislature bitter antagonists.
Long-standing differences on domestic issues paled before the
cleavage on foreign policy. In 1951 committees in each house
even refused to report a civil rights measure, and the prospects
dimmed for legislation on lynching, the poll tax, and FEPC.[53]

The nation was succumbing to vicious illiberalism, and Mc-
Carthy seemed to be running rampant. With Americans fearful
of communism, suspicious of reform, and identifying most opponents of segregation as reds, Truman remained cautious. His
prestige was damaged, his influence waning; he had almost no
political capital. But despite his plight, his administration did not
retreat before these new tides. When the citizens and officials
of Cicero, a Chicago suburb, attacked a Negro war veteran who
moved into the previously all-white area, Truman's Attorney
General, prodded by public outrage, sought action after a local

grand jury had exonerated the hoodlums and officials and had indicted the Negro's attorney for defending his client's right to rent a home.[54]

There was much to admire in Truman's willingness to allow the Department of Justice to place the government on the side of Negro rights, but some Americans wanted even more vigorous action. A handful demanded that the President act as energetically to advance the Negro's cause as had the government in opposing communism at home and abroad. (Walter White pointed to one of the disturbing paradoxes of Truman's government— "an increasing tendency on the part of government agencies to associate activity on interracial matters with disloyalty." Even Negroes working for the federal government and opposing segregation were frequently investigated as security risks.) Though Truman's interest in civil rights never approached his commitment to anti-communism, he did refuse to let the forces of reaction and segregation triumph. He pocket-vetoed a bill requiring some integrated federal schools in the South (such as those in Oak Ridge) to accept segregation. Continuing the struggle, in his 1952 State of the Union message he told Congress, "As we build our strength to defend the freedom in the world, we ourselves must extend the benefits of freedom more widely among all our own people." He was careful not to antagonize the South and generally silent about racial violence, but he did not abandon his occasional pleading for equality. Nevertheless, the Democratic record, when judged by legislative accomplishment, was bleak indeed. In 1952 civil rights bills were again bottled up in hostile committees and did not reach the floor of either house.[55]

IV

For Truman the promise of equality and protection against discrimination (though he construed these rights narrowly) remained the "essence of the American ideal and the American Constitution." In the spring and early summer of 1952 he campaigned sporadically for a strong civil rights plank. He was unwilling to see his party split again, and he seemed conscious of his record and perhaps anxious about how historians would judge him. But he yielded to exigency, and he succumbed ultimately, but uncomfortably, to the politics of accommodation. He gave up trying to place pledges for compulsory FEPC and a simple majority for cloture in the party's 1952 platform, and let other party leaders work out a compromise with the Southern wing. Whatever fears, however mild, had lingered of a Southern bolt in civil rights, the actions of the Democratic chiefs soon quashed them.[56]

The party retreated from the platform of 1948. By promising "equal opportunities for education, for economic advancement, and for decent living conditions," and leaving unspecified its efforts to eradicate racial discrimination, the Democrats yielded to caution. Their standard bearer, Adlai Stevenson, opposed compulsory federal FEPC, and John Sparkman of Alabama was placed on the national ticket. The party recognized its obligation to the South and restored temporarily the uneasy sectional alliance. At the convention, liberals won a weak loyalty pledge to the party, but when delegates from three Southern states balked, they did not bolt, nor did they lose their voting rights. In 1952 the bolters on civil rights were few, and they were not disgruntled Southerners but Negroes. Unable to halt the politics of capitulation, lacking adequate support from liberal allies who were anxious to heal the party, Adam Clayton Powell, Negro congressman from Harlem, and some other Negro delegates left in dismay. "Juggling with the favor of one group as against another, and maneuvering toward the tolerable compromise, the [white] politicians equivocated and lost sight of principle," concluded Oscar Handlin.[57]

In the campaign both parties competed for the important Negro vote which could swing the election. Stevenson moved beyond the platform and agreed, if elected, to try to influence the Senate to reform its rule on filibusters. Though the party had not endorsed the civil rights plank that Truman had urged, the President continued to condemn the Republicans for shying away from civil rights and for refusing to join the struggle for equality. He criticized the General and the GOP, but actually there was little to choose (at least as judged by promises) between the positions of Eisenhower and Stevenson on civil rights. Nevertheless, Truman went to Harlem and to the Negro section of Chicago to assail the Republicans on civil rights, to emphasize the achievements of his administration, and to plead for Democratic votes. He had become a conscience for the Democrats. He was bolder on civil rights than his party and its presidential candidate. Pushed years before to take a stand on civil rights and eager to defend his own record (which included many defeats on civil rights by the Congress), the President was now unwilling to abandon the issue. "You can't cure a moral problem, or a social problem, by ignoring it," he warned the nation.[58]

But the issue in 1952 was not civil rights. That challenge could not rekindle the passions of 1948. Instead, as the nation moved from the domestic-oriented politics of the thirties and the postwar forties to a new politics, the issues were communism, corruption, and Korea. No Democratic candidate, certainly not the scholarly and reflective Stevenson, aided by the slashing and discredited Truman, could have prevented the triumph of Dwight D. Eisenhower and the Republican party. The new President and his victorious party would face many challenges in the next eight years. On the domestic front, aside from McCarthyism, the major test would be in civil rights, and later generations might well judge the Republicans more by their failure and lack of vision in this realm than even by their ability to vanquish McCarthy, to cleanse politics, and to protect dissent. Truman, in some measure, had dimly foreseen the future. Appraising his own contributions, he had concluded:

> The civil rights report and the civil rights program give voice and expression to this great change of sentiment. They are the necessary instrument of progress. They are the trumpet blast outside the Walls of Jericho—the crumbling walls of prejudice.[59]

V

"No occupant of the White House since the nation was born has taken so frontal or constant a stand against racial discrimination as has Harry S. Truman," Walter White said in 1952.

Truman's rhetoric and his efforts fell far short of the promise of American democracy, and his actions were not even as bold as his words. But his contributions were still significant. He was the first President in the twentieth century to assail discrimination against Negroes, to condemn violence and intimidation directed at them, to proclaim their legal equality. Though his vision was limited and his motives frequently political; though his concern about the American image abroad influenced his actions; though he was reluctant to lead the nation on a crusade for equality and never vigorously attacked Jim Crow, he did advance the quest for civil rights. As President he started to desegregate the armed services and moved to end federal discrimination in federal employment. It was his Department of Justice, despite Truman's apparent lack of interest, that placed the weight of the national government against segregated schools and argued that separate-but-equal was self-contradictory and unconstitutional. The government had moved to a redefinition, a broader view of equality which presaged the end of the *Plessy* doctrine.[60]

In all, the Truman program was moderate, and its defects left the nation with a great burden of unresolved problems. Viewed from the perspective of today, Truman's views seem unduly restrained and his government excessively cautious; viewed even by the standards of his own time, he was a reluctant liberal, troubled by terror and eager to establish limited equality. He was ahead of public opinion in his legislative requests, but not usually in his actions. In that imbalance there is some evidence to support cynical charges but not enough to minimize his contributions. While lagging behind the new liberalism which found an important place for racial equality, Truman struggled with the racial problems of America.

The recipient of an ambiguous heritage, Truman bestowed a similar legacy upon the generation which followed. In emphasizing the ambiguity of that legacy, he focused American attention on the moral dimension of its dilemma. By his occasional advocacy, he educated the nation and held high the promise of equality. By kindling hope, he also may have prevented rebellion and restrained or delayed impulses to work outside the political system. In a limited sense he encouraged the reform forces which relied upon legalism; by yielding partly to their pleas and by granting them frequent audiences, he dignified them and their methods. He also helped—often in spite of himself—to educate a nation to its obligations and its failures. In another sense, he unleashed expectations he could not foresee, desires he could not understand, and forces which future governments would not be able to restrain. The injustices he revealed, the evils he tried occasionally to correct would soon demand new efforts and a new vision which would leave an aging Truman an embarrassing anachronism and many Negro leaders and their white allies as painfully outdated as their techniques. To remedy the injustices which the federal government did not correct and would not protest, some Americans would take to the streets to dramatize the evils a nation had too long endured. Ultimately these failures would compel blacks to reconsider their assumptions about the promise of American life and their quest for a color-blind society. Many would conclude that dignity and racial pride could be achieved only in separation from, and in antagonism to, white America. For too long, Americans had reneged on their commitment to equality; for too long they had denied human aspirations. The bold efforts and the troubling events of the late fifties and the sixties may have been at least as much the result of the failure of Harry S. Truman's administration as of its successes.[61]

NOTES

1. On the Negro and the New Deal, see Allen Kifer, "The Negro Under the New Deal, 1933–1941" (unpublished Ph.D. dissertation, University of Wisconsin, 1961); and Arthur M. Schlesinger, Jr., *The Politics of Upheaval* (Boston, 1960), pp. 409–446.

2. On FEPC, see Barton J. Bernstein, "America in War and Peace," in Bernstein, ed., *Towards a New Past* (New York, 1968), pp. 296–299;

and Gunnar Myrdal, *An American Dilemma: The Negro Problem in Modern Democracy* (New York, 1944), also at p. 1021 for the quotation. Urban League, "Racial Aspects of Reconversion," August 27, 1945, PPF 2685, Truman Library (source of all of the President's Personal Files). On new aspirations, see Richard M. Dalfiume, "The 'Forgotten Years' of the Negro Revolution," *Journal of American History*, LV (June 1968), 90–106.

3. On Truman's vote in 1938, see Samuel Lubell, *The Future of American Politics* (New York, 1951), p. 9; the quote is from his speech of July 14, 1940, to the Convention of the National Colored Democratic Association, in David Horton, ed., *Freedom and Equality: Addresses by Harry S. Truman* (Columbia, Mo., 1960), pp. xi–xxx; for a similar view in 1944, see *Common Sense* (October 1944), quoted in John O'Donnell, *Boston Daily Record*, September 15, 1948. See also interview in *Pittsburgh Courier*, August 5, 1944. For public attitudes toward the Negro, see Hadley Cantril, with Mildred Strunk, eds., *Public Opinion, 1935–1946* (Princeton, 1951), pp. 508–510.

4. President's News Conference, April 17, 1945, Files of the White House Reporter, Truman Library (all future news conferences cited are from the same source); Will Maslow, "FEPC—A Case History in Parliamentary Maneuver," *University of Chicago Law Review*, XIII (April 1946), 422–433; *Congressional Record*, 79th Cong., 1st sess., pp. 5734–5735, 5751, 5794–5798, 5812, 6820–6822, 7062–7065; FEPC, *Final Report* (Washington, 1947), pp. ix–x. Also, Walter White to Truman, June 1, Official File (OF) 413, Truman Papers, Truman Library (the source of all future citations of OF); Representative Mary Norton to Truman, June 1, OF40; Truman to Fred Vinson, June 2, OF122; Truman to Rep. Adolph Sabath, June 5 (and an identical letter to Senator Denis Chavez), OF40; Malcolm Ross (FEPC chairman) to Truman, June 7, OF40. Cf. Louis Ruchames, *Race, Jobs and Politics: The Story of FEPC* (New York, 1953), pp. 122–135.

5. Of about four thousand letters between June 1 and June 23, only nineteen opposed FEPC. "Analysis of Presidential Mail on FEPC," OF40. On Truman's avoidance of antagonism and meetings with partisans, see Frank Boykin to Truman, and reply, June 29, 1945; Randolph to Truman, August 31, September 30; Matthew Connelly to Randolph, September 4, 6, 10, October 16, 1945; Randolph to Matthew Connelly, October 10 and 19, all in OF40. For Truman's speech of September 6, see *Public Papers of the Presidents: Harry S. Truman* (hereafter *Truman Papers*), *1945* (Washington, D.C., 1961), pp. 263–309. For Truman's later interpretation, see his *Memoirs* (Garden City, 1955), I, 481–485.

6. On Negro fears of depression, see *Negro Digest*, III (November, 1944), 36. On the NAACP, see *NAACP Bulletin*, January 1946, and Walter White's testimony, in Senate Banking and Currency Committee Hearings, *Full Employment Act of 1946*, 79th Cong., 2nd sess., pp. 615–621.

7. On the Hazel Scott affair, see Powell to Truman, October 1; Truman to Powell, and reply, October 12; Powell to Mrs. Truman, October 11, and reply, October 12, 1945, all in OF93; *Newsweek*, XXVI (October 22, 1945), 31; *Crisis*, LII (November 1945), 313.

8. On the dispute, see Charles Houston to Truman, December 3, and reply, December 7; White House press release (Truman to Houston), December 17, 1945, all in OF40. For an affirmation of the committee, see

Executive Order 9664 of December 20, 10 Federal Register 15301; Thomas Emerson to John Snyder, August 30, 1945, Office of War Mobilization and Reconversion (OWMR) Records, Box 116, Record Group (RG) 240, National Archives (NA); Tom Clark to Truman, November 29; Ross to Harold Smith, November 9; Samuel Rosenman to Truman, December 3; and Rosenman, undated memo, all in OF40; cf. White to Truman, December 19, 1945, OF40; *Crisis*, LIII (January 1946), 9; Ruchames, *Race, Jobs*, p. 134; William Berman, "The Politics of Civil Rights in the Truman Administration" (unpublished Ph.D. dissertation, Ohio State University, 1963), pp. 23–25.

9. Speech of January 3 is reprinted in *Truman Papers 1946*, pp. 1–8, and see particularly pp. 3–4. For pressure on Truman to support FEPC vigorously and condemn the filibuster, see Mary McLeod Bethune to Truman, February 3, 1946; National Council for FEPC to Truman, February 6, 1946, both in OF40. On Truman's responses, see Truman to Randolph, February 6, 1946, and Truman to Mrs. J. Borden Harriman, January 29, 1946, OF40. On Truman and the filibuster, see also I. F. Stone, "Where There Is No Vision," *Nation*, CLXII (February 9, 1946), 111–119; Maslow, "FEPC," p. 440, which is the source of the quotation about the filibuster. On the defection of liberals, see NAACP Minutes, February 11, 1946, NAACP Papers, Library of Congress. At the FEPC rally of February 28 in Madison Square Garden, Secretary of Labor Lewis Schwellenbach represented the administration. Department of Labor press release, February 28, 1946, Philleo Nash Files, No. 21, Truman Library (all Nash Files are in the Truman Library).

10. Truman to Niles, July 22, 1946, and drafts (undated); and Nash to Niles, July 19, 1946, Nash Files, No. 20; and see Executive Order 9346, May 27, 1943. On segregation in federal employment, see President's Committee on Civil Rights, *To Secure These Rights* (Washington, D.C., 1947), pp. 57–61; on segregation in USES, see "Memorandum on the Washington Office, USES," August 26, 1946, Office of the Secretary (Schwellenbach) Files, Records of the Department of Labor, RG174, NA, and on Labor's promise to correct the situation, NAACP press release, September 19, 1946, NAACP Files, Schomburg Library (source of all NAACP Files). Quotation from *Pittsburgh Courier*, April 27, 1946, called to my attention in Berman, "Civil Rights," p. 33. On violence against Negroes, see *To Secure These Rights*, p. 22; and *Pittsburgh Courier*, October 6, 1945; February 2, March 9, 1946. On Truman and the poll tax, see News Conferences, April 6 and 11, 1946; and Truman to Irving Brant, March 29, 1946, OF465B.

11. For NAACP message, Truman to White, June 11, 1946, President's Personal File (PPF) 393, Truman Library (source for all PPF citations). The white press virtually disregarded the incident in Tennessee, *New York Times*, February 27, 1946, p. 44. *To Secure These Rights*, p. 22, is the source of the first quotation. See OF93 for more than two hundred telegrams protesting violence in Georgia, and NAACP press release, August 8, 1946. Other quotation from *New York Times*, July 31, 1946.

12. For the quotation, see White to Donald Harrington, September 12, 1946, White Papers, Yale University. For the message to the Urban League, see Truman to Lester Granger, September 12, 1946, PPF2868. On the meeting, see *Pittsburgh Courier*, September 28, 1946; NAACP press re-

lease, September 20, 1946; Walter White, *A Man Called White* (New York, 1948), pp. 330–332, also the source of the quotation attributed to Truman. Nash, in an interview of September 19, 1966, revealed that the plan was formulated in advance. Negro leaders were viewed by the administration as men of considerable power, as leaders of a bloc vote. For evidence of this belief, see Clark Clifford, "Memorandum for the President," November 19, 1947, Clifford Papers (used while in his possession but now at the Truman Library). For Negro grievances with the Democratic party, see *New York Times*, October 18, 1946.

13. Clark to Truman, October 11, 1946, OF596A; on the dating of the first three appointments, see Francis Matthews, "Memorandum" (n.d.), Matthews Papers No. 15, Truman Library. "Noah's Ark" was Nash's characterization. On Wilson, see White House Appointment Book, October 18, 1946. On Carr's appointment ,see Nash to Charles Mazley, Nash Files, No. 24. Luckman, because of the pressure of other commitments, later withdrew from the committee.

14. Executive Order 9809, 11 F.R. 14153. Also see Truman, *Memoirs*, II, 180–182. *Atlanta Constitution, Atlanta Journal, Mobile Register, Gulfport* (Miss.) *Daily Herald, Nashville Banner,* and *Charlotte Observer*, December 5–8, 1946, neither reported the President's act nor commented upon it. *Birmingham News*, December 7, was favorable, and the *Raleigh News and Observer*, December 6, 1946, mentioned it. The White House received about forty letters, and all but three were favorable. OF596. Address of January 6, 1947, is in *Truman Papers 1947*, p. 9. For Southern responses, see *New York Times, Washington Post, Baltimore Sun*, January 7–9, 1947.

15. On discrimination in the federal government, see n. 8 and complaints of the United Public Workers, in *New York Times*, January 11, 1947; also *Pittsburgh Courier*, May 18, 1946; October 18, 1947. On his statement of January 15, 1947 (to the committee), see *Truman Papers 1947*, pp. 98–99; there was no Southern response. *Charleston* (S.C.) *News and Courier, New Orleans Times-Picayune, Birmingham News, Mobile Register*, and *Atlanta Journal*, January 15–20, 1947. Advice on Truman's speech is in Niles to Connelly, June 4, 1947, OF419B, and June 16, 1947, Clifford Files, Truman Library. Truman's address of June 29 is in *Truman Papers 1947*, 311–313.

16. On responses to the speech, see *Pittsburgh Courier*, July 5, 1947; "Truman to the NAACP," *Crisis*, LIV (August 1947), 233. In 1946 the National Negro Congress had filed a complaint with the U.N. Economic and Social Council. The NAACP petition, "A Statement on the Denial of Human Rights to Minorities in the Case of Citizens of Negro Descent in the United States of America and an Appeal to the United Nations for Redress," was first submitted in preliminary form on January 27, 1947, and, after revisions, formally presented on October 23. The council, rejecting a Soviet motion, refused to investigate. Carey McWilliams, *Brothers Under the Skin* (New York, 1951), p. 38. On NAACP pressure, see White to Niles, November 5, 1947, Nash Files.

17. *To Secure These Rights*, pp. 1–95.

18. *Ibid.*, pp. 100–103.

19. *Ibid.*, pp. 139–173. On the compromise, Stephen Spingarn, "Recommendations of the President's Committee on Civil Rights," [n.d.], Spin-

garn Papers, No. 37, Truman Library. On FEPC, see "Telephone Conversation Between Mr. Matthews and Mr. Lowenstein," April 26, 1950, Matthews Papers, No. 43.

20. Curiously, there is no record—in the files of the Bureau of the Budget or in the papers at the Truman Library—of the recommendations which led to the selection of the committee's personnel. Perhaps there is information in the papers of David K. Niles at Brandeis University, but the collection is closed. On the committee's independence and the expectation throughout its history that the report would be published, see Robert Carr to Bernstein, August 11, 1966; Henry Knox Sherrill to Bernstein, July 2, 1966; "Minutes, the President's Committee on Civil Rights," March 6, 1947, p. 15, and April 17, 1947, pp. 179–180, Nash Files, No. 28; Carr to Maurice Latta, September 15, 1947, Nash Files, No. 24; Carr to Latta, October 21, 1947, files of the President's Commission on Civil Rights, No. 4, Truman Library; Nash to Niles, September 29, 1947, Nash Files No. 4. On surprise at the course of the committee, see interview with Nash. For the committee reports, A Program for National Security: Report of the President's Advisory Commission on Universal Training (Washington, D.C., 1947), p. 42; A Report of the President's Commission on Higher Education, Higher Education for American Democracy (Washington, D.C., 1947), II, 29–35.

21. Truman's statement of October 29, 1947 is in Truman Papers 1947, pp. 479–480; cf. report by Tobias, NAACP Minutes, November 17, 1947, NAACP Papers.

22. On Wallace's strength, see American Institute of Public Opinion poll of June 1947, in Public Opinion Quarterly, XII (Fall 1947), 490. On the efforts of advisers, see author's interviews with Clifford and Nash; Ewing to Bernstein, December 1, 1966; and interviews by Berman, "Civil Rights," pp. 64–70. For strategy, see Clifford, "Memorandum for the President," November 17, 1947. On Southern reactions, see New York Times, Baltimore Sun, Washington Post, New Orleans Times-Picayune, Atlanta Journal, Atlanta Constitution, Greensboro (N.C.) News, Richmond Times-Dispatch, Birmingham News, Louisville Courier-Journal, Alexandria (Va.) Gazette, October 29–November 10, 1947; Nashville Banner, October 30; Gulfport (Miss.) Daily Herald, October 31; Mobile Register, October 30; Charlotte Observer, October 30; and F. H. Vass to Harry Vaughn, October 30, 1947, OF596A. The mail on the report was about 5 to 1 in favor. OF596A. Also see Jack Redding, Inside the Democratic Party (New York, 1958), p. 76.

23. Clifford, "Memorandum for the President," November 19, 1947.

24. Speech of January 7, in Truman Papers 1948, pp. 1–10. On responses, see New York Times, Washington Post, Birmingham News, January 7–10, 1948. For misreading of sentiment, see interviews with Clifford and Nash.

25. On the ministers, see Pittsburgh Courier, January 19, 1948. Truman's address of February 2 is in Truman Papers 1948, pp. 121–126. The mail received at the White House was about 4 to 1 in favor of the President's speech (OF596A). On Truman's move left, see William Helm, ed., Mr. President (New York, 1952), p. 134, and Jules Abels, Out of the Jaws of Victory (New York, 1959), pp. 4–6. On the Civil Rights Section, see New York Times, November 28, December 8, 1947; May 9, 1948. On the

contents of the legislative program, see Stephen Spingarn, "Suggested
Outline of the Omnibus and Rights Bill of 1948," January 22, 1948,
Spingarn Papers, No. 36. For support of FEPC by prominent businessmen,
see *New York Times,* February 16, 1948.

26. See Arthur Krock, *New York Times,* February 4, 1948. On the
South, see *New Orleans Times-Picayune, Mobile Register, Altanta Constitution,* February 2–10, 1948.

27. On Barkley, see *New York Times,* March 10, 1948. On the maneuvering, see V. O. Key, *Southern Politics* (New York, 1949), pp. 329–334;
New York Times, February 7–11, 24, 1948, and February 24 for the first
quote. Laney, quoted in Hugh Gloster, "The Southern Revolt," *Crisis,* LV
(May 1948), 137. On the Progressive victory, see Lubell, *Future of American Politics,* pp. 85–87.

28. Key, *Southern Politics,* pp. 332–336; *New York Times,* February
24, 1948.

29. On Truman, see *New York Times,* March 8, 1948; and news conference, March 11, 1948. The assistant is Nash, in an interview. The
quotations are from Randolph, *New York Times,* March 23, 1948, and
Senate Committee on Armed Services, *Hearings on Universal Military
Training,* 80th Cong., 2nd sess., p. 688; and see p. 677 for Reynolds' agreement. For the (possibly unreliable) poll, see *Negro Digest,* VI (August
1948), 7. On the NAACP's response, see "Fighting the Jim Crow Army,"
Crisis, LV (May 1948), 136; and *Congressional Record,* 80th Cong., 2nd
sess., pp. 4317–4318; and see pp. 4314–4318 for other Negro responses.

30. On the meeting, see transcript of National Defense Conference on
Negro Affairs, April 26, 1948, Records of the President's Committee on
Equality of Treatment and Opportunity in the Armed Services, Truman
Library. For the quotes, see *New York Times,* April 27, 1948; March 28,
1948.

31. For the statement of William Joyner, see Royall to Truman, June
21, 1948, Clifford Papers. On the delayed orders, see news conference,
May 13, 1948. For protests, see White to Truman, April 7, 1948, OF413;
NAACP press release, July 22, 1948, and William Batt, Jr., to Gael Sulli-
van, April 20, 1948, Clifford Papers. For the plank, see Kirk Porter and
Donald Johnson, eds., *National Party Platforms* (Urbana, Ill., 1956), p.
404. On thoughts about the order, see Oscar Ewing to Charles Murphy,
January 2, 1948, Murphy Papers; Nash to Clifford, April 9, 1948, Nash
Files No. 10; Niles to Clifford, May 12, 1948, Nash Files No. 11.

32. See Porter and Johnson, *National Party Platforms,* pp. 452–453.
On Dewey's record, see Lubell, *Future of American Politics,* pp. 94–95.
On Wallace quotation, see *New York Times,* June 22, 1948; on defections,
see Batt to Sullivan, April 20. On the parties and FEPC, see Lee Mc-
Donald, "Congress and F.E.P.C.: A Case Study in the Legislative Process"
(unpublished Ph.D. dissertation, Harvard University). For fears of the
GOP and not the Progressives in Philadelphia, see Raymond P. Alexander
to Sen. Frank Myers, May 11, 1948, McGrath Papers.

33. On the NAACP's splits, see *New York Times,* March 20, June 27,
1948; "Annual Meeting," *Crisis,* LV (August 1948), 246–247.

34. On the battle, see Clifton Brock, *Americans for Democratic Action:
Its Role in National Politics* (Washington, D.C., 1962), pp. 94–99; cf.
Truman, *Memoirs,* II, 181–182; William Batt, Jr., to Clifford, July 9 (?),

1948, Clifford Papers. For the platform, see Porter and Johnson, *National Party Platforms,* p. 435.

35. Key, *Southern Politics,* pp. 321–335.

36. Truman's speech is in *Truman Papers 1948,* pp. 406–409.

37. For a weaker order on federal employment, see Donald Dawson to Clifford, March 8, 1948, OF596. Executive Orders 9980, 9981, in 13 F.R., 4311, 4314; for the Bradley episode, see news conference, July 29, 1948; Bradley to Truman, July 30, 1948, and Truman to Bradley, August 4, 1948, CS291.2, Army General Staff Papers, RG319, NA; last two items called to my attention in Richard M. Dalfiume, "Desegregation of the United States Armed Forces, 1939–1945" (unpublished Ph.D. dissertation, University of Missouri, 1966). For Randolph's renewed threat, see *Pittsburgh Courier,* July 3, 1948; for other pressures, see Leon Henderson to Truman, July 22, 1948, OF93B. On the meeting, see Grant Reynolds, "A Triumph of Civil Disobedience," *Nation,* CLXXVII (August 28, 1948), 365–366, and *Black Worker,* November 1948. On the announcement of the committee, see *New York Times,* September 19, 1948, p. 61; *Pittsburgh Courier,* September 25. For an earlier judgment, see Dawson to Truman, September 9, 1948, Nash Files No. 1.

38. For Truman's speeches, *Truman Papers 1948,* pp. 462–939, particularly 923–925. Advice from Batt to Clifford, August 11, 1948, Clifford Papers. On the campaign and election, also see Cecelia Van Auken, "The Negro Press in the 1948 Presidential Election," *Journalism Quarterly,* XXVI (December 1949), 431–435. For NAACP's estimates, see Henry Moon, "What Chance for Civil Rights," *Crisis,* LVI (February 1949), 42–45.

39. On Negro leaders, see *Pittsburgh Courier,* January 8, 1949. Truman's message of January 5, 1949, is in *Truman Papers 1949,* pp. 1–7. On the House, see *Congressional Record,* 81st Cong., 1st sess., pp. 10–12.

40. On the Senate, see *Congressional Record,* 81st Cong., 1st sess., pp. 863–866, 2724; McDonald, "Congress and F.E.P.C.," pp. 361–371; Berman, "Civil Rights," pp. 130–143. On Truman, see news conference, March 3, 1949; *New York Times,* March 16, 1949; and Jay Franklin [John Franklin Carter], "What Truman Really Thinks of Negroes," *Negro Digest,* VII (June 1949), 10–12.

41. On the Russell offer, see Malcolm Ross to Truman, February 5, 1949, OF596A; Jack Allen in *Washington Post,* July 13, 1949; Brooks Hays, *A Southern Moderate Speaks* (Chapel Hill, 1959), pp. 45–50; and Henry Silver to Truman, September 28, 1949, Clifford Files, Truman Library.

42. On Truman's hopes, see Truman to Representative Mary Norton, April 5, 1949, OF596. On FEPC, see Herbert Northrup, "Progress Without Federal Compulsion," *Commentary,* XIV (September 1952), 206–211; cf. Ruchames, *Race, Jobs,* pp. 142–143, 183–184. On FEPC and competing priorities, see NAACP Minutes, July 14 and September 12, 1949.

43. On public housing, see (unsigned) "The Housing Bill of 1949 and the Struggle over Segregation," July 7, 1949, Clifford Files; on "Negro clearance," see NAACP press release, July 2, 1952. Negro leaders did not generally protest segregation in public housing, but for an exception see NAACP press release, February 2, 1950. On January 3, 1949, the NAACP

withheld active support for federal legislation in housing, health, or education which required segregation. NAACP Minutes, May 9, 1949. For occasional concern in the administration about "Negro clearance," see Richard Neustadt to Nash, June 5, 1950, Spingarn Papers, No. 38.

44. For a more complete discussion, see Barton J. Bernstein, "Economic Policies," in Richard S. Kirkendall, ed., *The Truman Period as a Research Field* (Columbia, Mo., 1967), pp. 86–147. On labor unions, see John A. Davis, "Negro Employment: A Progress Report," *Fortune*, LXVI (July 1952), 102ff; *CIO News*, April 17, May 1 and 22, 1950. On Negro income, see Marion Hayes, "A Century of Change: Negroes in the U.S. Economy, 1860–1960," *Monthly Labor Review*, LXXXV (December 1962), 1364; Arthur Ross, "The Negro in the American Economy," in Ross and R. A. Gordon, eds., *Employment, Race and Poverty* (New York, 1967), p. 18. On the Cosmos Club, see its *List of Members* (Washington, D.C., 1945).

45. On the ride-in, see George M. Houser and Bayard Rustin, "Journey of Reconciliation," (mimeo, n.d., probably 1947), CORE files, Schomburg Library. Also see address by Walter White, June 29, 1947, Clifford Files. In 1951 the NAACP asked U.S. Steel to use its influence, through its subsidiary, Tennessee Coal and Iron, to stop "the reign of terror [in Birmingham] against Negro citizens." U.S. Steel "misunderstood" the request and shunted the NAACP to its subsidiary, which did nothing. (NAACP press release, July 12, 1951. Also see *ibid.*, March 26, 1950.)

46. On sincerity of Democratic legislators, see *New York Times*, July 13, October 4, 1949. Truman's statement is in NAACP press release, January 19, 1950. On the course of the measure, see Ruchames, *Race, Jobs*, pp. 206–213. The quote is from Berman, "Civil Rights," p. 152.

47. Krock in the *New York Times*, May 8, 1950, and see NAACP press releases, March 16, April 13, 1950. The second quotation is from *New York Times*, May 8, 1950; A. Philip Randolph's comment is in *Chicago Defender*, May 6, 1950. On Truman's reluctance to battle for FEPC, see Spingarn to Charles Murphy, March 11, 1950; *Washington Post*, April 14, 1950; Spingarn to Truman, May 16 and 19, 1950, all manuscripts in Spingarn Papers, Truman Library. On the July efforts, see Spingarn, "Memorandum for the FEPC File," July 5, 1950, Nash Files, No. 4; *Pittsburgh Courier*, July 22, 1950. For public attitudes to FEPC, see Scott Fowler, "Congress Blocks the Civil Rights Program," *Commentary*, IX (May 1950), 397–406. On continued complaints about segregation in federal employment, see Thomas Richardson to David Niles, January 29, 1949, Nash Files, No. 8; Therese Robinson to Truman, April 19, 1949, OF93; NAACP press release, March 22, 1951; Dan Kimball to Lester Granger, Admiral Dennison Papers, Truman Library.

48. On the swimming pool, see *Washington Post*, July 13, 1949.

49. Justice Department in brief for *Shelley* vs. *Kraemer* (signed by Tom Clark, Attorney General, and Philip Perlman, Solicitor General), 334 U.S. 1 (1948), which is a minor landmark because of the federal government's decision to intervene in a private case involving construction of the Fourteenth Amendment; brief for *Henderson* vs. *United States* (signed by Perlman and McGrath, Attorney General), 339 U.S. 816 (1950), the first federal attack on the *Plessy* doctrine; brief for *McLaurin* vs. *Board*

of Regents (signed by Perlman and Philip Elman), 339 U.S. 629 (1950); brief for *Sweatt* vs. *Painter* (signed by Perlman and Elman), 339 U.S., 629 (1950). On the President's apparent lack of interest, see interview with Philip Elman, December 21, 1966. Charles Murphy, a close presidential adviser, as well as Nash and Spingarn, two White House assistants on civil rights, disclaimed any contact with the Solicitor General's office, but Spingarn, at a public meeting on December 28, 1966, belatedly claimed almost daily contact with Perlman. On Charles Murphy, see letter to Bernstein, October 25, 1967; cf. Arnold Raum to Bernstein, October 23, 1967. According to the White House appointment book, Perlman never had a business appointment with the President until August 17, 1949, and then he had only eighteen in the next three years. On FHA, see NAACP press release, February 4, 1949, and Nash to Dawson, June 16, 1952, Nash Files, No. 8. The revision of FHA policy applied only to new houses, and FHA was not scrupulous in enforcing it. (Hortense Gabel to Raymond Foley, February 26, 1953, Foley Papers, Truman Library.) Also see White to Truman, December 28, 1951, Nash Files, No. 6; Housing and Home Finance Agency, *Fifth Annual Report* (Washington, D.C., 1952), p. 413; U.S. Commission on Civil Rights, *Civil Rights '63* (Washington, D.C., 1963), pp. 95–98.

50. Two other members were later unavailable for service. On the first meeting, see "Meeting of the President and the Four Service Secretaries with the President's Committee on Equality of Treatment and Opportunity in the Armed Services," January 12, 1949, OF1285(0). Report by the President's Committee on Equality of Treatment and Opportunity in the Armed Forces, *Freedom to Serve* (Washington, D.C., 1950), pp. 11–13, 24–29, 52–55, 67. On the promise, see Gordon Gray to Truman, March 1, 1950, OF1285B. In his news conferences of February 9 and April 13, 1950, Truman avoided attacking segregation, and he continued this policy in his address of May 15, 1950, reprinted in *Truman Papers 1950*, p. 413.

51. The telegram is excerpted in *CIO News*, June 25, 1951. For continued demands, Senator Hubert Humphrey to Truman, January 12, 1951; National Council of Negro Women, November 18, 1950; Albert Fitzgerald to Truman, October 25, 1950, all in Nash Files, No. 17; also many letters in OF40; *Chicago Defender*, November 25, 1950; and *Pittsburgh Courier*, January 6 and 13, 1951. The legislative impediment, the so-called Russell amendment, was Public Law 358, sec. 213, 78th Cong., 2nd sess. On Truman, see also news conference of January 18, 1951.

52. Executive Order 10210, in 16 F.R. 1049. For demands, see "Statement [by Negro Americans] to President Truman at the White House Conference on February 28, 1951," Nash Files, No. 17; Senator William Benton to Truman, October 21, 1951, OF526B; James Carey to Truman, April 12, 1951; *CIO News*, June 25, 1951; and Patrick M. Malin, Francis Biddle, Walter White, *et al.* (leaders of twelve other liberal organizations) to Truman, June 24, 1951, OF40, which includes many more letters of complaint; *Chicago Defender*, April 28, May 19, June 2 and 30, December 8, 1951; *Pittsburgh Courier*, June 8, 1951; "Where Is FEPC?" *Crisis*, LVIII (April 1, 1951), 258. Executive Order 10308, in 16 F.R. 12303. For criticisms that Truman had not created an FEPC, see *Pittsburgh Courier*, December 15, 1951; NAACP press releases, December 6, 1951,

January 3, 1952; Randolph to Truman, December 4, 1951, OF526. Cf. Channing Tobias to Truman, December 6, 1951, and other correspondence in OF526 and 526B. On the committee's experiences, see "Résumé of the Committee's letter of January 30, 1952 . . . ," March 17, 1952; for resistance by officials of the Department of Defense, see "Suggestions from Contracting Agencies," (n.d., about July 1952); Palmer to Nash, September 2, 1952, all in Records of Committee on Government Compliance, No. 3, RG325, NA. See its *Equal Economic Opportunity* (Washington, D.C., 1953), pp. 3–5, for quotations, and also pp. 42–46 and 63–76.

53. State of the Union message of January 8, 1951, calling for "equal rights and equal opportunities," is in *Truman Papers 1951*, and the quotation is on p. 12; the budget message, which asked for FEPC, is in *ibid.,* and see particularly p. 80.

54. Events at Cicero are discussed by Charles Abrams in *Forbidden Neighbors: A Study of Prejudice in Housing* (New York, 1955), pp. 103–106; also see pp. 150–164 for the code of the National Association of Real Estate Boards, which asserted as a principle that realtors should not act to establish interracial neighborhoods.

55. White to Truman, November 26, 1948, OF258K; and Carl Murphy to Truman, April 10, 1950, OF93 misc.; NAACP Minutes, November 8, 1947. The bill was HR 5411, and advice from officials is in bill file 107 and Nash Files, No. 31. Veto is in the White House press release, November 2, 1951. Address of January 9 is in *Truman Papers 1952–1953*, p. 16.

56. The quotation is from his address to the Jefferson-Jackson Day dinner on March 29 and repeated to the ADA on May 17, 1952, *Truman Papers 1952–1953*, pp. 224, 346; and Truman reaffirmed his position in a speech at Howard University on June 13, 1952, White House press release, and in his news conference of June 19, 1952. For Negro praise, see *Chicago Defender*, May 24, June 21, 1952. On the efforts in May by the chairman, see *Nation*, CLXXIV (May 24, 1952), 489.

57. The Democratic platform is in Porter and Johnson, *National Party Platforms*, pp. 473–489, and the Republican is on pp. 496–505. For *Chicago Defender*, July 12, 1952. On the convention, see *New York Times* and *Washington Post*, July 16–28, 1952; *Chicago Defender* and *Pittsburgh Courier*, July 19–August 9, 1952; Oscar Handlin, "Party Maneuvers and Civil Rights Restrictions," *Commentary*, XIV (September 1952), 197–206.

58. On Stevenson, see *New York Times*, August 5, September 3, 1952; Stuart Brown, *Conscience in Politics: Adlai E. Stevenson in the 1950's* (Syracuse, 1961), pp. 76–112; NAACP press release, September 11, 1952. Powell returned to the Stevenson camp. (*New York Times*, August 30, 1952.) For Truman's statement, see speech of June 13.

59. Quotation from speech of June 13. Also see his farewell address, White House press release, January 15, 1953. On the Negro vote, see Henry Moon, "Election Post-Mortem," *Crisis*, LXIV (December 1952), 616–617; Louis Harris, *Is There a Republican Majority?* (New York, 1954), pp. 152–153.

60. White's statement began, "Although he has appeared to soft-pedal the civil rights issue in recent months . . ." It is from NAACP press release, April 3, 1952. For other praise, see Wilkins to Truman, January

12, 1953, OF596. When the first of the primary school cases arose, Perlman, the Solicitor General, had boggled at filing a brief urging desegregation at the primary level, though he had previously endorsed briefs for integrated higher education. When he resigned, the new Attorney General, James P. McGranery, endorsed this brief. The Department waited until after the election before filing it in order to keep the issue removed from any appearance of partisan politics. Interview with Elman.

61. On Truman's responses to new tactics and demands, see *New York Times,* June 3, 1961; March 3, 1965.

Index

A NOTE ON THE CONTRIBUTORS

BARTON J. BERNSTEIN, Associate Professor of History at Stanford University, has edited *Towards a New Past: Dissenting Essays in American History* (1968) and, with Allen J. Matusow, *The Truman Administration: A Documentary History* (1966) and *Twentieth-Century America: Recent Interpretations* (1969). He is preparing a history of the Truman administration. Born in New York City in 1936, Mr. Bernstein attended Queens College (B.A., 1957), Washington University (St. Louis), and Harvard University (Ph.D., 1963), where he studied under Frank Freidel and Oscar Handlin. Formerly a member of the Bennington College faculty and a Fellow at the Charles Warren Center for American Studies (Harvard), he has also been a Woodrow Wilson Fellow and the recipient of grants from the American Council of Learned Societies and the Harry S. Truman Library Institute.

LLOYD C. GARDNER, Professor of History at Rutgers University, is the author of *Economic Aspects of New Deal Diplomacy* (1964) and *Architects of Illusion: Men and Ideas in American Foreign Policy, 1941–1949* (1970), editor of *A Different Frontier: Selected Readings in the Foundations of American Economic Expansion* (1966), and a contributor to *Towards a New Past: Dissenting Essays in American History* (1968). Born in Delaware, Ohio, in 1934, he is a graduate of Ohio Wesleyan University (B.A., 1956) and the University of Wisconsin (Ph.D., 1960), where he studied with William Appleman Williams. Mr. Gardner has also taught at Lake Forest College and has held a Woodrow Wilson Fellowship and a Social Science Research Council Fellowship.

DAVID GREEN, Special Lecturer in History at the University of Saskatchewan, is the author of *The Containment of Latin America: A History of the Myths and Realities of the Good Neighbor Policy* (1971). Born in New York City in 1942, a graduate of Cornell University (A.B., 1962), he did graduate work at Stanford University (M.A., 1963) before returning to Cornell (Ph.D., 1967), where he studied with Walter LaFeber. A recipient of a Herbert Lehman Fellowship and a Woodrow Wilson Fellowship, Professor Green has also taught at Ohio State University and Cornell.

THOMAS G. PATERSON, Assistant Professor of History at the University of Connecticut, is the author of "The Abortive American Loan to Russia and the Origins of the Cold War, 1943–1946," *Journal of American History* (1969), and, with Les K. Adler, "Red Fascism: The Merger of Nazi Germany and Soviet Russia in the American Image of Totalitarianism, 1930's to 1950's," *American Historical Review* (1970). He is completing a book on American economic foreign policy and the origins of the Cold War, and editing and contributing to a forthcoming volume, *Cold War Critics: Alternatives to American Foreign Policy in the Truman Era.* He is also editor of *The Origins of the Cold War.* Born in Oregon City, Oregon, in 1941, Professor Paterson attended the University of New Hampshire (B.A., 1963) and the University of California at Berkeley (Ph.D., 1968), where he studied with Armin Rappaport and Richard Abrams. At the University of California he was both a Brown and Bolton Fellow; he has also received grants from the Harry S. Truman Library Institute.

ATHAN THEOHARIS, Associate Professor of History at Marquette University, is the author of *Seeds of Repression: Harry S. Truman and the Origins of McCarthyism* (1971) and *The Yalta Myths: An Issue in American Politics* (1970), and co-author of *Anatomy of Anti-Communism* (1969). Born in Milwaukee, he attended the University of Chicago (A.B., 1956 and 1957, Ph.D., 1965), where he studied under Walter Johnson. Mr. Theoharis has also taught at Texas A & M, Wayne State University, and Staten Island Community College, and has received grants from the University of Chicago, Wayne State University, and the Harry S. Truman Library Institute.